George W. Schwartz

Office Routine and Bookkeeping

A Method of Teaching the Science of Accounts and of Illustrating the....

George W. Schwartz

Office Routine and Bookkeeping
A Method of Teaching the Science of Accounts and of Illustrating the....

ISBN/EAN: 9783337143985

Printed in Europe, USA, Canada, Australia, Japan

Cover: Foto ©Lupo / pixelio.de

More available books at **www.hansebooks.com**

WILLIAMS & ROGERS SERIES

OFFICE ROUTINE

AND

BOOKKEEPING.

A METHOD OF TEACHING THE

SCIENCE OF ACCOUNTS

AND OF ILLUSTRATING THE

ROUTINE IN BUSINESS OFFICES.

For use in Business Colleges and Commercial Departments

COMPLETE COURSE.

BY

GEORGE W. SCHWARTZ,

Principal Commercial Department, Public Schools, Louisville, Ky., and Expert Accountant.

SCRIPT ILLUSTRATIONS BY E. C. MILLS.

NEW YORK .:. CINCINNATI .:. CHICAGO

AMERICAN BOOK COMPANY

W. P. 2

PREFACE.

Pedagogical principles require that correct mental impressions of business transactions, and the documents that vouch for such, be produced in the mind of the student before he attempts to make a record of them. The methods employed to produce such impressions may vary; in this work it was thought best to reproduce the routine work of the bookkeeper as nearly as possible. To that end, and for that purpose, hundreds of elegantly engraved business documents accompany this book, which represent the proprietor's incoming mail, and from which the student — his bookkeeper — is to make entries. In addition, the necessary blank forms are furnished, and the student is required to write up all the documents that represent the proprietor's outgoing mail, and to make the records therefrom.

When the student has had sufficient practice in making records from business documents they are dispensed with, as it is believed that the advanced student will derive valuable mental discipline in making records from historical data; besides, the use of vouchers with which he has become familiar, will tend to make the work monotonous if continued too long.

The independent price lists, the uniform script in the text book and on all the vouchers, and the persistent emphasis that is placed on the importance of superior mechanical work can not fail to have a beneficial influence on the student's work.

The Introductory Course of this work came from the press one year ago, and was most enthusiastically received by teachers. Since then there have been added 130 pages devoted to Commission, Department Store, Manufacturing, Corporation and Banking businesses. Many modern, labor-saving features, which have never before been given, are introduced, and it is believed that they will meet the approval of teachers. Special attention is called to the practical treatment of corporation bookkeeping.

The author and publishers hereby express their thanks to the many teachers who have used the Introductory Course in the past year, and trust that this, the Complete Course, will prove equally satisfactory to all who use it.

ROCHESTER, N. Y.,
August 15, 1898.

SUGGESTIONS TO THE STUDENT.

Accuracy. The first essential of a bookkeeper is to be *absolutely accurate*. To acquire the habit of being accurate will require constant, persistent effort on your part. Learn to concentrate your thoughts upon your business—that of learning office routine and bookkeeping—and never permit your mind to wander therefrom during your business (study) hours. It is in bookkeeping as in medicine: "An ounce of prevention is worth a pound of cure;" *careful thinking* before *doing* will prove a good *preventive* of errors, while much worry and waste of valuable time will be the *cure* for errors once made. It is better to spend a *minute* in thinking before doing than to spend an *hour* or more in detecting an error that has been made. Improvement is the direct result of thought and intelligent application; so, if you desire to improve you must think, *think*, THINK before acting. A practical knowledge of commercial calculations, and the ability to add correctly with ease and certainty are absolutely essential to insure accuracy in bookkeeping.

Neatness. A plain, business style of writing is the first and most important essential to neatness in bookkeeping. To acquire a good business style of writing will require much *thought* and *practice*. The script plates throughout the book will furnish you food for thought and material for practice. The arrangement of the work and attention to details are also very important and should receive considerable of your attention. Remember that "perfection is made up of trifles, and perfection itself is no trifle," hence, the importance of observing all the details and instructions that are given. Last, but not least, neatness will assist you in acquiring accuracy, besides errors are more readily detected in neatly kept books than in those that are not neatly kept.

Dispatch. First of all be accurate; second, be neat, and let speed and facility come with practice, experience, and a thorough familiarity with your business. Remember that dispatch without accuracy and neatness is absolutely *worthless*. An inaccurate clerk or bookkeeper is *worse* than worthless, while a careless, slovenly bookkeeper is very soon displaced by one who is accurate and neat. Never hurry in your studies. It is better to have your mind filled with properly assimilated knowledge than to have your books filled with work that you do not understand.

Your Teacher. The duty of your teacher is to guide and direct you in your studies, but *not* to do your work for you, as thereby he would be doing you a positive *injury*.

Yourself. Rely upon *yourself*. Be industrious. Do not *injure* and *disgrace* yourself or waste your time by trying to copy from others, as it can not be done in this system without being detected.

OFFICE ROUTINE AND BOOKKEEPING.

Bookkeeping is the art, method or practice of recording business transactions. By the term business transactions is meant dealings between two or more persons. The object of keeping books is to enable the proprietor to ascertain at any time with certainty and ease any particulars regarding the business.

Methods. There are two methods of keeping books, termed Double Entry and Single Entry. In Double Entry Bookkeeping accounts are kept with persons and things. In Single Entry Bookkeeping accounts are kept with persons only. Single Entry will be introduced later. The following pertains to Double Entry.

Books required. Originally three books were used in recording business transactions; viz, Day Book or Blotter, Journal and Ledger. The Day Book and Journal are now usually combined. This form of book is known as the Day Book-Journal.

The Day Book-Journal contains a statement of the business transactions and the Debits and Credits arising therefrom, arranged in convenient form for transferring to the Ledger. Deciding upon and arranging the Debits and Credits in the Day Book-Journal is called *Journalizing.* Debit is abbreviated Dr. Credit is abbreviated Cr.

The Ledger is the book of accounts.

An Account consists of Debits and Credits of a like nature, systematically arranged, and is a statement of debt, either owed to the business or owed by the business. The left side of an account is the Debit, and the right side the Credit. Transferring the debits and credits to the proper accounts in the Ledger from any other book is called *Posting.*

GENERAL RULES FOR DEBITING AND CREDITING.

1. *DEBIT* the account that has received value, because it has become indebted to the business.*

2. *CREDIT the account that has supplied value, because the business has become indebted to it.*

*To debit an account means to *charge* it with the value received. Many bookkeepers use the term *charge* instead of *debit.*

TO THE STUDENT.

Model Set. On the following four pages a set of books, consisting of a Day Book-Journal and Ledger, is illustrated. The object of this set is to give you a general idea of the arrangement and appearance of a simple set of books; also to serve as a model, which you are to copy a sufficient number of times to enable you to acquire a neat, business-like style of writing, to arrange your work properly, and to enable you to make good figures rapidly.

March 1, 89

L. F.	Journal Entry	Explanation	Dr. Amount	Cr. Amount
	Cash	Wm Wood commenced business	5000	
	Wm. Wood	investing cash		5000
	Mdse	Bot for cash	320	
	Cash	800 bu Wheat 40		320
	Expense	Bot books for office use	18 50	
	Cash			18 50
	2			
	Cash	Sold for cash	140	
	Mdse	200 bu Wheat 70		140
	3			
	Mdse	Bot on acct	340	
	J. W. Hunter	1000 bu Oats 25		340
		600 " Corn 40		
	Mdse	Bot on acct	1400	
	S. W. Snow	200 bbls Flour 7.00		1400
	4			
	Jas. Spring	Sold on acct	250	
	Mdse	500 bu Corn 50		250
	J. W. Hunter	Paid on acct	250	
	Cash			250
	M. Summer	Sold on acct	600	
	Mdse	100 bbls Flour 6.00		600
	Cash	Recd on acct	200	
	Jas. Spring			200
	Bills Rec	Recd his note	600	
	M. Summer	in full of acct		1600

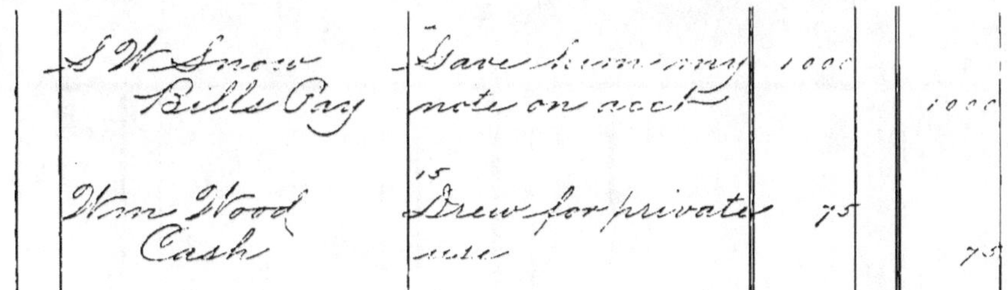

FIRST POSTING EXERCISE.

In performing the work outlined herewith, read the first direction, then do the work as instructed. Read the second direction and do the work. Continue taking up the directions *one* at a time, performing the work as directed. Consult your teacher on any point you do not fully understand.

1. Copy the Model Day Book-Journal given on pages 2 and 3, on journal paper, observing every detail closely as you proceed. 2. Write the headings or names of accounts on ledger paper as you find them in the Model Ledger, given on pages 4 and 5. 3. Begin with the first debit, *Cash*, in the Day Book-Journal, trace it to the Cash account in the Model Ledger, after which post it to *your* Ledger (on the Dr. side of Cash account) as you see it in the Model Ledger. 4. In *your* Day Book-Journal, in the column headed L. F. (Ledger Folio) write the number (1) of the page to which you have posted, opposite the word *Cash*, to show that it has been posted. Writing the number of the page opposite an item in the Day Book-Journal or any other book to show that it has been posted is termed *checking* or *post marking*. 5. Take the first credit, *Wm. Wood*, trace it to Wm. Wood's account in the Model Ledger, and post in *your* Ledger (on the credit side of Wm. Wood's account) as shown in the Model Ledger. 6. Check in *your* Day Book-Journal by placing *1* in the column to the left of Wm. Wood's name.

Trace the second debit, *Merchandise*, in the Day Book-Journal to the Merchandise account in the Model Ledger. 2. Post to *your* Ledger (on the Dr. side of Merchandise account) referring to the Model Ledger. 3. Check in the Day Book-Journal opposite the item just posted. 4. Trace the credit, *Cash*, to the Cash account in the Model Ledger. 5. Post to *your* Ledger (on the credit side of Cash account) as shown in the Model Ledger. 6. Check in the Day Book-Journal opposite the item just posted.

Trace the third debit, *Expense*, to the Expense account in the Model Ledger. 2. Post to *your* Ledger, observing all the details given in the previous instructions. 3. Check in the Day Book-Journal opposite the word Expense. Have you posted to the debit side of Expense account? 4. Trace the credit, *Cash*, to the Cash account in the Model Ledger. 5. Post to *your* Ledger, referring to the entry as given in the Model Ledger. 6. Check in the Day Book-Journal.

Continue until you have posted every entry in the Day Book-Journal to the Ledger, following the instructions as given above. Proceed to make a Trial Balance as explained on pages 6 and 7; after which present your work for approval. Then copy the Day Book-Journal, post to the Ledger and take a Trial Balance, referring to the script illustrations, carefully following the style of the writing and figures, the arrangement and general appearance of same. Copy several times more, or until you can produce work that is satisfactory to your teacher.

Wm. Hood.

Date						Date					
Mar			1	75		Mar			1	5000	

Cash

Date						Date					
Mar			1	5000		Mar			1	320	
			1	140			1		1	18	50
			1	200			6		1	250	
							15		1	75	50

Merchandise

Date						Date					
Mar			1	320		Mar	2		1	140	
	3		1	340			4		1	250	
			1	1400			5		1	1600	

Expense

Date						Date					
Mar			1	18	50						

J. W. Hunter, Main City

Date						Date					
Mar			1	250		Mar	3		1	340	

S. W. Snow, 45 Market, City

189– Mar	12		1	1000	189– Mar	3		1	1400

Jas. Spring, Detroit, Mich.

189– Mar	4		1	250	189– Mar	8		1	200

M. Sumner, Troy, N.Y.

189– Mar	8		1	1600	189– Mar	10		1	1600

Bills Receivable

189– Mar	10		1	1600					

Bills Payable

					189– Mar	12		1	1000

TRIAL BALANCE.

You will observe that in the Model Day Book-Journal the debits and credits are equal in amount—the total of the Debits is equal to the total of the Credits. This being the case, it is evident that if no errors were made in posting, the Ledger debits and credits must also be equal in amount. To ascertain whether the debit and credit sides of the Ledger are equal, we make a test by taking a *Trial Balance.* Trace the small pencil footings of each account in the Model Ledger to the Trial Balance given below. When there is but one item on either side of an account it stands to reason that no footings are required, as there is nothing to add, but do not fail to enter such items in the Trial Balance. Pencil foot (in very small, neat figures) the accounts in *your* Ledger, and proceed to make a Trial Balance. Add both sides of your Trial Balance to see that they agree, after which submit your work to your teacher for approval, and ask questions on any point you do not fully understand.

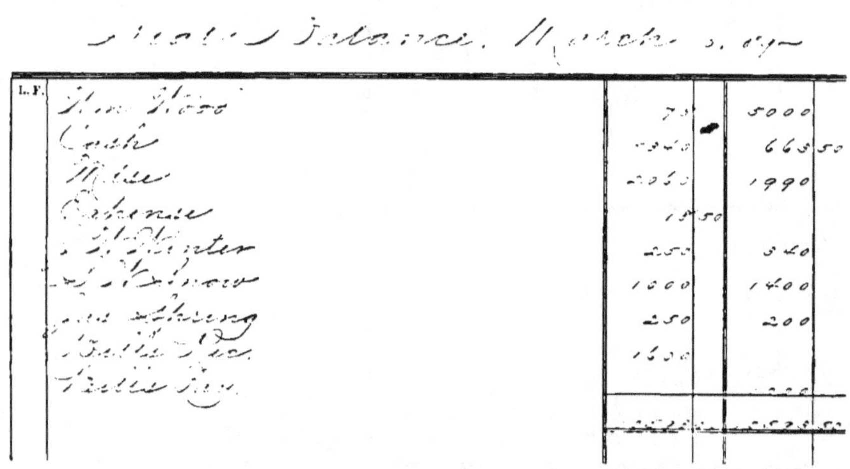

[illegible]

L. F.					
	[illegible]	75		5000	
	Cash	[illegible]		665	50
	Mdse	[illegible]		1990	
	Expense	15	50		
	[illegible]	[illegible]		540	
	[illegible]	1000		1400	
	[illegible]	250		200	
	[illegible]	1500			
	[illegible]			[illegible]	
		[illegible]		[illegible]	[illegible]

NOTE.—All ruling should be done in red ink unless otherwise instructed by the teacher.

Instead of carrying the footings of the Ledger accounts to the Trial Balance, it is the practice among bookkeepers to carry only the balances (differences between the debit and credit footings) to the Trial Balance. The Trial Balance of the Model Ledger, when balances are used instead of footings, will appear as given on next page. Compare same with your Ledger balances, and employ this method when taking Trial Balances in your subsequent work.

TRIAL BALANCE, MARCH 15, 189–. (Balance Method.)

L. F.					
1	Wm. Wood,			4925	
	Cash,	4676	50		
	Merchandise,	70			
	Expense,	18	50		
	J. W. Winter,			90	
	S. W. Snow,			400	
	Jas. Spring,	50			
	Bills Receivable,	1600			
	Bills Payable,			1000	
		6415	00	6415	00

Having copied the preceding Day Book-Journal, posted the Ledger and taken the Trial Balance the required number of times, you will lay aside your book and all of your bookkeeping work, except one copy of your Day Book-Journal, from which you are to post up a Ledger and take a Trial Balance without referring to any model. After this is done, and you have satisfied yourself and your teacher that you can post readily and accurately, consult him in regard to proceeding. Your writing should show a marked degree of improvement by the time you have reached this point; if not, you will have to improve it, as good writing is one chief essential of good bookkeeping. It would be a waste of time to proceed without being able to do creditable work. You should establish correct habits at the very beginning. Preserve the best copy of your Model Ledger and Trial Balance, as you will need them later.

OBSERVATIONS.—Since the primary object of business is to acquire wealth, it is the custom of most merchants "to close" their books once a year to ascertain whether their business for the year has been prosperous or not. To close the model set in a systematic manner, you would be obliged to employ the processes for closing books as explained on pages 33 to 40 inclusive. To acquire a thorough understanding of those processes, it will be necessary for you to first learn and put into practice the fundamental principles of making bookkeeping records as presented and explained on pages 9 to 28 inclusive.

While you will not be able to employ the systematic processes used by the practical bookkeeper in determining whether Wm. Wood's business has been a prosperous one or not, you can, however, ascertain for yourself, by the aid of the instructions given below, what the condition of the business is.

Looking at the first entry in the Model Journal you find that Mr. Wood put into the business $5000 in cash. The Trial Balance shows the amount of cash on hand at the close of the business period to be $4676.50, which makes it appear that there has been a loss. But you are to consider that there is now $50 due the business from Jas. Spring; also M. Sumner's note for $1600. (See Trial Balance.) You will find by referring to the Model Journal that the goods purchased have not all been sold; 500 bu. Wheat have been bought, while 200 bu. have been sold. The remaining 300 bu., valued at 64¢ (the cost price), amount to $192. (See Model Journal.) The Oats purchased remain unsold, 400 bu., valued at 25¢, amount to $100. Of the 600 bu. Corn bought, 500 bu. have been sold; the remaining 100 bu. at 40¢ amount to $40. Adding $4676.50, the cash on hand; $50, amount due from J. Spring; $1600, amount due from M. Sumner on note; $192, value of Wheat unsold; $100, value of Oats on hand; and $40, value of Corn not sold, you have $6658.50, which would be the present value of Mr. Wood's business were there nothing due other parties.

You will find by referring to the Trial Balance that there is due J. W. Winter $90, and S. W. Snow $400; also a note favor S. W. Snow for $1000, making a total of $1490. Subtracting $1490, the amount due other parties, from $6658.50 gives you $5168.50, the present value of the business.

Mr. Wood started in business with $5000; he withdrew for private use $75, thereby reducing the value of his interest in the business to $4925. Subtracting $4925 from $5168.50, the present value, gives you $243.50, the amount gained.

SECOND POSTING EXERCISE.

Make a neat copy of the following Journal, post same to a Ledger, placing four accounts on a page; then test the accuracy of your posting by taking a Trial Balance, using the balances instead of the footings. When completed, present to the teacher for approval: then preserve same for future use.

SEPT. 16, 189–.

Accounts	Explanation	Dr.	Cr.
Cash,	Jos. Winter commenced business	8500	
Jos. Winter,	and invested,		8500
Expense,	Paid one month's rent,	75	
Cash,			75
	17.		
Mdse.,	Bo't for cash	850	
Cash,	200 yds. Broadcloth at 4.25,		850
	18.		
Cash,	Sold for cash	250	
Mdse.,	50 yds. Broadcloth at 5.00,		250
	19.		
Mdse.,	Bo't on account	765	
H. M. Royal,	300 yds. Fancy Cass. at 2.55.		765
	20.		
H. M. Royal,	Paid on account,	500	
Cash,			500
Mdse.,	Bo't on account	645	
A. G. Rudolph,	150 yds. Broadcloth at 4.30,		645
	21.		
A. G. Rudolph,	Gave him my note	500	
Bills Payable,	on account,		500
	22.		
B. Hermann,	Sold on account	440	
Mdse.,	80 yds. Broadcloth at 5.50,		440
	23.		
Cash,	Received on account,	250	
B. Hermann,			250
	24		
Jno. Frey,	Sold on account	525	
Mdse.,	175 yds. Fancy Cass. at 3.00,		525
	25.		
Bills Receivable,	Received his note	400	
Jno. Frey,	on account,		400
	26.		
Mdse.,	Bought on account	720	
Jacob Hauser,	300 yds. Blk. Cass. at 2.40,		720
	27.		
Jno. Hauser,	Sold on account	300	
Mdse.,	100 yds. Blk. Cass. at 3.00,		300
	28.		
Jno. Frey,	Sold on account	240	
Mdse.,	80 yds. Blk. Cass. at 3.00,		240
	29.		
Jos. Winter,	Took for private use	12 75	
Mdse.,	3 yds. Broadcloth at 4.25,		12 75
	30.		
Expense,	Paid drayage bill,	6 50	
Cash,			6 50

KEEPING BOOKS FOR C. W. HAMMOND.

You are now to become the bookkeeper for C. W. Hammond, Wholesale and Retail dealer in General Merchandise, 122–124 Main Street. City. Mr. Hammond, having confidence in your ability and integrity, gives you a Power of Attorney to transact business and sign all the business papers requisite to carry on the business. He will make all purchases and sales, and you are to receive the goods purchased, and deliver the goods sold; also, make all records in the books.

Being a novice in business, you will be subject to the directions of those who are able to direct you. Do every thing you are told to do. Remember you are a learner, not a business man. Business can not be done in the school room, and is represented only to teach business routine and make bookkeeping more practical than it is possible without the vouchers (business papers) and the representatives of the commodities in which you are dealing.

You will practically get the same experience you would get were you engaged in a real business, and will be confronted with the same problems that confront the bookkeeper in a business house. Bills of the goods bought and other business papers will be handed to you by the teacher, just as the letter carrier delivers the mail to the bookkeeper or manager in an office. These papers are similar in every respect to those used in business. All business papers issued are to be written up by you, and the records made in the books just as this work is done by the bookkeeper in business.

The work in your books will not be like any other student's work. The capital invested will be different in amount. Your selling list will be assigned to you by your teacher, and you must adhere strictly to it if you desire to get correct results. No advantage is to be derived from comparing your work with that of other students, as of necessity the work is different. Be self-reliant and you will succeed.

Before making an entry in your books, it will be necessary for you to determine the *debit* and *credit* to which the transaction gives rise. This you will do by applying the Special Rules for the accounts to be debited and credited, to which you will be referred by number. After you have made the entry, your next step will be to learn the *reason* for debiting and crediting as you did, which may be done by studying the General Rules for debiting and crediting.

Carefully study the following accounts and answer the questions.

Cash. Under this title everything considered money is to be entered; as Specie, Bank Bills, Checks, Bank Drafts, Postal, Express, and Telegraph Money Orders, etc.

The Special Rules for debiting and crediting Cash are as follows:

3. *Debit Cash when it is received by the business.*

4. *Credit Cash when it is parted with by the business.*

The difference between the sides of the Cash account will show the the cash on hand. The credit side of this account can not be greater than the debit side, since it is impossible to pay out more than has been received. Cash on hand is a *Resource.* An account exhibits a Resource when it represents property on hand, or an amount owing to the business.

TRANSACTIONS ILLUSTRATING THE CASH ACCOUNT.

March 1. Received cash of the Proprietor, $500. March 2. Paid cash for rent, $20. March 3. Received cash for merchandise, $140. March 4. Paid Jas. Harris cash on account, $50. March 5. Received cash of John West on account, $80.

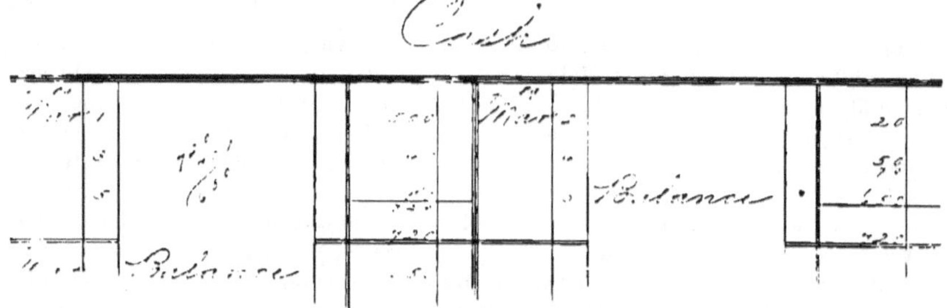

* Write the above line in red ink unless otherwise instructed by the teacher. It has been a prevailing custom to balance accounts in red ink and to bring the balances below the ruling in black ink. There are many good bookkeepers, however, who use but one color of ink on their books. The tendency at the present time seems to be toward one color. You are to use red ink in all your work wherever directed to do so, unless you receive instructions to the contrary from your teacher.

The above illustration shows that Cash account has received $720 and parted with $70, leaving a balance of $650, which is a *Resource*. The balance as shown by the Cash account should agree with the actual amount on hand.

QUESTIONS.—What is to be entered in the Cash account? What is considered money? When is cash debited? When credited? What does the difference between the two sides of the Cash account show? Is cash on hand a resource or a liability? Which side of Cash account must be the greater, when there is any difference? Why?

The Proprietor's Account. The person engaging in business has an account opened under his own name, in which are to be entered the sum or sums by him invested or withdrawn, and, at stated periods, the net gain or net loss resulting from the prosecution of the business. The title STOCK was formerly used instead of the proprietor's name. When several persons are engaged in a business they are known as partners, and each partner is credited for his investment and debited for all withdrawals.

The Special Rules for debiting and crediting the Proprietor's account are as follows:

5. *DEBIT the Proprietor for his liabilities assumed by the business.*
6. *DEBIT the Proprietor for amounts drawn from the business for his private use.*
7. *DEBIT the Proprietor for the Net Loss.*
8. *CREDIT the Proprietor for his investment at commencing business.*
9. *CREDIT the Proprietor for subsequent investments.*
10. *CREDIT the Proprietor for the Net Gain.*

The difference between the sides of the Proprietor's account at commencing business is called the Net Investment. The difference in the account at the close of business, after the Net Gain or Net Loss has been transferred to it, is called the Net Capital or Present Capital.

TRANSACTIONS ILLUSTRATING THE PROPRIETOR'S ACCOUNT.

James Munsey, Proprietor. June 1. Invested: Cash, $5,000; Merchandise per Inventory, $2450; H. J. West's note, $500. His Liabilities are: Note favor of E. W. Martin, $1000, with interest accrued, $60. June 15. Withdrew for private use, $75. June 30: On closing books the Net Gain is found to be $632.

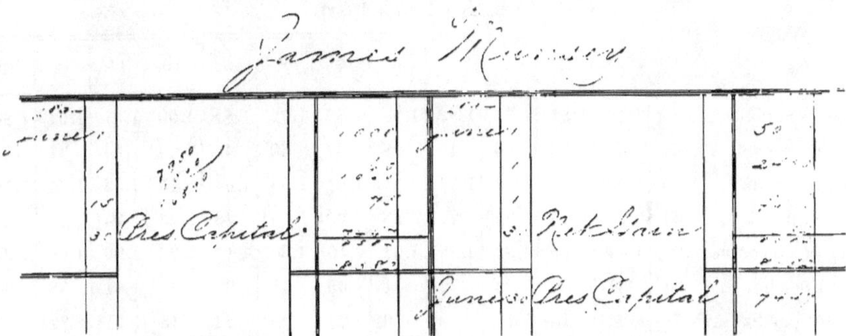

*To be written in red ink.

The above account shows that the total investments are $7950, and the total liabilities are $1060, making a Net Investment or Capital of $6890. This Capital is diminished by the withdrawal of $75, and increased by the Net Gain of $632, making the Present Capital $7447.

QUESTIONS. For what is the Proprietor credited? For what is he debited? What is the difference between the sides of the Proprietor's account at commencing business called? What is the difference called after the Net Gain or Net Loss has been entered in the account? What title is sometimes used instead of the Proprietor's name? What is a partnership?

Explanations in Ledger Accounts. Formerly it was the custom of bookkeepers to write the name of the credit account of an entry in the explanation column of the debit account of the same entry. Likewise in the explanation column of the credit account of an entry, the name of the debit account was written. As the writing of the names of opposite accounts in the explanation columns of ledger accounts conveys no *practical* information, and only creates unnecessary labor, it has been discontinued by progressive bookkeepers.

Other information of a more practical character may be, and often is, written in the ledger accounts; such as the terms on which a bill of goods was purchased or sold, the amount of discount received from or allowed to a person, and the initials of the books from which postings are made when there is more than one book of original entry, so that reference to the original entry can be made with ease and certainty, etc. The original part of a *closing* entry should be written in red ink to distinguish it from those items that are transferred from other books or accounts, and should have the name of the account to which it is transferred written in the explanation column. The record in the account to which it is transferred should be made in black ink, and should include the name of the account which contains the original part of the entry.

In posting from the books of original entry the student will observe the instructions given, unless otherwise directed by the teacher.

NOTE.—In law the book containing the original entry is the Day Book, whether such book is the Day Book, so called, or the Day Book-Journal, Sales Book, Cash Book, or any other book or record. Such books of original entry become the basis for all explanations, and are the only business records admitted as evidence in court. Such records to possess value as evidence must be clear and complete and *free from erasures*. A material alteration in an entry in a book of original entry taints the record, and sometimes makes it worthless. When a mistake is made in a book of original entry it should be corrected in such a manner as will make the fact that it was a mistake apparent; in other words, the evidence of the mistake should be preserved. Erasing should never be resorted to in a book of original entry.

Selling Price Lists.

	1	2	3	4	5	6	7	8	9	10	11	12	13
Apples per bbl....	1.80	1.76	1.81	1.77	1.82	1.78	1.83	1.79	1.84	1.90	1.97	1.91	1.86
Barley per bu....	38	48	39	50	40	28	37	30	42	29	43	31	44
Beans per bu.....	1.75	1.52	1.59	1.62	1.74	1.51	1.61	1.58	1.64	1.73	1.53	1.65	1.56
Butter per lb.....	21	22⅓	25	26⅔	22⅔	28	27⅓	25⅓	26	23	25⅔	29⅓	26⅓
Clover-s'd per bu.	4.02	4.14	4.18	4.32	4.38	4.04	4.40	4.30	4.12	4.26	4.06	4.28	4.34
Corn per bu.	34	31	36	38	32	41	45	48	53	33	51	35	50
Coffee per lb.....	18¾	24¼	18¼	19	20¼	19½	21	20½	22	18½	21¾	22½	23
Eggs per doz.....	16⅕	17⅕	18⅕	16⅗	17⅕	18⅗	19	20⅕	20⅕	18⅕	17	19⅕	21
Flaxseed per bu.	1.81	1.69	1.65	1.51	1.45	1.79	1.43	1.53	1.71	1.57	1.77	1.55	1.49
Flour per bbl. ...	4.50	4.74	4.72	4.61	4.52	4.71	4.69	4.53	4.65	4.57	4.67	4.59	4.55
Hams per lb.	18	17	16	17⅕	16⅗	15⅕	15⅕	14	13⅗	15⅗	17⅕	14⅗	13⅕
Lard per lb......	12⅔	14⅓	11⅔	10	14	08⅔	09⅓	11⅓	10⅔	13⅔	11	07⅓	10⅓
Molasses per gal.	49½	48	47	45½	37½	38½	41	43½	45	48½	42½	38	39½
Oats per bu......	46	49	44	42	48	39	35	32	27	47	29	45	30
Peas per bu......	1.41	1.64	1.57	1.54	1.42	1.65	1.55	1.58	1.52	1.43	1.63	1.51	1.60
Potatoes per bu.	41	45	40	44	39	43	38	42	37	31	24	30	35
Rye per bu......	41	31	40	29	39	51	42	49	37	50	36	48	35
Sugar per lb.....	10¾	05¼	11¼	10½	09¼	10	08½	09	07½	11	07¾	07	06½
Tea per lb.......	27	28½	29½	31	39	38	35½	33	31½	28	34	38½	37
Wheat per bu....	99	75	77	88	97	78	80	96	84	92	82	90	94

Amounts to be Invested.

1	2	3	4	5	6	7	8	9	10	11	12	13
8100	7300	9500	7500	7100	8200	7600	8000	8800	7400	8900	8300	7200

C. W. HAMMOND'S BUSINESS.

To the Student. Bear in mind that you are about to keep the books of the "business" of which Mr. Hammond is the Proprietor, and not merely the accounts of Mr. Hammond. The *business* receives and parts with (supplies) value, and, so far as the books are concerned, Mr. Hammond is merely one of the persons with whom the business has dealings. As you have learned, an account is kept with him, and he is credited with the capital he invests (value supplied to the business) and is charged (debited) for what he receives from the business.

SELLING PRICE LISTS (Continued).

	14	15	16	17	18	19	20	21	22	23	24	25
Apples per bbl.	1.92	1.87	1.93	1.88	1.94	1.89	1.95	2.00	1.96	1.99	1.85	1.98
Barley per bu.	32	46	33	45	34	47	35	26	36	49	41	27
Beans per bu.	1.63	1.72	1.54	1.67	1.60	1.68	1.71	1.55	1.69	1.66	1.57	1.70
Butter per lb.	27	30⅓	23⅓	29⅔	28⅓	30	27⅔	29	28⅔	24⅔	24⅓	23⅔
Clover-seed per bu.	4.08	4.22	4.48	4.16	4.46	4.44	4.36	4.50	4.20	4.24	4.42	4.10
Corn per bu.	43	52	40	55	47	54	46	49	44	39	42	37
Coffee per lb.	20	23½	21½	23¾	20¾	22¾	23¼	22¼	21¼	19¾	24	19¼
Eggs per doz.	19⅗	20⅗	16⅕	17⅗	20	18⅗	20⅘	19⅗	17⅗	19⅕	18	16⅘
Flaxseed per bu.	1.75	1.61	1.35	1.67	1.37	1.39	1.47	1.33	1.63	1.59	1.41	1.73
Flour per bbl.	4.64	4.60	4.58	4.63	4.70	4.56	4.66	4.62	4.68	4.54	4.73	4.51
Hams per lb.	14⅘	13⅗	17⅚	16⅗	14⅙	15⅗	13⅚	14⅚	16⅕	15	16⅙	17⅚
Lard per lb.	09⅔	06⅓	13⅓	07	08⅓	06⅔	09	07⅔	08	12	12⅓	13
Molasses per gal.	42	46½	44	41½	40	46	44½	43	40½	39	47½	49
Oats per bu.	37	28	40	25	33	26	34	31	36	41	38	43
Peas per bu.	1.53	1.44	1.62	1.49	1.56	1.48	1.45	1.61	1.47	1.50	1.59	1.46
Potatoes per bu.	29	34	28	33	27	32	26	21	25	22	36	23
Rye per bu.	47	33	46	34	45	32	44	53	43	30	38	52
Sugar per lb.	09½	06	08	05¾	08¾	06¾	06¼	07¼	08¼	09¾	05½	10¼
Tea per lb.	34½	30	32½	35	36½	30½	32	33½	36	37½	29	27½
Wheat per bu.	85	89	91	86	79	93	83	87	81	95	76	98

AMOUNTS TO BE INVESTED (Continued).

14	15	16	17	18	19	20	21	22	23	24	25
7900	8600	9200	7700	8500	9400	8700	7800	9100	9300	9000	8400

Having carefully studied pages 9, 10 and 11, consult your teacher in regard to proceeding, and answer all questions he may ask you. If you answer his questions satisfactorily, he will hand you the cash Mr. Hammond is to invest in the business, your Power of Attorney, and the receptacles for your business papers and merchandise, also, assign you the price list you are to use. Count the cash and place it in the Cash Drawer. File the Power of Attorney on the Voucher File.

NOTE.—After having been assigned by the teacher the price list to be used, the pupil is advised to copy it on a separate sheet of paper. This will put the list in a form convenient for use, and render mistakes less liable to occur in making the extensions.

(This entry is similar to the first entry in the Model Journal.)

Give the reason mentally for the above debit. (*Read rule 1, page 1.*) Give the reason mentally for the above credit. (*Read rule 2, page 1.*) Give your reasons similar to the following: "Cash account is debited because it has received value from the business, and is, therefore, indebted to it. Mr. Hammond is credited because he has supplied the value, and, therefore, the business is indebted to him." Be sure to give the reason every time you are instructed to do so.

Carefully study the following account and be prepared to answer the questions.

Merchandise. This title is usually applied to all goods the proprietor is dealing in as a business. If it is desired to show results in detail, separate accounts should be opened; as Flour, Corn, Wheat, etc., instead of including all under the general heading, Merchandise.

The Special Rules for debiting and crediting Merchandise are:

11. *Debit Merchandise when received (bought) by the business.*

12. *Credit Merchandise when parted with (sold or supplied to others) by the business.*

Since the debit side of Merchandise shows what the goods cost, and the credit side what they sell for, the difference must show the Gain or Loss—providing the goods have all been sold. When some of the goods remain unsold, deduct their *current* value from the debit side—or add it to the credit side—and the difference between the sides, after this has been done, will show the gain or loss. If the credit side of the account is the larger, the difference shows a gain: if the debit side is the larger, the difference shows a loss. Property remaining on hand is called an *Inventory*.

TRANSACTIONS ILLUSTRATING MERCHANDISE ACCOUNT.

May 1. Bought goods of L. Warwick for Cash, $200. May 2. Bought goods of Wm. Macy on account, $350. May 3. Sold John Kress merchandise for Cash, $150. May 4. Value of the goods on hand (Inventory), $450.

Note.—In every computation if there is a fraction of one-half cent or more in the result, add another cent; if less than one-half cent, drop the fraction.

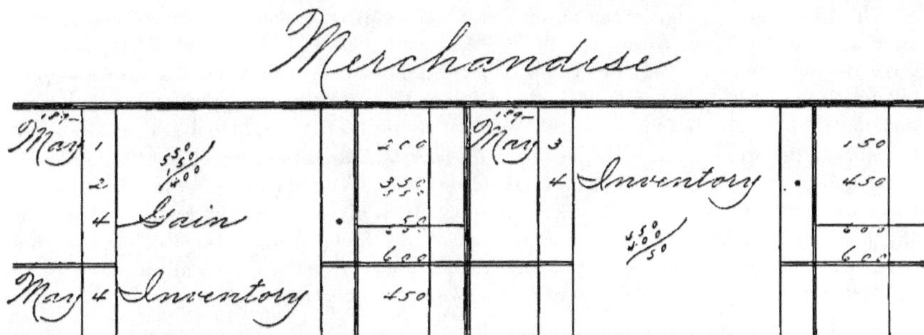

*To be written in red ink.

The above account shows that goods amounting to $550 have been purchased, and goods amounting to $150 have been sold. Since the cost is in excess of the sales, it is evident that there would be a loss of $400 were there no goods on hand. Subtracting the excess of cost ($400) over sales from the inventory, we have a gain of $50. Why?

QUESTIONS. To what is the title Merchandise applied? Why are separate accounts sometimes opened with the different articles, instead of including them all under the general heading, Merchandise? For what is Mdse. debited? For what credited? What does the difference between the debit and credit sides show? When a portion of the goods remain unsold, what must be done to find the gain or loss? What is property remaining unsold called? When the credit side of Mdse. is larger than the debit, does the difference show a Gain or a Loss?

No. 2.—CASH PURCHASE. Mr. Hammond has bargained with your teacher for 300 bu. Wheat, at 60¢ per bu., and 200 bbls. Flour, at $4.10 per bbl. He wishes you to pay for same, receive the Mdse. and a receipted bill. Make the calculations to find the cost, then hand the required amount of cash to your teacher, and get the bill and the representative Mdse. Check the items of the bill (using pen and ink and placing the check marks in the vertical column to the left of the items) with the Mdse. to see that what is called for is received. Go over the calculations and the addition of the bill to see that no errors exist, placing a check mark to the right of every extension found to be correct. If found correct, write "O. K." with your initials underneath in the lower left-hand corner. Place the Mdse. in the "Store Room." Determine the account to be debited by reading *rule 11, page 14.* Determine the account to be credited by reading *rule 4, page 9.* Make the entry as follows, substituting the correct amounts for the amounts given.

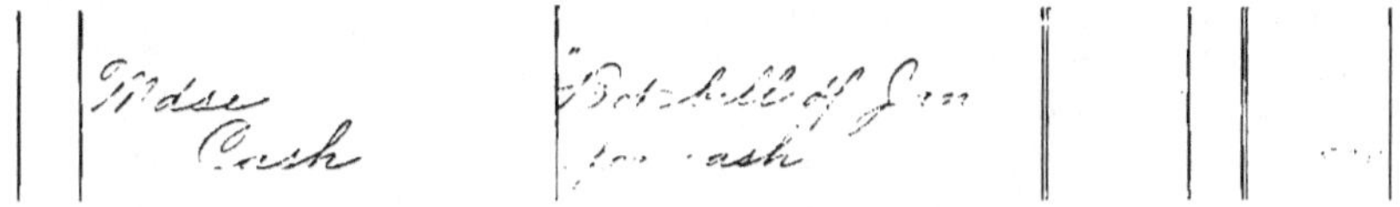

Give the reason mentally for the above debit. (*Read rule 1, page 1.*) Give the reason mentally for the above credit. (*Read rule 2, page 1.*) Fold your bill lengthwise, face outward, and write across the face "Entered," placing the date underneath. Place it on the Voucher File.

No. 3.—Merchandise Purchased for Cash. Mr. Hammond has given your teacher an order for 1300 bu. Corn, at 30¢ per bu., and 100 bbls. Flour, at $4.10 per bbl Take the necessary cash, pay for it, and get the representative merchandise and receipted bill for same. Check the bill with the merchandise. Verify the calculations and addition of the bill, and if found correct, O. K. it as previously instructed. Place the merchandise in the Store Room. Debit—*Rule 11, page 14.* Credit—*Rule 4, page 9.* Make the entry underneath the entry for the second transaction. With the exception of the amounts, this entry is identical with No. 2, therefore no model is given. Give the reason mentally for the debit (*rule 1*); also for the credit (*rule 2*). Fold the bill lengthwise, face outward, and write across the face "Entered," placing the date underneath. File the bill properly.

Follow all directions in the exact order in which they are given.

No. 4.—Cash Sale. Your teacher has received an order for Flour and Wheat from an out of town customer. Not having either in stock, he has arranged with Mr. Hammond to purchase from him 50 bbls. Flour and 100 bu. Wheat at the prices given in your selling price list. Select the goods from the stock in the Store Room. Make out the bill on one of Mr. Hammond's bill heads, using one of the bills on your Voucher File as a model. Always go over your calculations and addition a second time to make certain that your work is correct. Receipt the bill as follows:

"*Received Payment,*
C. W. Hammond,
per (*your name*)."

Hand the bill and the goods to your teacher. If he approves your work he will pay you; if not, you will have to rewrite the bill. When he has paid you, determine the account to be debited by reading *rule 8, page 9.* Also the account to be credited by reading *rule 12, page 14.* Make the entry as follows, substituting the correct extensions and amounts for the ones given:

Cash	Sold for cash		[illegible]	
Mdse	50 bbls Flour [illegible]	[illegible]		[illegible]
	100 bu. Wheat [illegible]	[illegible]		

Give the reason mentally for the debit—*Rule 1;* credit—*Rule 2.* Place the cash in the Cash Drawer, recounting it before doing so. Always count cash a second time, both in receiving and paying it out.

Follow the instructions of your teacher and those given herewith to the letter. All business papers or vouchers and merchandise representing the business transacted by Mr. Hammond will come to you through your teacher. Apply for the first lot. Take up each transaction in the order it is given.

No. 5.—Merchandise Bought for Cash. The first bill (No. 5) represents a cash purchase which Mr. Hammond has made. Take the merchandise (No. 5) and check up the bill. Verify the calculations and addition, and if found correct, O. K. it as you did No. 2. Store the merchandise. Mr. Hammond's O. K. indicates that the prices are the ones agreed on when he made the purchase, but it does not signify that the calculations and addition are correct. That is left for you to ascertain. Never enter a bill that has not had the prices

O. K.'d by the buyer. Pay the bill, placing the cash in the Cash Paid Out receptacle. In paying parties other than your teacher, always place the cash in this receptacle, from which it will be delivered to your teacher, who represents these parties. Debit—*Rule 11, page 14.* Credit—*Rule 4, page 9.* This entry is similar to entry for No. 2.

NOTE.—The student is requested to write his address where indicated and complete the date on each and every voucher received.

Give the reason mentally for the debit—*Rule 1;* credit—*Rule 2.* File the bill, following instructions given for No. 2. Do not proceed with the next transaction until you thoroughly understand this one.

Study the following account and be prepared to answer the questions.

Expense Account. Under this title are to be entered all amounts expended for carrying on the business; as rent, office books and office furniture, clerks' salaries, postage, etc. If it is desired to show results in detail, separate accounts must be kept with Salaries, Rent, Office Furniture, etc., instead of including them all under the general heading, Expense. When separate accounts are kept, apply the rules for Expense account, as they are subdivisions of this account.

The Special Rules for debiting and crediting Expense account are:

13. *DEBIT Expense when it costs the business value.*

14. *CREDIT Expense when it supplies value from anything previously debited to Expense.*

TRANSACTIONS ILLUSTRATING EXPENSE ACCOUNT.

Oct. 1. Paid rent, $12. Oct. 2. Bought two tons coal, $9.50. Oct. 3. Bought postage stamps, $5. Oct. 7. On selling out the business, sold the coal on hand for $6.

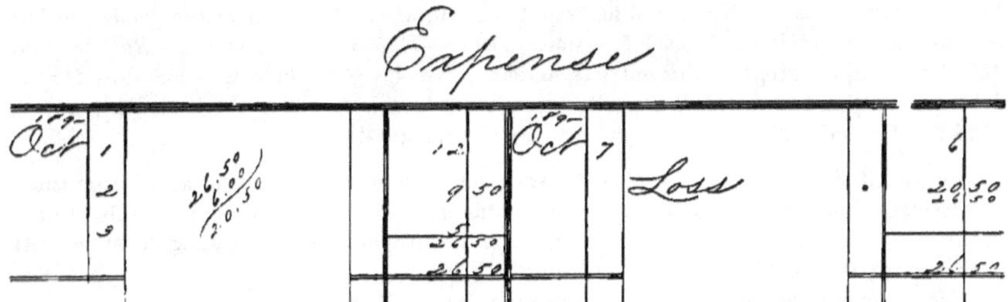

*To be written in red ink.

This account shows the expenditures (value received by Expense) for carrying on the business to be $26.50, and the amount "supplied" by selling the coal to be $6. Deducting the credit amount from the debit gives $20.50, the loss. Expense account generally shows a loss.

QUESTIONS. What is to be entered under the title Expense? What must be done if it is desired to exhibit results in detail? For what is Expense debited? For what credited? What does Expense account generally show?

JANUARY 2, 189–.

No. 6.—Cash Paid for Stationery and Books. Bill No. 6 is for stationery and books, which were received yesterday. It has been checked and O. K.'d by Mr. Hammond, which shows that all the items were received by him and the prices are correct. Examine the bill to see that no errors exist. Pay the bill, placing the cash in Cash Paid Out. Determine the account to be debited by reading *rule 13, page 17.* Determine the account to be credited by reading *rule 4, page 9.* Substituting the proper amounts, make the following entry:

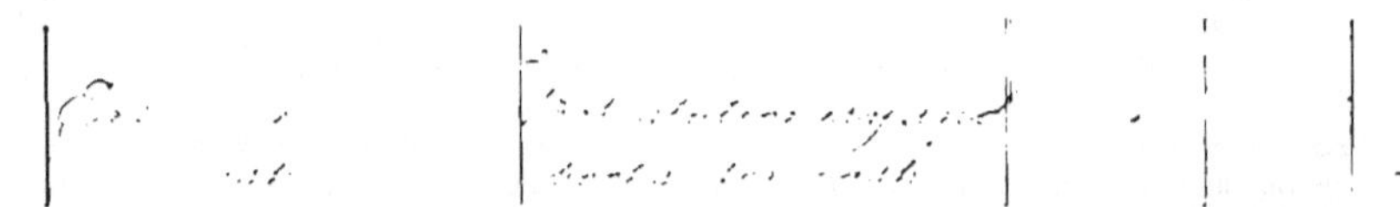

Give the reason mentally for the debit—*Rule 1;* credit—*Rule 2.* File the bill as previously instructed. Consult your teacher about anything that you do not fully understand.

No. 7.—Rent Paid in Cash. According to the terms of his lease, Mr. Hammond is to pay $100 per month for rent of store at 122–124 Main Street. Pay the rent for the month of January, placing the cash in Cash Paid Out, and take a receipt (No. 7) for same. Debit—*Rule 13, page 17.* Credit—*Rule 4, page 9.* This entry is similar to the entry for No. 6, with the exception of the explanation (Day Book entry), which is as follows: "Paid January rent." Give the reason mentally for the debit—*Rule 1;* credit—*Rule 2.* Place the receipt on the Voucher File. Are you doing everything in the exact order indicated?

JANUARY 3, 189–.

No. 8.—Merchandise Sold for Cash. Mr. Hammond has sold your teacher the following: 1000 bu. Oats, 1000 bu. Corn, for cash at the prices given in your selling price list. Follow instructions for No. 4 and make out the bill, after which deliver the goods and bill to your teacher, receiving the cash for same. Debit—*Rule 8, page 9;* credit—*Rule 12, page 14.* Explanation excepted, this entry is similar to No. 4. Give the reason mentally for the debit (*Rule 1*) and credit (*Rule 2.*) Recount the cash and place it in the Cash Drawer.

Study the following and be prepared to answer the questions.

Personal Accounts. If a person buys goods from us, to be paid for at a future time, he receives value from the business. At the time he pays for them he supplies value to the business. If we buy of a person, in like manner he supplies the business with value. At the time we pay him, he receives value from the business.

For personal accounts we have the following Special Rules:

15. *DEBIT a person when he receives value from the business on account.*

16. *CREDIT a person when he supplies value to the business on account.*

When a person buys goods, without paying for them at the time of purchase, the transaction is said to be on account (on credit). If the debit side of a personal account is larger than the credit, he owes us the difference, and this difference is a *Resource.* If the credit side of a personal account is larger than the debit, we owe him the difference, and this difference is a *Liability.* An account exhibits a Liability if it represents an amount owing by the business. Accounts with firms and corporations are considered Personal accounts.

TRANSACTIONS ILLUSTRATING A PERSONAL ACCOUNT.

Dealings with Edward F. Becker. Aug. 1. Sold him merchandise on account, $65. Aug. 2. Received cash of him on account, $25. Aug. 3. Received his note at 60 days for $40. Aug. 4. Loaned him $30.

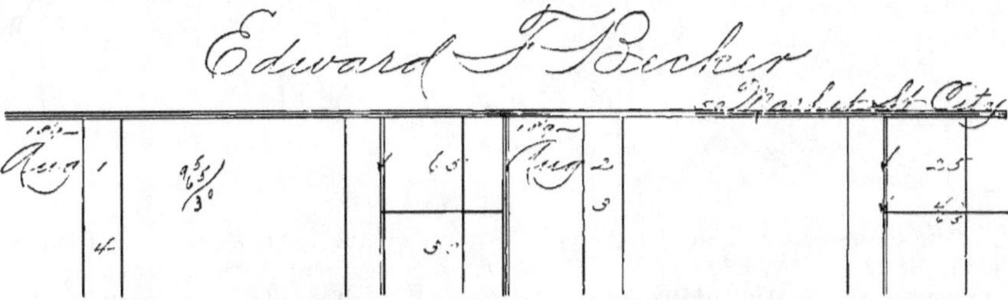

The debit side of this account shows that Edward F. Becker has received value amounting to $95 from our business, and the credit side shows that value amounting to $65 has been supplied to our business by him, leaving a balance of $30, which is a resource to the business. Why? Never rule a personal account unless it balances. See above illustration. In many business houses personal accounts are never ruled.

When personal accounts are not ruled, it is a good plan to check the payments when such payments equal one or more items on the opposite side. This is done by placing neat check marks (√) at the time of posting on the double vertical rulings directly to the left of both the debit and credit items that are equal to each other, as illustrated above.

NOTE.—In the above illustration the items that balance are both ruled and checked. You are to either check or rule the items that balance, as your teacher may direct. Do not fail to consult your teacher.

TRANSACTIONS ILLUSTRATING A PERSONAL ACCOUNT.

Dealings with Frank J. George. Nov. 1. Bought merchandise of him on account, $450. Nov. 2. Paid him cash on account, $150. Nov. 3. He sold us merchandise on account, $200.

The credit side of this account shows that Frank J. George has supplied value to our business amounting to $650; the debit side shows that he has received value amounting to $150 from our business, leaving a balance of $500, which is a liability to the business. Why?

QUESTIONS. When is a person to be debited? When credited? If a person buys goods and does not pay for them at the time of purchase, what is said of the transaction? When a person's account is debited for more than it is credited, does he owe us or do we owe him? Is the difference a resource or a liability? How is it when the credit side of a personal account is the larger? Is the difference a resource or a liability?

January 4, 189–.

No. 9.—Merchandise Bought on Account. This bill (No. 9) of merchandise Mr. Hammond has bought on account. He will owe the parties until the bill is paid. Are the prices correct? How can you tell? Verify the addition and calculations and O. K. it, if found correct. Store the merchandise if found to agree with the bill. Debit—*Rule 11;* credit—*Rule 16.* Make an entry like the following, substituting the correct amounts for the amounts given:

[illegible]	Bot bill of Jan [illegible]	[illegible]		
To [illegible] & Son	on acct			

Give the reasons mentally for the debit (*Rule 1*) and the credit (*Rule 2*). This bill is not receipted. Why not? Fold the bill lengthwise, face outward, and write across the face "Entered" and the date. Place same on the Invoice File. Place all subsequent bills bought *on account* on this file.

No. 10.—Merchandise Sold on Account. This order (No. 10) Mr. Hammond has secured from A. P. Batson. Make out the bill, using the prices given in your price list, but do not receipt it. No terms are placed on the bill when the sale is on account and the time is not given. Place the number (10) of the order on the bill. Go over the calculations and addition to see that you have made no errors. Debit—*Rule 15;* credit—*Rule 12.* Make the entry as follows, placing the correct prices, extensions and amounts instead of the ones given:

A P Batson	Sold on acct	[illegible]	
Mdse	120 bu Potatoes [illegible]		[illegible]
	50 " Wheat [illegible]		
	200 " Corn [illegible]		
	25 bbls Flour [illegible]		
	" " Apples [illegible]		

Give the reason mentally for the debit (*Rule 1*) and credit (*Rule 2*). Select the merchandise and place it together with the bill in "Vouchers for Others" receptacle. Fold the order lengthwise, face outward, write across the face "Filled" and the date; after which place it on the Voucher File.

January 6, 189–.

No 11.—Merchandise Sold on Account. Make out the bill for this order (No. 11) following previous instructions. Place the order number on this and every subsequent bill. Verify your extensions and addition. Debit—*Rule 15;* credit—*Rule 12.* Excepting the items and amounts, this entry is similar to entry for No. 10.

Give the reasons for the debit (*Rule 1*) and the credit (*Rule 2*). File the order as previously instructed. Place bill and the required merchandise in Vouchers for Others.

First Report. Carefully review the General Rules for debiting and crediting and the classes of accounts which have been presented. Take a Report Blank and make a report of cash and all merchandise and vouchers intended for parties with whom the business has had dealings. Present same, together with the vouchers, cash, and merchandise intended for others, and your bookkeeping work to your teacher for inspection and approval; before so doing, examine every voucher carefully to see that you are not presenting work that is a discredit to your ability. Poor work will not be accepted; your best work will be none too good. Rewrite all work that is not your best before handing it in.

If your work meets your teacher's approval, make a neat and careful transcript of your journal sheet into your regular Journal. When completed, present it to your teacher, and be prepared to answer all questions he may ask you pertaining to the Cash account, Proprietor's account, Merchandise account, Expense account, Personal accounts, and the General Rules for debiting and crediting. You may then take up the next transaction.

JANUARY 8, 189–.

No. 12.—MERCHANDISE PURCHASED ON ACCOUNT. Bill No. 12 is bought on account. When the terms are not given, it is understood that the purchase is on account. Check the bill with the merchandise (No. 12). Verify the calculations; if everything is found to be correct, O. K. it and store the merchandise. In case you discover an error, report same to your teacher. Debit—*Rule 11;* credit—*Rule 16.* This entry is similar to entry for No. 9.

Give the reasons mentally for the debit (*Rule 1*) and credit (*Rule 2*). File the bill, following instructions for No. 9.

No. 13.—CASH RECEIVED ON ACCOUNT.—This cash (No. 13) is received in part payment of the bill purchased on the 4th inst. Count it carefully. Debit—*Rule 3;* credit—*Rule 16.* Make the entry as follows, substituting the correct amounts for the amounts given:

Cash	Rec'd on acct	...	
A P Batson			...

Give the reasons mentally for the debit (*Rule 1*) and credit (*Rule 2*). Place the cash in the proper receptacle. Write a receipt for the same, using voucher No. 7 as a model. Excepting the amount, your receipt should read as follows:

$500\frac{00}{100}$. .... (Your place) ...., JAN. 8, 189–.

Received of A. P. Batson, Five Hundred $\frac{00}{100}$ .... Dollars, to apply on acct.

C. W. HAMMOND,

per ...... (your name)

Place the receipt in Vouchers for Others.

No. 14.—CASH PAID ON ACCOUNT. Pay Redfield & Son $300 as part payment of bill No. 9. Count out the cash. Debit—*Rule 15;* credit—*Rule 4.* Make the entry as follows:

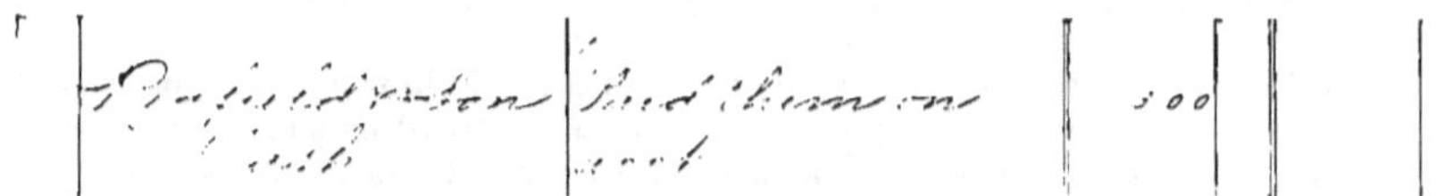

Give the reasons mentally for the debit (*Rule 1*) and credit (*Rule 2*). Recount the cash, place it in Cash Paid Out and take a receipt (No. 14) for same. File the receipt following the instructions for No. 7.

No. 15.—MERCHANDISE BOUGHT ON ACCOUNT. Look at the terms of bill No. 15. Check merchandise (No. 15) with the bill. Verify the additions and extensions of the bill, and, if found correct, O. K. it and store the merchandise. What do Mr. Hammond's check marks and O. K. indicate? Debit—*Rule 11;* credit—*Rule 16.* This entry is similar to Nos. 9 and 12. Give the reasons mentally for the debit (*Rule 1*) and credit (*Rule 2*). File the bill, following instructions for No. 9.

Study the following account and be prepared to answer the questions.

Bills Receivable. Under this title are entered the written promises of other parties, payable at a future time, which come into the business, as Notes and Accepted Time Drafts.

The Special Rules for debiting and crediting this account are:

17. *DEBIT Bills Receivable when received by the business.*

18. *CREDIT Bills Receivable when disposed of, because value is supplied to other accts.*

The difference between the sides of the account will show the Bills Receivable on hand. The amount of Bills Receivable on hand is a Resource. The credit side of Bills Receivable account can never be larger than the debit, because a greater amount cannot be disposed of than has been received. Bills Receivable account is debited and credited with the face value of the bills (notes), the account will therefore balance when all have been disposed of. The term Notes Receivable is sometimes used instead of Bills Receivable.

TRANSACTIONS ILLUSTRATING BILLS RECEIVABLE ACCOUNT.

Dec. 1. Proprietor invests Chas. Smith's note of $400. Dec. 3. Received of W. J. Solly his note, on account, $350. Dec. 4. Loaned Sam'l Eichert on his note cash, $100. Dec. 6. Chas. Smith paid his note in cash, $400. Dec. 8. Gave J. A. Luman, W. J. Solly's note, on account, $350.

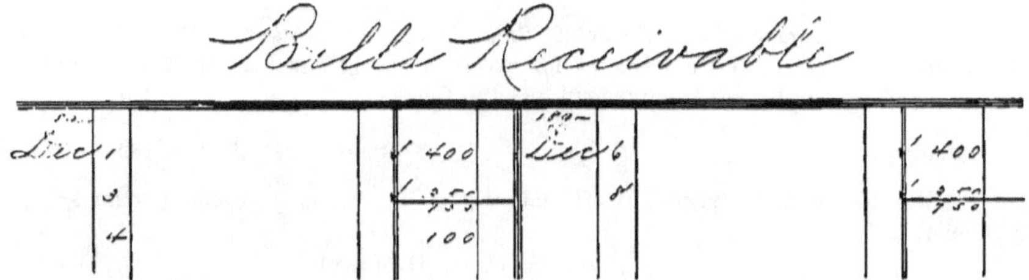

The debit side of this account shows that other persons' notes amounting to $850 have been received by the business. The credit side shows that other persons' notes amounting to $750 have been disposed of, leaving one note of $100 on hand, which is a Resource. Why? Either rule the account or check the debit and credit items that are equal, as illustrated above.

QUESTIONS. What are included under the title Bills Receivable? When is Bills Receivable account debited? When credited? Why cannot the credit side of Bills Receivable account be larger than the debit? What does the difference in Bills Receivable account show? Is the amount of Bills Receivable on hand a resource or a liability? When will the account balance?

JANUARY 10, 189–.

No. 16.—NOTE RECEIVED ON ACCOUNT. This note (No. 16) is in part payment of No. 11. Examine the note carefully. Whose written promise is it? Who should receive credit for this note? Debit—*Rule 17;* credit—*Rule 16.* Excepting the amounts and the credit, make the entry as follows:

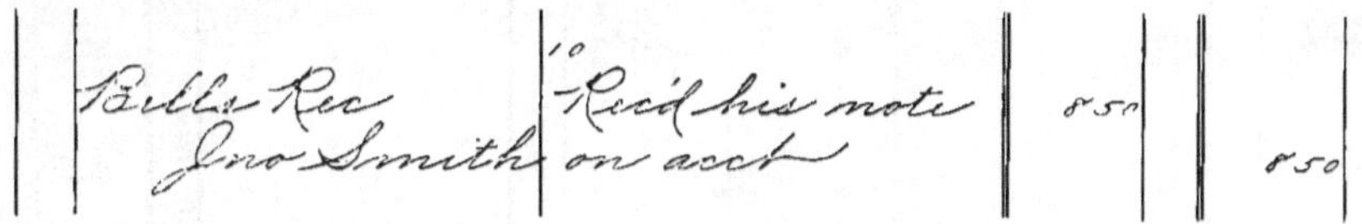

10
Bills Rec
Jno Smith
Rec'd his note
on acct
850
850

Give the reasons mentally for the debit (*Rule 1*) and credit (*Rule 2*). Place the note in the Cash Drawer, where all notes received from others will be kept until paid or otherwise disposed of. Notes are not cash, and are kept in the Cash Drawer for convenience only. No receipt is given when a note is received, as when the note is paid it will be indorsed and returned to the maker, thus becoming a receipt.

JANUARY 11, 189–.

No. 17.—MERCHANDISE SOLD ON ACCOUNT. Following previous instructions, make out a bill for this order (No. 17). Satisfy yourself that you have made no error in calculations. Debit—*Rule 15;* credit—*Rule 12.* This entry is similar to what entry? Give the reasons mentally for the debit (*Rule 1*) and credit (*Rule 2*). Place the bill and required merchandise in the proper receptacle. File the order properly, observing previous instructions.

JANUARY 12, 189–.

No. 18.—MERCHANDISE PURCHASED ON ACCOUNT. Check this bill (No. 18) with merchandise (No. 18). Verify the calculations, and, if found correct, O. K. the bill, observing previous instructions. Store the Merchandise. Note the terms of the bill. Debit—*Rule 11;* credit—*Rule 16.* Make the entry, relying upon the information obtained from reading the above rules. Give the reasons mentally for the debit (*Rule 1*) and credit (*Rule 2*). File the bill properly.

Study the following account so that you will be able to answer the questions.

Bills Payable. Under this title are to be entered our own written promises issued to other parties, by the business, payable at a future time, as Notes and Accepted Time Drafts.

The Special Rules for debiting and crediting this account are:

19. *DEBIT Bills Payable when redeemed (received back) by the business.*

20. *CREDIT Bills Payable when issued, because value is supplied to other accounts.*

The difference between the sides of the account will show the amount of Bills Payable outstanding. The amount outstanding is a Liability. The debit side of the Bills Payable account cannot be larger than the credit, because a greater amount cannot be redeemed than has been issued. Bills Payable account is debited and credited for the face value of the bills (notes). The account will therefore balance when all have been redeemed. This account is sometimes called Notes Payable instead of Bills Payable.

TRANSACTIONS ILLUSTRATING BILLS PAYABLE ACCOUNT.

May 1. Gave W. W. Scott our note on account, $400. May 2. Accepted Jos. Frey's draft on us, $200. May 3. Gave John Hauser our note for $350. May 30. Paid note favor of W. W. Scott, $400.

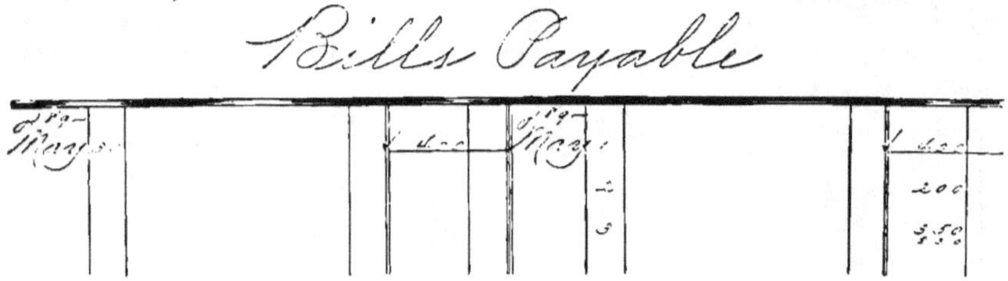

The above account shows that notes (written promises) amounting to $950 have been issued by the business, and one note of $400 has been redeemed (paid), leaving a balance of $550 unpaid, which is a Liability. Bills Payable account is ruled or checked similar to Bills Receivable account or personal accounts.

QUESTIONS. What are included under the title Bills Payable? When is Bills Payable account credited? When debited? Why cannot the debit side of Bills Payable account be larger than the credit? What does the difference in Bills Payable account show? Is the amount outstanding a Liability or a Resource?

JANUARY 14, 189–.

No. 19.—NOTE GIVEN ON ACCOUNT. Using voucher No. 16 as a model, write a note for $325 favor of Kaufman, Straus & Co. to apply on account. Your note will read as follows:

$325 $\frac{00}{100}$. ....(Your place)........, JAN. 14, 189–.

Thirty days after date I promise to pay Kaufman, Straus & Co., or order, Three Hundred Twenty-five $\frac{00}{100}$ Dollars, in college currency, value received, at my office.

No. 1. Due Feb. 13, 189–.

C. W. HAMMOND.

(your name) Attorney.

NOTE.—Do not add days of grace to notes and time drafts, in this work.

Debit—*Rule 15*; credit—*Rule 20*. Make the entry as follows:

Kaufman Straus & Co	Gave them our	325		
Bills Pay	note on acct			325

Give the reasons mentally for the debit and credit. Place the note in Vouchers for Others. Replace the note used as a model.

No. 20.—Opening an Account with the City Bank. Mr. Hammond has made arrangements with the City Bank of this city to deposit therein for safety and convenience the cash received by the business. All transactions with the bank are recorded in the Check Book. No journal entry is required when a deposit is made, the cash so deposited being considered practically as on hand, because it is not paid out in the sense of being disposed of, as the bank simply becomes the custodian of it in place of our Cash Drawer. You will now make a deposit of $5000. Count out the cash. Study the following form of deposit ticket, after which write one like it. Next take your Check Book and make a record of your deposit on the stub as follows:

DEPOSIT TICKET.

DEPOSITED
IN THE
→CITY BANK←
—BY—
C. W. HAMMOND.
(Your own name here) ____________ Attorney.
Jan. 14, 189—

	Dollars	Cents.
Currency	5000	
Checks		

STUB OF CHECK BOOK.

Deposited Jan. 14 189— | 5000
No.________
Date ________ 189—
Order of ________

For ________
Amount of Bill, $________
Discount____% $________
Amount of Check, $________

Deposited ________ 189—
No.________
Date ________ 189—
Order of ________

For ________

Take the cash, deposit ticket and Pass Book to the bank. In case there is no regular bank, your teacher will receive your deposits and give you credit for them in your Pass Book. You will be required to write the firm's signature in a book for that purpose; as you write it in this book, you must always write it when signing the business papers of the firm. Before leaving the bank, see that you have been credited with the proper amount in your Pass Book.

January 15, 189–.

No. 21.—Merchandise Sold on Account. Make out a bill for this order (No. 21). Verify your calculations. What account has received value? What account has supplied value? In making this entry apply the General Rules for debiting and crediting. Place the bill and the required merchandise in the proper receptacle. File the order as previously instructed.

JANUARY 16, 189–.

No. 22.—CHECK RECEIVED ON ACCOUNT. This check (No. 22) is received in part payment of No. 17. Examine and study the form carefully so as to be able to draw up one properly when required to do so. Debit—*Rule 3;* credit—*Rule 10.* This entry is similar to No. 13. Give the reasons mentally for debiting and crediting. Place the check in the Cash Drawer. Why? No receipt is necessary when payment is made by check. When the check is returned to the maker by the bank on which it is drawn, it is filed as evidence of payment.

A Check is a written order by a depositor on his bank requesting the bank to pay a certain sum out of his deposit to the party named in the check.

Second Report. Review the classes of accounts which have been presented and the General Rules for debiting and crediting. Carefully inspect all the vouchers intended for others and rewrite those which do not show evidence of your best efforts. Make a report, using a Report Blank, and present same, together with the business papers for others and all your bookkeeping work, to your teacher.

Having had all your work approved, proceed to copy it into your regular Journal. Be prepared to answer all questions pertaining to the classes of accounts which have been presented. Having answered all questions satisfactorily, you may proceed with the next transaction.

JANUARY 17, 189–.

No. 23.—CHECK GIVEN ON ACCOUNT. Pay Henry Knefely & Son by check $250 to apply on account. Take your Check Book, fill out the stub of the check as shown below, then write the check.

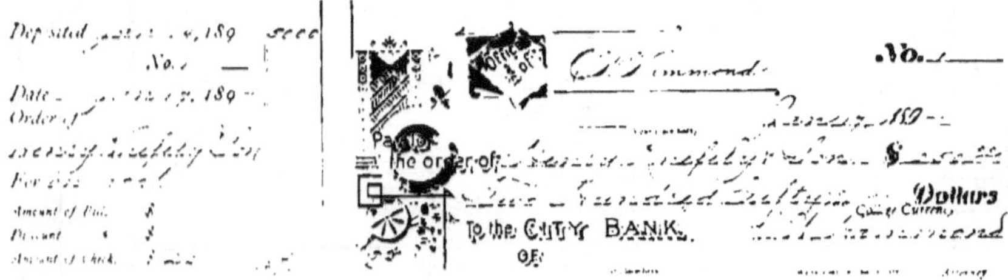

Tear out the check and place it in the Cash Paid Out receptacle. Always fill out the stub before writing a check. Subtract the amount of the check from the deposit. When Knefely & Son present this check at the bank it will be paid out of the deposit you have made, and in order to keep the amount in the bank and your Check Book balance alike, you must subtract every check that is issued. Make all entries for checks issued from the stubs of the checks. Debit—*Rule 15;* credit—*Rule 4.* This entry is similar to all entries for cash paid out.

JANUARY 18, 189–.

No. 24.—MERCHANDISE SOLD ON ACCOUNT. Bill the goods called for in this order (No. 24). Place the terms, "20 das.," on your bill. Recalculate the items. What account has received value? What account has supplied value? In making this entry apply the General Rules (*1 and 2*) for debiting and crediting. Place the bill and required merchandise in Vouchers for Others. File the order.

JANUARY 20, 189–.

No. 25.—CHECK RECEIVED ON ACCOUNT. This check (No. 25) is in part payment of No. 24. What account has received value? What account has supplied it? Make this entry, applying the General Rules for debiting and crediting. Place the check in the Cash Drawer.

JANUARY 21, 189–.

No. 26.—NOTE GIVEN IN FULL OF ACCOUNT. Write a 30-day note in favor of Henry Knefely & Son for the balance due them, making it payable at Mr. Hammond's office. Examine it carefully to see that you have made no error. Debit—*Rule 15;* credit—*Rule 20.*

Excepting the explanation, this entry is similar to No. 19. Give the reasons mentally for the debit and credit. Place the note in Vouchers for Others.

JANUARY 22, 189–.

No. 27.—MERCHANDISE PURCHASED ON ACCOUNT. Check this bill (No. 27) with the merchandise (No. 27). Verify the calculations of the bill; if found correct, O. K. it. Store the merchandise. What account has received value? What account has supplied it? In making this entry apply the General Rules. File the bill properly.

JANUARY 23, 189–.

No. 28.—CHECK GIVEN IN PART PAYMENT. Pay A. Paul, Jr., $300 by check. Fill out the stub of the check, deduct the amount from the amount in the bank, then write the check. Tear it out and place it in Cash Paid Out. What account has received value? What account has supplied it? Make this entry from the stub of the check, applying the General Rules. Are you certain that you have not omitted any of the details?

JANUARY 25, 189–.

No. 29.—MERCHANDISE BOUGHT ON ACCOUNT. Check bill No. 29 with the merchandise (No. 29). Verify the addition and extensions of the bill. O. K. it if no errors are discovered. Store merchandise. What account has received value? What account has supplied it? In making this entry apply the General Rules. Place the bill on the Invoice File.

JANUARY 27, 189–.

No. 30.—MERCHANDISE SOLD ON ACCOUNT. Bill the merchandise called for in this order (No. 30). Go over your calculations. Does your writing show evidence of your best efforts? What account has received value? What account has supplied it? In making this entry apply the General Rules. Place the bill and the required merchandise in the proper receptacle and file the order.

JANUARY 29, 189–.

No. 31.—PROPRIETOR DRAWS CASH FOR PRIVATE USE. Mr. Hammond wishes $100 for private use. Take your Check Book, fill out the stub of the check; after deducting the amount write the check making it payable to C. W. Hammond. Place it in Cash Paid Out. Debit—*Rule 6*; credit—*Rule 4*. Make the entry as follows:

C. W. Hammond	Loan for private	100		
Cash	use			100

Give the reasons mentally for the debit and credit.

JANUARY 30, 189–.

No. 32.—MERCHANDISE SOLD ON ACCOUNT. Make out the bill for order No. 32. Place the terms, "15 das.," on the bill. Verify your calculations. What account has received value? What account has supplied it? Apply the General Rules in making this entry. Be sure to place the bill and required merchandise where they belong and file the order properly.

JANUARY 31, 189–.

No. 33.—BOOKKEEPER'S SALARY PAID IN CASH. Pay yourself $50 by check as salary for the first month. Fill out the stub, deduct the amount, and write the check. Debit—*Rule 13*; credit—*Rule 4*. This entry is similar to entry for No. 7. Give the reasons mentally for the debit and the credit. Place the check in Cash Paid Out.

No. 34.—DRAYAGE BILL FOR THE MONTH PAID IN CASH. This bill (No. 34) is for hauling done for the business during the month. The bill is receipted and Mr. Hammond has O. K.'d it. Pay it in currency, placing the cash in the proper receptacle. Debit—*Rule 13*; credit—*Rule 4*. This entry is similar to entry for No. 33. Give the reasons mentally for the debit and credit. Place the bill on the Voucher File.

No. 35.—NOTE RECEIVED ON ACCOUNT. This note (No. 35) is to apply on account of No. 32. Debit—*Rule 17*; credit—*Rule 16*. Make the entry similar to the entry for the 16th transaction. Give the reasons for debiting and crediting. Place the note in the Cash Drawer.

No. 36.—MERCHANDISE SOLD ON ACCOUNT. Bill the merchandise called for in this order (No. 36). Calculate the items of the bill a second time. What account has received value? What account has supplied it? Apply the General Rules and make the entry. File the order and place the merchandise and bill in the proper receptacle.

No. 37.—CASH ITEMS DEPOSITED IN BANK. You will now indorse all the checks you have in the Cash Drawer, by writing

"*Pay to the order of City Bank,*
C. W. Hammond,
..........your name.......... *Atty.*"

across the back of each check, beginning near the left-hand end. Be careful not to indorse the notes. Note the difference between checks and notes. Count all the currency in the Cash Drawer. Make out a deposit ticket, entering the amount of currency opposite the word "Currency." Enter each check separately where indicated on the deposit ticket. Add the items, including the currency. Enter the amount of the deposit on the right-hand stub of your Check Book, following previous instructions; directly opposite on the left-hand stub make a duplicate of the items on the deposit ticket. This is done that you will have a detailed record of your deposits in case you have made an error and wish to know of what items your deposits consist. Consult your teacher about this or any instructions that you do not fully understand. Take your deposit, deposit ticket, and Pass Book to the bank. See that you are credited with the proper amount in the Pass Book, and leave it at the bank to be written up.

Third Report. Make a report on a Report Blank of all vouchers, merchandise, and cash intended for other parties. Present your report, together with the vouchers, etc., and your bookkeeping work for inspection and approval. Do not present any work which is not your best. Be prepared to answer any questions that your teacher may ask you on the work gone over. Next make a careful transcript of your journal sheet into your regular Journal; when completed, present your Journal for approval.

Directions for Posting. Your next work will be to post the journal debits and credits to your Ledger. You have had considerable practice in posting from the Model Journal and the one following it. If you have been diligent and exercised a constant watchfulness as you proceeded, you ought to experience no difficulty, as the process is purely mechanical and the method never varies. However, to make certain that you will start aright, and that any wrong impression you have formed may be corrected, a guide for posting the work for this month is presented herewith. Read the first direction, then perform the work exactly as directed before reading further. Read the second direction and perform the work. Continue in this way until you are able to proceed without directions.

FIRST ENTRY. 1. Place your Journal and Ledger before you on the desk, turn to page 2 of your Ledger and write *Cash* in a plain, bold hand on the upper line. By so doing you have opened the Cash account. 2. On the debit side of this account; *i. e.*, on the left-hand side, enter in the date column, *Jan. 1*, placing the year above. 3. In the journal-page column, enter the page of the Journal, *1*. 4. In the amount column, enter the amount invested. 5. Turn to your Journal and enter the page of the Ledger, *2*, in the column at the left of Cash to indicate that this item has been posted.

1. Turn to page 1 of your Ledger. In a bold, plain hand write *C. W. Hammond* on the upper line. 2. On the credit side of the account; *i. e.*, on the right-hand side, enter in the date column the date, *Jan. 1*, placing the year above. 3. In the journal-page column, enter the page of your Journal, *1*. 4. In the amount column, enter the amount invested. 5. Turn to your Journal and enter the page of the Ledger, *1*, in the column at the left of C. W. Hammond's name as a check to indicate that the item has been posted. This completes the posting of the first entry. Keep a clean blotter under your hand when making records in your books.

SECOND ENTRY. 1. Open an account with Merchandise at the top of page 3 in your Ledger. 2. On the debit side — that is, on the left-hand side — enter in the date column the date, *Jan. 1*, placing the year above. 3. Enter the journal page, *1*. 4. Enter the amount. 5. Turn to the Journal and enter the ledger page, *3*, in the column at the left of Merchandise as a check to show that it has been posted.

1. Turn to Cash account on page 2 in the Ledger and enter on the credit side; *i. e.*, right-hand side, the date, *Jan. 1*, placing the year above. 2. Enter the journal page, *1*. 3. Enter the amount. 4. Turn to the Journal and enter the ledger page, *2*, at the left of Cash as a check.

THIRD ENTRY. This entry is essentially the same as the second entry, therefore, follow the same instructions for posting.

FOURTH ENTRY. 1. Turn to Cash account on page 2 in your Ledger and enter on the debit side; *i. e.*, the left-hand side of the account the date, *1*. 2. Enter the journal page, *1*. 3. Enter the amount. 4. Turn to your Journal and postmark as before by entering the ledger page, 2, at the left of Cash.

1. Turn to Merchandise account on page 3 and enter on the credit side the date, *Jan. 1*, placing the year above. 2. Enter the journal page, *1*. 3. Enter the amount. 4. Turn to your Journal and check opposite Merchandise by entering the ledger page, *3*.

FIFTH ENTRY. This entry is similar to entries 2 and 3, therefore, no instructions for posting are given; follow previous instructions.

SIXTH ENTRY. 1. Open an account with Expense at the top of page 4. 2. Enter on the debit side the date, *Jan. 2*, writing the year above. 3. Enter the journal page. 4. Enter the amount. 5. Check in the Journal.

Turn to the Cash account on page 2 and enter on the credit side the date, *2*, the journal page, *1*, the amount; then check in the Journal.

SEVENTH ENTRY. Follow instructions for No. 6.

EIGHTH ENTRY. Follow instructions for No. 4.

NINTH ENTRY. On the debit side of Merchandise account enter the date; the journal page; the amount; then check in the Journal. Next open an account with Redfield & Son, 141 Dock St., City, on page 14, and enter on the credit side the date, including the year; journal page; amount; then check in the Journal.

NOTE.—By following the directions for opening accounts as given, the accounts in your Ledger will be grouped under four divisions. The first, beginning on page 1, contains the Proprietor's account; the second, beginning on page 2, contains the Property and Loss & Gain accounts; the third, beginning on page 9, contains the Personal Accounts Receivable; and the fourth, beginning on page 14, contains the Personal Accounts Payable. Loss & Gain accounts are the accounts that show either Losses or Gains; Personal Accounts Receivable are the accounts with persons who become indebted to the business; and Personal Accounts Payable are the accounts with persons or firms to whom the business becomes indebted. It is, however, not absolutely necessary that the ledger accounts be grouped in the above manner. See Model ledger, pages 4 and 5.

TENTH ENTRY. Open an account with A. P. Batson, 944 Market St., City, on page 9, and enter on the debit side the date; journal page; the amount; then check in the Journal. Next, turn to Merchandise account and enter on the credit side the date, journal page and amount. Check in the Journal.

ELEVENTH ENTRY. Follow instructions for No. 10.

TWELFTH ENTRY. Open an account with Thos. J. Johnston & Co., 715 Broadway, City, on the 14th line of page 14, then post the debit and credit, following instructions for No. 9.

THIRTEENTH ENTRY. Post to the debit side of Cash account on page 2, following the instructions previously given. Post to the credit side of A. P. Batson's account, observing previous instructions. Have you postmarked both the debit and the credit in the Journal?

FOURTEENTH ENTRY. Post to the debit of Redfield & Son's account; post to the credit of Cash account. Have you done everything in the exact order indicated in previous instructions?

FIFTEENTH ENTRY. Post to the debit of Merchandise account and check in the Journal. Open an account with Henry Knefely & Son, 5 E. Pratt St., City, on the 29th line of page 14: post to the credit of their account and check in the Journal.

SIXTEENTH ENTRY. Open an account with Bills Receivable on the 19th line of page 2 and post to the debit side, after which check in the Journal. Post to the credit of A. P. Batson's account.

SEVENTEENTH ENTRY. Open an account with Frey & Thomas, 620 Jefferson St., City, on the 19th line of page 9 and post to the debit of their account, after which check in the Journal. Post to the credit of Merchandise account and check in the Journal.

EIGHTEENTH ENTRY. Post to the debit of Merchandise account and check in the Journal. Open an account with Kaufman, Straus & Co., Fourth Ave., City, top of page 15 and post to the credit of their account, after which check in the Journal.

NINETEENTH ENTRY. Post to the debit of Kaufman, Straus & Co.'s account and check in the Journal. Open an account with Bills Payable on the 31st line of page 2 and post to the credit of that account. Do not forget to check in the Journal.

TWENTIETH, TWENTY-FIRST AND TWENTY-SECOND ENTRIES. Instructions for similar entries have been given.

TWENTY-THIRD ENTRY. Open an account with H. B. Philips & Co., S. W. Cor. 8th & Main, City, on the 32d line of page 9 and post to the debit of their account; post to the credit of Merchandise. Do not forget to check in the Journal.

TWENTY-FOURTH AND TWENTY-FIFTH ENTRIES. Instructions for similar entries have been given.

Either check or rule Henry Knefely & Son's account, as it balances. Do not fail to either check or rule (as your teacher may direct) all personal accounts found to balance while posting your subsequent work.

TWENTY-SIXTH ENTRY. Post to the debit of Merchandise. Open an account with A. Paul, Jr., 54 Grace Ave., City, on the 14th line of page 15 and post to the credit of his account.

TWENTY-SEVENTH ENTRY. Instructions for a similar entry have been given.

TWENTY-EIGHTH ENTRY. Post to the debit of Merchandise. Open an account with Barlow, Henderson Co., Cor. 3d Ave. & 11th St., City, on the 29th line of page 15 and post to the credit of their account.

TWENTY-NINTH ENTRY. Open an account with Harry Powell, 420 Chestnut St., City, on page 10. Post to the debit of his account; post to the credit of Merchandise.

THIRTIETH ENTRY. Post to the debit of C. W. Hammond's account; post to the credit of Cash.

For the remaining entries, consult instructions for entries of a similar nature.

Having finished the posting of your Ledger, carefully review same, placing a check (√) in pencil at the left of the amount of each item in the Ledger as you proceed. The points to be noted while reviewing your posting are as follows: 1. See that the journal debits have been posted to the debit side of the proper accounts in the Ledger. 2. That the journal credits have been posted to the credit side of the proper accounts in the Ledger. 3. That none of the details necessary to make the work complete have been omitted. 4. That the proper amounts have been posted from the Journal to the Ledger. 5. That no entries have been omitted. 6. That no entries have been posted twice.

Monthly Statements. It is the custom of business houses to render statements to their customers once a month. A monthly statement contains the name of the customer, together with his address, and a copy of the Ledger debits and credits of his account. The energetic bookkeeper will prepare his statements so as to have them ready for mailing or delivery to customers promptly on the first of each month. He, also, exercises great care in preparing these statements so as to make them appear as attractive as possible.

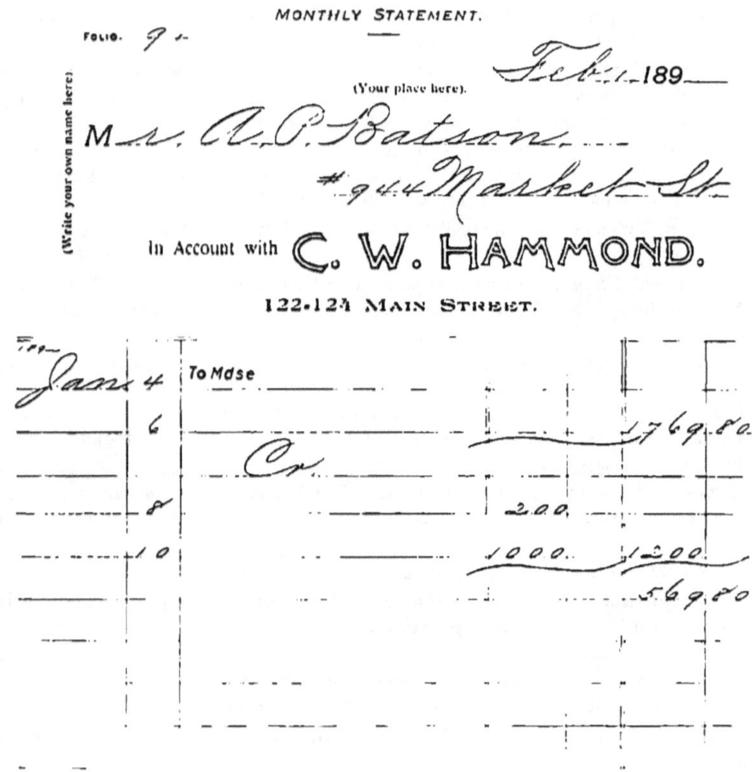

MONTHLY STATEMENT.

Folio. 9

(Your place here). Feb. 1 189

(Write your own name here)

Mr. A. P. Batson
#944 Market St.

In Account with C. W. HAMMOND.

122-124 MAIN STREET.

Jan.	4	To Mdse			
	6				1769.80
		Cr.			
	8		200.		
	10		1000.	1200	
					569.80

Carefully study the form of statement given herewith. Turn to page 9 of your Ledger and make a statement of A. P. Batson's account, as shown in the above illustration. Be sure to place on the statement the two debit items left blank in the illustration. Make out statements against all parties who owe the business, and present them for inspection and approval.

Having had your statements approved, insert them in envelopes neatly and properly addressed, but do not seal them. Place the envelopes in Vouchers for Others.

Taking a Trial Balance. Pencil foot all the accounts in the Ledger preparatory to taking a Trial Balance. Use a sharp pointed pencil for work of this kind, as the figures can be made much smaller and more legible than with a dull pointed one. Make your pencil footings plain and distinct, but quite small; do not draw lines in the columns to be added, as the size and peculiar position of the footing serves to distinguish it from the other items in the account. When there is but one item, no pencil footing is necessary.

Take a journal sheet, head it as follows: *Trial Balance, Jan. 31, 189–.* Commencing with the first account in your Ledger, proceed to make a Trial Balance, using the form on page 7 as a Model. Copy the number of the page on which the account is found in the Ledger, the name of the account, and the debit or credit balance. Compare the balance as shown by the Cash account with the balance of cash on hand as shown by the Check Book. Proceed until all the balances have been entered, after which add the sides to see if they are equal. If found to be equal, submit your Trial Balance for approval. Should it fail to balance, it will be necessary for you to go over the work and locate the error. Do not ask your teacher to aid you before you have made a diligent effort to find your mistakes. When your work is approved, place the sheet containing your Trial Balance in your Balance Book and proceed to take an account of the Resources and Liabilities of the Model Set as explained in the following paragraphs.

Inventory of Resources and Liabilities—Model Set. As you have already learned, a Resource is either property on hand or an amount due the business. A Liability is an amount owed by the business. The difference between the Resources and Liabilities of any business is the Proprietor's present capital.

The first thing to be done in ascertaining the Inventory of Resources and Liabilities is to find the current value of the merchandise remaining unsold. The merchandise on hand belonging to the business represented by the Model Set and its value is given below.

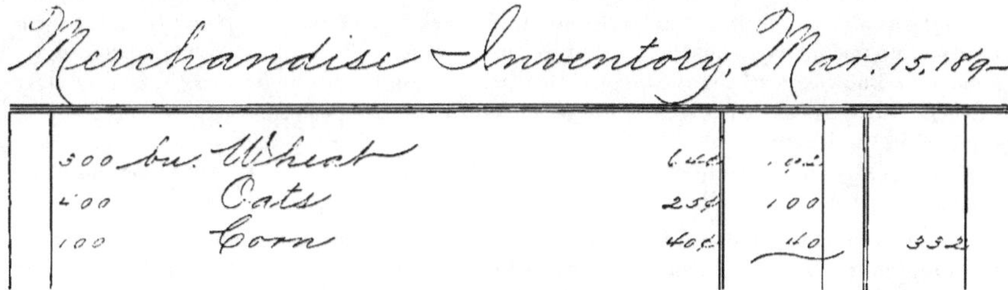

Merchandise Inventory, Mar. 15, 189–

300 bu. Wheat	64¢	192		
400 Oats	25¢	100		
100 Corn	40¢	40	332	

In business the amount of goods on hand is usually ascertained by going through the store, measuring, weighing, or counting the various articles, their value usually being estimated at *current* cost. When the merchandise inventory includes a long list of goods a separate book called a Stock or Inventory Book is employed.

Having ascertained the value of property on hand, the remainder of the facts can be ascertained from the books, or more readily from the Trial Balance. Refer to the Model Trial Balance No. 2 and trace the items to the Inventory given below. Observe that Wm. Wood's capital, the merchandise and expense debits are not taken from the Trial Balance. Why not? Wm. Wood's capital is the difference between the Resources and Liabilities. His capital when he began business was $5000, he withdrew $75, leaving a capital of $4925. Subtracting $4925 from $5168.50 equals $243.50, the amount he gained.

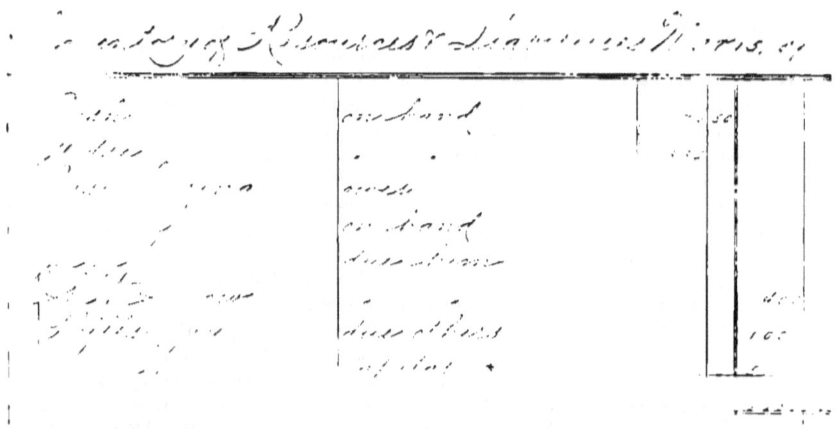

* To be written in red ink.

The above Inventory of Resources and Liabilities gives the results of the business, but it does not show the *sources* of Losses and Gains.

Model Balance Sheet. To ascertain the *sources* of Losses and Gains it will be necessary to make a detailed analysis of the various ledger accounts. This will be best accomplished by making a Balance Sheet. Your attention is now directed to the Model Balance Sheet given on page 36.

The first step to be taken is to make an exact copy of the Model Trial Balance No. 2 on a Balance Sheet blank, first heading it as in the Model. Before reading further you will do the work as above indicated. In performing this work it is of the utmost importance to you that you do not merely copy the form of Balance Sheet. To do the work understandingly, securing a knowledge of the relations of the various accounts to the business, it is absolutely essential that you take each step in the order indicated, and perform the work precisely as directed in the instructions.

Your next step will be to extend the Losses, Gains, Resources and Liabilities as shown by the various accounts, as follows:

CASH.—Commence with Cash, it being the first account on your Balance Sheet following the Proprietor's account. You have on hand $4676.50, which you will extend to the Resource column, because property on hand is a Resource.

MERCHANDISE.—First enter in the Resource column the Merchandise Inventory, $332, as shown on page 33, because property on hand is a Resource. Make the entry in red ink, to distinguish it from the Resources shown by the ledger accounts. Note that the debit (cost) side shows a balance of $70; therefore the goods purchased amount to $70 more than those sold. Were there none on hand, the business would have lost $70 on merchandise. There is, however, a Merchandise Inventory valued at $332; subtracting $70 from the value of the goods on hand gives $262, the amount gained. Extend this amount to the Gain column.

EXPENSE.—The debit footing, $18.50, shows the total outlay. Extend this amount to the Loss column, because an account which costs more than it produces exhibits a Loss.

J. W. WINTER.—The credit balance, $90, is the amount the business still owes him, which you will extend to the Liability column, because an amount owing by the business is a Liability.

NOTE.—In extending S. W. Snow's account, consult the explanation given for J. W. Winter, above.

JAMES SPRING.—The debit balance, $50, is the amount he owes the business, which you will extend to the Resource column, because an amount owing to the business is a Resource.

BILLS RECEIVABLE.—The debit balance, $1600, shows the total amount of notes on hand. Extend this amount to the Resource column, because an amount owing to the business is a Resource.

BILLS PAYABLE.—The credit balance, $1000, shows the total amount of notes outstanding. Extend this amount to the Liability column, because an amount owing by the business is a Liability.

Net Gain and Present Capital. Foot the Resource, Liability, and Loss and Gain columns of the Balance Sheet, and extend the results as shown in the form on page 36.

Extend into the Loss column, in red ink, the Net Gain, $243.50, which is the difference between the total Gains and the total Losses.

To the Proprietor's credit balance, $4925, add the Net Gain, and extend the amount, $5168.50, which is the Present Capital, into the Liability column.

The Net Gain is found, as shown in the accompanying Balance Sheet, by subtracting the total Gains from the total Losses, as exhibited by the different accounts showing Losses and Gains. As illustrated by the Inventory of Resources and Liabilities, the Net Gain may also be found by subtracting the Proprietor's capital on commencing from the Present Capital: the Present Capital at any time being the difference between the Resources and Liabilities.

It will also be seen that the Present Capital in double entry bookkeeping may be found in two ways: either by adding the Net Gain to the Net Credit or Capital on commencing, or by finding the difference between the Resources and Liabilities, as illustrated by the Inventory of Resources and Liabilities.

When the Losses exceed the Gains the difference is called the "Net Loss:" in such cases, when making out the Balance Sheet, the Net Loss must be deducted from the Net Credit or Capital on commencing, to find the Present Capital.

When the Liabilities exceed the Resources, the Proprietor is Insolvent: *i. e.*, he is unable to pay what is due others.

As the Present Capital of any business belongs to the proprietor or stockholders, it is in that sense a Liability to the business. This Liability, however, must not be confounded with the regular Resources and Liabilities, the difference between which is the Present Capital, or the value of the business belonging to the proprietor.

NOTE.—Read *Observations* on page 7 if you had any difficulty in understanding the work given on pages 33 to 35. To do so will aid you in comprehending the work on the following three pages.

* *Net Gain*, 243.50 and 332 are to be written in red ink.

Having ascertained by the foregoing Balance Sheet the sources of Losses and Gains and the true condition of the business at the present time: *i. e.*, what the Net Gain has been, how much the proprietor is worth, and of what his worth consists, it is desired to make the Proprietor's account in the Ledger exhibit the Present Capital.

To do this, the accounts showing Losses and Gains must be closed and the Net Gain entered in the Proprietor's account. It is only necessary to close the accounts which show Losses and Gains, because in them have been entered all transactions making the proprietor worth more or less. The other accounts, those exhibiting Resources and Liabilities, simply show of what the Present Capital consists, and closing them would in no way affect the Proprietor's account.

Closing the Accounts Showing Losses and Gains. Following the last account in your Ledger for the Model Set, open an account with Loss & Gain, to which are to be carried the Losses and Gains from the various accounts as they are closed, and from which the Net Gain is to be finally transferred to the Proprietor's account. Proceed to close your best Ledger of the Model Set, observing the following instructions and referring to the Model on page 38.

MERCHANDISE.—The Inventory is first to be entered on the credit side of this account, that it may be added to the sales. (This is equivalent to deducting it from the debit or cost side.) Proceed as follows: On the credit side of the account enter the Inventory. Write in red ink, *Mar. 15, Inventory, 332.* Then to close the account, on the smaller side—which is the debit—enter the difference between the sides, that is the Gain. Write in red ink, *Mar. 15, Gain, 262.* Next rule and foot the account. (See Merchandise account closed and ruled on page 38.)

In ruling an account, draw the red line directly on the blue line. In the double ruling, draw the lines as close as possible and not have them run together. Rule on the same line on both sides of the account, even if there be a larger number of entries upon one side than on the other.

The two entries just made have put the Ledger out of balance, and, to restore the balance, entries for like amounts must be made on the opposite sides, as follows: First, transfer the Inventory below the ruling on the debit side. Write in black ink, *Mar. 15, Inventory, 332.* Next transfer the Gain to the credit side of the Loss & Gain account. Write in black ink, *Mar. 15, Mdse., 262* (enter in page column the page of Mdse. account.) By these two entries we have not only placed the Ledger again in balance, but we have caused the Loss & Gain account to show, as it should, on the credit side, the gain produced by an account (Mdse.) which has been closed.

EXPENSE.—To close this account, on the smaller side—which is the credit—enter the loss. Write in red ink, *Mar. 15, Loss, 18.50.* (Enter page of Loss & Gain account.) Next, rule the account. (See Model.) Transfer the Loss to the debit side of Loss & Gain account. Write in black ink, *Mar. 15, Expense, 18.50.* (Enter page of Expense account.)

LOSS & GAIN.—Having closed all the accounts which show Losses and Gains into the Loss & Gain account, you will now proceed to close this account. On the smaller side, which is the debit, enter the difference between the sides, that is the Net Gain. Write in red ink, *Mar. 15, Wm. Wood* (the page) *243.50.* Next rule and foot the account. Transfer the Net Gain to the credit side of Wm. Wood's account. Write in black ink, *Mar. 15, Net Gain* (the page) *243.50.*

WM. WOOD'S ACCOUNT.—The Net Gain having been carried to it, this account now contains the Present Capital, and that it may be shown in a single amount, you will close the account. Proceed as follows: On the smaller side, which is the debit, enter the difference between the sides, that is the Present Capital. Write in red ink, *Mar. 15, Present Capital, 5168.50.* Next, rule and foot the account. Transfer the Present Capital to the opposite side (credit side) below the ruling. Write in black ink, *Mar. 15, Present Capital, 5168.50.*

This completes the work of closing the accounts which contained the Losses and Gains growing out of the preceding business, and the Net Gain—the difference between the Losses shown on the debit side and the Gains shown on the credit side of the Loss & Gain account—has been entered in the Proprietor's account, causing it to show the Present Capital. It is evident that the Proprietor's account will continue to show its true relation to the business—that is, the Present Capital, or exact difference between the Resources and Liabilities—only until such time as a Gain or Loss has been produced in the course of trade; because such Gain or Loss is not immediately entered in the Proprietor's account, but it is permitted to remain in the account producing it until a general closing of the accounts showing gains or losses is made, such as has just been explained and illustrated.

Submit your Model Balance Sheet and Model Ledger, just closed, for inspection and criticism.

NOTE.—In case your work in closing the Model Ledger is not up to the standard, your teacher will require you to make an Inventory of Resources and Liabilities and a Balance Sheet for the set given under Second Posting Exercise on page 8, after which you will close the Ledger and submit your work for approval. The Inventory of Merchandise consists of the following: 217 yds. Broadcloth @ 4.25; 125 yds. Fancy Cass. @ 2.55; 120 yds. Black Cass. @ 2.40.

[illegible]

Mar		Pres. Capital		[illegible]	Mar		Net Gain		[illegible]
				[illegible]					[illegible]
					Mar		Pres. Capital		[illegible]

Merchandise

Mar				[illegible]	Mar	2			[illegible]
				[illegible]		4			[illegible]
				[illegible]					[illegible]
		Gain		[illegible]			Inventory		[illegible]
				[illegible]					[illegible]
Mar		Inventory		[illegible]					

Expense

Mar				[illegible]	Mar		Loss & Gain		[illegible]

Loss & Gain

Mar		Expense	1	[illegible] 50	Mar	15	Mdse	1	[illegible]
		Net Gain		[illegible] 50					
				[illegible]					[illegible]

* To be written in red ink.

Directions for Taking Merchandise Inventory. You will now proceed to take an Inventory of the goods on hand (in Store Room) preparatory to making your regular Balance sheet for Mr. Hammond's business. The current cost prices of your commodities are as follows: Apples $1.50, Potatoes 20¢, Barley 25¢, Rye 28¢, Corn 30¢, Oats 24¢, Flour $3.75, Wheat 65¢. Do the work on a journal sheet before copying into your regular Journal, and submit it, together with the representative merchandise, to your teacher. After your work is approved, copy it into your Journal. Refer to the Merchandise Inventory for the Model Set while doing this work.

Directions for Taking Inventory of Resources and Liabilities. Having ascertained the value of the Merchandise on hand, the remainder of the Resources and Liabilities you will determine from your books or from the Trial Balance. Make the Inventory of Resources and Liabilities, using the one given for the Model Set as a guide. The difference between the Resources and Liabilities will give you Mr. Hammond's worth or capital. Subtracting his Capital on commencing from the Present Capital gives the Gain. To ascertain the sources of Losses and Gains, you will make a Balance Sheet. Before doing so, present your Inventory for approval.

Directions for Making Balance Sheet. Head a blank Balance Sheet as follows: "C. W. Hammond's Balance Sheet, Jan. 31, 189–." 2. Copy the Trial Balance on the Balance Sheet, following the directions given for the Model Balance Sheet. (Keep Model Balance Sheet before you while doing this work.) 3. Extend the balance of Cash to the Resource column. Why? 4. Enter the Inventory of Merchandise in the Resource column in red ink. Ascertain the Gain by subtracting the debit balance from the value of the merchandise on hand. Why is this amount a Gain? 5. Extend the total of Expense account to the Loss column. Why? 6. Extend the credit balances of the following accounts to the Liability column: Redfield & Son, Thos. J. Johnston & Co., Kaufman, Straus & Co., Bills Payable, A. Paul, Jr., Barlow, Henderson Co. Why are these accounts extended to the Liability column? 7. Extend the debit balances of the following accounts to the Resource column: A. P. Batson, Bills Receivable, Frey & Thomas, H. B. Philips & Co., Harry Powell. Why are these balances extended to the Resource column? 8. Rule and foot all six of the columns as shown in the Model. 9. Subtract the Loss from the Gain to find the Net Gain and extend it into the Loss column in red ink, referring to the Model to make sure that you are arranging your work properly. 10. To the Net Credit or Capital on commencing of Mr. Hammond's account add the Net Gain and extend the amount, which is his Present Capital, to the Liability column. Present your Balance Sheet for approval.

Directions for Closing Accounts Showing Losses and Gains. Open an account with Loss & Gain on page 5 of your Ledger.

MERCHANDISE ACCOUNT.—1. Enter the Merchandise Inventory as shown by the Inventory in the Balance Sheet on the credit side of the Merchandise account in *red ink*, following the directions as given for closing the Model Ledger. (*See page 37.*) 2. On the debit side enter in *red ink* the Gain, which is the difference between the sides including the Inventory, writing it as follows: "Jan. 31, Gain, 5," and the amount. 3. As the sides of the account are now equal, rule and foot same properly. (*See Mdse. Acct., page 38.*) 4. Transfer the Inventory in ***black ink*** to the debit side below the ruling. 5. Transfer the Gain to the credit side of Loss & Gain account; writing in ***black ink***, "Jan. 31, Mdse., 3," and enter the amount in the money column.

EXPENSE ACCOUNT.—1. On the smaller side write in *red ink*, "Jan. 31, Loss, 5," and the amount which is required to balance the account, which is a Loss. 2. Rule the account as shown on page 38. 3. Transfer in *black ink* the Loss to the debit side of the Loss & Gain account as follows: "Jan. 31, Expense, 4, 177.00."

LOSS & GAIN ACCOUNT.—1. On the smaller side enter the difference between the sides *in red ink*, writing, "Jan. 31, C. W. Hammond, 1," and the amount. 2. Rule and foot the account, referring to the Loss & Gain account on page 38. 3. Transfer in *black ink* the Net Gain to the credit side of C. W. Hammond's account, writing "Jan. 31, Net Gain, 5," and the amount.

C. W. HAMMOND'S ACCOUNT.—1. On the debit side write in *red ink*, "Jan. 31, Present Capital," and the amount. 2. Rule and foot the account. 3. Bring down the Present Capital in *black ink* to the credit side below the ruling.

Having finished closing the accounts that show Losses and Gains, check their balances as shown in the Ledger with those shown in the Resource and Liability columns of the Balance Sheet to see that you have made no errors in closing.

Present all your books for inspection.

While your teacher is examining your books prepare yourself for an examination upon the leading principles involved in the work of the foregoing pages. The following questions will aid you materially in this.

QUESTIONS FOR REVIEW.—What is bookkeeping? What is the object in keeping books? What is double entry bookkeeping? Define the Day Book-Journal. The Ledger. What is a debit? A Credit? What is an account? What is Journalizing? Posting? Give the general rules or principles for debiting and crediting. What is the object in taking a Trial Balance? Why is it a good plan to check over your postings before taking a Trial Balance? Why is it a better plan to take a Trial Balance, using the balances instead of the footings? In case your balance would not prove when you used the balances, would you try to get it by using the footings? Give your reasons for your answer. What is a Balance Sheet? What is the object of making a Balance Sheet? What is a Merchandise Inventory? How is the Merchandise Inventory ascertained? What is an Inventory of Resources and Liabilities? What does the difference between the total Resources and Liabilities show? When does an account show a Loss? A Gain? A Resource? A Liability? How is the Net Gain found? When would there be a Net Loss? How is the Present Capital determined? What is the next step after the Present Capital has been found? Why are the Loss and the Gain accounts in the Ledger closed? Into what account are they closed? Into what account is Loss & Gain account closed? Review all the questions given under the accounts previously presented.

FEBRUARY 1, 189–.

Continuation of Mr. Hammond's business. The amount of business transacted, the profits arising therefrom, and the success of the business generally, has induced Mr. Hammond to employ Mr. Frank Winter as salesman and receiving clerk, leaving you to devote your entire time to the books and office work. Mr. Winter will attend to the shipping and the receiving of all goods, O. K. bills, and sell to customers who buy at retail. Mr. Hammond, as heretofore, will attend to the soliciting of orders, make the purchases, and attend to the financial matters pertaining to the business. Mr. Winter will take charge of the stock as shown by your Inventory, and you will have nothing whatever to do with the handling of goods. Never enter an order or bill unless it has been O. K.'d either by Mr. Hammond or Mr. Winter.

The Cash Book is now introduced as the first of labor-saving books. It is generally considered a subdivision of the Day Book, and takes the place of the Cash account in the Ledger. All cash entries are to be recorded in this book and posted directly to the Ledger without being carried to the Journal. (*See pages 42 and 43.*)

The Method. Whenever cash is received, the amount is entered on the left or debit side (page) of the Cash Book, with the title of the account to be credited in posting, and an appropriate explanation. Whenever cash is paid out, the amount is entered on the right or credit side (page) of the Cash Book, with the title of the account to be debited in posting, and an appropriate explanation. The difference between the sides of the Cash Book should exhibit, at any time, the cash on hand. In business it is customary to prove cash every day; *i. e.*, ascertain whether the cash on hand agrees with the balance as shown by the Cash Book. The Cash Book is ruled daily, weekly, or monthly, usually the latter. The Cash Book is a great convenience in proving cash, as proving it when the cash entries are made in the Journal could be accomplished only with difficulty, because it would be necessary to collect the debit items and the credit items before their difference could be ascertained.

Model Cash Book. Carefully study the Model Cash Book illustrated on pages 42 and 43, make a transcript of it, and post same to a Ledger, on a sheet of ledger paper, referring to Ledger on pages 42 and 43, after which take a Trial Balance to test the correctness of the posting. You will observe that the items appearing on the debit side of the Cash Book are posted to the credit of the ledger accounts; also, that the items appearing on the credit side of the Cash Book are posted to the debit side of the Ledger. Excepting the amounts, the transactions recorded in the Model Cash Book are identical with the cash transactions recorded in the Day Book-Journal for January. Compare the Model Cash Book with the cash transactions recorded in the Day Book-Journal to learn why the cash book items are posted to the opposite sides of the ledger accounts. As no account of Cash is kept in the Ledger, the Cash Book, in which all receipts and payments of cash are recorded, is to be considered as the Cash account in the Ledger, and in taking a Trial Balance start by bringing the receipts and payments of Cash, or the balance on hand, to the Trial Balance, just as you would were the account kept in the Ledger. Then proceed as previously instructed with all other accounts in the Ledger. The Ledger of itself will not balance when it does not contain the Cash account, so always get the balance on hand from the Cash Book, which, as before stated, takes the place of the Cash account in the Ledger. Submit your work to the teacher. (Continued on page 44.)

Cash

Jan. 1	C. W. Hammond invested		5000	
1	Mdse	cash sales	324	
3	Mdse	"	765	
8	A. P. Batson	on acct	200	
11	Frey & Thomas	"	600	
20	H. B. Phillips & Co	"	150	7040
			7040	
				7040
Jan. 31	Balance			3797 25

C. W. Hammond.

189 .			189 .		
Jan. 29	C.	100	Jan. 1	C.	5000

Merchandise.

189 .			189 .		
Jan. 1	C.	900	Jan. 1	C.	324
1	C.	720	3	C.	766
1	C.	500			

Expense.

189 .					
Jan. 2	C.	17 75			
2	C.	90			
31	C.	50			
31	C.	15			

A. P. Batson.

			189 .		
			Jan. 8	C.	200

Cash

189-		L.F.						
Jan	1		Mdse	cash purchase	900			
			Mdse	" "	720			
			Mdse	" "	500			
	2		Expense	office books	17	75		
			Expense	rent	90			
	9		Redfield & Son	on acct	300			
	17		H Knefely & Son	" "	250			
	22		A Paul Jr	" "	300			
	29		C W Hammond	private use	100			
	31		Expense	student's salary	50			
			Expense	drayage bill	15			
					3242	75	3242	75
			Balance *	on hand			3797	25
							7040	

*To be written in red ink.

Redfield & Son.

189-. Jan.	9	C.	300				

Frey & Thomas.

				189-. Jan.	16	C.	600

H. Knefely & Son.

189-. Jan.	17	C.	250				

H. B. Phillips & Co.

				189-. Jan.	20	C.	150

A. Paul, Jr.

189-. Jan.	22	C.	300				

Having had your work approved, you will now balance the Cash account in the Ledger in red ink, writing on the smaller side, " Feb. 1, Balance to C. B.," and the amount. Rule the account and bring the balance to the debit side (left-hand page) of your journal sheet representing the Cash Book, writing in black ink, " Feb. 1, Balance on hand," and place the amount in the column nearest the center of the page. Write the word *Cash* on the top line of each page as you find it in the Model Cash Book.

Call for your Pass Book at the bank if you have not already received it. Compare the balance in the Pass Book with the balance in the Check Book, and if found to agree, write in *red ink* " O. K. with Bank Balance " opposite the balance in the Check Book. If there is a discrepancy, compare the checks returned by the bank with the amounts shown by the stubs to locate the error. If you fail to locate the discrepancy, consult the teacher.

Carefully file away the checks returned by the bank on the Voucher File. Remember that no receipts were taken when payments were made by check, therefore you will preserve these checks as evidences of payment. A check paid by the bank and returned to the depositor is the best kind of receipt, and should, therefore, be carefully preserved.

No. 38.—Proprietor's Additional Investment. Mr. Hammond wishes to make an additional investment. Your teacher will hand you the amount your price list calls for in the following table. Apply for same and count the cash carefully.

Additional Amounts to be Invested.

No. of Price List.	1	2	3	4	5	6	7	8	9	10	11	12	13
Amount.	5000	5800	3600	5600	6000	4900	5500	5100	4300	5700	4200	4800	5900
	14	15	16	17	18	19	20	21	22	23	24	25	
	5200	4500	3900	5400	4600	3700	4400	5300	4000	3800	4100	4700	

What account has received value? (*Rule 3.*) What account has supplied value? (*Rule 9.*) Excepting the amount, make the entry as follows on the debit side of the Cash Book:

	[illegible] Hammond	Invested		

By this entry, Cash is debited and Mr. Hammond is credited. While the form varies, this entry does not differ in effect from the entry to be made in the Journal, in case there were no Cash Book kept. Give the reasons mentally for the debit and credit. (*Rules 1 and 2.*) Recount the cash and place it in the proper receptacle.

No. 39.—Gas Bill for January Paid. Read this bill, No. 39, carefully. Mr. Hammond wishes you to pay it to-day to take advantage of the discount allowed when payment is made on the first day of the month. Write the check for the net amount, first filling the stub properly, and deduct the amount from the balance in the bank. File the bill on the Voucher File and place check in proper receptacle. Determine the account to be credited by reading rule 4; the account to be debited by reading rule 13. Make the entry from the stub of the Check Book on the credit side of the Cash Book as follows:

Feb.		Expense	Furniture Bill		

Give the reasons mentally for the debit and the credit.

No. 40.—Rent for February Paid. Pay the rent for the current month by check. Write the check, first filling the stub properly and deducting the amount from the previous balance. Examine your check carefully to see that you have made no errors. Tear it out and place it in the proper receptacle. No receipt is necessary. Why not? What account is to be debited? (*Rule 13.*) What account is to be credited? (*Rule 4.*) Make the entry from the stub of the check book on the credit side of the Cash Book. Why? Have you written the proper explanation?

No. 41.—Sale on Account. Make out the bill for this order (No. 41). Place the terms (15 das.) asked for on your bill. Re-calculate the items to see that you have made no errors. Note the check marks to the left of the items, and Mr. Winter's initials under the word "Filled:" these indicate that the order has been filled and the goods sent. In making this entry apply the General Rules. Make the entry in the Journal, using a journal sheet for that purpose. Place the bill in the proper receptacle and file the order as previously instructed.

No. 42.—Purchase on Account. Examine carefully bill No. 42 and go over the calculations. Note that the items have been checked off by Mr. Winter, which indicates that all the goods called for have been received by him. Mr. Hammond's O. K. and check marks opposite the prices indicate as usual that the prices charged are satisfactory to him. He does not examine the extensions and additions of the bills; that is the duty of the book-keeper. You will O. K. the bill as usual if the calculations prove to be correct. Apply the General Rules for debiting and crediting, and make the entry in the Journal. File the bill properly.

No. 43.—Sale on Account. Bill the goods called for in this order (No. 43). Go over your calculations a second time. Mr. Winter's check marks and initials under "Filled" indicate that the goods have been sent. Never make out a bill for an order that is not checked off, as that clearly indicates that it has not been filled. Apply the General Rules for debiting and crediting and make the entry in the Journal. Place the bill in the proper receptacle and file the order.

February 2, 189–.

No. 44.—Purchase on Account. Examine this bill, verify the calculations and O. K. it. Are the items checked off in the vertical column to the left of the items, and has it been O. K.'d to show that the prices are correct and all the goods have been received? Never enter a bill that is not checked off and O. K.'d, as there is nothing to indicate that the goods have been received, as two or more bills may be sent for the same lot of goods, or the bill sent and the goods not delivered by oversight. Were you to credit the parties for every bill sent, you would very likely pay out money for goods that were not received. Apply the General Rules for debiting and crediting and make the entry in the proper book. File the bill.

No. 45.—Cash Received on Account. This check is in part payment of bill sold on the first inst. What has been received? Who supplied it? Note the indorsement on the back. The indorser is the one who supplied value to the business. Apply the General Rules for debiting and crediting and make the entry on the debit side of the Cash Book as follows: "2, T. A. Cooke, on acct.," and the amount. Why is this entry made on the debit side of the Cash Book? Place the check in the Cash Drawer.

No. 46.—Cash Received in Full of Account. Check No. 46 is in full payment of balance due by the party who sends the check. Refer to his account in your Ledger and see if the amount named in the check is the amount required to balance the account. Report to your teacher if you find that there is a discrepancy. What account has received value? (*Rule 3.*) What account has supplied it? (*Rule 16.*) Explanation excepted, this entry is similar to the entry for No. 45. The explanation should read "in full of acct." Place the check in the proper receptacle.

February 3, 189–.

No. 47.—Deposit. You will now make a deposit. Count the currency in your Cash Drawer, fill out a deposit ticket, entering the amount opposite the word "Currency." Indorse the checks as instructed on page 28, and enter each separately where indicated on the deposit ticket. Foot the items, then carefully recount your currency and checks and re-add the items to make certain that there is no error. Enter the total amount of your deposit on the right-hand stub of your Check Book and add it to the last balance. On the left-hand stub make a copy of the items (names and amounts) on your deposit ticket, so that reference can be made to them when desired. Take your deposit together with your Pass Book to the bank.

No. 48.—Cash Paid on Account. Pay Thos. J. Johnston & Co. by check $750 to apply on account. First fill the stub, deduct the amount from the previous balance, then write the check. Examine it carefully to see that you have made no mistake. Place it in the proper receptacle. Who has received value? What account has supplied it? Make the entry on the right-hand side of the Cash Book as follows: "3, Thos. J. Johnston & Co., on acct., 750." Give the reasons mentally for the debit and credit. Why is this entry made on the credit side of the Cash Book?

February 4, 189–.

No. 49.—Cash Paid in Full of Account. Turn to Barlow, Henderson Co.'s acct. in your Ledger and ascertain the amount the business owes them. Fill the stub of the Check Book, deduct the amount, then write the check for the balance due them. Examine it carefully to see that it is correct, then place it in the proper receptacle. Who has received value? What account has supplied it? Make the entry on the credit side of the Cash Book, similar to the entry for No. 48. The explanation should read "in full of acct." Why is this entry made on the credit side of the Cash Book?

No. 50.—Purchase on Account. Examine this bill to see if all of the goods have been received. How can you tell? Are the prices correct? Go over the calculations of the bill and if found correct O. K. it as per previous instructions. Make the entry in the Journal, applying the General Rules for debiting and crediting. File the bill properly.

Proving Cash. In small pencil figures, foot the sides of your Cash Book. Determine the balance by subtracting the credit from the debit footing. See if this balance agrees with the amount on hand, as shown by the check book stub, plus the amount in the Cash Drawer. Always exercise the utmost care in proving Cash so as not to make an error.

Fourth Report. Fill a report blank properly and hand it together with the vouchers and cash for others to your teacher. Have your cash book and journal sheets examined and approved. Copy them into your regular Cash Book and Journal. Re-write any of the vouchers that your teacher may reject on account of errors or poor appearance of work.

Posting. Open an account with T. A. Cooke, Cor. 8th & Market Sts., City, on the 15th line of page 10 of the Ledger; on page 16 open an account with Ballard & Ballard Co., Cor. 10th & Main Sts., City; on the 30th line of page 10, with J. E. Grimm, 948 State St., City; on the 14th line of page 16 with J. J. Disosway & Co., City. Post the items in the Day Book-Journal to the Ledger as previously instructed, and place the letter "J" in the explanation column of the Ledger accounts with all items posted from the Journal, to distinguish them from those to be posted from the Cash Book. Post your Cash Book next, making certain that you carry the items on the debit side to the credit side of the Ledger and the credit items to the debit side of the Ledger. Place the letter "C" in the explanation column of the ledger accounts with all items that are posted from the Cash Book, to distinguish them from those that are posted from the Journal. Check over your posting carefully to make sure that you have made no errors. Present your Ledger, Journal and Cash Book for inspection. If your work meets with approval you will proceed with the following transactions.

FEBRUARY 5, 189–.

No. 51.—CASH SALES, RETAIL DEPARTMENT. This cash Mr. Winter turns over to you as the amount received from cash sales for the week in the retail department. Count it carefully. What account receives value? (*Rule 3.*) What account supplies it? (*Rule 12.*) Make the entry on the debit side of the Cash Book, writing "Feb. 5, Mdse., retail sales, 50.25." Place the cash in the Cash Drawer.

No. 52.—SALE ON ACCOUNT. Examine this order to see if it has been filled. Make out the bill. Re-calculate the items of the bill. Apply the General Rules for debiting and crediting and make the entry. Place the bill in the proper receptacle and file the order.

No. 53.—CASH RECEIVED ON ACCOUNT. This check is to apply on account. What account has received value? What account has supplied it? Make the proper entry in the Cash Book. On which side is the entry made? Why? Place the check in the proper receptacle.

FEBRUARY 6, 189–.

No. 54.—DEPOSIT. Make a deposit of all currency and checks on hand, following instructions for No. 47. Have you made a detailed record on the left-hand stub of the Check Book?

No. 55.—CASH PAID IN FULL OF ACCOUNT. Turn to Thos. J. Johnston & Co.'s account in the Ledger and ascertain the amount the business owes them. Take your Check Book, fill the stub, deduct the amount from the last balance and write the check. Carefully examine it and place it in the proper receptacle. Apply the General Rules for debiting and crediting, and make the entry similar to the entry for No. 49. Why is this entry made on the credit side of the Cash Book?

FEBRUARY 7, 189–.

No. 56.—NOTE RECEIVED ON ACCOUNT. This note is to apply on account. Examine it carefully. Apply General Rules and make the entry. Place the note in the Cash Drawer. Is a note cash?

FEBRUARY 9, 189–.

No. 57.—CASH RECEIVED FOR NOTE DUE TO-DAY. This check is in payment of note due to-day. You will find the note in the Cash Drawer. Cancel the note by writing "Paid, Feb. 9, 189–, C. W. Hammond, (your name) , Attorney," across the face, and place it in Vouchers for Others, from where it will be delivered to Mr. Batson, who will hold it as a receipt.

FEBRUARY 11, 189–.

No. 58.—NOTE GIVEN ON ACCOUNT. Write a note at 60 days for $825, favor Ballard & Ballard Co., payable at City Bank, to apply on account. Notes made payable at the bank will be paid out of C. W. Hammond's deposit when due, the same as a check. Examine it very carefully. What account is to be debited? (*Rule 15.*) Credited? (*Rule 20.*) Make the proper entry, being careful to give the correct explanation. Place the note in the proper receptacle.

No. 59.—CASH PAID IN FULL OF ACCOUNT. Consult Redfield & Son's account in the Ledger and ascertain the amount the business owes them. In your Check Book fill the stub, deduct the amount and write the check for the balance due them. Carefully examine it and place it in the proper receptacle. Make the entry from the stub, applying the General Rules. This entry is similar to entries for Nos. 49 and 55.

FEBRUARY 12, 189–.

No. 60.—CASH SALES, RETAIL DEPARTMENT. Mr. Winter turns over to you the cash received from sales at retail. Count it carefully. This entry is similar to entry for No. 51. Where will you place the cash?

No. 61.—DEPOSIT. Deposit all the cash in the Cash Drawer, observing instructions in detail as given for No. 47. Be sure that you omit nothing.

FEBRUARY 13, 189–.

No. 62.—SALE ON ACCOUNT. Order No. 62 has been filled. Make out the bill, placing the terms, "20 das.," where indicated. Go over the extensions and addition. Apply the rules and make the entry. Place the bill in the proper receptacle. File the order.

No. 63.—NOTE DUE TO-DAY PAID BY CHECK. Kaufman, Straus & Co. have left their note due to-day with your teacher for collection. Fill the stub properly, deduct the amount, and write the check, making it payable to Kaufman, Straus & Co. Take the check to the teacher and get him to cancel the note. File the note as a receipt. Make the entry from the stub of the Check Book. Debit—*rule 19*; credit—*rule 4*. In what book is the entry made?

FEBRUARY 14, 189–.

No. 64.—NOTE RECEIVED ON ACCOUNT. This note is in part payment of what the maker owes the business. Carefully examine it. Make the entry, applying the General Rules. Place the note in the Cash Drawer.

Proving Cash. Add the sides of your cash book sheet in neat pencil figures and ascertain whether the balance agrees with the amount on hand (in the bank). If found to agree, balance, rule (in red ink) and foot the Cash Book as shown in the Model on pages 42 and 43. Bring the balance down below the ruling in black ink.

Fifth Report. Make a report on a report blank and hand same to your teacher, together with your cash and vouchers for others. Rewrite all vouchers that do not meet with approval. Submit your cash book and day book-journal sheets for inspection and approval. Copy them into your regular Cash Book and Day Book-Journal, then balance and rule the Cash Book. In doing this, observe any suggestions your teacher made while examining your work.

Posting. Post all items from the Day Book-Journal to the Ledger, as previously instructed, placing the letter "J" in the explanation column. Post from the Cash Book, using the letter "C" as explanation to indicate that the items came from the Cash Book. Be sure to post the items on the debit side of the Cash Book to the credit of the proper accounts in the Ledger; also post the items on the credit side to the debit of the ledger accounts. Do you clearly comprehend why this is done? After the posting is completed, check over your work as you have been previously instructed.

Trial Balance. As the Cash Book takes the place of a part of your Ledger—the Cash account—it will be necessary to treat it as you would the Cash account in taking a Trial Balance. On a journal sheet start your Trial Balance with Cash, bringing in the balance as shown by the Cash Book. Proceed as previously instructed with all accounts in the Ledger that do not balance. Foot the sides. When found to be equal, submit your Trial Balance to your teacher for approval. Never ask anyone to assist you in finding errors in your trial balances until you have made every effort to find them yourself.

Errors in Trial Balances. Much time is spent in correcting errors that are due, not to a lack of knowledge of the work in hand, but simply to lack of care. A bookkeeper must learn to find mistakes, although a constant effort should be made to avoid them. If the Trial Balance does not at first balance, he should not be discouraged, for a systematic search will always disclose the error. The instructions given below should be followed explicitly and in the order given. Poor figures cause many of the errors in bookkeeping. Errors may be made because figures are improperly formed, and therefore are misread; figures may not be written in columns, thus causing mistakes in addition; or corrections may be carelessly made, rendering the figures illegible. A good bookkeeper will make good figures. The acquiring of a habit of accuracy is one of the valuable things that bookkeeping teaches, and a constant effort should be made to improve in this particular. A permanent record of errors, kept perhaps on one of the fly leaves of a text-book, will be of value in showing what errors you are most liable to make, and thus enable you to guard against them.

To Find Errors when the Trial Balance Does Not Balance.

First.—Review carefully the addition of the Trial Balance.

Second.—Find the exact amount out of balance. Look for this amount in the Journal, and in all other books from which posting is done; also, look for one-half the amount, and see if such amounts are posted correctly.

Third.—Review the additions of the Ledger accounts, and see if all footings have been transferred correctly from Ledger to Trial Balance.

Fourth.—See if all previous balances and inventories have been brought down below the rulings on the proper side.

Fifth.—See that no amount has been entered on the wrong side, omitted, or entered twice in the Trial Balance.

Sixth.—Check the posting in the order of dates, beginning at date of last Trial Balance, as follows:

(a) See that the Journal entries of each transaction balance;

(b) Check each entry in Ledger, in the order of original posting, as found to be correct. Place a check mark in pencil, thus, √, in the Ledger against each item examined and found to be correctly posted. (Sharpen your pencil and make very small, light check marks that may afterwards be erased.) *Never review the posting without checking in the Ledger.* The probable location of an error may frequently be determined by its amount. An error of several thousand dollars could only be in accounts containing large amounts, or a balance placed on the wrong side, or the omission of an account. An error of only a few cents is likely to be in Interest or Discount, or the omission of the cents in posting some account. If the amount out of balance is exactly 1.00, 10.00, 100.00, 1000.00, etc., the error is usually in addition. If the amount out of balance is divisible by nine, the error may be a transposition of figures.

In case it becomes necessary to review and check the posting, and an error is found in this process, but which is not the amount required to make the trial balance prove, correct the error thus discovered; then find the exact amount still required to make the Ledger balance, and again apply the short tests given above before going on with the examination of the posting. Continue in this way until the Trial Balance balances.

Correction of Errors. The manner of correcting an error depends upon the nature of it, and upon the book in which it appears. As a rule, erasures should not be made in any of the books, and particularly in the books of original entry.

In case of an error, consult the teacher for instructions regarding its correction.

When your Trial Balance has been approved, copy it into your Trial Balance Book, but do not make an Inventory of Resources and Liabilities, and Balance Sheet.

Trial Balances and Balance Sheets in Business. In business it is customary to take a Trial Balance once a month, and to make an Inventory of Resources and Liabilities and a Balance Sheet to ascertain the gain or loss and the true standing of the business once or twice a year. To give you ample practice in taking Trial Balances and making Balance Sheets, you will be required to perform these operations oftener than is necessary and customary in business.

Carefully read and study the following, preparatory to the continuation and handling of the new features of the business.

Classification of Orders. Our written order requesting our bank to pay money out of our deposit to some person named therein is called a *Check*. You have already become acquainted with this class of orders.

Our written order requesting a person to deliver goods or valuables of any kind to some person (either himself or some one else) named therein is called an *Order*. You are also familiar with this class of orders.

Our written order requesting a person (usually some one who owes us) to pay to some person (either ourselves or some one we owe) named therein is called a *Draft*.

A bank or banker's written order requesting some other bank or banker to pay money to some person named therein is called a *Bank Draft* or *Bill of Exchange*.

Drafts. A draft is a written order on a person requesting him to pay a certain sum of money to another person. A draft differs from a check in that it is drawn on an individual, while a check is drawn on some bank or banker. When a bank or banker draws a draft on another bank or banker it is known as a Bank Draft or Bill of Exchange.

When Payable. There are two kinds of drafts. Those payable when made, are termed sight drafts or demand drafts; those payable at some future time are termed time drafts.

Object. The primary object of drafts is to facilitate the collection and payment of debts, and obviate the inconvenience, expense, risk and delay incident to transmitting money from place to place.

Form of Draft. The following is the form of draft in common use.

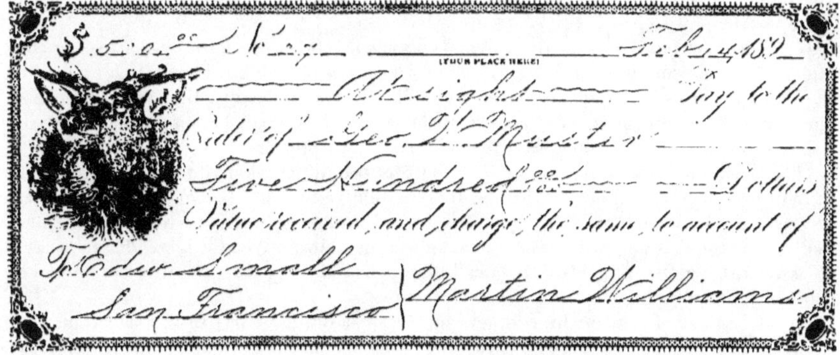

$500.00 No. 27 (YOUR PLACE HERE) Feb. 4 189

At sight Pay to the

Order of Geo. W. Muster

Five Hundred 00/100 Dollars

Value received and charge the same to account of

To Edw. Small
San Francisco

Martin Williams

In the above draft Martin Williams requests Edward Small to pay George W. Muster $500. The presumption is that Small owes Williams or Williams would not request him to pay Muster, whom Williams must be owing or he would not order the money to be paid to him.

Martin Williams is the *drawer* of the draft, Edward Small is the *drawee*, and George W. Muster, the *payee*. The drawer is the one who gives the order, the drawee is the one on whom it is drawn and who is expected to pay to the payee, who is to receive the money.

When Martin Williams mails this draft to Geo. W. Muster, of San Francisco, he debits Geo. W. Muster on his books and credits Edward Small, because Muster will *receive* value, and Small will *supply* value when he pays the draft.

When Muster receives the draft he takes it to Small, who resides in the same city, and receives the cash for same. On his books he will debit cash and credit Williams, because Williams ordered the value to be supplied to him. It would have been impossible for him to get money from Small without Williams' order, because Small is not one of Muster's debtors.

Small will debit Williams because he paid a debt for him, thereby indirectly supplying value to him, and credit cash.

NOTE.—If for some reason Small were to refuse to pay the draft, neither Small nor Muster would make any records on their books. Muster would mail the draft to Williams, stating that payment was refused. Williams would then be obliged to make an entry, crediting Muster and debiting Small, to cancel the entry made when the draft was sent.

The General Rules for debiting and crediting are to be applied to all drafts.

Special Instructions for Debiting and Crediting Drafts. (a) As you have already learned, when you give your check to a person, that person is debited, because he received the value, and Cash account is credited, because it supplied the value out of your deposit in the bank on which the check was drawn. Likewise when you order (draw a draft on him) one of your debtors to pay one of your creditors a certain sum of money, you debit the creditor because he receives the value, and credit the debtor because he supplies it. Apply these instructions to No. 66.

(b) When you draw a draft on one of your debtors payable to yourself and leave it at the bank for collection, you make no entry until the bank notifies you that the amount has been collected and placed to your credit, when you will debit Cash because that account received the value, and credit the party from whom the account was collected because he supplied the value. Should the bank fail to make the collection, no entry will be necessary. Apply these instructions to No. 151.

(c) When you receive a time draft drawn on some person and accepted by that person, and endorsed over to you by the payee (the one to whom it is payable), it is a written promise to pay you a certain sum of money. You debit Bills Receivable because that account received the value, and credit the party (the payee) who endorsed the draft because he supplied the value to your business. Apply these instructions to No. 116.

(d) When one of your creditors orders you (draws a draft on you) to pay a certain sum of money to some person named therein, it is nothing more than his request; when you pay it, the creditor who ordered you to pay it is debited because indirectly he received the value, and Cash account is credited because it supplied the value. When it is payable to himself the same rule applies, the only difference being that he receives the value directly instead of indirectly. Apply hese instructions to No. 89.

(e) When one of your creditors orders you (draws a draft on you) to pay a certain sum of money at a future time to some person named therein and you promise (in writing) to pay it, it becomes a Bills Payable. The party ordering you (drawing on you) to pay it is debited because either directly or indirectly he received the value—directly when payable to himself and indirectly when payable to some one else—and Bills Payable is credited because that account supplied the value. To promise to pay a draft in writing is to write across the face of the draft "Accepted," the date and your signature, which is equal in effect to giving a party your promissory note. It is customary to write the acceptance in red ink, although there is no necessity for so doing. Apply these instructions to No. 119.

The Bank Draft. When you wish to remit to a party in some distant place in payment for goods, and the party does not know of your financial standing, it would not be wise to send your check, as the party, not knowing that you have sufficient funds in the bank to pay the check, would hesitate and possibly refuse to accept it as payment, or would have the check collected by his bank before he would send the goods ordered. This would cause delay, inconvenience and annoyance. The better plan is to make your check payable to "New York Exchange" (or exchange on some other city, depending on where your bank has a correspondent), take it to your bank and receive a bank draft for same, and send it to the party from whom you desire to purchase. This will be accepted, although you are a stranger to him.

Suppose you wish to purchase 10 brls. New Orleans Molasses from Edwin J. Wright, of New Orleans, and the cost of same is $120. You will write your check for $120 payable to "Philadelphia Exchange," favor Edwin J. Wright; taking the check to the bank which in the illustration given on the next page is the German National Bank, you will receive a bank draft similar to the following:

The German National Bank

(YOUR PLACE HERE.) Feb 14, 189 . No

Pay to the order of Edwin J. Wright — $120 00/100

One Hundred Twenty 00/100 —— Dollars

THE CENTRAL NATIONAL BANK,
PHILADELPHIA, PA.

A. T. Williams.
Cashier

In the above the German National Bank, through its cashier, orders the Central National Bank of Philadelphia to pay $120 to Edwin J. Wright. This will be accepted by Mr. Wright, as his bank will receive it on deposit or cash it unhesitatingly, knowing that it will be paid by the Central National Bank of Philadelphia when presented. This bank draft is known as "Philadelphia Exchange" instead of "New York Exchange," as it is drawn on a Philadelphia bank. The German National Bank would not have drawn on the Central National Bank did it not have money on deposit there against which it may draw for the accomodation of its depositors, as illustrated in the above case. In this case the Central National Bank is known as the correspondent of the German National Bank. Sometimes banks make a slight charge for selling exchange; in that case, debit Expense for the charge. If desired to show results in detail, an account must be opened with Exchange.

No. 65.—Sale on Account. This order has been filled. Bill and enter same. Apply rules 1 and 2 in making the entry. Go over your calculations before placing the bill in its receptacle. File the order properly.

February 15, 189–.

No. 66.—Order on a Debtor to Pay a Creditor. Turn to A. Paul, Jr.'s account in the Ledger and ascertain the amount the business owes him. Take a blank form and write a draft, ordering A. P. Batson, who owes the business, to pay to A. Paul, Jr., at sight, the amount the business owes Mr. Paul. Examine it carefully to see that you have made Batson the drawee, Paul the payee, and C. W. Hammond, (your name) .... Atty., the drawer. By this operation the business ceases to owe Mr. Paul and Mr. Batson ceases to owe the business the amount named in the draft. Determine the accounts to be debited and credited by reading "a" under the instructions for debiting and crediting drafts, page 51. Make the entry, debiting the payee and crediting the drawee. Why? Write for explanation the following: "Drew draft on A. P. Batson favor A. Paul, Jr." Place the draft in an envelope and address it to A. Paul, Jr. Do not seal it. Place the envelope in Vouchers for Others. When Mr. Paul receives this draft he takes it to Mr. Batson and receives the amount called for.

Note.—It has been pre-arranged by Mr. Hammond that Mr. Batson is to pay the draft and Mr. Paul has agreed to accept it. It would be very unbusinesslike to draw on a debtor in favor of a creditor unless there is some assurance that the draft will be honored when presented.

FEBRUARY 16, 189–.

No. 67.—PURCHASE ON ACCOUNT. Examine this bill. Have all the goods been received? Are the terms and prices correct? How can you tell? Test the calculations, and if found correct, O. K. it and make the proper entry, applying the General Rules.

No. 68.—SALE ON ACCOUNT. If this order has been filled, make out the bill and enter in your Journal, applying the General Rules. Re-calculate the items of your bill and place it in the proper receptacle. Have you filed the order?

No. 69.—DRAFT REQUESTING A DEBTOR TO PAY A CREDITOR. H. B. Phillips & Co. are willing to honor (pay) our draft on them for the amount they owe the business. Turn to your Ledger and ascertain the amount. Using a blank form, write a draft requesting them to pay that amount to Kaufman, Straus & Co., whom the business owes. Inspect the draft critically. Who receives value by this operation? Who supplies the value? Read "a" under instructions for debiting and crediting drafts, page 51, and make the entry. This entry is similar to entry for No. 66. Place the draft in an envelope and address it to Kaufman, Straus & Co. Place the envelope in the proper receptacle.

FEBRUARY 17, 189–.

No. 70.—NOTE GIVEN ON ACCOUNT. Write a note favor of J. J. Disosway & Co. for one month for $1250, making it payable at the City Bank. Critically examine the note. Debit—*rule 15*; credit—*rule 20*. Make the entry, being careful to give the proper explanation. Place it in the proper receptacle.

No. 71.—DRAFT ON A DEBTOR TO PAY A CREDITOR. Turn to Kaufman, Straus & Co.'s account in the Ledger and ascertain the amount the business owes them. Do not fail to deduct the amount of the Journal entry on the 16th inst., as that entry has not been posted. Mr. T. A. Cooke has agreed to honor (pay) our draft on him for any amount he owes the business. Draw a draft on him at sight for the amount the business owes Kaufman, Straus & Co. Examine your draft carefully: read "a" under instructions for debiting and crediting drafts, page 51, and make the entry. This entry is similar to entries for Nos. 66 and 69.

FEBRUARY 18, 189–.

No. 72.—SALE ON ACCOUNT. Bill the goods called for in this order if they have been sent. How can you tell? Make the entry, applying rules 1 and 2. Re-calculate the items on the bill, then place it in the proper receptacle. File the order.

No. 73.—CASH SALES RETAIL DEPARTMENT. Mr. Winter turns over to you this Cash (No. 73), being the amount received from cash sales in the retail department. Count it carefully and make the entry in the proper book, applying rules 1 and 2. Place the Cash in the Cash Drawer.

Study the following and be prepared to answer all the questions.

Interest and Discount. Interest is the compensation received or paid for the use of money *when or after it is due*. Discount is the compensation received or paid for the use of money *before it is due*. The object of this account is to show the gain or loss resulting from loaning or borrowing money, or discounting and buying Commercial Paper. By Commercial Paper is meant notes, drafts, etc. The Special Rules for debiting and crediting Interest & Discount are:

21. *DEBIT Interest & Discount when either costs the business value.*

22. *CREDIT Interest & Discount when either supplies value to the business.*

When the debit side of the account is the larger the difference is a Loss; when the credit side is the larger the difference is a Gain. The above rules for debiting and crediting will apply also to Exchange, Premium, Collection, Storage, Commission—in fact to all allowance accounts. It is customary to keep Interest and Discount in one account, although some prefer to keep an account with Interest and another with Discount.

NOTE.—In calculating interest and discount the rate to be employed is 6%, and days of grace are not to be considered.

TRANSACTIONS ILLUSTRATING INTEREST & DISCOUNT ACCOUNT.

Jan. 1. Paid interest on note favor Joseph Winter, $6.25. Jan. 2. Received cash for interest on John Keller's note, $7.20. Jan. 8. Purchased a note from Jos. Frey for $400, less discount to maturity, $3.80. Jan. 12. Discounted my note at bank for $6000, the discount being $5.60. Jan. 18. Received cash from H. Stadler for his note due to-day, $800, and interest, $48. Jan. 23. Paid annual interest on my note favor Martin Schwartz, $21. Jan. 26. Purchased a note from August Schreiber for $650, less discount to maturity, $4.60. Jan. 30. Discounted Jacob Hauser's note at bank, the discount being $6.75.

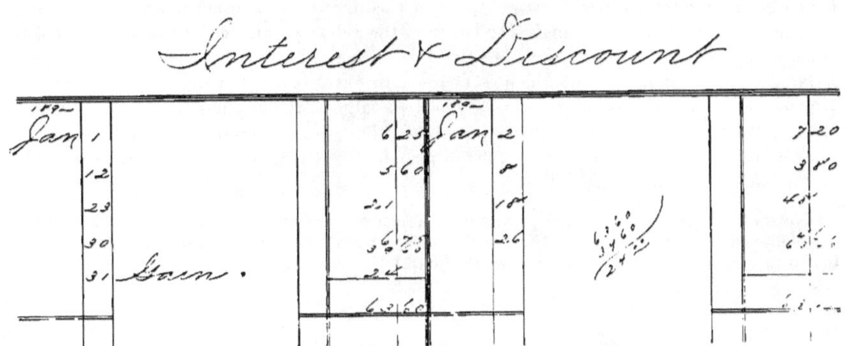

*To be written in red ink.

The debit side of the above account shows that Interest & Discount has cost the business value to the amount of $39.60; the credit side shows that value has been supplied to the business to the amount of $63.60; the difference between what has been supplied (63.60) and what has been paid out (39.60) is $24, which is a Gain. In case more has been paid out than has been received, the result is a Loss.

QUESTIONS. What is Interest? What is Discount? When is Interest & Discount account debited? When credited? When the debit side of the account is the greater, is the difference a Loss or a Gain? To what other accounts will the above rules apply? What is the object of keeping the Interest & Discount account?

No. 74.—Note Discounted at Bank. Mr. Hammond wants you to have discounted at bank H. B. Phillips & Co.'s note of the 31st ult. Take the note from your Cash Drawer and find how many days it has to run, including the day it falls due. Calculate the discount at 6% for the number of days it has to run. Endorse the note *in blank* (on the left-hand end): *i. e.*, write "C. W. Hammond, (your name) Atty." Take it and your Pass Book to the bank. The bank will discount it (purchase it, less the discount to maturity). Tell the clerk what the discount amounts to, and have him enter the amount of the proceeds in your Pass Book. Having received the proper credit in your Pass Book, return to your desk and enter the following on the left-hand stub of the Check Book: "Feb. 18, discounted H. B. Phillips & Co.'s note $400 less discount, 80¢, 399.20." Add the net proceeds (399.20) to the amount in bank. In your Cash Book on the debit side record the following: "18, Bills Receivable, Dis. H. B. Phillips & Co.'s note, $400." (Take more than one line for explanation whenever necessary.) On the credit side of your Cash Book record the following: "18, Interest & Discount, H. B. Phillips & Co.'s note, 80¢." Why do you debit cash for $400? (*Rule 3.*) Why do you credit Bills Receivable for $400? (*Rule 18.*) Why do you debit Interest & Discount? (*Rule 21.*) Why do you credit Cash for 80¢? (*Rule 4.*) Look up these rules carefully and do not pass by this transaction before you understand it thoroughly.

The bank gives you $399.20 for the note; *i. e.*, it increased your deposit that amount, which is equal to paying you $400 and you paying it 80¢ discount, just as the records in your Cash Book make it appear you did. Remember that a note is always debited and credited for its face; therefore, when you sell a note to a bank or to some other person for less than its face it will be necessary to make the entry on the debit side of the Cash Book for the full amount; on the credit side make the entry for the amount allowed the party to whom you sell it, for the accommodation, which is charged to Interest & Discount. Did Interest & Discount *cost* the business value, or has it *produced* value to the business, by this transaction? What is the bank going to do with the note that it has just discounted for you? Who will pay the note when it becomes due? In case they fail to pay it, who will be held responsible by the bank for its payment? Why?

Note.—In Philadelphia, Baltimore, Louisville and some other cities it is customary to include both the day of discount and the day of maturity when computing the bank discount on commercial paper. Follow the instructions as given above unless otherwise directed by the teacher.

February 20, 189–.

No. 75.—Note Paid by Check. The note favor of Henry Knefely & Son, which is due to-day, has been left with your teacher for collection. After filling the stub of your Check Book properly, write the check, making it payable to Henry Knefely & Son. Take it to the teacher and get him to cancel the note. File the note as a receipt. What account is to be debited? (*Rule 19.*) What account has supplied value? (*Rule 4.*) Make the entry in the Cash Book. When entries are made for checks issued, on which side of the Cash Book are they always made? Why? Have you written the proper explanation for this entry?

February 20, 189–.

No. 76.—Purchase from an Out of Town Party. Mr. Hammond has ordered the goods called for in this bill. The goods have all been received and the freight has been prepaid and added to the bill. In order to receive the goods it was necessary for Mr. Winter to present the shipping receipt that accompanied this bill, at the local freight office. Go over the calculations and addition, and if found correct O. K. same. Make the entry, applying rules 1 and 2. File the bill.

No. 77.—CASH REMITTED TO A CREDITOR. Write a check favor A. Engelhard & Son for $200 to apply on account. Have you filled the stub and deducted the amount? Write them a letter as follows:

(Your place here), February 20, 189–.

Messrs. A. ENGELHARD & SON,
Louisville, Ky.

Gentlemen,—

Enclosed please find my check for $200 to apply on account. Please acknowledge receipt of same, and oblige,

Yours truly,

C. W. HAMMOND,
per (your name)

Place the check on the letter sheet, then fold the letter properly, and after addressing the envelope correctly, insert it but do not seal it. Place the envelope in Vouchers for Others. Make the entry, applying rules 1 and 2. In what book is the entry made?

No. 78.—PURCHASE FROM AN OUT OF TOWN PARTY. The goods called for in this bill have been ordered by Mr. Hammond from C. Wilt & Son's salesman, who was in the city last week. Have the goods been received? Are the prices correct? How can you tell? Notice that the freight has been prepaid and added to the bill. Test the calculations and O. K. the bill. What would you do in case you discovered an error? Make the entry, applying the General Rules. File the bill.

No. 79.—NOTE DISCOUNTED AT BANK. Discount Frey & Thomas' note at bank. Find how many days it has to run, including the due date. Take it and your Pass Book to the bank and tell the clerk what the discount amounts to. Also see that you receive proper credit in your Pass Book for the net proceeds. Return to your desk and make a record on the left-hand stub of your Check Book as instructed for No. 74. Have you added the net proceeds to the amount in bank? What has the business parted with (supplied to others)? What account cost the business value? (*Rule 21.*) What has the business received in return for the note (Bills Receivable) it sold to the bank? On the debit side of the Cash Book enter the face of the note as instructed for No. 74; on the credit side enter the discount as per instructions for No. 74. Have you written the proper explanation? Why not enter the actual amount received from the bank on the debit side of the Cash Book and omit the entry on the credit side?

FEBRUARY 22, 189–.

No. 80.—SALE TO AN OUT OF TOWN PARTY. Order No. 80 is from an out of town party. His references speak well of him, and his ratings by Dun and Bradstreet (Mercantile Agencies) are good. Mr. Hammond has ordered the goods to be shipped to him. Bill and enter same, applying General Rules. Go over your calculations. It will be necessary for you to fill out a triplicate set of Shipping Receipts (sometimes called Bills of Lading) in the blank book furnished for that purpose as follows:

SHIPPING RECEIPT.

YOUR PLACE HERE — Feb. 25, 189

Received from C. F. Hammond

BY INTER-STATE TRANSPORTATION COMPANY,

The property described below, in apparent good order, except as noted (contents and condition of contents of packages unknown), marked, consigned, and destined as indicated below, which said Company agrees to carry to the said destination, if on its road, otherwise to deliver to another carrier on the route to said destination.

It is mutually agreed, in consideration of the freight charged for this service, as to each carrier of all or any of said property over all or any portion of said route to destination, and as to each party at any time interested in all or any of said property, that every service to be performed hereunder shall be subject to all the conditions, whether printed or written, shown or endorsed hereon, and which are hereby agreed to by the shipper and by him accepted for himself and assigns as just and reasonable.

MARKS, CONSIGNS AND DESTINATION.	DESCRIPTION OF ARTICLES.	WEIGHT SUBJECT TO CORRECTION.
A. J. Gouley	160 bu Beans	
Louisville	250 " Corn	
Ky.	670 " Peas	
	200 " Oats	

For Inter-State Transportation Company,

Freight Agent.

Observe that your forms are printed in triplicate. The first is designated as *Original*, the second as *Forwarding Order*, and the third as *Duplicate*. After you have the set filled out as illustrated above, take your book to the freight agent, or in case there is none, take it to your teacher, who will act as freight agent, and have him receipt for the goods. In business no freight agent would sign a shipping receipt or bill of lading unless accompanied by the goods to be shipped.

The freight agent will keep the *Forwarding Order*; you will leave the *Duplicate* in the book as a receipt in case any dispute arises or the goods fail to reach their destination; and you will detach the *Original* and enclose it with the bill. Place both in an envelope addressed to the party who ordered the goods, and put the envelope in Vouchers for Others.

Proving Cash. In neat pencil figures foot the sides of your Cash Book and ascertain whether the balance as shown by the Cash Book agrees with the amount on hand (in the bank and Cash Drawer). In case there is a discrepancy which you can not locate after making a diligent effort, report same to your teacher, but do not be disappointed if he refuses to find your error for you. It may be of such a nature as not to warrant his assistance, and be due entirely to your carelessness.

Sixth Report. Make a report on a Report Blank and hand it to your teacher together with the vouchers and cash for others. Re-write any of the vouchers that do not meet with approval. Have your journal sheet and cash book sheet examined, after which copy them into your regular Journal and Cash Book, being careful to make your work look as neat as possible.

Posting. Open accounts as follows: Interest & Discount on the 29th line of page 4; A. J. Gouley, Louisville, Ky., on page 11; Renaker & Heinrich, City, on the 29th line of page 16; A. Engelhard & Son, Louisville, Ky., on page 17; and C. Wilt & Son, Philadelphia, Pa., on the 14th line of page 17. Post to your Ledger, being sure that you make no errors in posting from the Cash Book. Remember the items on the debit side of the Cash Book are posted to the credit of your Ledger accounts; also the items on the credit side of the Cash Book are posted to the debit of the Ledger accounts. Check over your posting carefully; never fail to check over your posting, as thereby you will save much worry, annoyance and time.

No. 81.—Office Furniture Purchased for Cash. The items called for in bill No. 81 have been received and the prices are correct. Verify the addition and O. K. the bill if found to be without error. This furniture is for use in Mr. Hammond's private office and in the shipping department. Pay the bill by check. Place the check in the proper receptacle and file the bill on the Voucher File. Make the entry from the stub of the Check Book, applying *rule 13* for the debit and *rule 4* for the credit, and charging to Furniture & Fixtures account. Furniture & Fixtures account is treated exactly like Expense account, as it is a subdivision of that account and is opened to show what amount has been expended for furniture and fixtures instead of being included under the general heading of Expense. (*See explanation and illustration of Expense account, page 17.*)

No. 82.—Purchase on Account. Calculate the items of bill No. 82 to see that no error exists. Have the goods been received? Make the entry, applying the General Rules. File the bill properly.

February 23, 189–.

No. 83.—Sale to an Out of Town Party. Bill and enter this order. Go over your calculations a second time and make the entry, applying rules 1 and 2. Make out three (3) shipping receipts, applying the instructions as given for last order. Take them to the freight agent and have him receipt the same. Enclose the *Original* with the bill for the goods in a correctly addressed envelope, but do not seal it.

No. 84.—Order on a Debtor to Pay a Creditor. Write a draft ordering A. J. Gouley, of Louisville, Ky., to pay A. Engelhard & Son of the same city the amount the business owes them. Turn to the proper book and find the amount. As both parties reside in the same city it will obviate the necessity of Mr. Gouley remitting to C. W. Hammond the amount he owes our business, and C. W. Hammond in turn remitting to A. Engelhard & Son the amount the business owes them. When A. Engelhard & Son receive this draft they will take it to Mr. Gouley, who will pay them the amount as he agreed to when he gave us the last order. (*See order on file.*) What account receives value? What account supplies value? Make the entry, debiting the party who receives value and crediting the party who supplies value. Inclose the draft in a properly addressed envelope. To whom will you send the draft, the Payee or the Drawee? Why not send it to the other party? Your teacher will tell you if you can not determine for yourself.

No. 85.—Cash Received on Account. Enter this check (No. 85) and place it in the Cash Drawer. What account received value? What account supplied value? In what book are all checks entered? Do you examine all checks carefully as to the form, wording and proper method of filling or writing same?

Ask questions at the proper time on all points you do not fully understand. A good student should be a good questioner. In performing this work never regulate your pace by that of some other student or endeavor to accomplish more than you can understandingly, and not sacrifice the appearance of your work. Work with dispatch but never hurry; remember, "What is worth doing at all is worth doing well."

FEBRUARY 24, 189–.

No. 86.—CASH RECEIVED IN FULL OF ACCOUNT. This check (No. 86) is sent in full for the amount the debtor owes the business. Turn to his account and determine whether the amount of the check is equal to the amount as shown by his account. If found to agree, make the entry, applying rules 1 and 2. Place the check in the proper receptacle. Why are checks more commonly used by business men than currency or specie? Give two reasons.

No. 87.—DEPOSIT. Make a deposit. Count all the currency in the Cash Drawer. Fill out a deposit ticket, entering the amount opposite the word "currency." Endorse the checks as previously instructed, and enter each check separately where indicated on the deposit ticket. Foot your deposit ticket, then carefully re-count your currency and checks, also re-add the items to make certain that there is no mistake. Enter the total amount of your deposit on the right-hand stub of your Check Book, and add it to the amount in bank. On the left-hand stub make a copy of the items on your deposit ticket so that reference can be made to it when desired. Take your deposit and Pass Book to the bank. Have you received proper credit for your deposit?

No. 88.—NOTE DISCOUNTED AT BANK. Take from your Cash Drawer J. E. Grimm's note dated Feb. 14, and calculate the discount preparatory to having it discounted at the bank. First, determine the time it has to run including the due date. After you have found the discount, endorse the note in blank as previously instructed. Take it to the bank and state what the discount amounts to. After receiving credit for the net proceeds in your Pass Book, return to your desk and make the proper record on your Check Book, as per instructions for Nos. 74 and 79. Be sure to refer to Nos. 74 and 79 so that you will make no error. From the stub of the Check Book enter the face of the note on the debit side of the Cash Book, applying previous instructions as per above numbers, and write the proper explanation. On the credit side of your Cash Book debit Interest & Discount for the proper amount, being careful to refer to previous instructions, and write the explanation correctly. Why is Bills Receivable credited? (*Rule 18.*) Why is Cash debited for $1500? Why is Interest & Discount debited? (*Rule 21.*) Why is Cash credited for the amount of the discount? Do not fail to consult your teacher in case you do not clearly understand any of the details given for this class of transactions.

No. 89.—SIGHT DRAFT PAID IN CASH. No. 89 is a written order requesting Mr. Hammond to pay a certain sum of money to the drawers of the draft. As the business is indebted to them for that amount and over, you will pay the draft, by check. The entry for this transaction is similar to the entry made when cash is paid to a party on account, as the draft is nothing more than a request, and should Mr. Hammond for some cause or other refuse to pay it, no entry would be required. Notice the endorsements made on the back of the draft. The last one was made by the bank's messenger who brought the draft to your office to receive payment for same. When making this entry write for explanation "Paid sight draft." File the draft on the Voucher File as a receipt.

FEBRUARY 26, 189–.

No. 90.—CASH SALES, RETAIL DEPARTMENT. This cash (No. 90) the salesman turns in as the amount received for cash sales for the past week. Count it carefully. Make the entry correctly in the proper book. Re-count the cash and place it in the Cash Drawer. Have you made the proper entry? Have you written the proper explanation for this entry?

No. 91.—Proprietor Draws Cash for Private Use. Mr. Hammond wishes $100 for private use. Pay him the amount, placing the currency in Cash Paid Out. Who has received value? What account supplied it? Make the entry in the proper book, applying rules 1 and 2.

No. 92.—Proprietor Takes Merchandise for Private Use. Mr. Hammond has requested Mr. Winter to send one barrel of Flour to his residence by the City Carting Co. No bill will be necessary. You will charge him cost price for the flour and credit the account that supplied the value. Be sure to make the proper explanation, as this is a very important part of any entry.

February 27, 189–.

No. 93.—Check Received on Account. This check (No. 93) has been sent to apply on account. Carefully read the letter (No. 93) that accompanied the check. Write a letter on one of Mr. Hammond's letter heads acknowledging receipt of the check and state that you have given him proper credit for the amount. Your letter should be similar to the following:

(Your place) , *Feb. 27, 189–.*

Mr. Paul Frey,
Owensboro, Ky.

Dear Sir,—

I am in receipt of your favor of the 26th inst. enclosing check for $1500, which has been placed to your credit. Please accept my thanks for same.

Soliciting your further favors, I am,

Respectfully,

C. W. Hammond,

per (Your name) .

Inclose your letter in a properly addressed envelope and place it in Vouchers for Others. Make the entry for the check, applying rules 1 and 2, after which place the check in the Cash Drawer.

February 28, 189–.

No. 94.—Drayage Bill Paid. This bill (No. 94) has been found to be correct and it has been O. K.'d by the shipping clerk. Go over the calculations. Pay the bill by check. Write the check and place it in the Vouchers for Others. File the bill on the proper file. Make the entry from the stub in the Check Book. Debit—*Rule 13;* credit—*Rule 4.*

No. 95.—Clerk's Salary Paid. Pay Mr. Frank Winter $60 by check as salary for the month. Place the check in Vouchers for Others. Debit—*Rule 13;* credit—*Rule 4.* Why is Expense debited for clerk's salary?

No. 96.—Bookkeeper's Salary Paid. Mr. Hammond has increased your salary, and you will pay yourself $75 for the month instead of $50, as in the previous month. Write the check and place it in the proper receptacle. Make the entry from the stub of the Check Book.

No. 97.—Deposit. You will now make a deposit of all the cash on hand. Endorse the checks in your Cash Drawer as previously instructed. Count the currency and fill out a deposit ticket, placing the amount on the proper line. Enter the check on the deposit ticket. Re-count your currency and re-add the items on the deposit ticket. Add the deposit to the amount in bank as shown by the Check Book stub. On the left-hand stub make a detailed record of your deposit ticket. Take your deposit and Pass Book to the bank. After satisfying yourself that you have received proper credit, leave your Pass Book at the bank to be written up.

Seventh Report. Fill out a Report Blank properly and hand same, together with the cash and vouchers for others, to your teacher for examination. Rewrite all vouchers that do not meet with approval. Have your journal and cash book sheets approved, and copy same into your regular Journal and Cash Book.

Proving Cash. Test the correctness of the entries in your Cash Book by comparing its balance with the balance on hand. If found to agree, you will balance and rule the Cash Book as previously instructed and bring the balance below the ruling in black ink.

Posting. Open accounts as follows: Furniture & Fixtures on the 29th line of page 5, and Lerch Bros., 7 East Pratt St., City, on the 29th line of page 17.

Post to your Ledger from the Journal. Post from your Cash Book, observing previous instructions. Having finished the posting you will check (in pencil) over same to locate any error you may have made.

Statements. Make out statements against all parties who are indebted to the business. Do not include either debit or credit items that are checked or ruled off, as they balance and have, therefore, been settled for in full. Be careful, however, lest you have made errors by checking or ruling items that do not balance, or in failing to check or rule those that do balance. Have your statements approved.

Trial Balance. Pencil foot all the accounts in the Ledger that do not balance preparatory to taking a trial balance. Begin the trial balance on a journal sheet with the balance of cash as shown by the debit side of the Cash Book. Continue with all the accounts in the Ledger that do not balance. Have your trial balance approved before proceeding to close your books.

Inventories. Preparatory to making a Balance Sheet and closing the books to ascertain the standing of the business, Mr. Hammond has ordered the shipping clerk to take an account of stock. Mr. Winter has done this and found the stock on hand to consist of the articles named in the February Inventory (No. 97a).

Make the calculations of the inventory on a sheet of paper and have same approved before copying into your regular Journal. File the inventory on the Voucher File.

Make an Inventory of Resources and Liabilities, per previous instructions, and submit same, for approval.

Balance Sheet. 1. Head a blank Balance Sheet as you were instructed for January balance sheet. 2. Copy the Trial Balance on the Balance Sheet, observing previous instructions. 3. Enter the inventories in the Resource column in red ink. 4. Extend the balances of the various accounts to the proper columns, referring to previous instructions. 5. Find the Net Gain. 6. Find Mr. Hammond's Present Capital. 7. Rule and foot all the columns. 8. Critically inspect your Balance Sheet and compare it with the Model as given on page 36, and if its appearance is not good make another copy of same. 9. Present for approval.

Closing Accounts Showing Losses and Gains. 1. Enter the merchandise inventory on the credit side of Mdse. account in red ink. 2. On the proper side enter (in red ink) the Gain. 3. Carry this Gain to the Loss & Gain account, referring to previous instructions. 4. Bring down the Inventory below the ruling to the debit side of Mdse. account.

Close Expense account and carry the Loss to the Loss & Gain account. Do not fail to rule every account that closes into Loss & Gain account.

Close Interest & Discount account and carry the balance to the Loss & Gain account. This account is treated similarly to Expense account.

Furniture & Fixtures account. 1. Enter the inventory on the credit side of Furniture & Fixtures account. 2. Enter the Loss on the proper side in red ink. 3. Carry the Loss to the proper account. 4. Have you ruled Furniture & Fixtures account and brought down the Inventory in black ink? This is a property account and is treated similarly to Merchandise account.

Close the Loss & Gain account as instructed for January, properly ruling it and carrying the Net Gain to Mr. Hammond's account.

Balance Mr. Hammond's account as you did in January and bring down the Present Capital. Check the balances of the accounts just closed with the balances as they appear in the Resource and Liability columns of the Balance Sheet to satisfy yourself that you have made no error in closing. Present all books for inspection.

REVIEW QUESTIONS. In business how often is it customary to make a balance sheet and close accounts showing losses and gains? What reasons are there for not keeping account of Furniture & Fixtures in the Expense account? What is a draft? What other kinds of orders are there? When is a bank draft preferable to a check? Of what advantage is a draft? What is the advantage of having a note discounted at a bank? What disadvantage do you see in discounting a note when you do not need the money? How often is it customary to take a trial balance in business? How would you close an account that does not show a loss or a gain, if you desired to do so? What property accounts do not, as a rule, show a loss or gain? Do personal accounts, as a rule, show losses or gains? When a debtor fails and cannot pay all that he owes you, what would you do with the balance he cannot pay? Would the business gain or lose in that case? What is the object of the Cash Book? In what way does it save labor? What is a shipping receipt? By what other name is a shipping receipt sometimes known?

THE BUSINESS OF C. W. HAMMOND & CO

MARCH 1, 189–.

No. 98.—By this bill of sale Mr. Hammond sells his business to the firm of C. W. Hammond & Co., the members of which are yourself and Mr. Hammond, as he has decided to take you into the business as partner. Read the bill of sale, attach the Inventory of Resources and Liabilities, then file it on the Voucher File. You will make a cash investment equal to Mr. Hammond's investment. (*See February Balance Sheet.*) Get a check for the amount of your investment from your teacher, made payable to your order, which you will endorse over to the firm of C. W. Hammond & Co. as follows: "Pay to the order of C. W. Hammond & Co.," then sign your name underneath. Credit yourself for this check on the sheet representing your Cash Book. Have you written the proper explanation? In the C. W. Hammond check book write a check favor of *C. W. Hammond & Co.* for the amount Mr. Hammond has in bank. Deduct the amount to show that Mr. Hammond individually has nothing in bank. Place both checks in the Cash Drawer.

Your rights and privileges will be the same as Mr. Hammond's, and you are to share the Gains, Losses and Assets equally. Study form No. 1 in the appendix, then write a partnership agreement between yourself and Mr. Hammond on practice paper. Have it inspected by the teacher before copying on the blank provided in your package of supplies. Your teacher will sign for Mr. Hammond and show you how to fold and where to brief your partnership agreement. Brief it by writing where directed "Partnership Agreement between C. W. Hammond and (your name)...., March 1, 189–." Place it on the Voucher File.

NOTE.—In business two copies of the partnership agreement would be made and signed by both partners, so that each would have a copy.

Hereafter sign all checks and business papers as follows: "C. W. Hammond & Co.," and place your name on the form wherever indicated. Be sure that you never omit writing your name on each and every paper issued by the business. Do not sign your name as Att'y hereafter, which is not necessary, as you are one of the proprietors and your rights are equal to Mr. Hammond's.

Get your Pass Book at the bank and compare the balance with the balance as shown by the Stub of the Check Book. If found correct, write in red ink "O. K. with bank balance, Mar. 1." If there is a discrepancy, follow instructions as given for last month.

No. 99. You will now deposit the checks on hand. Endorse them as follows: "Pay to the order of the City Bank, C. W. Hammond & Co., per (your name) ." Fill out a deposit ticket, using the C. W. Hammond & Co. form. Enter the amount of your deposit on the right-hand stub of your C. W. Hammond & Co. Check Book. On the left-hand stub of your Check Book make a detailed record as previously instructed. Take your deposit to the bank and see to it that *C. W. Hammond & Co.* receive credit instead of C. W. Hammond. This is very important.

No. 100.—By this deed the building occupied by the business at 122-124 Main St., and the lots upon which it is located, are transferred to C. W. Hammond & Co. Read the deed carefully and ask questions on any points you do not fully understand. Read it a second time, then write the check for same and place it in the proper receptacle. Make the entry from the stub in the Check Book, applying the General Rules. Debit Real Estate instead of Merchandise, as this is a kind of property entirely different from the commodities you are dealing in as a business, and is not purchased with the intention of selling it for speculative purposes. Brief and fold the deed properly and place it on the Voucher File. In what book have you made the entry? Have you written the proper explanation?

No. 101.—This bill is for gas consumed during the month of February. You will pay it to-day to take advantage of the discount allowed when payment is made on the first day of the month. Write the check and place it in the proper receptacle. Make the entry as previously instructed. File the bill.

NOTE.—Ordinarily this bill would be paid by the former proprietor who had the use of the gas. In this case you and Mr. Hammond agree that the partnership is to bear the expense. Partners may agree to do anything that is legal.

No. 102.—This bill is for coal Mr. Hammond has purchased to heat the building. It has been O. K.'d and receipted and therefore you will pay it by check. Apply *rules 13 and 4* in making this entry. File the bill.

Sales Book. This is the second of the labor saving books to be introduced. In this book are entered the purchasers' names and addresses, the terms on which the goods are sold, and a detailed record of the goods and prices of same, whenever a bill is rendered for the purchase. When no bill is rendered and the goods are paid for at the time of purchase, it is to be considered a part of the cash sales for the day, and Cash is debited and Merchandise is credited for the total of such sales, at the close of the day's business. In retail business houses the bulk of the sales are made to persons not known to the proprietors, and are paid for at the time of purchase. Such sales are never entered in the Sales Book, as it would involve unnecessary labor and inconvenience. The proper thing to do in cases similar to the above is to debit Cash and credit Merchandise for the total of the sales at the close of the day's business.

In posting from the Sales Book debit each purchaser with the amount of his purchase, and at the end of the month, or when a Trial Balance is taken, credit Mdse. account for the total sales. It will be seen that this book takes the place of the credit side of the Mdse. account in the Ledger.

No. 103.—Using the *C. W. Hammond & Co.* form of bill head, make out the bill for this order, as the goods have been sent. Re-calculate the items of your bill. Make the entry as given below on a journal sheet representing your Sales Book, making the correct extensions instead of the ones given.

March 1, 189–

A. P. Batson 2/10 net 30 days.			
Market St. City.			
100 brls. Flour	4.00	400	
160 " Apples	2.00	320	
70 bu Wheat	1.00	70	
144 " Flaxseed	2.00	288	1078

Note every detail closely in the illustration and be sure that your entry is made absolutely correct. Place the terms as you see them in the illustration. The figures "2/10" indicate that a discount of 2% will be allowed if the bill is paid within 10 days. "Net 30 days" signifies that 30 days is the time allowed in which the bill may be paid, and it should be paid at the end of that time. Observe the greatest care in placing the terms both on your bill and in your Sales Book so that no discrepancy will occur. Place the bill in the proper receptacle and file the order. No detailed explanation for entries in the Sales Book will be given hereafter, and you will be expected to refer to the above for any information regarding the details of such entries.

MARCH 2, 189–.

Invoice Book. This is the third of the labor saving books to be introduced, and in it are entered all purchases of merchandise. Expense bills and the like are never entered in this book. Many different forms are in use in the business houses of the present day, and they are known by different names, some firms calling them Purchase Books. The form used herewith is one in common use, and possesses many advantages over most other forms. (*See form on page 67.*) In this book the bills are pasted in consecutive order after they are received and have been O. K.'d. When a bill is ready for credit, paste it into the Invoice Book, taking care not to extend the right-hand end of the bill beyond the first rulings of the money columns. To properly do this it may be found necessary to trim the edges of the bills, as bills from different houses are not uniform in size. In preparing the invoice to be pasted into the book, first apply the mucilage along the lower edge of the bill and then let it dry. Then apply the brush a second time and paste the invoice into the book. By observing these directions a smooth, even surface will be secured. The paper would shrink if pasted in at first. Care should be taken to apply as little mucilage as possible.

No. 104.—Go over the calculations of this bill and make sure that no error exists. Take your Invoice Book and see whether the bill fits in the space intended for it in the book; if not, trim it to the proper size. Apply a very small quantity of mucilage to the back of the bill (on the lower edge) and let it dry. Apply the mucilage a second time, being careful not to use too much. Place the bill in the proper position, even with the upper edge of the first page of the Invoice Book. Extend the total amount of the purchase directly opposite where the firm's name appears. (*See illustration on opposite page.*) Be sure to do this with each and every bill.

MARCH 3, 189–.

No. 105—Bill the goods called for in this order. Go over your calculations. Enter in the proper book and be sure to place the terms correctly, both in the book and on the bill. Always apply rules 1 and 2 for debiting and crediting when no others are given. Have you filed the order?

No. 106.—Bill and enter this order in the proper book and place the order on file. Place the terms asked for in the order on the bill.

No. 107.—This draft is in settlement of the amount the drawer owes the business. Turn to your Ledger and ascertain if the amount is correct. When is the amount to be paid to the business? Is it an order to pay or a promise to pay? Read *rules 17 and 16* and make the entry. In what book is it made? The word "Accepted," etc., with the party's signature is equal to his signing his name to a promissory note, as thereby he promises to pay you a sum of money on a certain date as absolutely as if he had given you his note.

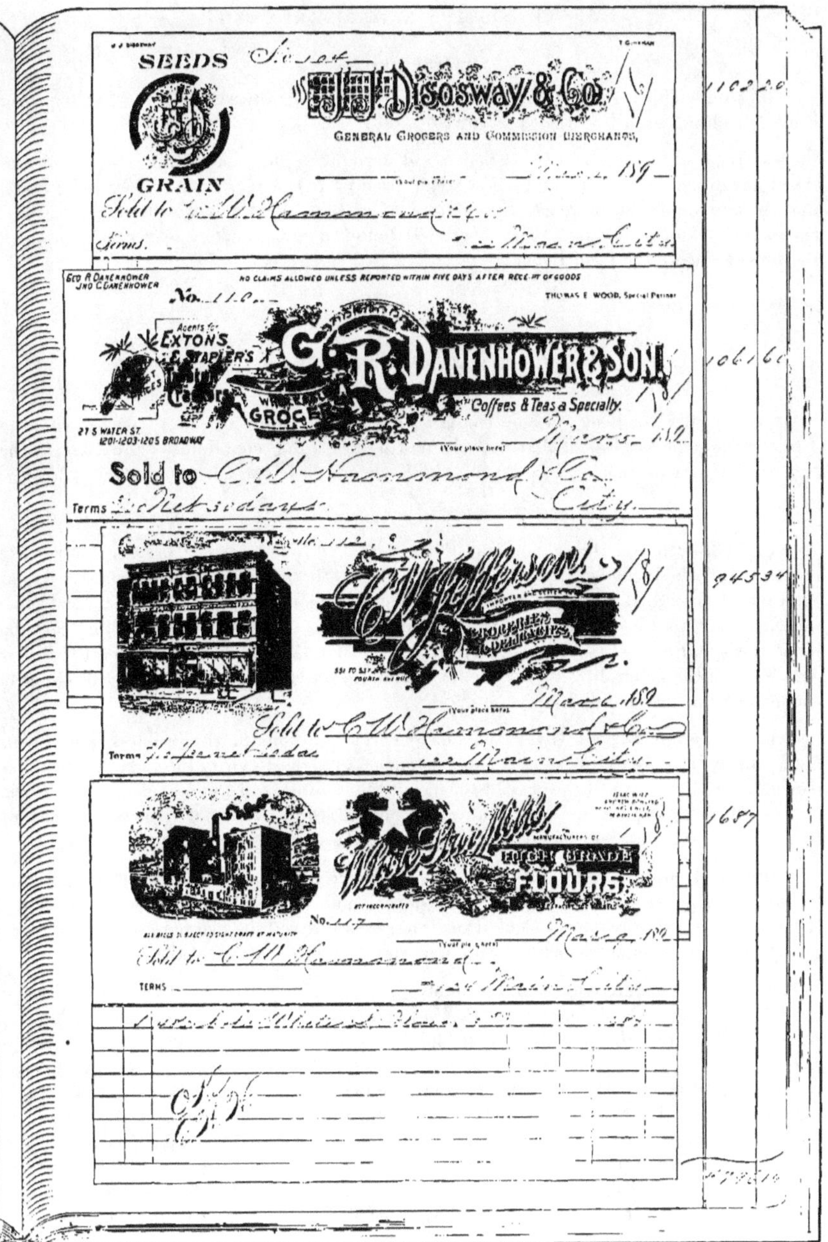
SEEDS
GRAIN
J. W. Disosway & Co.
General Grocers and Commission Merchants,
(Your place here)
Sold to
Terms
No claims allowed unless reported within five days after receipt of goods
Geo. R. Danenhower
Jno. C. Danenhower
Thomas E. Wood, Special Partner
No.
Agents for Exton's & Stapler's
G. R. Danenhower & Son
Wholesale Grocers
Coffees & Teas a Specialty.
27 S. Water St.
1201-1203-1205 Broadway
(Your place here)
Sold to C. W. Hammond & Co.
Terms Net 30 days
City.
C. W. Jefferson
Groceries & Delicacies
(Your place here)
Sold to C. W. Hammond & Co.
Terms
High Grade
Flours
No.
All bills subject to sight draft at maturity
(Your place here)
Sold to C. W. Hammond & Co.
Terms

MARCH 5, 189–.

No. 108.—This cash is the amount of the retail sales for the week. Enter in the proper book and place the cash in the Cash Drawer.

No. 109.—This check is in settlement of account. The party signing the check has taken advantage of the discount allowed for prompt payment. Turn to your Sales Book, find the amount of his purchases, then take 2% of that amount and subtract to see if it equals the amount called for in the check. If found to agree, make the entry as follows on the proper side of the Cash Book.

In case your Cash Book does not contain the rulings for the discount, you will rule the columns the same as illustrated above. In posting items that contain discounts, observe the special instructions that will be given. Place the check in the Cash Drawer.

MARCH 6, 189–.

No. 110.—Go over the calculations of this bill. If found correct, prepare for pasting into the Invoice Book by applying a very small quantity of mucilage on the lower edge of the back of the bill. Let it dry, then apply another small quantity and paste the bill so that it will cover the first bill up to the double ruling that divides the heading from the body of the bill. (*See illustration, page 67.*) See that the right-hand edge of the bill is parallel with the first ruling of the money column. Extend the amount directly opposite the firm's name on the bill.

No. 111.—Pay Barlow, Henderson Co. by check the amount the business owes them. Make the entry. In business it is not customary to make an entry for a check when it is issued, but to leave it until the close of the day or the beginning of the next day, when all the checks issued for the day are entered at once from the stubs. Therefore it is very important that a complete record be made on the stub, before the check is issued.

Eighth Report. Make a report and hand same together with the vouchers and cash for others to the teacher. Have your cash, journal, and sales book sheets approved and copy them neatly into your regular books. Prove your cash to ascertain whether the amount called for by the Cash Book agrees with the amount you have in bank and in the Cash Drawer.

Posting. Open accounts with the following: (Your name) on the 20th line of page 1; Real Estate on page 6, and C. R. Danenhower & Son, 1201 Broadway, City, on page 18. Post from the Sales Book first, debiting each person to whom you have made a sale. Do not forget to postmark in the Sales Book. Place the letter "S" in the explanation column of the accounts to which postings are made from the Sales Book. Do not credit Merchandise for the total until the end of the month.

Post from the Invoice Book, crediting each party from whom you have purchased. Do not forget to postmark on each bill directly opposite the extension. (*See illustration, page 67.*) Place the letter "I" in the explanation column of all accounts that have received postings from the Invoice Book. Next post from the Journal, following previous instructions.

Post from your Cash Book as previously instructed. When you come to A. P. Batson's account, credit him with cash received, $2197.41, using the letter "C" as explanation. On the next line below credit him for discount, $44.85, using the term "Dis't" as explanation. This is the best method of handling merchandise discounts, as every account shows how much discount was allowed to it or received from it by the business.

NOTE.—If we were to treat this entry as it is often treated by some business houses and authors on bookkeeping; *i. e.*, credit Mr. Batson for $2242.26, the amount he owes the business, and debit Mdse. Discount for $44.85, we would make a record that would not be strictly true. Were we to post the $2242.26 to Mr. Batson's account, it would appear that he had paid us that amount and that no discount was allowed.

Check over your posting.

MARCH 7, 189–.

No. 112.—Verify the calculations of this bill and O. K. same, if found correct. Paste it into the Invoice Book, as previously instructed. Cover the second bill as far as the double ruling which divides the heading from the body of the bill. (*See illustration, page 67.*) Extend the amount directly opposite the party's name on the bill.

No. 113.—Bill and enter this order, being careful to place the terms asked for on the bill. Make the entry, file the order and place the bill in the proper receptacle.

No. 114.—Turn to T. A. Cooke's account in the Ledger and ascertain the amount he owes the business. He has consented to honor our drafts so long as he owes the business. Draw on him at sight for the amount he owes the business, making it payable to J. J. Disosway & Co. Debit the party who receives the value and credit the party who supplies the value. Place the draft in Vouchers for Others.

MARCH 9, 189–.

No. 115.—Bill and enter this order, placing the terms asked for on the bill. Have you filed the order and placed the bill in the proper receptacle?

No. 116.—This written promise to pay the business a certain sum of money is to apply on account. Why is it payable to the business? Debit—*Rule 17*; credit—*Rule 16*. Be sure to credit the party who ordered this draft payable to the business, as he is the one who owes the business. Have you written the proper explanation? Consult your teacher whenever in doubt as to what the proper explanation should be, as that is a very important part of the entry. Place the draft in the Cash Drawer.

MARCH 10, 189–.

No. 117.—O. K. this bill if the extensions are correct and paste it into the Invoice Book. Follow previous instructions in detail. Have you extended the amount directly opposite the firm's name?

MARCH 11, 189–.

No. 118.—Bill and enter this order, being careful that the terms and calculations are correct. Make out a set of shipping receipts and take them to the freight agent or teacher and have him receipt same. Enclose the original with the bill in a properly addressed envelope. File the order.

No. 119.—Accept this draft in red ink. Write "Accepted payable at City Bank, March 11, 189–, C. W. Hammond & Co., per ....(your name)............." Make this entry, applying the instructions given in paragraph "c" under drafts, page 52. Place the acceptance in Vouchers for Others. Have you written the proper explanation for this entry?

MARCH 12, 189–.

No. 120. Cash sales for the week. Count the cash and make the entry.

No. 121. Make a deposit of all checks and currency on hand. Be sure that you have endorsed all the checks properly.

No. 122. Pay C. R. Danenhower & Son's bill by check less the discount allowed for prompt payment. Turn to their bill in the Invoice Book and ascertain what the terms and rate of discount are. Calculate the discount and deduct it from the amount of the bill. Write a check for the net amount, being sure to explain on the stub that a discount was allowed. Make an entry similar to the entry made when the business received a check less discount, from A. P. Batson. Why is this entry made on the credit side of the Cash Book?

MARCH 13, 189–.

No. 123. –Bill and enter this order, placing the terms asked for on the bill. Place all vouchers in the proper receptacles.

No. 124.—Accept this draft, following instructions for No. 119. Have you made the proper explanation for this entry? Place the acceptance in Vouchers for Others.

Ninth Report. Make a report and hand all vouchers and cash for others to the teacher. Have your work on the journal sheets examined and copy same into your regular books. Prove cash to ascertain if the balance as shown by the Cash Book agrees with the actual balance on hand.

Posting. Open the following accounts: C. W. Jefferson, 551 Fourth Ave., City, on the 14th line of page 18, and White Star Mills, City, on the 20th line of the same page.

(1) Post from the Sales Book.

(2) Post from the Invoice Book.

(3) Post from the Journal.

(4) Post from the Cash Book. When you post the entry on the credit side apply the instructions given for Mr. Batson's account in your previous posting, being careful that you post to the debit of C. R. Danenhower & Son's account instead of the credit. Have you placed the initials of the books from which you posted in the explanation column of the ledger accounts?

Check over your posting.

MARCH 14, 189–.

No. 125. Verify the extensions of this bill, O. K. it if found correct, and enter in the Invoice Book. Have you extended the amount directly opposite the firm's name?

No. 126. Bill and enter this order. Make out a set of shipping receipts and have the freight agent receipt for the goods. Enclose the original with the bill in a properly addressed envelope. File the order.

MARCH 15, 189–.

No. 127. –Pay Lerch Bros. by check the amount the business owes them and make the entry.

MARCH 16, 189–.

No. 128. Ascertain from the Ledger the amount Frey & Thomas owe the business. They have consented to honor our draft for that amount. Draw a draft at ten days' sight, making it payable to Ballard & Ballard Co., whom the business owes. Debit the party who receives the value and credit the party who supplies the value. Place the draft in the proper receptacle.

MARCH 17, 189–.

No. 129.—Note favor of J. J. Disosway & Co. for $1250 made payable at your bank is due to-day. As it is made payable at City Bank it is paid out of the firm's deposit and charged to the firm the same as when the bank pays the firm's checks. At the end of the month when your pass book is written up it will be returned to you with the checks. To keep your check book balance even with your bank balance it will be necessary for you to deduct the amount, and write an explanation. On the left-hand stub write "March 17, 189–. Bank paid note favor J. J. Disosway & Co., $1250.00." On the right-hand stub deduct the amount from the last balance. Make the entry on the credit side of the Cash Book, applying *rules 19 and 4*. Why?

NOTE.—In many places the banks require their depositors to pay notes made payable at the bank by check. When this is done the notes are cancelled and delivered to the depositor at the time they are paid instead of holding them until the pass book is written up. In that case the stub of the check takes the place of the detailed record explained above. Follow the instructions as given above unless otherwise directed by the teacher.

MARCH 18, 189–.

No. 130.—Verify the calculations and O. K. this bill. Paste into the Invoice Book, following previous instructions. Do not forget to extend the amount directly opposite the firm's name every time you paste a bill into the Invoice Book.

No. 131.—Pay Renaker & Heinrich by check the amount the business owes them and make the entry.

MARCH 19, 189–.

No. 132.—Amount received for cash sales during the past week. Do not forget to make the entry.

MARCH 20, 189–.

No. 133.—This check is to apply on account. Make the entry and place the check in the Cash Drawer.

No. 134.—This check is in full settlement of account.

No. 135.—Deposit all checks and currency on hand. Do not fail to endorse the checks properly.

MARCH 21, 189–.

No. 136.—Turn to Coyle, McCandlish & Co.'s bill in the Invoice Book and ascertain the terms and rates of discount allowed when prompt payment is made. Calculate the discount and deduct from the amount of the bill. Write a check for the net amount, being certain that you make a proper record of the discount on the stub, so that you will be able to make a proper record therefrom in the Cash Book. This entry is similar to entry for No. 122.

MARCH 22, 189–.

No. 137.—Go over the calculations of this bill and O. K. same if found correct. Note the terms of the bill; also the discount allowed. Although the terms are cash, do not pay it until instructed. In business the term "Cash" is frequently construed as meaning any time within ten days. This lapse of time enables the purchaser to receive the goods before paying for them. Enter as previously instructed, extending the amount of the bill directly opposite the party's name.

MARCH 23, 189–.

No. 138.—Pay C. Wilt & Son by check the amount the business owes them and make the entry. Write them a letter similar to the following:

(Your place) , *Mar. 23, 189–.*

C. Wilt & Son,
Philadelphia, Pa.

Gentlemen,

Enclosed find our check for $555.35, in full settlement of account. Please acknowledge same.

Yours truly,
C. W. Hammond & Co.,
per (your name).

Enclose the check and letter in a properly addressed envelope and place it in Vouchers for Others.

No. 139.—Pay Edward P. Genung's bill of yesterday by check and make the proper entry.

MARCH 24, 189–.

No. 140. Hammond & Co. desire to buy stock in a corporation, and not having the required amount of cash on hand (in bank), they wish to have the firm's note discounted at the bank. Write a note for $1000.00 at 30 days, making it payable to the City Bank. Calculate the discount at 6% for 30 days. Take it to the bank and state what the discount amounts to and see that you receive proper credit for the proceeds. On the left-hand stub of the Check Book make a record of the transaction. For details see No. 74. Add the proceeds to the amount in bank. Make the entry in the Cash Book, debiting according to *rule 3* and crediting according to *rule 20* for the face of the note. On the credit side of the Cash Book make the usual entry for the discount. Have you written the proper explanation for these entries?

No. 141.—Read this certificate of stock carefully. It has been purchased at par (face value). Write a check for same, making it payable to the Worcester Coal Co. This is a kind of property different from the commodities you are dealing in as a business, and it would not be proper to charge it to Merchandise. Apply the General Rules for debiting and crediting and debit Worcester Coal Co. Stock. File the certificate on the Voucher File.

MARCH 25, 189–.

No. 142. The goods called for in this order have been sent. Bill, enter and file all the papers properly.

No. 143.—In payment of No. 142 less discount. See the rate of discount in the Sales Book and go over the calculations to see that no errors were made. Enter similar to No. 109.

No. 144.—Deposit all checks and currency on hand. Endorse the checks properly.

No. 145.—To get the benefit of the discount, you will prepay the draft favor of Thos. W. Dryden accepted on the 13th inst. Ascertain the number of days it has to run until due, and find the discount for that number of days. Write a check for the proceeds, making it payable to the holders of the draft. Take the check to your teacher and you will receive the draft properly endorsed. Do not fail to debit the draft for the full amount (face value), and credit Discount on the opposite side of the Cash Book. File the draft on the Voucher File.

Tenth Report. Make a report and hand in the cash and vouchers for others. Have your work on the journal sheets approved, and copy same neatly into your regular books. Prove your cash to ascertain whether the balance as shown by the Cash Book agrees with the balance on hand.

Posting. Open accounts as follows: Worcester Coal Co. Stock on the 14th line of page 6; Dennis & Herring, West Washington Market, City, on the 14th line of page 11; Coyle, McCandlish & Co., 615 Market St., City, on page 19, and Edward P. Genung, 283 Washington St., City, on the 14th line of the same page. Post all books in the order previously indicated. Always refer to previous instructions when in doubt how to proceed. Check over your posting in pencil.

MARCH 26, 189–.

No. 146.—Go over the calculations of the bill and if found correct O. K. it and enter in the proper book.

No. 147.—For cash sales of retail department. Make the entry in the proper book.

No. 148.—Take draft favor of Harry Powell and accepted by E. K. Shoop from your Cash Drawer, and have same discounted at bank. Ascertain the number of days it has to run. Calculate the discount. Endorse the draft. See that you receive proper credit in your Pass Book. Make the usual record on the left-hand stub of the Check Book and add the proceeds to the balance in bank. Credit the draft for the full amount and be sure to debit Interest & Discount on the opposite side of the Cash Book. Refer to *rules 3, 18, 4 and 21* if you experience any difficulty with this entry.

No. 149.—The firm's acceptance favor J. J. Disosway & Co., made payable at City Bank is due to-day. The bank has paid same out of the firm's deposit, and will return it to you, with the checks paid, at the time your Pass Book is written up. To keep your Check Book balance and bank balance alike you will deduct the amount from the last balance on the Check Book stub. Make the usual record on the left-hand stub. (*See No. 129.*)

MARCH 27, 189–.

No. 150.—Bill and enter goods called for in this order as per terms written on the order by Mr. Hammond. Always verify your calculations and file all papers before taking up the next transaction.

No. 151.—Draw a draft at sight on A. J. Gouley, Louisville, for the amount he owed the business on the first day of the month. Make the draft payable to "Ourselves" and endorse it as you endorse a check for deposit, and leave it at the bank for collection. No record will be necessary except the record on the draft book stub, although it is the custom of some banks to give credit "in short" for all paper left for collection.

MARCH 28, 189–.

No. 152.—Make out the bill for this order, taking off the discount asked. This bill will be made out similar to bill No. 137 in the Invoice Book. Make the record in the Sales Book similar to the bill. File the order and place the bill where it belongs.

No. 153.—In payment of No. 152. Make the entry.

No. 154.—Bill and enter on the same terms as their previous order. Verify the calculations and file all papers.

No. 155. [illegible] allowed for prompt payment [illegible] M[illegible] N[illegible] [illegible]

[illegible]

No. 156.—[illegible] Merton Schwartz, Co. [illegible] Take [illegible] [illegible] Make the entry [illegible] Interest & Discount [illegible]

No. 157. [illegible] take advantage of the discount [illegible] [illegible] Make the entry [illegible]

No. 158.—[illegible] in the proper book.

No. 159.—[illegible] this order, deducting the discount asked for. This entry [illegible] entry for No. 15[illegible].

No. 160.—[illegible] payment of No. 15[illegible].

March 31, 18[illegible]

No. 161.—Pay Frank W[illegible] $[illegible] by check as salary for the month instead of $[illegible], as his salary has been increased. Make the proper record.

No. 162.—Write a check for C. W. Hammond for $[illegible], which he wants for private use. Do not forget to make the entry as per rule [illegible]

No. 163.—Pay yourself $[illegible] by check for private use and make the entry, applying rule [illegible]

No. 164.—[illegible] pay it by check and make the usual entry.

No. 165.—Deposit [illegible] cash on hand [illegible] properly.

No. 166.—[illegible] City Bank [illegible] take advantage of the discount allowed [illegible] for the unexpired time and [illegible] "Note of March 24." Take it to [illegible] Make the entry [illegible] Credit Interest & Discount for [illegible]

Eleventh Report. Make [illegible] vouchers [illegible] and cash to the [illegible] when approved [illegible] balance on [illegible] and bring [illegible]

Posting. Open the following accounts: Merchandise Discounts on the [illegible] line of page [illegible]; Benjamin Sterling & Co., [illegible] W. Main St., City, on the [illegible] line of page [illegible]; [illegible], City, on page [illegible]; Curry, Davis & Norwood, [illegible] W. Main St., City, on the 13th line of page [illegible]; and Fred Bowley, City, on page [illegible]. Post from the books in the usual order and always refer to posting instructions when in doubt as to the proper method. Post the total of the Invoice Book to the debit of the Mdse. account, writing the word "Purchases" in the explanation column, and the total of the Sales Book to the credit side of the Mdse. account, writing the word "Sales" in the explanation column. Post the total of the [illegible] column on the debit side of the Cash Book to the debit of Mdse. Discounts and the total of the credit column to the credit of the Mdse. Discounts. Check over the posting, that you may locate any errors you have made.

Statements. Make out statements against all customers owing the firm. Be sure to omit the debit and credit items of [illegible] balance. Do not depend entirely upon your ruling or checking when determining the items that balance. Have your statements approved and dispose of them as previously instructed.

Trial Balance. Pencil foot all accounts that [illegible] balance and take a trial balance. Be sure [illegible] the cash balance [illegible] expect to have your trial balance prove.

Inventory and Balance Sheet. Make an Inventory of Resources and Liabilities and a Balance Sheet to ascertain the standing of the business. For amount of property on hand, see Inventory No. 1 [illegible] taken by Mr. [illegible] and approved by Mr. Hammond.

Find the amount of the merchandise inventory and have same approved before proceeding with the Inventory of Resources and Liabilities. After the Inventory of Resources and Liabilities has been approved, proceed with the Balance Sheet as previously instructed until you reach the summary. Arrange the summary of your Balance Sheet as shown in the form given below.

		44256	14	44256	14	[illegible]	[illegible]	[illegible]	[illegible]	[illegible]	[illegible]	[illegible]	[illegible]
Hammond's Net Gain						[illegible]	[illegible]						
Students						[illegible]	[illegible]						
						[illegible]	[illegible]	[illegible]	[illegible]				
Hammond's	Net Credit			4600	[illegible]								
"	Net Gain			[illegible]	[illegible]								
"	Present Capital											[illegible]	
Students	Net Credit			4000	[illegible]								
	Net Gain			[illegible]	[illegible]							[illegible]	[illegible]
	Present Capital									[illegible]	[illegible]	[illegible]	[illegible]

Have your Balance Sheet approved when completed, after which make a neat transcript of same into your regular Trial Balance Book and proceed to close the accounts in the Ledger showing Losses and Gains. Apply the instructions given in the first set when in doubt how to proceed. Check the balances of the accounts just closed with the balances as obtained by the Resource & Liability columns of the Balance Sheet to satisfy yourself that you have made no errors.

Present all books for inspection.

THE BUSINESS OF C. W. HAMMOND & CO., CONTINUED.

APRIL 1, 189–.

No. 167. Mr. Frank Winter has decided to purchase an interest in the business, and invests the amount he has on deposit in the Bank of Marion, as shown by this certificate of deposit, which he has endorsed over to the firm. Read it carefully and examine the endorsement. Make the entry, applying *rules 1, 2 and 8.* Place the certificate of deposit in the Cash Drawer.

Study form 2 in the appendix, then draw up a partnership agreement embodying the following points: (1) The partnership is to continue for five years, unless sooner dissolved by consent of all the partners. (2) The net gain or loss is to be divided equally. (3) Owing to the unequal investments of the partners, interest is to be allowed each partner on his investment, and interest is to be charged on his withdrawals. (4) Each partner is entitled to draw $150 per month. Make a draft of your partnership agreement and submit it for inspection before copying on the form in your package of supplies. When it is copied on the form it should be signed by Mr. Hammond, yourself and Mr. Winter. (Your teacher will sign for Mr. Hammond and Mr. Winter.) Brief and file on the Voucher File.

NOTE. In business three copies of the partnership agreement would be made and signed by each of the partners, so that each partner would have a copy.

Using form No. 98 as a model, write a bill of sale on practice paper, transferring the personal property of the firm to the members of the new firm. Have it approved before copying on the form furnished in your supplies. It should then be executed by Mr. Hammond and yourself in the presence of a witness. (Your teacher will sign for Mr. Hammond.) Brief and file on the Voucher File.

Using form No. 100 as a model, write a warranty deed on practice paper, making the members of the new firm the grantees. After the deed has been approved, copy it on the regular blank. It should then be executed and acknowledged by Mr. Hammond and yourself. (Your teacher will sign for Mr. Hammond and for the commissioner of deeds.) Brief and file on the Voucher File.

No. 168.—Verify the calculations of this bill and paste it into the Invoice Book at the top of page 4.

No. 169.—Pay this bill by check. You are expected to file all papers hereafter and make the entry at the proper time, as all instructions regarding same will be omitted except in special cases. See note under No. 101, page 65.

No. 170.—Deposit the certificate of deposit after properly endorsing it.

APRIL 2, 189–.

No. 171.—Bill the goods called for in this order on the terms asked.

Selling Goods on Commission. Many merchants do not purchase the goods they deal in as a business, but act as the agent for the owner of the goods. They receive as compensation for their services a certain percentage on the gross sales, called a commission. Hence they are known as Commission Merchants. They often receive goods to be sold from parties in other cities, where there is no ready market for same, as it is expected a readier and better market can be secured in their localities.

No. 172.—It has been arranged by Mr. Hammond to have the firm sell goods on commission for other parties. The goods called for by this invoice of shipment have been received to be sold for the account and risk of the consignors, Emmons, Hawkins & Co. Read the invoice of shipment carefully and compare it with an ordinary bill. Note that no prices are given. The reason for this is that the business is not purchasing the goods, but is receiving them to be sold for the consignors, and all that the business will receive will be a certain per cent. of the gross sales, called a commission. You make no entry because the goods belong to the consignors and not to C. W. Hammond & Co. When the goods are sold, the amount received for them less the firm's commission and other charges will be remitted to the consignors. File the shipping invoice on the Voucher File.

No. 173.—Turn to your Ledger to ascertain if the amount called for by this statement agrees with your records. If found to agree, pay same by check. Write a letter asking the parties to receipt the statement. Enclose it together with the check and statement in a properly addressed envelope.

No. 174.—Turn to your Ledger and verify the correctness of this statement. If found correct proceed as with No. 173.

APRIL 3, 189–.

No. 175.—Cash sales for the week.

No. 176.—Read this letter carefully. Not finding a ready sale for the Beans and Peas on hand, Mr. Hammond has ordered the quantity desired of each to be shipped. Make out the shipping invoice similar to the one received from Emmons, Hawkins & Co. Enter the shipment in the Sales Book, making the extensions at the current cost prices as given in the March Inventory. Prefix the word "Shipt." to the party's name to distinguish it from the sales. Make out a set (3) of shipping receipts and prepay the freight, which amounts to $13.12 by check. Take the check and Shipping Receipt Book to the Freight Agent. In the Cash Book charge Shipt. Philip Lindeman with the freight. Enclose the original shipping receipt with the shipping invoice in a properly addressed envelope.

NOTE.—When Philip Lindeman receives this consignment he makes no entry, as the goods belong to C. W. Hammond & Co. When he sells the goods he credits C. W. Hammond & Co.'s Consignment for the sales and debits it for his commission and the net proceeds. See No. 172 for similar transaction.

No. 177.—The draft drawn on A. J. Gouley, Louisville, Ky., on the 27th ult. has been collected. Go to the bank and have the amount placed to your credit in your Pass Book. On the left-hand stub of the Check Book write "Collection, A. J. Gouley, Louisville," and the amount. Add the amount to the balance in bank and credit A. J. Gouley for the same in the Cash Book.

APRIL 4, 189–.

No. 178.—Read this order carefully and examine the bank draft. Have the goods been sent? If so, bill and enter the order, allowing the discount asked and make the entry for the bank draft. Note the endorsement on the back of the bank draft. Make out a set of shipping receipts and have the freight agent receipt for the goods. Enclose the original with the bill in a properly addressed envelope.

No. 179.—Verify the calculations and enter in the proper book.

No. 180.—Pay Curry, Tunis & Norwood by check the amount of their bill, less the discount allowed for prompt payment. Be sure to make the proper record of the discount in the Cash Book.

APRIL 5, 189–.

Note Ledger or Bill Book. The fourth of the labor saving books to be introduced is the Note Ledger, or the Bills Receivable and Bills Payable Book, as it is commonly called. In this book are entered all the notes received and issued by the business. When the same are paid or redeemed in any manner, the record is made in this book from the Cash Book or other posting book, and no account, either of the notes received or given, will be kept in the regular Ledger hereafter. The notes received are posted to the credit of the proper personal accounts in the regular Ledger, and those issued to the debit of the proper personal accounts. For form of Note Ledger see the blank furnished you in your supplies and the illustration given on opposite page. Study same carefully.

No. 181.—Write a 30-day note favor of Fred Bowley for the amount the business owes him, dating it March 30, and making it payable at the City Bank. Make the entry on the Bills Payable side of the Note Ledger, filling all the blanks from the note, except the one headed "Drawer and Endorser." (*See opposite page.*)

No. 182.—For annual dividend on 25 shares of Worcester Coal Co. Stock. Credit Worcester Coal Co. Stock. Why?

No. 183. In response to an inquiry made by Mr. Hammond, the Quaker City Milling Co. has quoted the following price on flour: 4.00 per brl. less 10% when cash accompanies order. Write a letter ordering 200 brls., telling them you enclose bank draft in payment less the discount allowed. Write a check for the net cost of the flour, take it to the bank and receive bank draft for same. After endorsing the draft properly if made payable to your order, enclose it with your letter in a properly addressed envelope. Make the entry, charging the parties who have received the value. Why would it not be as well to send your check in place of the bank draft?

Twelfth Report. Make a report and hand it to the teacher with the cash and vouchers for others. Copy your bookkeeping work into your regular books after it has been approved. Post the cash as previously instructed.

Posting. Open accounts as follows: Frank Winter on the 34th line of page 1; Shipt. Philip Lindeman, New York City, on page 7; Jno. G. Leake, Marion, Ky., on the 14th line of page 12; E. Levering & Co., 102 Commerce St., City, on the 14th line of page 20; Bremer & Mahis Co., 1405 Main St., City, on the 29th line of page 20, and Quaker City Milling Co., Philadelphia, on page 21. Post your books in the order previously indicated. In posting from the Note Ledger, debit Fred Bowley for the amount of the note, writing the word "Note" for explanation. Be sure to place the Ledger page in the proper column in the Note Ledger. Check your posting.

APRIL 6, 189–.

No. 184.—Bill and enter this order. Do you always verify your results?

No. 185.—Pay C. W. Jefferson by check the amount due him less the discount allowed for prompt payment.

No. 186.—In full of account to April 1st.

No. 187.—To apply on account. Enter in the Bills Receivable Book, filling in the blanks from the note itself, excepting the one headed "Drawer and Endorser."

APRIL 7, 189–.

No. 188.—Verify the extensions and enter in the proper book.

(Left-Hand Page.)

BILLS

No.	When Given.		Drawer and Endorser.	Drawee or Maker.	In Whose Favor.	For What Given.	Where Payable.
	189-.						
181	Apr.	5		C. W. Hammond & Co.	Fred Bowley.	in full of %.	City Bank.

(Right-Hand Page.)

PAYABLE

Date.			Time.	When Due.													L. F.	Amount.		When and How Disposed Of.		
Year.	Month.	Day.		Year.	Jan.	Feb.	Mar.	April	May	June	July	Aug.	Sept.	Oct.	Nov.	Dec.				Amount.	Date.	Explanation.
189-.	Mar.	30	30 da.	189-				29										1138	68			

APRIL 8, 189–.

No. 189.—The goods asked for in this letter have been consigned by Mr. Winter to be sold on our account and risk. Make out the invoice of shipment and enter in the Sales Book at current cost prices as shown by the March Inventory, prefixing the title "Shipt." Make out the shipping receipts and have the freight agent receipt for same. Do not prepay the freight; it will be paid at the other end of the line and charged to our consignment.

No. 190.—The goods called for in this invoice of shipment have been received and are to be sold on account and risk of the shipper. Pay the freight as per the freight bill. Sign and detach the receipt and place in Vouchers for Others. Examine and file freight bill. Charge Const. Geo. Brown for the freight.

APRIL 9, 189–.

No. 191.—Bill and enter this order, deducting the discount asked. Record the check in the proper book. Make out a set of shipping receipts and have the agent receipt for the goods. Enclose the original with the bill to the party who gave the order.

No. 192.—To apply on account. Enter similar to No. 187.

APRIL 10, 189–.

No. 193.—Cash sales for the week.

No. 194.—Verify and enter. Why is this bill receipted? Pay the freight.

APRIL 11, 189–.

No. 195.—Bill and enter.

No. 196.—Write a 30-day note payable at City Bank to balance White Star Mills' account, and make the entry similar to entry for No. 181.

APRIL 12, 189–.

No. 197.—In full of account.

No. 198. Pay Edward P. Genung's bill of the 7th inst. by check, less the discount allowed for prompt payment.

No. 199.—Deposit all cash items on hand.

APRIL 13, 189–.

No. 200.—Verify and enter as usual.

No. 201.—Pay H. Knefely & Son's bill of March 14 by check.

Thirteenth Report. Make a report and have your journal sheets approved. Copy same into your regular books. Prove the cash.

Posting. Open the following accounts: Shipt. R. A. Golden, Louisville, Ky., on the 14th line of page 7; Wm. J. Cooke, Asheville, N. C., on the 29th line of page 12; Const. Geo. Brown, New Orleans, La., on the 14th line of page 21, and Mast, Crowell & Kirkpatrick, City, on the 29th line of the same page. Post as previously instructed. Check your posting.

APRIL 14, 189–.

No. 202.—Bill and enter this order in the Journal, at the price named, debiting the party who receives value and crediting Emmons, Hawkins & Co.'s Const. This entry is made in the Journal in order that you may give proper credit to the Consignors, instead of crediting the Merchandise account, as would be the case were you to make the entry in the Sales Book.

NOTE.—In business, when the commission sales are numerous, a Commission Sales Book is kept for all sales on commission. In the absence of the Commission Sales Book a special column is used in the regular Sales Book to receive the sales on commission.

No. 203.—In full payment of amount due. Read the note carefully. What difference do you observe between this and other notes that you have received? This note is interest bearing, and consequently we gain the interest that will accrue by extending the time, while the maker loses thereby the amount of the interest.

No. 204.—Write a note favor Mast, Crowell & Kirkpatrick in full of account, at one month from date of their bill, and make the proper record.

APRIL 16, 189–.

No. 205.—Bill and enter.

No. 206.—Verify the extensions and enter.

No. 207.—Invoice of shipment for merchandise received to be sold for the account and risk of the consignor. Make no entry. Why not? The merchandise belonging to this consignment will be designated as Const. No. 2 to distinguish it from a previous consignment received from the same parties.

No. 208.—Pay Henry Rohner's bill by check, less the discount allowed for prompt payment. Do not fail to make the proper record of the discount.

APRIL 17, 189–.

No. 209.—Cash sales for the week.

No. 210.—Account Sales and check for the net proceeds of shipment made on the 3d inst. Credit the shipment for the amount of the check, and, after examining the account sales, carefully file it on the Voucher File.

No. 211.—In payment of bill less discount. Verify the discount calculation.

APRIL 18, 189–.

No. 212.—Bill and enter. Make out shipping receipts, and proceed as previously instructed.

No. 213.—As you have received payment from Weber & Co. for the merchandise sold them belonging to Emmons, Hawkins & Co.'s Const. No. 1, you will render them an account sales and remit them the net proceeds after your charges for commission, etc., and the discount allowed Weber & Co. for prompt payment have been deducted. Calculate the commission, etc., at 5% on the total sales. Debit Emmons, Hawkins & Co.'s Const. for the total of commission and merchandise discount, and credit these accounts for their respective amounts, in the journal. With the exception of the amounts, make the entry as follows:

		18		
	Emmons, Hawkins & Co.'s Const. No. 1,		24	
	Commission,	5% on sales,		15
	Mdse. Discts.,	allowed Weber & Co.,		9

Give the reasons mentally for the above debit and credits. Write a check for the net proceeds and place it, with the account sales, in an envelope properly addressed. Charge the consignment from the stub of the Check Book for the remittance. When the entries just made are posted the account should balance.

APRIL 19, 189–.

No. 214.—Verify the extensions and enter.

No. 215. To apply on account. Enter similar to No. 203.

APRIL 20, 189–.

No. 216.—Account sales and check for the proceeds. Verify the calculations and enter as previously instructed, crediting Shipt. R. A. Golden.

No. 217.—To balance account less discount for prompt payment. Verify the discount.

APRIL 21, 189–.

No. 218.—Bill and enter this order on the terms asked. As the goods sold do not belong to us, do not credit Merchandise, but credit the consignment to which they belong and debit the party who gave the order. In what book is this entry to be made? Why?

No. 219.—Write a 60-day note favor Curry, Tunis & Norwood for $1000 to apply on account, and make the entry in the proper book.

Fourteenth Report. Make a report and hand in all vouchers. Have your work approved and copy into your regular books. Prove the cash.

Posting. Open accounts as follows: Commission on the 29th line of page 7; H. Weber & Co., City, on page 13; Chas. Y. Kay, 349 Main St., City, on the 14th line of page 13; Const. Emmons, Hawkins & Co. No. 1, Omaha, Neb., on page 22, and Henry Rohner, N. E. Cor. 5th & Race Sts., City, on the 14th line of page 22. Post and check as previously instructed.

APRIL 22, 189–.

No. 220.—Verify the calculations and enter.

No. 221.—In full, less the discount allowed for prompt payment. Verify the discount.

No. 222.—Render an account sales to Geo. Brown and send him the net proceeds by check. Commission to be 5% of gross sales. Deduct the merchandise discount allowed Chas. Y. Kay. In the Journal debit the Const. for commission and merchandise discounts and credit Commission and Mdse. Discounts for their respective amounts.

Write the check for the net proceeds and make the proper record of same in the Cash Book. Place the check with the account sales in a properly addressed envelope.

APRIL 24, 189–.

No. 223.—Bill and enter.

No. 224.—Cash sales for the week.

No. 225.—The goods asked for have been sent. Make out the invoice of shipment but make no extensions. Enter in the Sales Book at current cost prices as shown by the March Inventory, prefixing the title "Shipt." Make out the shipping receipts and prepay the freight, which amounts to $18.64, by check. Have the freight agent receipt for same. Place the original with the invoice of shipment in a properly addressed envelope.

No. 226.—Deposit all cash on hand.

APRIL 25, 189–.

No. 227.—Verify the calculations and enter.

No. 228.—Write a 30-day note favor J. J. Disosway & Co. for $1000, payable at City Bank to apply on account, and make the usual entry.

APRIL 26, 189–.

No. 229.—To apply on account. Make the usual entry.

No. 230.—In payment of note due to-day. Endorse the note properly and place in Vouchers for Others.

APRIL 27, 189–.

No. 231.—Make out one bill for this order. Charge him with the firm's merchandise in the Sales Book. For the merchandise belonging to the consignment, debit him in the Journal and credit the consignment (No. 2). Make out the shipping receipts and have the freight agent receipt for same. Enclose the original with the bill in a properly addressed envelope.

No. 232.—Verify and enter. This method of billing is in use in many business houses.

APRIL 28, 189–.

No. 233.—Make out an invoice of shipment for the goods asked for in this letter, as they have been sent, but do not make any extensions on same. Enter in the Sales Book, prefixing the title "Shipt.," and make the proper extensions at the current cost as shown by the March Inventory. Prepay the freight amounting to $17.04 by check. Make out the shipping receipts and have the freight agent receipt for same. Enclose the invoice of shipment and the original shipping receipt in a properly addressed envelope.

APRIL 29, 189–.

No. 234.—Render an account sales to Emmons, Hawkins & Co. for Const. No. 2, but do not send them the proceeds, as you have not received pay from A. J. Gouley, to whom you sold the goods. In the Journal charge (debit) the consignment with the commission and net proceeds, and credit Commission for the commission, and Emmons, Hawkins & Co., Principals, for the net proceeds. The word Principal is affixed to their firm name to indicate that the firm of C. W. Hammond & Co. is bound to them *in trust*, instead of owing them a simple debt. Write a letter explaining that the proceeds have been placed to their credit and that you will forward same as soon as the goods are paid for by the party to whom you sold them. Enclose the letter with the account sales in a properly addressed envelope.

No. 235.—Note due to-day is paid by the City Bank out of the firm's deposit. Make the proper records on the stub of the Check Book and in the Cash Book. If in doubt, refer to a previous entry similar to this one.

APRIL 30, 189–.

No. 236.—Bill and enter.

No. 237.—Pay by check.

No. 238.—Pay yourself, Mr. Hammond and Mr. Winter each $150 by check for private use.

No. 239.—Calculate the interest on your investment for 30 days—the time it was invested; also on Mr. Hammond's and Mr. Winter's. Add the three interests and divide the amount by three to find the average. Observe that Mr. Winter's interest is as much below the average as yours and Mr. Hammond's combined are above. It will be readily seen that Mr. Winter is indebted to you and Mr. Hammond for the amount that his interest is less than the average. Therefore you will debit him in the Journal for that amount and credit yourself and Mr. Hammond for the amounts above the average. Be sure to write an appropriate explanation of this entry.

No. 240.—Deposit all cash on hand. Leave your Pass Book at bank to be written up.

Fifteenth Report. Make a report and hand all cash and vouchers for others to the teacher. Have your bookkeeping work examined and approved, after which copy into your regular books. Prove the cash, then balance and rule the Cash Book.

Posting. Open the following accounts: Shipt. E. Spencer, St. Louis, Mo., on page 8; Shipt. Bower & Moore, Chicago, Ill., on the 14th line of page 8; Miller, Lippincott & Co., 134 S. Front St., City, on the 29th line of page 22; Emmons, Hawkins & Co.'s Const. No. 2, Omaha, Neb., on page 23, and Emmons, Hawkins & Co., Principals, Omaha, Neb., on the 14th line of the same page. Post in the order previously indicated. Post the last entry on each side of the Cash Book to the Note Ledger in the columns ruled for that purpose, as no account of either Bills Receivable or Bills Payable is kept in the regular Ledger. Do not fail to post the totals of the Merchandise Discount columns in the Cash Book to the proper account in the Ledger. Post the total purchases and sales for the month to the Merchandise account.

Statements. Make out statements as previously instructed and have them approved.

Trial Balance.—Take a trial balance and have it approved. Be sure to include the cash on hand, the notes on hand, and the firm's notes outstanding.

Inventories and Balance Sheet. Make the extensions on the Inventory of Merchandise and other property (No. 240*a*) as furnished you by Mr. Winter and have it approved. Copy same into your Journal. Make an Inventory of Resources and Liabilities and have it approved. Make a Balance Sheet. Have it approved and close the accounts showing losses and gains.

Present all books and your vouchers on file for inspection and approval.

QUESTIONS. What is Real Estate? What instrument is necessary to transfer Real Estate? Why is Real Estate not kept under the Mdse. account? Why is a separate account kept for Stock purchased instead of including it in Mdse? What is the object in allowing a discount on bills paid within a certain time? What advantage is there in discounting your note at bank? What is the object in keeping the Sales Book? The Invoice Book? What is a certificate of deposit? Why is the Pass Book more frequently used by banks in giving credit to depositors for their deposits than the certificate of deposit? What is a consignment? To whom is a consignment known as a shipment? What is the object in shipping goods to a Commission Merchant in another city to be sold? What is an Invoice of Shipment? What is the difference in use between an Invoice of Shipment and an ordinary bill? What is an Account Sales? On what is the commission always reckoned? What is meant by the Net Proceeds? Are the net proceeds always remitted to the consignor when the account sales is rendered? Why is it not necessary to make an entry when we receive goods to be sold on commission for other parties? What is the object in keeping a Note Ledger or Bill Book? When is it customary to allow partners interest on their investments and charge them interest on their withdrawals? Give a good reason for filing all the vouchers received by the business.

The Business of C. W. Hammond & Co. Dissolved.

May 1, 189–.

Dissolution of Partnership. You will now assume that a fire has destroyed the entire business block of which 122–124 Main Street is a part. Your stock of merchandise and all the fixtures, except the fire proof safe and its contents, have been consumed. Owing, either to negligence or imprudence, you and your partners failed to carry insurance on your property, and consequently will have to bear the loss.

Mr. Hammond has been offered the management of the City Grocery Company at a good salary and has decided to discontinue business. The Tropical Fruit Company have made Mr. Winter a very flattering offer to go to South America as their purchasing agent. Glad to avail himself of the opportunity to travel, he has decided to accept, if you and Mr. Hammond will agree to discontinue the business or purchase his interest.

J. D. Creager, doing business as a retail grocer at 228 Walnut St., is desirous of increasing his business; with that end in view he makes you a proposition to take you into partnership and open a larger and better store at 620–622 Broadway.

You and your partners meet and confer. They propose that as you are thinking of continuing as a merchant, you would better attend to the closing up of the late business. Mr. Hammond proposes to accept as his share of the remaining assets the real estate, valued at $3250, and the 25 shares of Worcester Coal Co. stock, valued at $2625, making a total of $5875. Mr. Winter agrees to take as his share of the assets the two notes drawn by A. J. Gouley, for $1000 and $2152.08, respectively. You are to receive the remainder of the assets and assume all the liabilities. Ascertain from the April Balance Sheet the amount of your share of the assets, provided you accept their proposition.

You will observe that your share of the remaining assets after the liabilities have been discharged will be greater in proportion to the investments than either Mr. Hammond's or Mr. Winter's; but you are to consider that you will be put to the trouble of closing up the business, and should you fail to collect all or part of any of the accounts you will be the loser.

You decide to form the partnership with J. D. Creager. You, also, agree to the terms proposed by Mr. Winter and Mr. Hammond. Endorse the A. J. Gouley notes over to Frank Winter, by a full endorsement, *i. e.*, write "Pay to the order of Frank Winter, C. W. Hammond & Co., per ......(your name)......," and place them in Vouchers for Others. Transfer the Worcester Coal Co. Stock to Mr. Hammond by assignment; *i. e.*, fill out the blank form of assignment on the back of the certificate, complying with all the requirements. Write up a quit-claim deed, quit-claiming your and Mr. Winter's interests in the real estate to Mr. Hammond. (*See form 3 in the appendix.*) Make a copy and submit your work for approval before copying on the form provided in your supplies. Get your teacher to sign for Frank Winter. Place all papers in Vouchers for Others.

Prepare an Inventory of the Resources and Liabilities, which you are to submit to your future partner, Mr. Creager Have it approved. Prepare a bill of sale in which C. W. Hammond and Frank Winter transfer to you your share of the effects as scheduled in the Inventory of Resources and Liabilities you have just prepared. (*See form 4 in the appendix.*) Have it approved before copying on the form furnished you in your supplies. Your teacher will sign for your partners. Place it on the Voucher File. Endorse the notes drawn by Harry Powell and Frey & Thomas, making them payable to your order. Write a check payable to your order for the amount of cash on hand but do not detach it.

Closing Accounts Showing Losses and Gains. Turn to your Ledger and close the accounts (Merchandise, Furniture & Fixtures and Real Estate) affected by the fire into Loss & Gain account. There are no inventories of Furniture & Fixtures and Merchandise, as everything belonging to these accounts has been destroyed; the inventory of Real Estate is $3250.

Closing Partners' Accounts. Close the Inventories of Real Estate and Worcester Coal Co. Stock into Mr. Hammond's account, making use of red ink and explanations, as you do when closing an account into Loss & Gain account. Next, on the debit side of his account, write "Loss" and the amount required to balance his account. Rule his account and transfer this balance to the credit of Loss & Gain account. Next transfer the A. J. Gouley notes from the Bills Receivable account in the Note Ledger to the debit of Frank Winter's account. Write in the Note Ledger opposite the respective notes in red ink, "Frank Winter, L," and the amount. Transfer the total to the debit of Frank Winter's account, writing "A. J. Gouley notes" and the amount. Transfer the balance of his account to the Loss & Gain account. The remaining part of the Loss, as shown by the Loss & Gain account, you will now close into your account, which is the amount you have lost. Bring down the balance of your account, which should be equal to your part of the Resources less the Liabilities, as shown by the Inventory of Resources & Liabilities which you have prepared.

Notice of Dissolution. Your relations with C. W. Hammond and Frank Winter as partners are now at an end, and the law is that neither of you may by any act bind the late firm as to any new transaction, but this presupposes that the person with whom the transaction occurs knows of the dissolution. It follows, therefore, that notice of the dissolution should be given. It is customary to mail a circular notice to all persons with whom the firm had any dealings, and also to insert a notice of dissolution in the advertising columns of one of the local newspapers so as to inform the general public, although it is not necessary to give notice of the dissolution to those who have had no dealings with the firm.

The following is a convenient form for giving notice of the dissolution, and may be sent to the persons with whom the firm has been doing business, or it may be published in the paper, or both.

NOTICE OF DISSOLUTION.

Notice is hereby given that the copartnership heretofore existing under the firm name of C. W. Hammond & Co., at (your place).... is this day dissolved. All accounts due the firm are to be paid to ....(your name)......, and all liabilities should be presented to him for payment.

Dated ....(your place)........., May 1, 189–.

C. W. HAMMOND.
(Your name.)
FRANK WINTER.

Prepare a notice similar to the above but do not sign for your partners. Present it with your books for inspection.

RETAIL GROCERY BUSINESS.

MONDAY, MAY 10, 189–.

The New Firm. It is agreed between Mr. Creager and yourself that the firm name under which you are to do business shall be *J. D. Creager & Co.* Each partner is to invest his entire Resources, and the Liabilities of each are to be paid by the firm. All losses or worthless resources are to be charged to the partner investing same. Both partners are to share gains, losses and assets equally, and each partner is entitled to draw $25 per week for private use. Mr. Creager will make all purchases, sell to customers who buy for cash, and make all deposits for the firm. You are to keep the books and sell to persons who buy on account. Mr. Creager is to be credited for Good Will for an amount sufficient to make his capital equal to yours.

By Good Will is meant the good name, the trade, the acquaintance and the standing which J. D. Creager's business at 228 Walnut Street has acquired. The good will of some business concerns is their most valuable resource.

No. 241.—By this bill of sale Mr. Creager sells the entire effects of his late business at 228 Walnut Street to the firm of J. D. Creager & Co. Read it carefully, then draw up one transferring your share of the effects of the late business, 122–124 Main Street, to the firm of J. D. Creager & Co. Have your bill of sale approved. After folding it properly, brief both documents, *i. e.*, fill out the blanks on the back of same. Place them on the Voucher File.

Carefully read form 5 of partnership agreement given in the appendix, then draw up a partnership agreement between Mr. Creager and yourself, observing every detail as given in the form. Have your Partnership Agreement approved, then brief it and file on the Voucher File.

Take Mr. Creager's bill of sale from the Voucher File and make the proper records for his investment in the books as explained in the following:

Opening Entries. In the Cash Book credit J. D. Creager for the amount of cash invested. (*See form of Cash Book, pages 88 and 89.*) In the Note Ledger, on the Bills Receivable side, on page 2, credit him in the "Drawer & Endorser" column for the note he invests. Credit him for the remainder of his resources and for Good Will in the Journal as illustrated below. You are to determine the amount of Good Will by subtracting his Net Capital from your Net Capital. Debit him for his liabilities as illustrated.

MAY 10, 189–.

J. D. Creager and (your name) commenced business under the firm name of J. D. Creager & Co.					
J. D. Creager's Resources are:					
Cash, $2482. 40.	(*See Cash Book.*)				
J. P. Hinolf's note, $450.	(*See Bill Book.*)				
Furniture & Fixtures	on hand	500			
Horse & Wagon	"	250			
U. S. Bonds	"	2500			
J. D. Tuckey	owes him	20	50		
Waverly Hotel	"	82	40		
Mrs. E. K. Shoop	"	16	20		
Mdse.	per Inventory	335	16		
Good Will					
J. D. Creager					
His Liabilities are:					
J. D. Creager		902	66		
Curry, Tunis & Norwood	owes them			621	50
Ballard & Ballard Co.	"			281	16

RETAIL CASH BOOK.

DATE		L. F.	LEDGER ACCOUNTS AND EXPLANATIONS.	GENERAL.		MDSE.
189-						
May	10	25	J. D Creager, invests	2000		
		25	Student, "	5000		
			Cash sales for the day			120
		2	Bills Receivable, M. Mahoney's note	500		
		32	J. D. Tuckey, in full	42	50	
	11		Cash sales for the day			145
		32	Waverly Hotel, in full	86	25	
	12		Cash sales for the day			205
		32	Mrs. E. K. Shoop, in full	17	25	
	13		Cash sales for the day			240
		33	Harry Powell, in full	72		
		25	Mdse., total cash sales	710		710
				8428	00	
May	13		Balance	7485	70	

You will now enter the Resources and Liabilities of your late business as shown by the bill of sale you executed. Take your bill of sale from the Voucher File and replace the one you have been using. Observe the instructions and illustrations given for entering J. D. Creager's Resources and Liabilities when making the entry for your investment. Be sure to transfer the Bills Receivable on hand to page 2 of the Note Ledger, crediting yourself in the "Drawer & Endorser" column for each note invested. Likewise transfer the Bills Payable outstanding to page 2 of the Note Ledger, charging yourself in the "Drawer & Endorser" column for each note not redeemed.

No. 242.—By this check J. D. Creager turns over the cash he invests to the firm of J. D. Creager & Co. Transfer the check in your Check Book, made payable to your order, to the firm of J. D. Creager & Co. by endorsing it in blank. Make out a deposit ticket, using the proper form, and endorse the checks as follows: "Pay to the order of Farmers and Mechanics Bank, J. D. Creager & Co., per ....(your name)........" Enter the deposit on the stub of the check book where you find the first Farmers and Mechanics Bank check. Place the checks and deposit ticket in an envelope and write J. D. Creager's name on the envelope. Mr. Creager will make this and all subsequent deposits for the firm. The Farmers and Mechanics Bank will supply the Pass Book; banks as a rule supply their customers with pass books, and, if desired, check books.

Posting. Post the entries just made, placing the initial of the book from which you post in the explanation column of each account in the Ledger. Be sure to post the note invested by J. D. Creager to the credit of his account and the notes invested by you to the credit of your account; also post to the debit of your account all notes outstanding.

In opening accounts in the Ledger, place four accounts on a page, beginning with the Proprietors' accounts on page 25. Place all property and allowance accounts under this group. On page 28 begin with the personal accounts payable or accounts with persons to whom the business is indebted. On page 32 begin with the personal accounts receivable or accounts with persons who are indebted to the business.

RETAIL CASH BOOK.

DATE.		L. F.	LEDGER ACCOUNTS AND EXPLANATIONS.	GENERAL.		MDSE.		EXPENSE.	
189- May	10		Premium for insurance 5.00; postage 2.00					7	
			Baker's bill for the day			1	50		
			One week's rent in advance, ck. # 1					20	
			Apples and potatoes, ck. # 2			18			
		28	J. J. Disosway & Co., in full	72	40				
	11		Dried beef and peaches, ck. # 4			26			
			Moving telephone					5	
			Baker's bill for the day			3	60		
		2	Bills Payable, White Star Mills	500					
		28	Curry, Tunis & Norwood, in full	240					
	12		Butter and Eggs, ck. # 7			27	80		
			Horse feed					12	
	13		Cheese 5.00; apple butter 4.00			9			
		25	Expense, total for week	44				44	
		25	Mdse., total cash purchases	85	90	85	90		
			*Balance in bank**	*7485*	*70*				
				8428	00				

* Italics indicate red ink.

In case you are unable to decide under which division an account belongs, consult the C. W. Hammond & Co. Ledger or the teacher.

Trial Balance. Take a trial balance and have it approved.

Balancing Old Ledger. Turn to Shipt. E. Spencer account in the C. W. Hammond & Co. Ledger. Write on the credit side in red ink, *May 10* (with the year above), *J. D. Creager & Co. L., 27, 888.50.* Rule the account as heretofore instructed, but do not bring the balance down, as it is to be found in Creager & Co.'s Ledger where indicated by the folio number in the balancing entry you have just made. Continue in like manner with all accounts that do not balance. Be sure to include the number of the page to which the account has been transferred in your balancing entry so that the balance of the account can be readily traced to J. D. Creager & Co.'s Ledger. Balance both sides of the C. W. Hammond & Co. Note Ledger as per above instructions.

Books Used. The books used in this business do not differ materially from the ones used in the preceding business, the Journal and Note Ledger being identical in form.

Cash Book. Labor saving columns are used in the Cash Book. (*See illustration of Cash Book on pages 88 and 89.*) All items, the amounts of which are placed in either of the Merchandise columns or Expense column, are short-extended, *i. e.*, the entries are written farther to the right, away from the Ledger folio column, to indicate that they are not to be posted as separate items. In entering an item, the amount of which is to be placed in one of the Special Columns, make a full explanatory record of same and omit the title of the Ledger account, as the heading of the Special Column receiving the amount clearly indicates the account to be charged or credited. At stated periods, usually once a month, the Special Columns are footed and the footings carried to the General Column, when the totals are posted — the Mdse. total on the left side to the credit of Mdse. account, and the Mdse. and Expense totals on the right side to the debit side of the proper accounts.

Abstract Sales Book. Instead of making a detailed record of the sales in the Sales Book as heretofore, in this business you will make an abstract of each sale from the Sales Ticket; *i. e.*, write the party's name and the total of his purchase, together with the number and date of the Sales Ticket from which the abstract is made. (*See form of Abstract Sales Book given below.*) Instead of the Abstract Sales Book, Abstract Sales Sheets are often used.

ABSTRACT SALES BOOK.

DATE.		NO. OF SALE.	L. F.	NAME OF PURCHASER.	ADDRESS.	AMOUNT.		AMOUNT OF DAILY SALES.	
189 .									
May,	10	1		Mrs. Paul Frey,	200 Broadway,	2	05		
		2		Mrs. Simon Hart,	114 Walnut St.,	5	40		
		3		N. A. Eckler,	66 Marshall St.,	2	60		
		4		Waverly Hotel,	7th & Walnut,	26	50		
		5		Dennett's Lunch Rooms,	9th & Chestnut,	7	40	43	95
	11	6		Mrs. G. Brenner,	1216 8th St.,	2	40		
		7		Mrs. Simon Hart,		1	75		
		8		R. H. Lord,	53 Manhattan St.,	1	55		
		9		Mrs. Paul Frey,		1	30	7	00

Sales Tickets. The Sales Tickets used in business are printed in duplicate (sometimes in triplicate) and are usually bound in book form. By the use of carbon paper two or more copies are produced at one writing. The *original* is sent to the bookkeeper's desk to be charged, while the *duplicate* is delivered with the goods to the purchaser. After the Sales Tickets for the day have been entered in the Abstract Sales Book or on the Abstract Sales Sheet they are filed in numerical order so that reference to them can be readily made. Various appliances are used in business houses for filing sales tickets and other papers of a like nature. The following are forms of the original and duplicate forms of Sales Tickets.

J. D. CREAGER & CO.

Name

Address

Amount Received — Examined by

1

ORIGINAL.

J. D. CREAGER & CO.

Name

Address

Amount Received — Examined by

1

DUPLICATE.

In the larger retail houses the salesmen are designated by number. The salesman's number in the above case is 2. In this business Mr. Creager will be designated as salesman number 1 and you as salesman number 2.

Cash Tickets. For cash sales, Cash Tickets are used. While they differ in use they are identical in form to the Sales Tickets, and are also printed in duplicate or triplicate. The *original* is sent to the cashier's desk with the cash received, and the *duplicate* is enclosed with the purchase. The cashier makes an abstract on an Abstract Cash Sheet of the different Cash Tickets for the day, the total of which must agree with the actual amount of cash received from Cash Sales.

The cashier reports daily to the bookkeeper the amount of cash received, and the result is verified by him or by some other person by checking the Cash Tickets with the Abstract Cash Sheet and proving the addition. In this business Mr. Creager will verify the cashier's results. The method of filing the Cash Tickets is similar to that of filing the Sales Tickets. Following are the forms of original and duplicate Cash Tickets.

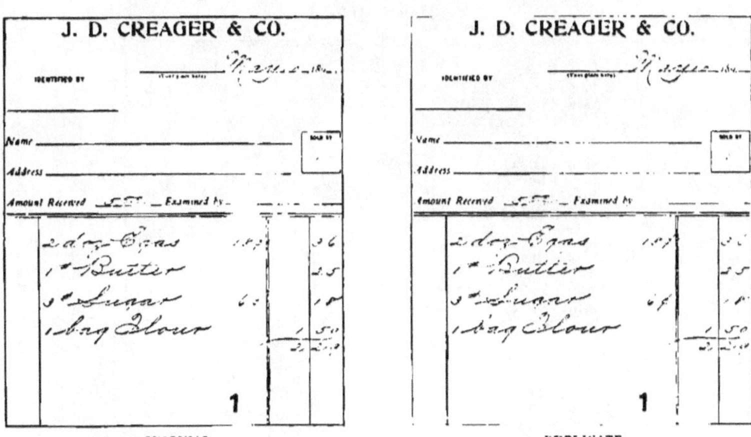

J. D. CREAGER & CO.

Identified by

Name

Address

Amount Received — Examined by

2 doz Eggs ... 36
1 # Butter ... 25
5 # Sugar ... 10
1 bag Flour ... 1 50

1

ORIGINAL. DUPLICATE.

Advantages of the Ticket System. The Ticket System which you are to use in this business is the one in use in the more progressive retail houses; especially is this true in dry goods establishments and department stores. It is a labor saving method, as the Tickets take the place of the Order Book, Customers' Ledger and Pass Book. Besides, Pass Books are an inconvenience, both to customers and merchants; but when they are not used the customers have no way of checking the articles purchased at the time of delivery, unless the Ticket System be used.

Other Books Sometimes Used. In some retail houses the Order Book, Accounts Payable Book, Petty or Customers' Ledger and Main Ledger are kept. Other books, as Petty Cash Book, Receiving Book, Clerks' Sales Record, Department Sales Book, Department Sales Ledger, Abstract Books, etc., are also kept in the larger retail houses.

Order Book. The Order Book used in most retail houses is a cheap, coarse book, made usually with a page twelve inches long and five inches wide, and lies upon the counter during business hours. Goods to be delivered, that are paid for when ordered, are entered regularly in the Order Book, and the word "Paid" is written across the order, but the amount is not extended into the outside column. If not paid for, the amount is extended into the outside column, and the items are entered in the purchaser's account in the Customers' Ledger at the close of the day's business, or at such other times as it may be convenient to post from this book. At the close of the day's business, or at the end of the month, the outside money column of the Order Book is footed, and the footing, which represents the credit sales of Mdse. for that period, is posted to the credit of Mdse. *(See form of Order Book below.)*

Some retail houses have two sets of Order Books. One set for use on Mondays, Wednesdays and Fridays, and the other for use on Tuesdays, Thursdays and Saturdays. When this is done, the books used in the store on one day are examined, checked and posted in the office on the next.

Order Book.

May 2, 189–.

	L. F.							
	16	Mrs. Paul Frey,	on a/c,					
		1 bag Flour,			1	50		
		1℔ Rio Coffee,				30		
		½℔ Oolong Tea,		50¢		25	2	05
Paid	✓	Mrs. Simon Hart,	cash,					
		2 bags Flour,		1.50	3			
		1 bu. Apples,				50		
		1 Sugar Cured Ham, 16℔.		11½¢	1	84		
					5	34		
	20	T. W. Dryden,	on a/c,					
		1 bu. Potatoes,				35		
		1 doz. Florida Oranges,				40		
		1℔ Rio Coffee,				30		
		1 bag Flour,			1	50	2	55
		3						
Paid.	✓	R. L. Long,	cash,					
		2℔ Butter,		25¢		50		
		1 bag Salt,				05		
		2 bags Flour,		1.50	3			
					3	55		

Customers' Ledger. The Petty or Customers' Ledger is, generally, a medium sized book, ruled like the ordinary Journal, and contains accounts with customers only. The purchases and payments of customers are entered in detail in this book, the former from the Order Book or Sales Tickets, the latter from the Cash Book. From a Ledger kept in this way an itemized statement of a customer's account can easily be made at any time. Such statements are rendered monthly in most retail houses where the ticket system is not used. *(See form of Customers' Ledger, page 93.)*

It will be observed that the left-hand money column is used for debit amounts, and the right-hand money column for credit amounts. The items are short-extended until the line is filled, when the sum of the items on that line is entered in the money column. Two or more dates may be entered on one line, thereby economizing space.

As a part of the accounts of the business are kept in the Customers' Ledger, the balance of these accounts must be carried to the Trial Balance when balancing the books. Instead of keeping a separate Ledger for customer's accounts, it is customary in the smaller retail houses to set aside a portion of the regular ledger for customers' accounts or personal accounts receivable as explained at the foot of page 88.

CUSTOMERS' LEDGER.

Mrs. E. K. Shoop, 2635 Columbia Ave., City.

189-.			Dr.		Cr.	
May	2	Mdse., per P. B.,	2	28		
	5	20 lb. A. Sugar, ^{95}; 4½ lb. C. Fish, ^{36}; 2 lb. J. Coffee, ^{70};	2	01		
		4 lb. Crackers, ^{40}; 5 gal. K. Oil, ^{75}; 8 bu. Potatoes, 2^{40};	3	55		
	6	Cash,			5	00
	8	Mdse., per P. B., 2^{10}; (9) Mdse., per P. B., 2^{27},	4	37		
	11	20 lb. G. Sugar, 1^{05}; 2 qt. Oysters, ^{80}; 1 pkg. Pepper, ^{25};	1	90		
		2 lb. J. Tea, 1^{10}; 1 Lemon ex., ^{20}; 5 lb. Butter, 1^{25},	2	55		
	12	Cash,			11	66
			16	66	16	66

The Pass Book. It is customary for some retailers, who do not use the Ticket System, especially those engaged in the grocery or market business, to furnish each regular customer a pass book, which is usually pocket size, and ruled like the ordinary Day Book. (*See form of Pass Book below.*)

The book is footed at the bottom of each page, and the footing carried forward until a payment is made, when it is deducted, and the balance brought down.

In case the credit items are numerous the Pass Book is kept similar to the Cash Book or Bank Pass Book; the debit items being placed on the left-hand page and the credit on the right-hand page. This method is usually employed when farm products are exchanged for groceries, etc.

When an order is given at the store to be delivered, the pass book is usually left with the order, and when the goods are delivered the pass book is returned, with the proper charges entered in it.

When the items are entered in the pass book it is not necessary to post in detail in the Customers' Ledger; the date, amount, and explanation "per Pass Book" or "per P. B.," being sufficient. But orders are often received and charged in the absence of the pass book, when the items should, of course, be posted in detail in the Customers' Ledger; and the details would indicate "not on Pass Book." Then when the pass book is left at the store to be "written up," the bookkeeper copies from the Customers' Ledger only the detailed charges, and then tests the footing of the pass book with the footing of the account in the Ledger, which should agree.

When pass books are used no bills are rendered for the month, as the pass book is a statement of account in itself. The page of the customer's account in the Ledger is usually written in large figures on the cover of the pass book, together with the customer's name, which enables the bookkeeper to turn to the customer's account without consulting the index.

PASS BOOK.

1 (Left hand page.)

189-.				
May	2	½ lb. Java Coffee,		18
		1 lb. G. P. Tea,		50
		1 sack Flour,	1	60
	5	20 lbs. A. Sugar,		95
		4½ lb. C. Fish,		36
		2 lb. J. Coffee,		70
		5 gal. K. Oil,		75
		4 lb. Crackers,		40
		8 bu. Potatoes,	2	40
		Forward,	7	84

(Right hand page.) 2

189-,				
May		Forward,	7	84
	6	Cash,	6	00
		Balance,	1	84
	8	2 Brooms,		50
		4 bu. Apples,	1	00
		1 lb. Raisins,		12
		1 doz. Eggs,		23
		1 cake Chocolate,		25

No. 243. Miss Emma Frey has been engaged as cashier and stenographer at a salary of $10 per week. She has given bond for the faithful performance of her duties, which meets with Mr. Creager's approval, and which you will also approve. Read the bond carefully so as to become familiar with the form, then fold, brief and file it.

Miss Frey is to have charge of the cash. She is to receive all currency and checks, pay out all currency, and render a statement of the cash received and paid out, to the bookkeeper at the close of each day's business.

No. 244. Read this lease (No. 244) carefully, then brief and file it. Pay the rent for one week in advance. Write the check and place it in Cash Paid Out. In this business do not enter checks issued until instructed at the close of the day's business.

Nos. 245, 246, 247, 248.—Mr. Creager has received the goods called for by these bills. Go over the calculations and if found correct O. K. the bills. Enter in the Invoice Book beginning on page 7.

Mr. Creager has purchased 40 bu. Potatoes at 25¢ and 30 bu. Apples at 40¢ from John Payne for cash. Write a check in payment of same.

Write a check making it payable to Frank J. Brown in payment of 40 doz. Eggs at 15¢ and 56 lbs. Butter at 20¢.

Pay J. J. Disosway & Co. by check the amount due them.

Make out the Sales Tickets for the orders received that are to be charged on account. In business the salesman receives the orders and makes out the Sales Tickets. You will now perform the work of the salesman who sells on account, and prepare the Sales Tickets for the sales on account for the day referring to the Model on page 90.

NOTE.—The duplicate Sales Tickets are dispensed with as they are not necessary to illustrate the method of keeping the books. If they were used you would write the original in pencil placing a carbon sheet on the duplicate, then detach and place it in Vouchers for Others.

Sales on Account.—(1.) Mrs. Paul Frey, 200 Broadway, 1 bag Flour, 1.50; 1 lb. Rio Coffee, 30¢; ½ lb. Oolong Tea at 50¢.

(2.) Mrs. Simon Hart, 114 Walnut St., 1 bottle Lemon Extract, 25¢; 2 bags Flour at $1.50; 1 bu. Apples, 50¢; 1 Sugar Cured Ham, 16 lbs., at 11½¢.

(3.) N. A. Eckler, 66 Marshall St., 1 bu. Potatoes, 35¢; 1 doz. Oranges, 50¢; ½ doz. Lemons at 40¢; 1 lb. Java Coffee, 35¢; 1 bag Flour, $1.50.

(4.) Waverly Hotel, 7th & Walnut Sts., 25 lbs. Butter at 22½¢; 1 brl. Gran. Sugar, $8.75; 20 lbs. O. Tea at 29¢; 2 brls. Flour at $4.80; 10 doz. Eggs at 18¢.

(5.) Dennett's Lunch Rooms, 9th & Chestnut Sts., 12 lbs. Butter at 24¢, 50 lbs. Sugar at 6¼¢; 12 bottles Tomato Sauce at 15¢.

Go over your Sales Tickets to see that you have omitted none of the details and that the extensions and calculations are correct. Have you numbered the Sales consecutively as given above and placed your number (2) on each ticket?

Enter the Sales in numerical order in the Abstract Sales Book, giving the date and number of the sale, the name and address of the party who made the purchase and the amount of the purchase. (*See illustration of Abstract Sales Book on page 90.*) Extend the total to the "Amount of Daily Sales" column. File the Sales Tickets in numerical order in the receptacle furnished you for that purpose in your supplies.

NOTE.—Your partner is supposed to sell to customers who buy for cash. He makes a set of Cash Tickets for each sale, encloses the *duplicate* with each purchase and sends the *original* with the cash received to the Cashier's desk. The total amount of cash received from Cash Sales should at any time equal the total of the Cash Tickets. These tickets are kept on file in numerical order by the Cashier so that reference can be readily made to them.

No. 249.—CASHIER'S STATEMENT. Examine voucher No. 249 carefully. See if the additions and subtraction are correct. Make the entries therefrom in the Cash Book as follows: 1. Credit Mdse. for the cash sales and place the amount in the Mdse. column. Short-extend this entry to indicate that it is not to be posted until the end of the week. (*For similar entry, see illustration of Cash Book, pages 88 and 89.*) 2. Credit Bills Rec. in the General Column for the amount received from Harry Powell as it is in payment of note due yesterday. (*See Note Ledger.*) 3. Credit J. D. Tuckey in the General column for the amount received. 4. Debit Expense for the amount paid for insuring the stock of merchandise, also for postage and place the amounts in the Expense column. 5. Debit Mdse. for the baker's bill and place the amount in the Mdse. column. Have you short-extended each of the entries on the credit side to indicate that they are not to be posted? File the statement on the Voucher File.

From the stub of the Check Book make entries for all checks issued to-day. Be sure to place the amounts in the proper columns and short-extend each entry the amount of which is to be placed in one of the Special columns. Prove cash to see that the balance as shown by the Cash Book agrees with the actual amount on hand, *i. e.*, in bank, and in safe as shown by the cashier's statement. If found to agree, present your Sales Book, Sales Tickets and Cash Book for inspection. Post the books. Do not post any items that appear in either of the Mdse. or Expense columns. Check over the posting.

TUESDAY, MAY 11, 189–.

Nos. 250 and 251.—Verify the calculations and additions of these bills. Paste them into the Invoice Book.

Pay note due to-day by check. (*See Note Ledger.*) Take the check to the teacher and receive the note properly cancelled.

Pay Curry, Tunis & Norwood the amount due them.

Make out Sales Tickets for the following:

Sales on Account.—(6.) Mrs. G. Brenner, 1216 8th St., 1 can Corn, 15¢; 2 doz. Eggs at 17½¢; 3 lbs. Sugar at 6¾¢; 1 bottle Salad Dressing, 30¢; 1 bu. Potatoes, 40¢.

(7.) Mrs. Simon Hart, 1 lb. Grenoble Walnuts, 30¢; 1 lb. Cheese, 22¢; 2 lbs. Dried Beef at 28¢.

(8.) R. H. Lord, 53 Manhattan St., 2 lbs. Java Coffee at 35¢; 1½ lbs. Butter at 25¢; 5 lbs. D. Peaches at 18¢; 1 bag Salt, 6¢.

(9.) Mrs. Paul Frey, 2½ lbs. Butter at 25¢; 1 bag Salt, 6¢; 2 lbs. Mixed Candy at 12½¢; 3 gal. K. Oil at 11¢.

(10.) Mrs. E. C. Mills, 55 Chestnut St., 3 bu. Potatoes at 40¢; 1 Broom, 30¢; 1 gal. Vinegar, 10¢; 3 doz. Eggs at 17½¢.

(11.) Waverly Hotel, 1 crate Eggs, 30 doz. at 16¢; 1 box Oranges, $3.95; 1 brl. Salt, $2.00.

(12.) Mrs. S. Eichert, 711 16th St., 1 brl. Flour, $4.85; ½ lb. Baking Powder at 50¢.

Verify your work. Enter the Sales Tickets in the Abstract Sales Book in numerical order, then file them numerically with the Sales Tickets of yesterday.

No. 252.—Verify the additions and substraction of this statement and make the entries in the Cash Book referring to previous instructions. Add the deposit to the balance in bank. File the statement on the Voucher File.

Enter the checks issued to-day from the stub of the Check Book. Prove cash. If found to agree present the Cash Book, Sales Book and Sales Tickets for inspection. Post the books. Check over the posting.

WEDNESDAY, MAY 12, 189–.

Nos. 253 and 254. Verify the calculations and O. K. these bills if found correct. Enter in the proper book.

Pay one-half of Invoice No. 245 by check.

Prepare Sales Tickets for the following:

Sales on Account.—(13.) Mrs. Philip Zoercher, 561 8th St., 1 cake Toilet Soap, 15¢; 2 loaves Bread at 5¢; 3 lbs. Sugar at 6¼¢; 1 lb. O. Tea, 50¢.

(14.) N. A. Eckler, 2 doz. Eggs at 17½¢; 1 bottle Chili Sauce, 20¢; 2 Lamp Chimneys at 8¢; 1 can Salmon, 18¢.

(15.) J. D. Tuckey, 2026 Brandywine St., 5 lbs. Oatmeal at 6¢; 1 package Toothpicks, 5¢; 2 loaves Bread at 10¢; 1 lb. Ground Pepper, 70¢; 1 bag Salt, 6¢; 2 cans Peaches at 28½¢.

(16.) Mrs. E. K. Shoop, 2635 Columbia Ave., 2 lbs. Mixed Nuts at 30¢; 1 doz. Bananas, 15¢; 1 doz. Pickles, 10¢; 3 lbs. Sugar at 7¼¢.

(17.) Mrs. E. C. Mills, 4 doz. Eggs at 17½¢; 1 brl. Flour, $4.75; 8 loaves Bread at 9¢; 2 lbs. Corn Starch at 8¢.

(18.) Waverly Hotel, 1 bunch Bananas, $1.40; 1 box Lemons, $3.25; 10 lbs. Mixed Candy at 8½¢; 25 lbs. Sugar at 6¼¢. 1 doz. bottles Olives, $6.40.

Verify the calculations, then enter same in the Abstract Sales Book as previously instructed. File the Sales Tickets in numerical order, with the Sales Tickets already filed.

No. 255. Verify the additions and subtraction. Make the entries as previously instructed. File on the Voucher File.

Make entries from the stub of the Check Book for all checks issued. Prove cash. Present books and Sales Tickets for inspection. Post the books and check over the posting.

THURSDAY, MAY 13, 189–.

Pay note due to-day by check Receive the note properly cancelled from the teacher.

Pay one-half of Invoice No. 246 by check.

Pay one-third of Invoice No. 247 by check.

Pay one-half of Invoice No. 248 by check.

Prepare Sales T'ckets for the following:

Sales on Account.—(19.) Mrs. Simon Eichert, 16 lbs. G. Sugar at 6¼¢; 2 lbs. W. Crackers at 12¢; 1 bag Flour, $1.50; 3 lbs. Currants at 12¢.

(20.) R. H. Lord, 3 cans Peaches at 28¢; 1 case Apollinaris Water, $1.25; 5 doz. Eggs at 16½¢; 5 lbs. Raisins at 12½¢.

(21.) Mrs. E. C. Mills, 2 lbs. Oolong Tea at 49¢; ½ lb. Baking Powder at 50¢; 1 bar Soap, 8¢; 1 bottle Salad Dressing, 30¢.

(22.) Dennett's Lunch Rooms, 1 doz. bottles Mustard, $1.50; 1 doz. Blue Label Catsup, $3.60; 1 brl. Sugar, $4.50.

(23.) Mrs. Paul Frey, 1 bunch Celery, 12¢; 4 lbs. Rice at 4½¢; 2 lbs. Mixed Nuts at 20¢; 1 lb. Cheese, 22¢; 1 Broom, 35¢.

(24.) Mrs. Simon Hart, 3 bu. Potatoes at 34¢; 2 loaves Bread at 8¢; 16 lbs. Sugar at 6¼¢; 2 lbs. Figs at 16¢; 1 gal. N. O. Molasses, 45¢.

(25.) Mrs. E. K. Shoop, 1 brl. Flour, $4.90; 1 Broom, 30¢; 1 lb. Vanilla Wafers, 20¢; 5 lbs. Oatmeal at 6¢.

(26.) Waverly Hotel, 12 cases Apollinaris Water at $1.25; 25 lbs. Mixed Nuts at 30¢; 1 box Oranges, $3.60.

After verifying your calculations enter the sales in the Abstract Sales Book, then file the Sales Tickets in numerical order.

No. 256.—Verify the additions and substraction of this statement. Make the entries therefrom. Add the deposit to the balance in bank as shown by the Check Book stub.

Make entries for all checks issued to-day. Prove cash. Have books and Sales Tickets inspected. Post and check over the posting.

FRIDAY, MAY 14, 189–.

Pay Invoice No. 250 by check.

Pay Invoice No. 251 by check.

Pay Bremer, Mahis & Co. in full by check.

Prepare Sales Tickets for the following:

Sales on Account.—(27.) J. D. Tuckey, 3 lbs. Dried Bartlett Pears at 7½¢; 3 doz. Eggs at 15½¢; 4 lbs. Sugar at 7½¢; 1 brl. Flour, $4.80; 2 lbs. Dried Beef at 26¢.

(28.) Mrs. Phil. Zoercher, 2 lbs. Rio Coffee at 29¢; 3 doz. Eggs at 16¢; 1 brl. Flour, $4.80; 5 lbs. Oatmeal at 6¢.

(29.) Mrs. G. Brenner, 1 brl. Flour, $4.80; 3½ doz. Eggs at 17¢; 2 lbs. Coffee at 32½¢.

(30.) R. H. Lord, 6 lbs. Oatmeal at 6¢; 3 lbs. Dried Beef at 26¢; 1 brl. Flour, $4.90.

(31.) Mrs. S. Eichert, 3 bu. Potatoes at 40¢; 2 cans Peaches at 27¢; 5 doz. Eggs at 18¢; 6 lbs. Soda Crackers at 12½¢.

(32.) Waverly Hotel, 50 lbs. Butter at 23¢; 50 lbs. Coffee at 27½¢; 2 crates Eggs, 60 doz., at 17¢; 20 lbs. Raisins at 12½¢.

(33.) N. A. Eckler, 3 lbs. Cheese at 23¢; 2 gal. Applebutter at 70¢; 10 gal. K. Oil at 9¢; 5 lbs. Coffee at 33¢.

(34.) Mrs. Paul Frey, 16 lbs. Sugar at 6¼¢; 10 lbs. Lard at 10½¢; ½ lb. Ground Pepper at 76¢; 5 doz. Eggs at 18¢.

(35.) Mrs. Simon Hart, 1 bottle Vanilla Extract, 25¢; 2 doz. Eggs at 18¢; 3 cans Peaches at 32¢.

Verify the calculations and enter in the Abstract Sales Book. File the Sales Tickets in numerical order.

No. 257. Verify the additions and subtraction. Make the entries. Enter the deposit on the Check Book stub.

Make the Entries for all checks issued to-day. Prove cash. Present books and Sales Tickets for inspection. Post books and check over the posting.

SATURDAY, MAY 15, 189–.

Pay one half of Invoice No. 253 by check.

Pay Invoice No. 254 by check.

Prepare Sales Tickets for the following:

Sales on Account.—(36.) N. A. Eckler, 3 cans Tomatoes at 8¢; 5 lbs. Sugar at 6¼¢; 2 cans Corn at 7¢; 3 lbs. Currants at 12¢.

(37.) Dennett's Lunch Rooms, 1 box Macaroni, $3.40; 1 box Chocolate, $12.00; 10 lbs. Butter at 21¢.

(38.) Mrs. P. Zoercher, 2 cans Peaches at 18¢; 2 doz. Pickles at 10¢; 3 loaves Bread at 8¢.

(39.) Mrs. G. Brenner, 5 lbs. Sugar at 6¼¢; 1 gal. Applebutter, 70¢; 1 gal. Vinegar, 20¢; 1 bottle Mustard, 20¢.

(40.) Mrs. E. K. Shoop, 2 loaves Bread at 8¢; 3 doz. Eggs at 18¢; 1 bottle Vanilla Extract, 25¢; 1 can Baking Powder, 20¢.

(41.) J. D. Tuckey, 2 loaves Bread at 10¢; 3 lbs. Coffee at 32¢; 4 lbs. Dried Peaches at 18¢; 1 lb. Figs, 15¢.

(42.) R. H. Lord, 3 heads Lettuce at 4¢; 1 can Salmon, 20¢; 1 Lamp Chimney, 8¢; 2 loaves Bread at 8¢.

(43.) Mrs. E. C. Mills, 2 loaves Bread at 8¢; 1 lb. Y. H. Tea, 55¢; 1 basket Fancy Fruits, $1.25; 2 lbs. Dates at 7¢.

(44.) Mrs. Simon Hart, 2 lbs. Crackers at 8¢; 3 heads Lettuce at 4¢; 1 bunch Celery, 9¢; 1 lb. Y. H. Tea, 55¢.

Verify the calculations and enter in the Abstract Sales Book. File the Sales Tickets in numerical order.

No. 258. Verify the additions and subtraction. Make the entries therefrom. Enter the deposit on the stub of the Check Book.

Make entries for all checks issued to-day. Prove cash. Balance and rule the Cash Book in pencil as illustrated on pages 88 and 89. Present Cash Book, Sales Book and Sales Tickets for approval. Balance and rule the Cash Book in ink, observing any suggestions or criticisms your teacher made while examining your work. Have you made proper use of red ink? Post the books. Do not forget to post the totals of the special columns in the Cash Book as instructed on page 89. Post the footing of both the Sales and Invoice Books. Check over the posting.

Trial Balance. Take a trial balance. Include the cash and notes on hand and the notes outstanding in your trial balance. Have it approved.

Inventories. Mr. Creager has taken account of the stock on hand, which is as follows: Merchandise, $406.35; Furniture & Fixtures, $500; Horse & Wagon, $250; U. S. Bonds increased in value 5 per cent; Shipt. E. Spencer, $888.50; Shipt. Bower & Moore, $1151.04; Good Will at the same value at which it was invested. Make an Inventory of Resources & Liabilities and have it approved.

Balance Sheet and Ledger Closed. Make a Balance Sheet and close the Ledger. Present all books and vouchers for inspection and approval.

QUESTIONS. How do you transfer a certificate of stock? Why is it not transferrable by endorsement? What is a quit-claim deed? What difference do you observe between a quit-claim deed and a warranty deed? When there is a dissolution of partnership, why is it a good plan to inform those persons of the dissolution with whom the firm has had dealings? Describe the different methods of giving notice of dissolution. Define Good Will. Why is it a good idea to classify accounts in the Ledger? What reasons can you assign for balancing and ruling the accounts in the old Ledger when they are transferred to the new Ledger? What is the object in having special columns in the Cash Book? Describe the Abstract Sales Book. Describe the Sales Tickets. Why are they usually printed in duplicate? What difference in use is there between the Sales Tickets and Cash Tickets? Name the other books sometimes used in retail houses. Describe the Order Book. Describe the Customers' Ledger. Describe the Pass Book. What is a bond? What is the object in requiring a cashier to give bond? What is a lease? What is meant by a cashier's statement? In what order are the Sales Tickets filed? Describe the method of making an entry the amount of which is placed in one of the Special Columns in the Cash Book. Describe the method of footing and ruling the Special Columns in the Cash Book. To which column is the footing transferred?

COMMISSION BUSINESS.

Branch House of J. D. Creager & Co. By consulting your books for the Retail Grocery Business, you will observe that the amount of cash invested is considerably more than is necessary to conduct that business successfully. In order to make a better use of your surplus capital, you and Mr. Creager decide to conduct a branch business for the purpose of selling goods on commission for other parties, and shipping goods, to be sold for your account, to parties in other localities. It is decided that you are to take charge of the branch Commission Business, and that Mr. Creager is to assume the entire management of the Retail Grocery Business located at 620-622 Broadway. The name of the new concern is to be the Creager Commission Co. (not incorporated) and is to be located at 624 Broadway, next door to the Retail Store.

NOTE.—As this business is a branch or part of the retail business no further articles of agreement are necessary, and you will continue to be governed by the partnership agreement of May tenth.

The Credit Man. Mr. Creager will act as credit man for the branch store. The duty of the credit man is to determine who shall receive credit and who shall not, also, the term and amount of credit to be given. The position of a credit man is usually a difficult one. The credit man obtains his knowledge of the prospective customers from the references they furnish, from the commercial agencies and the banking institutions, and from other sources. The banks usually have a pretty accurate knowledge of the financial condition of their customers.

Commercial Agencies. These agencies supply their subscribers with information pertaining to the moral and financial standing of individuals, firms and corporations who have gained a recognized standing in the commercial world. This information is of great assistance to credit men, and the greater part of it is usually contained in a bound volume, called a Reference Book, which is loaned to subscribers for a period of three or six months, when it is replaced by a revised edition, if the subscription continues in force. The information thus obtained is of a confidential nature, and is intended for the use of subscribers only. Reports of this kind are arranged alphabetically, first, according to states; second, according to cities, towns and villages; third, according to individuals and firms, thus enabling anyone to turn readily to the name of the party desired and ascertain his rating, etc., which is expressed in ciphers. A key to the ciphers is printed in the reference book. Besides the above, daily reports of failures, assignments, judgments, real estate transfers, etc., are furnished. When requested a stipulated number of reports are also furnished, giving additional information of anyone in the reference book or information of someone not contained therein. A great many business houses consider a subscription to a good commercial agency a necessary item of expense. A few of the commercial agencies are of a national or international character, supplying information of business men everywhere. Others are of a purely local character, and give information only of persons residing in the same city. This latter class is intended mainly for the retail trade, and usually gives the rating of all those who provide for themselves and others, especially householders residing within the city limits.

NOTE.—Honesty is necessary in any legitimate business. If you are engaged in business the commercial agencies will secure most of their information concerning you from those with whom you have had dealings, your bank, your creditors, etc. If you have not been honest, it will be proclaimed to the entire business world through the commercial reports.

Special Features of a Commission Business. The first thing you are to do is to acquaint yourself with the special features of commission bookkeeping. You are already familiar with the principles of keeping commission accounts. It is the purpose of this business to illustrate a labor saving system of keeping such accounts.

Loose Leaf Consignment Ledger. It is the custom of some commission merchants to enter a consignment when received in what is called a Receiving Book; then an account with each consignment is opened in the Ledger, in which is entered a detailed description of the goods as it appears in the receiving book. When all the goods belonging to a consignment are sold an Account of Sales is rendered, which is an exact copy of the consignment account as kept in the ledger. By the use of the Loose Leaf Method the Receiving Book, Consignment Ledger and Account of Sales are combined, whereby only one-third as much writing is required as by the first method. (*See illustration of page of Loose Leaf Consignment Ledger below.*)

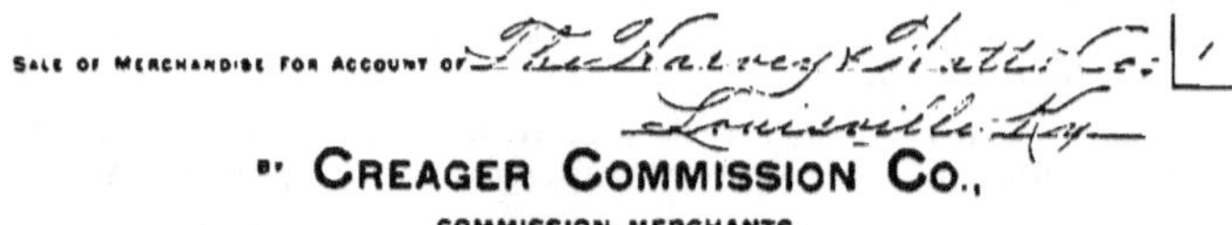

SALE OF MERCHANDISE FOR ACCOUNT OF [illegible] Co. 1
Louisville Ky.

BY CREAGER COMMISSION CO.,
COMMISSION MERCHANTS,
(Your place here.)

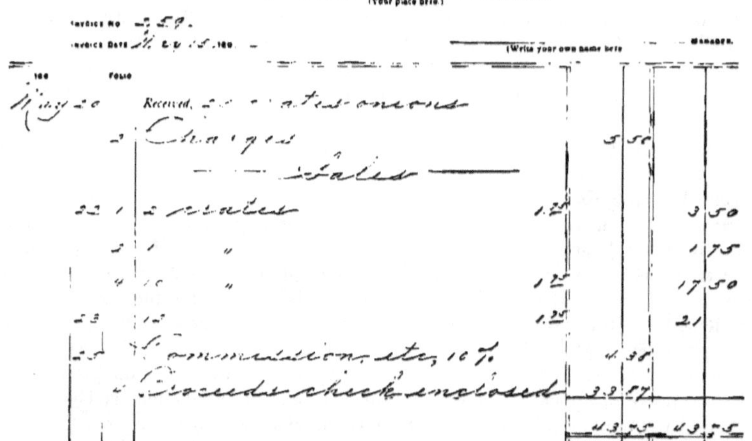

INVOICE NO. 259
INVOICE DATE May 25, 190
(Write your own name here) MANAGER.

190	FOLIO				
May 20		Received, [illegible] crates onions			
20		Charges		5 50	
		Sales			
22	1	2 crates	1.75		3 50
2	1	"			1 75
4	10	"	1.25		17 50
23	12		1.75		21
25		Commission, etc., 10%		4 38	
25		Proceeds check enclosed		33 87	
				43 75	43 75

These pages are printed in copying ink, and the sheets are usually numbered and padded consecutively. In case they are not numbered, the number is to be supplied by the bookkeeper. This number is also the *lot* number of the consignment and is stenciled or written on every package of goods belonging to the consignment. When the goods are not received in packages they are placed in stalls or other receptacles, on which are placed the proper lot numbers. Consignments are designated by lot numbers; first, for convenience; second, to prevent the commission merchant's customers from learning the source from which he gets his merchandise.

When a consignment is received it is checked up by the receiving clerk with the invoice of shipment, letter of advice, bill of lading, or any other document sent by the consignor. After he has verified the voucher referred to, or noted any irregularities thereon, it is sent to the office and from it the bookkeeper enters on a receiving blank the name and address of the consignor, the date of the shipping invoice (or other document of similar nature), usually the name of the transportation company, the date when received and a description of the goods. (*See illustration above.*) It is then filed in a binder and thereby becomes a part of the Loose Leaf Ledger. When all the goods belonging to a consignment have been sold, the commission and other charges are calculated and the net proceeds ascertained, all of which are entered in the account. The sheet is then removed from the binder and an impression taken of it in an Impression Account Sales Book, when it is sent as an *account of sale* to the consignor. In business all the writing on these sheets should be done with Japan ink, so as to insure a good impression in case considerable time elapses from the time a consignment is received until the account sales is rendered. In business these binders are made in various styles, and most of them are protected by patents. In this business instead of using a binder you will paste the sheets as instructed, and tear them at the perforation when removing them. The accounts in this book should be indexed both *alphabetically* and *numerically*. (*See separate index in your package of supplies.*)

Advantages of the Loose Leaf Method. The Loose Leaf Method may be used advantageously in any business. Some of the advantages are: first, only *live* accounts need be kept, because as soon as an account becomes inactive the sheet containing it may be removed and filed away. If at any time it should again become active it may be re-inserted in the binder wherever desired. Second, accounts may be arranged in alphabetical order, or classified in any other manner that may be desirable. Third, a binder may be used continuously, it only being necessary to supply the sheets or pages as needed. Instead of using binders the sheets (sometimes cards) are placed in draw cabinets similar in construction to the card index cabinets used in many of our libraries. Indeed, the innovations made by modern appliances of every description have been so great that it will be more appropriate in the near future, in speaking of the recording of business transactions, to call it *accounting* or *accountkeeping* instead of bookkeeping. It may be depended upon that in the progressive counting rooms of the future, books will be used *only* when they possess advantages over everything else.

Impression Account Sales Book. As has been stated, in this book an impression is taken of every account sales *before* it is sent to the consignor. This is done so that reference can be made to any account sales in case of dispute, or in case an account sales fails to reach the consignor, a duplicate can be made of it. (*See illustration of Account Sales Book, page 102.*)

These books are made of fine tissue paper so that they will absorb the ink readily. In the first column to the right are extended the proceeds of those accounts sales for which no remittances are made at the time they are rendered. Such proceeds are posted to the credit of the accounts of the persons to whom the accounts sales are rendered, while the total of the column is posted to the debit of Consignment account in the Main Ledger whenever a trial balance is taken. No extension is made in this column if the proceeds are remitted with the account sales. In most lines of business the proceeds are remitted with the account sales. Suppose the goods are sold on 30 days account and the commission merchant remits the proceeds to the consignor on the day of sale; he would lose the use of his money for 30 days. This is overcome by discounting the proceeds for 30 days. In cases like this, the discount would be deducted from the proceeds, the same as charges, commission, etc. In the outer column is entered the commission earned on each consignment. The total of this column is posted to the *debit* of Consignment account and to the *credit* of Commission account in the Main Ledger, at the time of taking a trial balance.

The accounts in the Account Sales Book should be indexed both numerically and alphabetically in the same index in which you index the accounts in the Consignment Ledger, as it is a decided advantage to use but one index for both of these books. Why? What advantage do you see in a numerical index?

Impression Account Sales Book.

Sale of Merchandise for Account of

By Creager Commission Co.,

Commission Merchants

43.75 43.75

Sale of Merchandise for Account of

By Creager Commission Co.,

Commission Merchants.

Sales Book. The sales book in a commission business differs from an ordinary sales book. A column to receive the *consignment* sales and a column in which are extended the *cash* sales are provided in addition to the usual merchandise column. The goods belonging to consignments are designated by their lot numbers in the column ruled for that purpose. (*See illustration of Sales Book.*) These lot numbers also indicate the pages of the Consignment Ledger to which the various *items* are to be posted, while the *amounts* of sales from consignments are extended to the *Sales* column, and the amounts of our merchandise to the *Merchandise* column. When a trial balance is to be taken the total of the Sales column is posted to the credit of the Consignment account in the Main Ledger, and the total of the Merchandise column to the credit of Merchandise account. When a sale is paid for at the time of sale it is checked in the folio column to show that it is not to be posted, and the total is extended to the Cash column. The Cash column should be footed each day independently of every other day, and the footing should equal the actual amount of cash received from cash sales for the day. This amount is carried to the General column in the Cash Book and checked in the folio column to show that it is not to be posted. Why? (*See illustration of Sales Book below.*)

SALES BOOK.

LOT NO.	L. F.	MAY 24, 189-.		EXTENSIONS AND AMOUNTS.	CASH.	SALES.	MDSE.
		Grainger & Co.,	Marion,				
		on account,					
		1 box Oranges,		6			
4		1 crate Onions,		1 75			
7		10 " Tomatoes,	2.00	20		21 75	6
				27 75			
	✓	Austin Thompson,	cash,				
		2 boxes Lemons,	4.50	9			
4		2 crates Onions,	1.75	3 50	12 50	3 50	9
				12 50			
		25					
		I. L. Whitehead,	Rome,				
		on account,					
6		5 crates Cucumbers,	1.40	7			
4		3 " Onions,	1.75	5 25			
		1 box Lemons,		4 50		12 25	4 50
				16 75			
	✓	H. H. Bielefeld,	cash,				
6		3 crates Cucumbers,	1.40	4 20			
		1 box Oranges,		6	10 20	4 20	6
				10 20			
		Mdse. Cr.,					25 50
		Consignments Cr.,				41 70	

Cash Book. The General columns of the Cash Book are to receive all amounts for which there are no special columns provided. In the *Shipments* columns are placed the amounts received and paid out on account of shipments. The *totals* of these columns are posted to the Shipment account in the Main Ledger, while the *items* are posted to the proper accounts in the Shipment Ledger. On the debit side of the Cash Book, columns for the losses and gains on shipments are provided. The gain or loss on a shipment is ascertained

CASH.

DATE		L. F.	NAME AND EXPLANATION.		GENERAL.	SHIPMENTS.	GAINS.	LOSSES.
189.								
May	24		H. S. West,	investment,	2500			
		√	Cash sales,	for day,	70 60			
	25		Grainger & Co.,	in full,	78			
			Shipt. J. K. Williams,	proceeds,		145	12 50	
		√	Cash sales,	for day,	52 90			
	26		Shipt. H. J. Pierrard,	recd. a/s sales,			8 50	
			Shipt. Grainger & Co.,	proceeds,		78 60		15 10
		√	Cash sales,	for day,	66 10			
	27		Austin Thompson,	on acct.,	67 50			
			I. L. Whitehead,	in full,	42 95			
		√	Cash sales,	for day,	70 45			
	29		Shipt. H. J. Pierrard	proceeds as per acct. sales of 26 inst.,	75			
			Shipments Cr.,		223 60	223 60	21 00	
							15 10	15 10
			Shipments, Dr., Loss & Gain Cr.,				5 90	
					3247 40			
May	31		Balance,		2281 80			

by referring to the account in the Shipment Ledger at the time the remittance for the proceeds is received. These columns are not to be considered when proving cash, as they contain journal entries and are placed in the Cash Book merely for convenience. At the time of closing the Cash Book the difference between the Gain and Loss columns is posted to the Shipment account and also to the Loss & Gain account in the Main Ledger. (*See illustration of Cash Book.*) The *Consignments* column on the credit side receives all amounts paid out on account of consignments. The total of this column is posted to the debit of the Consignment account in the Main Ledger at the time of closing the Cash Book. All amounts appearing in this column are also entered in the proper accounts in the Consignment Ledger. The Discount column on the credit side receives the discounts allowed to the business by others. The total of this column is posted to the credit of Merchandise Discounts account at the time of closing the Cash Book. (*See illustration of Cash Book on pages 104 and 105.*)

Shipment Ledger. Instead of using both a shipment book and a shipment ledger, the two are combined by using an itemized Shipment Ledger provided with a special merchandise column. (*See illustration of Shipment Ledger, page 105.*) When a shipment is made, the date of the shipment, the name and address of the consignee, the name of the transportation company, a description of the articles shipped and their valuation (usually current cost price) are entered in this book, and the amount extended to the merchandise column and also to the debit ledger column. If charges are paid on a shipment they are entered in the Cash Book and posted from it to this book. When an account of sales and a remittance for the proceeds are received, the amount of the proceeds and the net gain or net loss are entered in the Cash Book and from it posted to the Shipment Ledger. An account of sales not accompanied by a remittance for the proceeds is treated as a memorandum until the remittance is received. At the time of taking a trial balance the total of the Merchandise column is posted to the debit of Shipment account and also to the credit of Merchandise account in the Main

CASH.

DATE.		L. F.	NAME AND EXPLANATION.			DISC'TS.	GENERAL.	SHIP-MENTS.	CONSIGN-MENTS.
May	25		Shipt. J. C. Dodson,	freight,				6 50	
			Expense,	rent,			60		
			Freight,				17 50		
			T. P. McMenamim,	in full less 2%,		3	147		
	26		Shipt. H. J. Pierrard,	freight,				2 60	
			H. S. Weet,	private use,			50		
			Const. H. Bader,	net proceeds,					174 80
	27		Shipt. Jno. Malone,	freight,				4 25	
			Shipt. J. A. Luman,	"				2 70	
			Const. G. W. Dodson,	net proceeds,					182 65
			Expense,	cleaning store,			4 50		
			Wm. Becker,	in full less 2%,		1 60	78 40		
	29		Const. J. F. Brown,	net proceeds,					92 75
			Jno. P. Batson,	in full less 3%,		3 60	116 40		
			Consignments,	charges paid,					22 40
			Shipt. Vincent Smith,	freight,				3 15	
			Consignments, Dr.,				472 60		472 60
			Shipments, Dr.,				19 20	19 20	
	31		*Balance,*	*bank,* *safe,*	*2275.00* *6.80*		*2281 80*		
			Mdse. Discts., Cr.,			8 20	3247 40		

Ledger. Shipment account in the Main Ledger represents the Shipment Ledger and should prove an abstract of it. All accounts in the Shipment Ledger should be indexed immediately after they have been opened and checked in the column ruled for the purpose to show that they are indexed. At the end of the month this column is also used as a folio column for Shipment and Merchandise accounts in the Main Ledger. (*See illustration of Shipment Ledger below.*)

SHIPMENT LEDGER.

INDEX, CHECK & FOLIO.	MAY 24, 189-.		MDSE.	LEDGER ACCOUNTS. DEBITS.	CREDITS.	FOLIO & EXPLA'S.	DATE.	
							189 .	
✓	Frank J. Bower,	Tipton, Ind.		97				
	100 bu. Potatoes, 22¢,	22.		2 50		C 6	May	24
	50 brls. Apples, 1.50,	75.	97		102 50	C 8		27
	Union Line.			3		Gain		
	25			102 50	102 50			
✓	Edwin Dalton,	Newark, N. J.		160				
	40 boxes Oranges,	4 00	160					
	Merchants Dispatch.							
	26							
✓	C. F. Alcott,	Auburn, N. Y.		164				
	200 bu. Potatoes, 22¢,	44.		6 40		C 7	May	27
	40 boxes Lemons, 3.00,	120.	164		168 50	C 8		28
	Big Four Route.				1 90	Loss		
3	Shipments Dr.	Total.	421	170 40	170 40			
6	Mdse. Cr.	"						

Ledgers. In addition to the foregoing labor-saving forms which are common to the commission business, the method of using more than one ledger is presented, a feature that may be used to advantage in any kind of business where a division of labor is necessary.

Three ledgers will be used: Main Ledger, Shipment Ledger and Consignment Ledger. The Shipment and Consignment Ledgers have already been explained. The Main Ledger receives all accounts which do not classify in the Shipment and Consignment Ledgers, and in addition accounts with those ledgers are kept, a Consignment account representing the Consignment Ledger and a Shipment account representing the Shipment Ledger.

You will observe by consulting the books of original entry (Sales Book, Cash Book, Shipment Ledger and Impression Account Sales Book) that special columns are provided to receive all items that are to be posted to either the Shipment Ledger or Consignment Ledger, and that the totals of these columns are posted to the Shipment and Consignment accounts in the Main Ledger. This being the case it is apparent that the balances of these accounts should equal the sum of the net debit or credit balances of the Ledgers they represent.

Main Ledger. The ruling of the Main Ledger differs from the form presented in the preceding work. (*See illustration below.*) Some of the advantages of this form are: The money columns are brought together in the center of the page, making it easier to compare debit and credit amounts than when the credit column appears at the right-hand edge of the page. But one ruling is required when an account balances, whereas two or three are required by the other method. The explanation columns, which are used very little, are next to the edges of the page, where it is often very difficult to write in a large book.

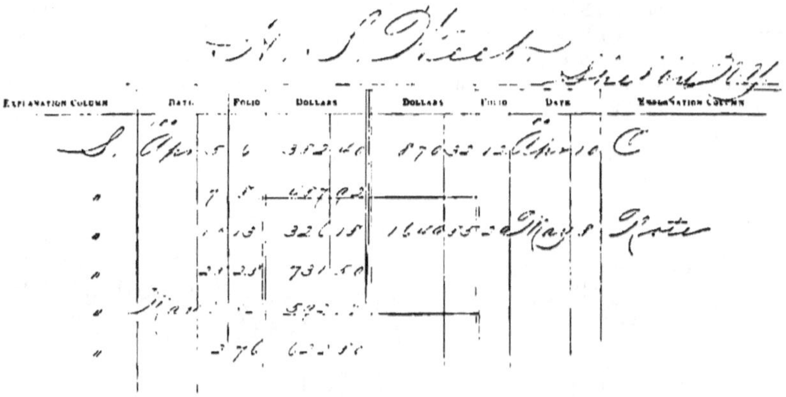

Letter Book. The letter book is a book made of fine tissue paper similar to the Impression Account Sales Book, in which an impression should be taken of every letter before it is mailed. Great care should be exercised in taking impressions, as the making of *good* copies with the letter press can be learned only by careful practice. In some lines of business, like railroading, ten or more copies are often required of certain documents, all of which are made with *one* impression of the letter press. To be able to make this number of copies successfully requires considerable skill. Every letter as soon as it is copied should be indexed and checked to show that it is indexed. (*See illustration of Letter Book on page 107.*)

NOTE.—In case you do not have the use of a letter press, you are to make a neat and accurate transcript with a lead pencil of every letter you write, in your letter book. This is done so that you will have a copy of your letter for reference.

A	E	I
Zaner C. P. & Co.	Zeller & Smith 9-27-36-41-52-87-110	Zink, Geo. & Co. 2-78
	Zeigler Thos. 83-129	

O	U	Y
Zoll, Jno. 7-142-179	Zurn, Chas 5-21-28	
	Zumm & Co. 17-99-198	
	Zucker, Jas. 6	

1

May 20, 188

C. P. Zaner & Co.
Columbus, O.

Gentlemen,—We are about to begin a produce commission business in this city and would be pleased to have you consign to us, not later than the first of June, 25 crates of good grade onions to be sold for your account and risk.

This concern is a branch of the well-known firm of Creager & Co. of this city. As to our responsibility, we refer to our bank, the Farmers and Mechanics.

Our charges for selling are 10 per cent of sales.

Yours truly,
Creager Commission Co.
per E. C. Mills

Indexing. Nothing is of more importance in counting-room work than the correct indexing of ledger accounts and other office records. There are a number of labor-saving indexes of various styles and makes on the market, some of which are patented or copyrighted, and all of which are based on the principle of alphabetical or numerical arrangement. Every account in your Main Ledger should be indexed *before* it is opened. This is very important and is done in order that no accounts will be omitted from the index. An index that does not contain *all* the accounts is very unreliable and almost useless. Do you see why?

NOTE.—In case the accounts or records occur in regular order as in the Letter Book, Consignment Ledger, Shipment Ledger, Invoice Book, Impression Account Sales Book, etc., the indexing may be done immediately after the record is made; but in that case every account that has been indexed should be checked so that none may be omitted from the index. Both an alphabetical and a numerical index can be used to good advantage with the Consignment Ledger and the Impression Account Sales Book. Do you see why?

Vowel Index. Probably the most widely used form of index is the vowel index shown in the illustration of letter book on page 107. In indexing C. P. Zaner & Co.'s letter you would open the index at the letter "Z." In a vowel index each letter is divided into six divisions, viz.: A. E. I. O. U. Y. Sometimes I and Y are considered as one division. The first vowel after the initial letter in the first surname of any title to be indexed decides the column in which it is to be entered. The first vowel in the word Zaner is "a", therefore, this firm name is indexed under the letter "Z" and in the vowel column headed "A". Turn to the illustration and see if you can ascertain for yourself why the remainder of the names are placed under the other vowel letters.

The same is to be observed in looking for a name in a vowel index. In looking for the page of Jas. Zucker's letter you would turn to the letter "Z" of the index and trace for the name in the vowel column headed "U", as the first vowel in the word Zucker is "u."

Paging before Posting. Before posting a day's records take the index and page each item to be posted by writing opposite it in the folio column the page of the account as shown in the index. After all the items which are to be posted have been paged, proceed to post each item to the page which you have indicated, and as each item is posted to its account place a check mark next to the folio figures, thus √21. Some bookkeepers consider it an advantage to do the paging in red ink, the check marks being in black will appear more distinctly, thus guarding against omissions and errors. By this method time will be saved, errors will be less likely to occur and neatness will be secured.

Other Books Sometimes Used. In many commission houses other books and forms than those described in the preceding paragraphs, are used. Those most frequently used are the Receiving Book, Consignment Ledger, Shipment Book and Shipment Ledger.

Receiving Book. This is usually a cheap, coarse book with ordinary journal rulings. In it is entered a detailed description of every consignment when received. The entries in this book are transferred to the Consignment Ledger.

Consignment Ledger. A detailed description of each consignment as it appears in the Receiving Book is transferred to the debit side of an account bearing the name of the consignor, in the Consignment Ledger. When sales are made they are transferred to the credit side of the account from the Sales Book. After all the sales have been entered the commission and other charges, if any, are calculated and an account of sales rendered, which is an exact copy of the account as it appears in the Consignment Ledger. The ruling of the Consignment Ledger is usually of the ordinary form of Ledger.

Shipment Book. The Shipment Book is ruled like an ordinary Journal. In this book a detailed description of every shipment is entered, and the entries are posted to the Shipment Ledger.

Shipment Ledger. The Shipment Ledger is usually of the ordinary form of Ledger.

Market Quotations. In this business the transactions for but one day of each week will be given. The following market quotations are to be used for all *sales*. Shipments are not to be entered at the selling price, but at *current cost* which will be specified in each case.

MARKET QUOTATIONS.

JUNE.	8	15	22	29
Cabbage, per crate, ...	3 50	3 20	3 10	3 10
Clams, per box,..........	1 20	1 20	1 25	1 20
Cucumbers, per crate.........	1 50	1 45	1 50	1 40
Lemons, per box, ...	5 00	5 00	5 00	4 90
Melons, each,..................	25	23	20	20
Onions, per crate,......	1 75	1 70	1 70	1 65
Oranges, per box.. ...	6 00	6 00	5 75	5 50
Oysters, per box, ...	1 20	1 20	1 25	1 25
Pineapples, per doz.,..	1 40	1 40	1 35	1 30
Potatoes, per bu.,.....	70	60	60	55
Sweet Potatoes, per brl.,.	3 00	3 00	2 75	2 60
Tomatoes, per crate, ...	2 00	2 00	1 95	1 95

Account with Main Store. No investment will be made for the Commission Business. All bills for this business will be paid by the Main Store and all cash will be received by it. As the Branch House keeps no bank account, no checks will be issued, but instead orders will be drawn on the Main Store for payments other than cash bills, which will be paid upon presentation, if O. K., without an order. These orders will be cashed upon presentation at the Main Store and charged to the Branch Store. When a remittance is to be made the order is drawn as usual and sent to the Main Store where a check will be drawn and sent in place of the order. The cashier will render a detailed statement each day, exhibiting the amount of cash received and paid out for account of Branch Store, from which the records will be made in the Cash Book. The Cash Book represents the account with the Main Store. The method of keeping this account is similar in every respect to the method of keeping the proprietor's account. The difference between the debit and credit sides of the Cash Book (excluding the amounts in the Loss and Gain and Merchandise Discounts columns) is either the amount the Branch Store owes the Main Store, or the net income of the Main Store from the Branch Store. At the time of closing the books the net gain or net loss should be carried to the Main Store account. The balance of this account should be carried to the trial balance whenever one is taken.

NOTE.—This balance could be transferred to the Main Ledger under the title *Main Store* and from there carried to the trial balance, but there can be no practical good resulting from this procedure, which only necessitates unnecessary labor.

MAY 20, 189–.

Preparatory to beginning business, you will order goods and request that they be consigned to you to be sold on commission for account of the consignors, as directed in the following paragraphs. Be very careful in composing your letters. It will be well for you to make neat drafts of your letters and have them inspected by the teacher before copying them on the letter heads furnished in your supplies. Have all letters approved *before* taking impressions of them in your letter book. Do not forget to *index* and *check* every letter as directed on pages 106 and 108.

Write a letter to The Harvey & Watts Co., Louisville, Ky., stating that you are about to begin a produce commission business and that you would be pleased to have them consign to you, not later than the first of next month, at least 25 crates of good grade Onions, to be sold on their account and risk. Tell them that your charges for disposing of same will be ten per cent. of sales. Mention the fact that your concern is a branch of J. D. Creager & Co., and give your bank (Farmers & Mechanics) as reference. (*See model illustrated in Letter Book on page 107.*)

Order from Frank J. Miller, New York City, 300 cans of Oysters and 600 cans of Clams on 60 days account, asking him to name his best discount if paid within 30 days. Tell him that your business is a branch of J. D. Creager & Co. and refer him to your bank and the leading mercantile agencies. Request that the goods be shipped in time to reach you by the first of June.

Write to Johnston & Brevillier, Chicago, Ill., asking them to ship to you, at the earliest possible date, 100 crates of marketable Tomatoes, to be sold on their account and risk. Give as references such parties as you think best to give.

After taking an impression of your letters insert them in neatly addressed envelopes. When you have your letter book properly indexed, submit it for inspection and hand the letters to the teacher to be mailed. You will be obliged to transcribe your letters in pencil if you do not have the use of a letter press.

Monday, June 1, 189–.

Your teacher will now hand you the incoming vouchers if your work to this point has been satisfactorily performed.

Mr. Creager has engaged Mr. Wm. Brenner as salesman in the Branch Store and to assist in the Main Store at a salary of $12 per week — each store to bear one-half of the expense. All bills and invoices of merchandise will be checked and O. K.'d by him if found to agree with the merchandise received. The Branch Store is also to pay one-half of the cashier's salary.

No. 259.—Examine this invoice of merchandise (sometimes called letter of advice) carefully. Has the merchandise been received? How do you know? Refer to your letter book to see if this invoice agrees with your order. If so make a record of same on a *receiving blank*, referring to the illustration on page 100. Place the lot number in the upper right-hand corner as a folio number. Paste this sheet, face upward, to the inside of the title page of the Consignment Ledger, which you will find in your supplies. File the invoice. Index this account *numerically* and *alphabetically* in the index furnished in your supplies, leaving blank the columns headed Account Sales Book.

No. 260. If this bill agrees with the goods received, turn to your letter book and ascertain if the terms are the ones you requested. Verify the extensions and additions, then paste the bill in the Invoice Book.

No. 261.—Proceed as instructed for number 259. Be sure to place the correct lot number in the upper right-hand corner. Have you indexed this account properly?

No. 262.—Read this letter carefully. Note that Mr. Creager as credit man approves of this request; also, that Mr. Brenner has not filled the order. You are glad to have the opportunity to make a shipment and, therefore, arrange to buy the quantity of apples desired.

for cash, from Wm. F. Menner, at $1.25 per barrel. Write an order in his favor for the amount. Make an entry in the Cash Book charging Merchandise and extend the amount to the General Column. Think, *think*, THINK before you make an entry in the Cash Book so that you will make a *good, complete* record, and place the amount in the *proper* column. By this entry you have credited the *Main Store* instead of Cash, because the Main Store supplies the cash to pay for the apples. Fill out an invoice of shipment (letter of advice) using one of the blanks in your package of supplies. On your invoice state that the goods have been shipped *via* the shortest route, you naming the actual route over which the goods would be shipped in business. File the letter on the Voucher File.

NOTE.—In business you would be required to prepare shipping receipts as you were previously instructed. Shipping receipts will be dispensed with as you have had sufficient practice in filling them.

Make an entry in the Shipment Ledger extending the amount into the Merchandise column and into the debit ledger column. Be sure to make this entry complete in every detail. (*See illustration of Shipment Ledger, page 105.*) Index the account and check it to show that it has been indexed. Place the shipping invoice in a properly addressed envelope. Place all documents in the Vouchers for Others receptacle.

No. 263.—Examine this statement carefully. The item marked "order" is not to be entered, as it was entered when the order was given. (*See No. 262.*) For all other payments the cashier has received vouchers (receipts) which she will file for reference. A cashier should preserve vouchers for money paid. Charge each consignment in the Consignment Ledger with the charges paid for its account; in the Cash Book enter the total amount as follows: "Cons't charges for day, 20.75," placing the amount in the Consignment column. Think twice before making an entry, so that you will place the amount in the proper column. Review and study the illustrated Cash Book if you experience any difficulty. Foot the columns of the Cash Book in pencil to see if your balance agrees with the balance as exhibited by the Cashier's Statement. File the Statement on the Voucher File.

Write to Ayrault's Produce Co., Baltimore, Md., requesting them to ship you 50 crates of Cucumbers to be sold on their account and risk; state that your facilities for disposing of same are exceptionally good, and that your total charges for commission, etc., will be ten per cent. of sales. Give such references as you deem most advantageous to your business.

Write a letter to A. H. Mason & Co., Richmond, Va., and ask them to consign to you as soon as possible 250 Melons to be sold on their account and risk. Mention the fact that you have a ready market for Melons in your locality at present, and that your total charges for disposing of them will be ten per cent. of the sales. Give such references as you may think best.

Order from the Quaker City Fruit Co., Philadelphia, Pa., 25 boxes of Oranges and 50 boxes of Lemons to be paid for on delivery. Give references and request them to send the goods with the utmost dispatch.

Have your letters approved and take an impression of them in your letter book. Place them in properly addressed envelopes. Do not forget to index your letter book.

Posting. Preparatory to posting, index and open the accounts required, placing four accounts on a page in the Main Ledger. Group the accounts, beginning with the Property and Allowance accounts on page 1, Accounts Receivable on page 3 and Accounts Payable on page 6. Post and check your posting.

Present your books for inspection.

MONDAY, JUNE 8, 189–.

No. 264.—Examine carefully, compare with your letter, then proceed as instructed for number 259. Have you written the lot number in the proper place?

No. 265. Compare with your letter: if correct, enter as usual.

No. 266. Compare with your order, verify the calculations and enter in the proper book. Do not pay the invoice before instructed to do so.

No. 267.—Read this letter carefully. Does the credit man approve of complying with this request? Have the goods been shipped? If so, make out the invoice of shipment and make the proper detailed entry in the Shipment Ledger. The current cost prices of the goods are as follows: Oysters, 90¢; Clams, $1.00; Oranges, $3.00; Lemons, $2.50. Write an order for $1 favor of the City Carting Co. for drayage and charge it to the Shipment in the Cash Book. Place the order and the shipping invoice in the proper receptacle, first inserting the invoice of shipment in a correctly addressed envelope.

Sales for the Day. The salesman has made the following sales for which you will render bills and make the proper entries in the Sales Book. Be very careful lest you make a mistake by entering amounts in the wrong columns. Place the bills in the proper receptacle.

NOTE.—Written orders are dispensed with in this business as it is supposed that the orders have been given in person or over the telephone by the purchasers. In business these orders would be entered in the Order Book or on order sheets by the party receiving the order. The credit man approves all time orders before the salesman is permitted to fill them.

Weet Bros., City, on account, 1 box Lemons; 1 box Oranges; 1 crate Cucumbers (lot 3); 10 crates Tomatoes (lot 2); 2 crates Onions (lot 1).

Use the market quotations for this date in making the extensions. (*See page 109.*) Omit the lot numbers on the bill but be *sure* to enter them in the Sales Book. Extend the sales from consignments to the Sales Column, and the sales from the firm's merchandise to the Merchandise column. Refer to the illustration of the Sales Book and the description of same when in doubt.

T. P. McMenamin, City, cash, 1 box Oranges; 1 box Lemons; 1 crate Onions (lot 1); 1 crate Tomatoes (lot 2).

No bill is to be rendered for this or any other cash sale, as a receipted bill is supposed to have been given when payment was received. Enter the total in the Cash column and make the extensions in the other columns as instructed above. Place a check mark in the folio column directly opposite the purchaser's name. Why?

Earl & Rogers, City, on account, 10 crates Onions (lot 1); 1 box Oranges.

Byrne & Collins, City, cash, 1 box Oranges; 2 crates Onions (lot 1).

J. K. Williams, City, on account, 10 crates Onions (lot 1); 5 crates Tomatoes (lot 2); 100 Melons (lot 4); 5 crates Cucumbers (lot 3).

Write an order favor of the Quaker City Fruit Co. for the amount of their bill.

No. 268. Make the entries from this statement as instructed for number 263. Be sure to enter the charges paid on consignments in the proper accounts in the Consignment Ledger, and enter the total in the Cash Book as previously instructed. Check in the folio column opposite the Cash Sales entry. File the statement.

Posting. First index, then open accounts with persons to whom sales on account have been made. Post from the Sales Book. Next post from the Sales Book to the Consignment Ledger all items belonging to consignments as indicated by lot numbers. Place a check mark to the left of each lot number to show that the amount has been carried to the Consignment Ledger. Proceed as usual in posting from the Cash Book and Invoice Book. Post the charges on the shipment to the proper account in the Shipment Ledger. Examine the indexes to make sure that you have *all* accounts *properly* indexed.

Write to T. & H. Smith & Co., Pekin, Ill., and give them an order for 250 bushels early Rose Potatoes at current market prices. Request that they bill the same to you on 30 days account, or allow a discount of 2 per cent. if paid within 15 days. Give such references and other information as you may think desirable to give with a first order. Request that the potatoes be forwarded by freight over the most direct route, you naming the actual route that would be employed in business.

Write to The Harvey & Watts Co., Louisville, Ky., requesting them to consign to you 50 additional crates of Onions. No references are required. State that you expect to render an account sales for their first shipment and remit for the proceeds in a few days. Make your letter as brief as possible.

Have your letters approved and take an impression of them. Index your letter book.

Present all books for inspection.

MONDAY, JUNE 15, 189–.

No. 269. Compare with your order, verify the calculations and enter in the proper book.

No. 270.—Enter as usual if found to be correct. Exercise care so that you will omit none of the details.

No. 271.—Read this letter carefully. If everything is found to be satisfactory, prepare the necessary document and make the proper record. The current cost price of potatoes is 40¢ per bushel. Write an order for $9.50 to prepay freight and drayage charges, and make the entry. Place all documents in the proper receptacle.

As all the merchandise belonging to The Harvey & Watts Co.'s Consignment (No. 1) has been sold, you will render them an account of sales. Calculate the commission at the agreed rate, ascertain the net proceeds and make the record for both in the account. Write an order for the amount of the proceeds, requesting that a bank draft be remitted in its stead. Remove the sheet containing the account by tearing on the perforated line, and take an impression of same in your Impression Account Sales Book. Extend the amount of the commission to the outer column. Index this account *numerically* and *alphabetically* in the same index used for the Consignment Ledger. Make the entry for the net proceeds in the Cash Book, extending the amount to the Consignment column. Write the folio number you have just placed in the index in the folio column of the Cash Book, opposite the entry just made to show where the account of which this entry is a part has been carried. Address an envelope to the consignors, place it, the account of sales and your order *unfolded* in Vouchers for Others. The cashier will insert the account sales and the remittance after she has secured the bank draft called for by the order.

Sales for the Day. The salesman has made the following sales. Render bills for all sales on account and make the entries for all sales.

Weet Bros., on account, 1 box Oysters; 3 boxes Clams; 1 crate Onions (lot 5); 10 crates Tomatoes (lot 2); 50 melons (lot 4); 5 crates Cucumbers (lot 3).

A. S. Longenecker, cash, 1 box Oranges; 2 boxes Lemons; 5 crates Cucumbers (lot 3); 10 crates Tomatoes (lot 2).

Earl & Rogers, on account, 50 Melons (lot 4); 1 box Lemons; 20 crates Tomatoes (lot 2); 10 crates Cucumbers (lot 3).

Write an order favor Frank J. Miller for the amount of his bill less the discount allowed. Make the proper record of both the discount and the amount of the order in the Cash Book.

No. 272.—Make the entries for all items on this statement that are not marked "order." Have you compared your Cash Sales with the amount received from that source?

Posting. Index, open accounts and post as previously instructed. Check over your posting.

Write a letter to F. S. Royster & Co., Columbus, Ga., requesting them to ship to you 25 barrels or more of Sweet Potatoes to be sold on their account. Give them all necessary information that need be given with a first request.

Write to Hancock & Co., Montgomery, Ala., and request them to ship to you, by express, you naming the express company, 10 crates of Cabbage to be sold on their account and risk. Give such information and references as you may think best.

Write to the Santa Clara County Fruit Exchange, San Jose, California, requesting them to consign to you 500 Pineapples to be sold on their account and risk. Give references and other necessary particulars.

Have your letters approved and take an impression of them. Do not forget to index your letter book to date.

Present all books for inspection.

MONDAY, JUNE 22, 189–.

No. 273.—Compare with your letter of June 15. Enter if found correct in every detail.

No. 274. Proceed as with number 273 if found to be correct in all details.

No. 275.—Examine very carefully. Note that the bank draft has been received by the cashier. File this document on the Voucher File, but do not make the entry for the proceeds until the cashier renders her daily statement.

No. 276.—Read this letter carefully. The merchandise necessary to fill this order was supplied by the Main Store and will be charged to the Branch Store in the cashier's daily report. Write an order for 75 cents favor of the City Carting Co. to pay for drayage and be sure to make the correct entry, placing the amount in the proper column. Prepare the shipping invoice and make the entry. The current cost price of Flour is $3.75 per barrel.

Sales for the Day. The salesman has made the following sales. Render bills for all sales on account and make the entries for all sales.

Peter Boyer, on account, 2 brls. Sweet Potatoes (lot 6); 1 box Lemons; 3 crates Cabbage (lot 7); 10 bu. Potatoes; 10 crates Cucumbers (lot 3).

Chas. A. Hall, cash, 3 boxes Clams; 2 boxes Oysters; 50 Melons (lot 4); 10 crates Cucumbers (lot 3).

H. H. Herdle, cash, 7 crates Cabbage (lot 7); 4 crates Cucumbers (lot 3); 10 boxes Clams; 10 boxes Oysters; 10 crates Tomatoes (lot 2); 1 brl. Sweet Potatoes (lot 6).

H. J. Parrard & Son, on account, 5 crates Onions (lot 5); 10 bu. Potatoes.

Write an order favor of T. & H. Smith & Co. for the amount of their invoice, less the agreed discount, and make the entry.

No. 277.—Verify this statement. Make the entries therefrom for all items not marked "order." Be sure to place all amounts in the proper columns. Refer to the illustration and explanation of the Cash Book when in doubt.

Posting. Index and post the books. Check over the posting.

Order from Wilhoyte, Barrett & Co., Rochester, N. Y., 100 barrels of Apples, requesting them to bill same on 30 days account and name their best discount if paid within 10 days. Give references and other requisite information.

Have your letter approved and take an impression of same. Index your letter book.

Present books for inspection.

MONDAY, JUNE 29, 189–.

No. 278.—Examine this account of sales carefully. Have the proceeds been received? Do not make an entry in the Cash Book for the proceeds until you receive the cashier's daily statement. File the account of sales on the Voucher File.

No. 279.—Refer to your order of the 22d instant. Note that the goods were not all received. Write to the parties requesting that they make good the shortage or that they send you a credit memorandum for the amount of the shortage. Do not enter the bill now.

No. 280.—Examine carefully. If found correct enter as usual.

No. 281.—Read this letter carefully. Has this request been complied with and is it approved by the credit man? If so, prepare the necessary document and make the entries. The current cost price of Lemons is $2.50.

No. 282.—Proceed as instructed for numbers 275 and 278.

Sales for the Day.—The salesman has made the following sales. Record all sales in the Sales Book and render bills for all sales on account.

S. H. Esarey & Co., on account, 2 boxes Oranges; 1 box Lemons; 5 crates Tomatoes (lot 2); 2 brls. Sweet Potatoes (lot 6); 2 boxes Oysters; 2 boxes Clams.

S. S. Neff, cash, 4 crates Onions (lot 5); 2 boxes Clams; 4 crates Tomatoes (lot 2); 1 box Oranges; 1 box Lemons.

J. P. Batson, on account, 10 crates Tomatoes (lot 2); 10 bu. Potatoes; 2 brls. Sweet Potatoes (lot 6); 10 doz. Pineapples (lot 8).

Philip Smith, on account 10 doz. Pineapples (lot 8); 5 brls. Sweet Potatoes (lot 6); 1 box Oranges; 1 box Lemons; 10 crates Onions (lot 5); 5 crates Tomatoes (lot 2).

Isaac Van Winkle, on account, 1 box Lemons; 2 brls. Sweet Potatoes (lot 6); 5 crates Tomatoes (lot 2); 5 crates Onions (lot 5); 4 dozen Pineapples (lot 8); 5 bushels Potatoes.

Herrmann Bros., cash, 5 dozen Pineapples (lot 8); 1 box Lemons; 3 brls. Sweet Potatoes (lot 6); 1 box Oranges.

Render an account of sales for consignment number 3. Calculate the commission, ascertain the proceeds and write an order for the amount of the proceeds, making it payable by bank draft. Prepare all the documents as instructed for consignment number 1 and do not fail to take an impression of the account of sales.

Render an account of sales for consignment number 4, referring to instructions given for numbers 1 and 3.

Render an account of sales for consignment number 7, following previous instructions. Don't fail to index every account in the Account Sales Book.

No. 283.—Examine carefully and make the entries for all items not marked "order." File on the Voucher File.

Posting. Index and post all the books. Check over the posting.
Present all books for inspection.

TUESDAY, JUNE 30, 189–.

No. 284.—Examine *very* carefully. Ordinarily the entry for this document would be made in the Journal, debiting the parties who sent it and crediting merchandise. In the absence of a Journal the entry may be made in the Sales Book because it is in effect the same as a sale; *i. e.*, you sold them the shortage. This you will do by writing the name of the parties and the description appearing on the document in your Sales Book, extending the amount into the Merchandise column. Enter voucher number 279.

Foot the special columns in all the books. Next rule all the books referring to the illustrations of the various books to make sure that you are doing it correctly. Post the totals of the various columns to their respective accounts in the Main Ledger.

Make an abstract of the balances of the various accounts in the Consignment Ledger. See if the total of these balances equals the balance of the Consignment Account in the Main Ledger.

Make an abstract of the accounts in the Shipment Ledger and prove it with the Shipment account in the Main Ledger.

Take a Trial Balance.

Mr. Brenner makes a verbal report of the goods on hand, not belonging to consignments, which are as follows: MDSE.—1 box Oranges, $3.00; 4 boxes Lemons at $2.50; 15 bu. Potatoes at 40¢; 96 brls. Apples at $1.10. FURNITURE AND FIXTURES (estimated) $120. COMMISSION. Earned on sales belonging to unclosed consignments, 31.20.

Make an Inventory of Resources and Liabilities and a Balance Sheet. Close all accounts that show losses or gains. Carry the Net Gain to the account with the Main Store in the Cash Book. Balance and rule the Main Store Account.

Present all books for examination and approval.

QUESTIONS.—What is meant by a Branch House? What is meant by the term Credit Man? From what sources do credit men obtain their knowledge of customers? Describe the commercial or mercantile agencies. How many kinds are there? Why is it necessary to know a person's moral as well as financial standing before giving him credit? Name some of the principal mercantile agencies. Describe the Loose Leaf Ledger. What advantage is there in using the Loose Leaf Method? Can it be used in other lines of business? Explain how a consignment is entered when the Loose Leaf Method is used. When a binder is not used, by what means are the accounts kept in order? Explain the use of the Impression Account of Sales Book. In what way is this a labor-saving book? What advantage is there in a numerical index? Wherein does a Sales Book for the commission business differ from an ordinary Sales Book? Why are cash sales checked in both the Sales Book and the Cash Book? Explain the use of Lot Numbers. What advantage is there in using special columns in the Cash Book? Describe the Shipment Ledger. What advantage do you see in combining the Shipment Book and the ordinary Shipment Ledger? Explain the method of using more than one Ledger. Why are accounts with the subordinate Ledgers kept in the Main Ledger? Is it necessary to take a Trial Balance of all the Ledgers? What is meant by an abstract of a Ledger? What is the object of a Letter Book? What is the object of indexes to books of account and record? When should an account or record be indexed? Do you understand the use of the vowel index? What advantage is there in paging before posting? Explain the method of keeping an account with the Main Store. If you were keeping the books of the Main Store would you be able to keep the account with the Branch Store? What is a Memorandum of Credit?

DEPARTMENT STORE BUSINESS.

To the Student. In your previous work you made all records from the business documents received and issued. In your subsequent work the use of vouchers will be discontinued, as it is believed that the advanced student will derive valuable mental discipline in making records from a statement or history of the transactions, instead of from the documents that vouch for and represent business transactions. In making records from a statement or history of the transactions the student should permit his imagination to supply the correct form of document for each transaction, if he desires to do the work effectively and intelligently. The ability to add accurately and with facility will be found to be essential to performing the following work successfully.

Plan of The Work. It is supposed that you will continue as manager of the Creager Commission Company J. A. Luman, one of the proprietors of the City Department Store, requests you to open the books for that business. This you agree to do after regular business hours.

City Department Store. The City Department Store is to be conducted by a partnership to commence on this date (July 1). The members of the partnership have previously been engaged in business for themselves in different parts of the city. They are as follows: J. A. Luman, dealer in shoes, 937 Spruce street; H. T. Williams, dealer in gloves, 1710 Broad street; Thos. H. Betts, dealer in hats, 1848 Twelfth street; C. R. Evans, dealer in dress goods, 112 Washington street; Abraham Levy, dealer in clothing, 265 South street. Each of the partners invests the resources and good will of his business and the liabilities of each are to be paid by the partnership. (*See page 132.*) As their investments are unequal in amount, each partner is to receive interest on his investment and is to be charged interest on all withdrawals for the time they are withdrawn.

NOTE.—In business a partnership agreement stipulating the rights and privileges of the partners and the conditions under which the partnership was formed would be drawn up and five copies executed, so that each of the partners would have a copy. As you have had ample practice in drawing up partnership agreements, it will not be necessary for you to draw up one in this case. When partnership agreements are of a complicated nature it may be well to have them drawn up by a competent attorney, in order to guard against litigation in the future.

Advantages of a Department Store. The advantages to be derived from merging several separate businesses into a department store are many. The advantages of a combined and increased capital are unquestioned in every line of business. Among the advantages that particularly pertain to the department store business may be mentioned the saving in advertising, as a department store can be advertised for proportionately less money than it would require to advertise as many separate businesses as there are departments in the store. Department store advertisements, as a rule, are more effective than specialty store advertisements; this is so because they are more interesting to a greater number of people, on account of the number and variety of articles to be advertised. Customers or visitors in one department are very apt to inspect and familiarize themselves with the goods in other departments; hence, each department assists in advertising every other department.

Subdivision of Merchandise Account. In this business the merchandise will be divided into five departments, as follows: Shoes, Gloves, Hats, Dress Goods, Clothing. A separate account will be kept with each department instead of including all the goods under the general title, Merchandise.

As the store and counting room are both divided into departments the student will be obliged to exercise care, so that he will not confuse the departments of the store with those of the counting room. He should remember that Shoe Department, Glove Department, Hat Department, Dress Goods Department, and Clothing Department are the departments of the store; the other departments mentioned in the following pages refer to the counting room work.

Object of This Business. The object of this business is to familiarize the student with the ordinary routine, forms, books and methods of keeping them, that are similar to those used in the best modern department stores. To accomplish this successfully the student will be called upon to do the work in each of the departments into which the counting room work is divided. One of the important things for the student to learn is the relation which one department, book or form sustains to the other departments, books or forms, as described in the following paragraphs.

Division of Labor. In the larger department stores the counting room work is divided into departments. While the number of departments varies in different counting rooms, yet the relation they sustain to each other will be fully exemplified and explained in this business where the work is divided into five departments, viz.: General Bookkeeping Department, Cash Department, Credit Man's Department, Time Sales Department and Purchases Department. Other departments, such as Rebate Department, Goods Returned Department, Collection and Dunning Department, etc., may be created whenever occasion demands. When the work that comes under these heads is not sufficient to justify the creation of a department it is attended to by the General Bookkeeping Department. The Credit Man's Department and the Collection and Dunning Departments are not, strictly speaking, counting room departments, but are here treated as such owing to their intimate relation to counting room work. Since the work of these departments pertains largely to the financial management of the business they are usually in charge of members of the firm.

General Bookkeeping Department. The General Bookkeeping Department is in charge of the general bookkeeper, or head bookkeeper, as he is sometimes called. He often has one or more assistants, the number depending upon the volume of work to be done. In this department the private accounts of the firm are kept, such as investment, property, and allowance accounts. In addition accounts with all the other counting room departments and also with the merchandise departments are kept so that synoptical or summary information of any part of the business may be obtained by consulting the books in the General Bookkeeping Department. To obtain detailed information of any department of counting room work it will be necessary to consult the books in that department. The books or accounts containing the detailed information should agree with the corresponding summary or synoptical accounts in the books of the General Bookkeeping Department. In the counting rooms of some department stores the agreement of the books is verified daily, in others weekly, and in others monthly.

Cash Department. This department is in charge of the cashier. When the volume of cash business is large several assistants are required. The duties of the cashier are briefly explained on pages 91 and 94. The cashier makes an abstract report to the General Bookkeeping Department daily; also, detailed reports to all other departments for whose account cash has been received or paid out. These detailed reports are verified and compared with the abstract report, in the General Bookkeeping Department, before they are handed to the other departments. The forms used to keep the accounts of the Cash Department, and the relation which this department sustains to other departments are explained and illustrated on pages 126, 127, 128 and 129.

Credit Man's Department. The credit man has charge of this department. Assistants are often employed to attend to the minor details and do the clerical work of the department. The duties of the credit man are fully explained on page 99. The relation which the Credit Department sustains to other departments of the counting room is explained on page 123.

Time Sales Department. The work in this department is divided alphabetically among as many bookkeepers as are necessary. In this business four Time Sales bookkeepers will be employed; the first will keep the accounts from A to G, the second from H to M, the third from Mc to R, and the fourth from S to Z. Frequently there are as many, or more, bookkeepers as there are letters in the alphabet; a large department store in one of our large cities has its Time Sales books divided alphabetically into one hundred and five divisions, each division being in charge of a separate bookkeeper. Some idea of the magnitude of a great department store may be formed when it is stated that in the above mentioned store only about one-seventh of all the sales are time sales. The documents from which the Time Sales bookkeepers make their records are all received from the General Bookkeeping Department, where they have been verified and compared with the abstract reports furnished by the other departments. The method of keeping the Time Sales accounts and the forms used are explained and illustrated on pages 122, 123, 124 and 126.

Purchases Department. The duty of the bookkeepers in this department is to verify the correctness of the invoices, keep a systematic account of them and see to it that they are promptly paid when due, or that they are discounted before the discount time expires. No invoices should be entered which have not been checked up by the receiving clerk and the prices on which have not been approved by the buyer. The head buyer usually has the supervision of the work in this department. The work in this department, like that in all other departments, is compared and verified by the General Bookkeeping Department. For illustration and explanation of forms and books used in this department see pages 120, 121 and 122.

Books and Forms Used. The books and forms used to illustrate a method of keeping the accounts in a department store are as follows: Abstract Purchase Book, Department Charges form, Abstract Purchase Ledger, Time Index, Clerks' Summary Sheets, Abstracts of Time Sales, Summary of Daily Sales, Sales Ledgers, General Ledger, Cashier's Abstract Statements, Cashier's Detailed Statements, Abstracts of Cash Sales, Abstract Cash Account, Pay Roll. Other books and forms than the above named are often used.

In no other line of business has there been so great an innovation made by the loose-leaf method of keeping accounts as in department stores. The reason is apparent. Were bound books used, duplicate sets for alternate days would be necessary, and these would be continually going the rounds of the counting room and the various departments of the store. When a book is in use by one clerk or bookkeeper the others who desire to use it are obliged to wait until he is through with it. Another objection is that the records are not continuous, owing to the fact that two sets are used; besides dishonesty is fostered, as false entries are not so easily detected in a fragmentary system of accounting, scattered about in two sets of books, as when the records are in consecutive order.

With the loose-leaf method all the vouchers and records are kept in consecutive order. The vouchers representing the transactions for each day pass from department to department until they reach their destination, when they are filed away in consecutive order. When this method is used it is a comparatively easy matter to refer to any voucher or record thereof. In short, when documents have to pass through several departments it is a decided advantage to use the loose-leaf method.

Abstract Purchase Book. In this book an entry is made for each invoice that is purchased. (*See illustration below.*) When a bill is ready to be entered a serial number is written upon it, or stamped upon it with an automatic numbering machine. This number is also written or printed in the column headed *No.* in the Abstract Purchase Book. The amount of each bill is entered in the *total* column, while the amount of goods belonging to each department is entered in the column bearing the proper heading. Whenever desired the entries in the department columns may be proven by ascertaining their total and comparing it with the footing of the total column, as shown in the illustration. All bills are filed in numerical order as soon as entered. When this method is used the entries are indexed and posted to ledger accounts.

If desired, the invoices could be pasted in an Invoice Book as previously instructed. When this is done the Invoice Book is so arranged that the invoices are pasted on the left-hand pages, while the department columns are ruled on the right hand pages.

ABSTRACT PURCHASE BOOK.

DATE.	NO.	L. F.	ACCOUNTS TO BE CREDITED.	TOTAL.	SHOES.	GLOVES.	HATS.	DRESS GOODS	CLOTHING.
189 .									
June 12	1		Marks Bros.,	922 80		922 80			
	2		Partridge & Richardson,	1345 96			1345 96		
	3		Lennon & Co.,	1722 92	1722 92				
	4		Lit Bros.,	612 20					612 20
	5		Strawbridge & Clothier,	889 69				889 69	
	6		Jno. C. Lewis,	787 34		787 34			
	7		Bacon & Co.,	1532 86					1532 86
	8		Gimbel Bros.,	719 41	719 41				
	9		Jno. A. Seeds & Co.,	827 89			827 89		
	10		Geo. Kremer & Co.,	1142 81				1142 81	
	11		Isaac Wittner	451 20	451 20				
	12		Andrew Meunier,	387 94			387 94		
	13		Thos. Hatfield & Co.,	1226 26		1226 26			
	14		Harold Dewesse & Son,	981 95				981 95	
	15		S. L. Sulzer & Bro.,	1482 25					1482 25
	16		Schwartz & Kratt,	1926 83					1926 83
	17		N. Knox & Sons,	1424 30			1424 30		
	18		Wright & Lackey	829 17	829 17				
			Shoes Dr.,		3722 70				
			Gloves Dr.,		2936 40	2936 40			
			Hats Dr.,		3986 09		3986 09		
			Dress Goods Dr.,		2964 45			2964 45	
			Clothing Dr.,		5584 14				5584 14
			Purchase Ledger Account Cr.,	19193 78	19193 78				

Department Charges Form. When the departments are quite numerous the above plans for entering invoices would not be practical, as but a few entries would appear in the department columns, consequently too much space would be wasted. In that event the department columns are omitted from the Abstract Purchase Book and a Department Charges form as illustrated on page 121 is used to receive all charges to departments. The columns headed *Serial No.* receive the serial number as it is written or stamped upon the invoice and entered in the Abstract Purchase Book, which will aid very materially in checking for errors or omissions, should the total of the department charges fail to agree with the footing of the money column in the Abstract Purchase Book. When this form is used an ordinary Journal, or a part of it, will serve the purpose of the Abstract Purchase Book. In the illustration on page 121 the numbers to the left of the footings are the folio numbers.

Department Charges—Month of *July*, 189–.

Shoes. Serial No.	Shoes. Amount.		Gloves. Serial No.	Gloves. Amount.		Hats. Serial No.	Hats. Amount.		Dress Goods. Serial No.	Dress Goods. Amount.		Clothing. Serial No.	Clothing. Amount.	
3	1722	92	1	922	80	2	1345	96	5	839	69	4	642	20
8	719	41	6	787	34	9	827	89	10	1142	81	7	1532	86
11	451	20	13	1226	26	12	387	94	14	981	95	15	1482	25
18	829	17				17	1424	30				16	1926	83
13	3722	70	14	2936	40	15	3986	09	16	2964	45	17	5584	14

Abstract Purchase Ledger. In this business the entries will be made in an Abstract Purchase Ledger as illustrated below. The advantages of this method are: (1) excepting the footing of the Amount of Purchases column, there is no posting to be done, (2) the terms, due date and discount time limit are recorded in connection with the entry, (3) provision is made to enter the payments and discounts directly opposite each bill, (4) accounts are indexed by their serial numbers instead of by the pages on which they are entered. As it is impossible to keep a systematic account of discounts in this book, the detailed account of them is kept on the cashier's detailed statements, while the total of each detailed statement is placed on the Cashier's Abstract Statement, and from there carried to the Abstract Cash Account. The footing of Discounts column of the Cash Account is posted to the debit of Purchase Ledger account and to the credit of Merchandise Discounts account in the General Ledger. (*See illustration of Cashier's Abstract Statement, page 127, and of Abstract Cash Account, page 129.*)

Abstract Purchase Ledger.

Date of Invoice.		No.	Index Check.	Accounts Credited and Terms.	Last Day of Disct.	Due Date.	Cr. Amount of Purchases.		Dr. Amount Paid.		Dr. Discount.		Date.
189–.													
July	1	1		Marks Bros., 2/10, net 30,	7/11	7/31	922	80	904	34	18	46	7/11
June	26	2		Partridge & Richardson, 2/5, net 30,	7/1	7/26	1345	96	1319	04	26	92	7/1
	28	3		Lennon & Co., 3/10, net 60 days,	7/8	8/28	1722	92	1671	23	51	69	7/8
	26	4		Lit Brothers, 2/5, net 30,	7/1	7/26	642	20	629	36	12	84	7/1
	29	5		Strawbridge & Clothier, 2/10, net 30,	7/9	7/29	839	69	822	90	16	79	7/9
	30	6		Jno. C. Lewis, 3/10, net 60,	7/10	8/29	787	34	763	72	23	62	7/10
July	1	7		Bacon & Co., 2/5, net 60,	7/6	8/30	1532	86	1502	20	30	66	7/6
	2	8		Gimbel Bros., 2/10, net 30,	7/12	8/1	719	41	705	02	14	39	7/12
	3	9		Jno. A. Seeds & Co., net 10 days,		7/13	827	89	827	89			7/13
	1	10		Geo. Kremer & Co., 30 days net,		7/31	1142	81	1142	81			7/31
	6	11		Isaac Witmer, 2/10, net 30,	7/16	8/5	451	20	442	18	9	02	7/16
	3	12		Andrew Meunier, 3/10, net 60,	7/13	9/1	387	94	376	30	11	64	7/13
	7	13		Thos. Hatfield & Co., 2/5, net 30,	7/12	8/6	1226	26	1201	73	24	53	7/12
	1	14		Harold Deweese & Son, 2/10, net 20,	7/11	7/21	981	95	962	31	19	64	7/11
	2	15		S. L. Sulzer & Bro., net 10 days,		7/12	1482	25	1482	25			7/12
	3	16		Schwartz & Kraft, 2/10, net 30,	7/13	8/2	1926	83	1888	29	38	54	7/13
	7	17		N. Knox & Sons, 10 days net,		7/17	1424	30	1424	30			7/17
	8	18		Wright & Luckey, 2/10, net 60,	7/18	9/6	829	17	812	59	16	58	7/18
									18878	46	315	32	
									315	32			
				Purchase Ledger Account Cr.,			19193	78	19193	78			

Time Index. Of the numerous forms of books and other devices that have been designed to keep track of the discount time limit and due date of bills purchased (or sold) none is as simple and effective as a Time Index. An ordinary diary, or a draw cabinet card index containing a card for each day on which the discount time limit and due date may fall will serve the purpose of a time index. When a bill is entered in the Abstract Purchase Book or Abstract Purchase Ledger, the serial number of such bill is entered in the index on the day the discount time limit expires and also on the due date. The first entry in the Abstract Purchase Ledger, illustrated on page 121, would be indexed as follows: Under date of July 11 write *1*, which is the serial number, in black ink, and under the date of July 31 write *1* in red ink. When an invoice is paid both numbers are canceled from the index. For the convenience of the manager of finances it may be well to also enter the amount of each invoice in the index, in connection with the serial number, so that the total amount due on any particular day may be readily ascertained by him. When either of these dates arrives it will be an easy matter to determine the number and amount of the invoices to be discounted, or that are due. It will greatly facilitate matters when a diary is used if the discount time limit is written in black ink and the due date in red ink, so as to readily distinguish one from the other. When a card index is used cards of two colors will serve the same purpose. The card index is the better of the two. Do you see why?

Sales Tickets. Sales Tickets will be dispensed with in this business. Historical data will be substituted in which the salesman's number, the number of the sale and the amount of each sale are given. If sales tickets were used they would be similar in form to those illustrated on pages 90 and 91.

(SUMMARY SHEET).

DATE, *July* .. CLERK NO. *1*.

Ticket No.	Amount.	Ticket No.	Amount.
1	3 00	26	
2	2 00	27	
3	2 50	28	
4	1 50	29	
5	3 00	30	
6	2 26	31	
7	14 26	32	
8		33	
9		34	
10		35	
11		36	
12		37	
13		38	
14		39	
15		40	
16		41	
17		42	
18		43	
19		44	
20		45	
21		46	
22		47	
23		48	
24		49	
25		50	

ABSTRACT OF TIME SALES.

A TO G LEDGER—SHOE DEPARTMENT.

July 2, 189

Clerks' Nos.	Ticket Nos.	L. F.	Accounts to be Charged.	Amounts.
5	20		Mrs. Henry Bader,	12 40
6	22		C. L. Behrns,	8 20
12	11		Mrs. Jno. R. Cassel,	9 26
14	13		R. S. Collins,	11 80
10	10		Henry Cutler,	15 25
4	9		C. O. Dinwiddie,	8 90
5	19		Chas. Dodson,	14 15
10	22		Geo. Engert,	17 26
1	12		Jno. E. Erhardt,	9 85
7	29		George Flynn,	4 22
8	23		Jno. B. Flower,	6 50
2	24		Jno. M. Gleason,	15 50
3	9		Mrs. A. K. Gilbert,	11 40
5	20		Chas. K. Gibson,	11 75
2	28		H. J. Glover,	3 25
3	23		Dr. D. S. Goble,	13 20
4	16		Miss B. Gutman,	4 85
6	14		C. F. Crainger,	7 35
				185 09

Clerks' Summary Sheets. Fifty sales tickets, printed in duplicate and numbered consecutively are usually put up in book form. For the convenience of the sales clerks a binder is used to hold these tickets, and a Summary Sheet is furnished (usually attached to the inside of back cover of binder) with each lot of fifty tickets. (*See illustration of Summary Sheet on page* 122.) When a sale is made the clerk enters the total on the Summary Sheet opposite the number that corresponds to the number on the Sales Ticket, before detaching the latter to send to the counting room department. There are usually two sets of tickets and Summary Sheets supplied to each clerk, so that one set may be left at the counting room to be compared with the corresponding sales tickets or entries for same, while the other is in use by the clerk. The total of all the Summary Sheets for a day should equal the total sales for that day. The daily footings of the Summary Sheets are entered on the Clerks' Daily Sales form, the total of which should equal the amount in the Summary of Daily Sales. (*See illustration of Clerks' Daily Sales form on page 125 and also illustration of Summary of Daily Sales form on page 124.*)

Sales on Account. In business when sales on account are made the sales tickets or bills must all pass through the hands of the credit man, before the goods are delivered to the buyers. Those persons who have not established a credit will be obliged to establish it or the goods will not be delivered. Those who have misused their credit will be denied the privilege of further credit, and no goods will be delivered to them unless paid for in cash.

When the credit man has approved the credit sales and the packing and shipping clerks have disposed of the goods, the tickets or bills for the same are turned over to the General Bookkeeping Department. Here the general bookkeeper and his assistants assort the tickets according to the merchandise departments, and, also, according to the sales ledgers, if more than one sales ledger is used.

Abstract of Time Sales. For the time sales in each merchandise department an Abstract of Time Sales sheet for each of the sales ledgers is required. On these sheets are entered the sales as shown in the illustration on page 122. This work is usually done by the General Bookkeeping Department. It may, however, be done by the managers of the various merchandise departments.

Summary of Daily Sales. The total of each Abstract of Time Sales sheet is charged to the proper Sales Ledger and credited to the proper merchandise department. This is done in the General Bookkeeping Department by entering the totals on a Summary of Daily Sales sheet as shown in the illustration on page 124. To ascertain the total daily sales of each Sales Ledger and of the Cash Sales it will be necessary to add the items in the department columns horizontally, and to ascertain the total of each department add them vertically. The footing of the Total column is the amount of the total sales for the day, and this footing should prove with the total of the footings of the department columns. The daily footings of all the columns are written in red ink to facilitate the addition of them. The monthly footings are posted to accounts in the General Ledger, bearing the same titles as the department columns of the Summary of Daily Sales, while the Sales Ledger totals in the Total column are posted daily. If thought expedient a form similar to Department Charges form, illustrated on page 121, could be employed to receive the charges to Sales Ledgers, and the footings of the columns posted once a month. The aggregate yearly sales are ascertained by consulting the accounts with the departments as kept in the General Ledger.

SUMMARY OF DAILY SALES MONTH OF *July*, 189

DATE, *July 1.*	SHOES.		GLOVES.		HATS.		DRESS GOODS.		CLOTHING.		TOTAL.		L.F.
A to G, Ledger Sales,	112	50	87	18	113	81	156	80	214	60	681	92	8
H to M, " "	97	22	104	29	129	30	172	10	184	27	687	48	9
Mc to R, " "	141	50	116	84	96	54	192	60	193	26	740	74	10
S to Z, " "	118	29	92	89	133	80	200	36	206	85	752	19	11
Total credit sales,	469	51	401	20	473	48	722	16	798	98	2865	33	
Cash Sales,	358	30	431	48	512	90	872	40	920	72	3095	80	
Total for day,	*827*	*81*	*832*	*68*	*986*	*38*	*1594*	*56*	*1719*	*70*	*5961*	*18*	

DATE, *July* [illegible]	SHOES.		GLOVES.		HATS.		DRESS GOODS.		CLOTHING.		TOTAL.		L.F.
A to G, Ledger Sales,	79	20	91	95	124	20	144	20	222	83	662	38	8
H to M, " "	118	29	99	26	116	69	167	65	176	40	678	29	9
Mc to R, " "	88	89	106	24	97	72	155	95	190	60	639	40	10
S to Z, " "	142	61	111	18	138	28	185	95	209	26	787	28	11
Total credit sales,	428	99	408	63	476	89	653	75	799	09	2767	35	
Cash Sales,	362	59	433	57	514	66	960	20	952	81	3223	83	
Total for day,	*791*	*58*	*842*	*20*	*991*	*55*	*1613*	*95*	*1751*	*90*	*5991*	*18*	

DATE, *July 6.*	SHOES.		GLOVES.		HATS.		DRESS GOODS.		CLOTHING.		TOTAL.		L.F.
A to G, Ledger Sales,	88	92	76	45	120	50	182	40	172	22	640	49	8
H to M, " "	92	88	99	25	130	75	384	20	196	50	903	58	9
Mc to R, " "	111	21	101	13	90	60	167	22	213	80	686	96	10
S to Z, " "	99	89	119	96	113	33	97	60	169	50	600	28	11
Total credit sales,	[illegible]	90	396	79	455	18	831	42	752	02	2831	31	
Cash Sales,	420	84	434	58	525	84	781	20	966	67	3132	13	
Total for day,	*816*	*74*	*831*	*37*	*981*	*02*	*1615*	*62*	*1718*	*69*	*5963*	*44*	

DATE, *July 7.*	SHOES.		GLOVES.		HATS.		DRESS GOODS.		CLOTHING.		TOTAL.		L.F.
A to G, Ledger Sales,	124	80	82	67	89	26	195	42	160	50	652	65	8
H to M, " "	98	72	116	42	112	81	193	20	267	30	788	18	9
Mc to R, " "	132	69	96	69	136	80	140	55	324	80	831	53	10
S to Z, " "	89	98	120	14	117	76	160	32	196	20	684	40	11
Total credit sales,	446	19	415	92	456	66	689	49	948	80	2957	06	
Cash Sales,	432	12	411	30	536	69	850	47	969	35	3202	93	
Total for day,	*878*	[illegible]	[illegible]	[illegible]	[illegible]	[illegible]	*1539*	*96*	*1918*	*15*	*6159*	*99*	

DATE, *July 8.*	SHOES.		GLOVES.		HATS.		DRESS GOODS.		CLOTHING.		TOTAL.		L.F.
A to G, Ledger Sales,	124	89	89	29	118	83	170	20	308	29	811	50	8
H to M, " "	88	72	109	19	98	38	180	24	364	20	837	73	9
Mc to R, " "	122	69	99	95	121	24	192	40	150	40	689	68	10
S to Z, " "	89	20	104	23	110	10	112	82	124	92	541	27	11
Total credit sales,	425	50	402	66	451	55	655	66	944	81	2880	18	
Cash Sales,	421	72	425	74	520	68	824	92	991	50	3184	56	
Total for day,	*847*		*828*	*40*	*972*	*23*	*1480*	*58*	[illegible]	[illegible]	*6064*	*74*	
Total for month,	4161	66	4164	87	4924	53	7844	67	9044	75	30140	48	
L. F.	13		14		15		16		17				

Clerks' Daily Sales. The book or sheets on which the clerks' daily sales are entered from the Summary Sheets, are ruled with vertical money columns, sufficient in number to accommodate the sales for each day of an entire month. In the illustration on page 125 but five columns for five days' sales and a Total column are ruled. The footings of each department should equal the footings of each department column on the Summary of Daily Sales sheet, while the monthly totals should equal the monthly totals of the Summary of Daily Sales. If errors exist, a comparison of the Clerks' Summary Sheets with the Sales Tickets and entries for same will be necessary. The department footings are written in red ink to facilitate the addition of them. Besides being a proof of the entries in the Summary or Daily Sales, the Clerks' Daily Sales record serves another important purpose. It enables the proprietors to ascertain the total daily, weekly, monthly or yearly sales of each and every clerk, thereby determining the value of the services of each clerk to the business and regulating his or her wages in proportion to the sales made.

Each clerk is given a number by which he is thereafter known, and the clerks for each department are supplied with numbers in consecutive order so that the sales from any department are clearly designated by the clerk numbers. In this business the clerk numbers for the Shoe Department range from 1 to 25; those for the Glove Department from 25 to 50; those for the Hat Department from 50 to 75; those for the Dress Goods Department from 75 to 100 and those for the Clothing Department from 100 to 125. In entering the numbers and names sufficient lines are left vacant for each department so that the names of extra clerks, employed temporarily during the busy season in any department, may be added in consecutive order at any time. (*See illustration of Clerks' Daily Sales record below.*)

CLERKS' DAILY SALES—MONTH OF *July*, 189

Clerk No.	NAMES OF CLERKS.	2		3		6		7		8		Total for Month.	
1	Clarence Small,	14	26	9	27	3	36	7	20	4	32	38	41
2	William Moore,	142	84	139	67	149	28	163	15	155	55	750	49
3	Miss Jennie Mission,	98	40	101	16	96	50	107	25	119	22	522	53
4	Miss Mary Murphy,	88	40	67	20	74	80	92	40	72	61	395	41
5	John Newlands,	91	20	75	60	69	75	88	50	77	79	402	84
6	Jas. O'Neill,	72	50	73	81	78	22	69	84	66	64	361	01
7	Miss Maud Young,	67	20	65	30	67	22	65	49	65	25	330	46
8	Elmer Winter,	79	20	78	79	77	82	79	92	81	81	397	54
9	Mrs. Kate Franklin,	65	26	71	20	72	50	71	16	70	70	350	82
10	Miss Mamie Robinson,	42	80	43	26	49	32	50	15	51	51	237	04
11	David White,	43	27	39	82	48	75	54	60	59	59	246	03
12	Jas. Ahl,	22	48	26	50	29	22	28	65	22	23	129	08
		827	*81*	*791*	*58*	*816*	*74*	*878*	*31*	*847*	*22*	*4161*	*66*
25	Miss Bertha Steele,	9	80	17	80	5	60	2	30	3	84	39	34
26	Miss Lottie Mason,	122	60	124	80	117	29	125	25	126	98	616	92
27	Henry Oliphant,	129	95	126	30	130	31	118	45	119	19	624	20
28	Chas. Hicks,	107	80	111	24	106	22	117	80	104	40	547	46
29	Miss Lucy Wade,	97	20	92	40	93	60	72	80	92	29	448	29
30	Miss May Greenfield,	78	40	79	80	81	30	92	60	89	89	421	99
31	C. C. Cunningham,	88	26	87	33	89	47	88	89	88	21	442	16
32	John Dwyer,	75	27	77	82	78	79	79	87	78	22	389	97
33	Joseph Mosby,	69	20	68	42	71	50	72	66	69	50	351	28
34	Edward Sebriefer,	54	20	56	29	57	29	59	60	55	88	283	26
		832	*68*	*842*	*20*	*831*	*37*	*830*	*22*	*828*	*40*	*4164*	*87*

Sales Ledgers. When the bookkeepers in the General Bookkeeping Department have charged the different Sales Ledgers and credited the various departments with the amounts of sales they enter the daily totals of the Clerks' Summary Sheets on the Clerks' Daily Sales record and compare the footings with the footings of the Summary of Daily Sales sheet. When found to agree, the Abstract of Time Sales sheets and the accompanying Sales Tickets are handed to the bookkeepers in charge of the Time Sales Department. These bookkeepers will enter and file the tickets for reference. In some business houses the entries in the Sales Ledgers are itemized as they appear on the Sales Tickets, in others only the footings of the Sales Tickets are posted. The method of filing the Sales Tickets, etc., varies, and the appliances in use are numerous and of various patterns. Generally the Sales Tickets and the Abstract of Time Sales sheets for each day are filed together in consecutive order. The ledgers used in this department are usually of the ordinary form of

ABSTRACT OF CASH SALES, *July 2*, 189

Shoes.				Gloves.				Hats.				Dress Goods.				Clothing.			
Clerk No.	Ticket No.	Amount.		Clerk No.	Ticket No.	Amount.		Clerk No.	Ticket No.	Amount.		Clerk No.	Ticket No.	Amount.		Clerk No.	Ticket No.	Amount.	
5	4	11	80	33	12	12	40	53	6	14	70	85	5	19	80	107	3	20	40
1	8	12	85	34	3	18	25	54	7	10	25	86	10	24	10	118	4	12	31
10	2	28	40	27	10	10	17	56	6	6	40	77	1	12	87	107	4	25	30
11	14	3	50	35	1	4	75	50	9	12	80	80	10	34	50	103	4	46	50
2	6	12	25	28	3	8	40	53	5	16	75	79	6	17	85	106	5	19	70
12	2	11	10	25	13	19	80	51	2	12	40	81	1	10	00	103	5	15	00
11	5	10	25	35	5	7	81	53	11	11	10	82	3	45	15	118	6	31	10
3	17	12	15	33	2	11	10	57	5	19	80	85	3	31	10	119	6	9	30
9	10	24	20	34	11	12	50	51	8	11	75	82	4	18	76	101	4	15	75
13	1	15	25	32	7	15	80	51	1	9	80	80	8	19	80	100	8	38	60
12	9	14	76	28	4	19	20	53	12	4	67	85	4	11	85	118	7	63	00
13	2	4	70	31	6	6	75	60	6	8	14	81	2	11	90	101	8	14	75
15	13	6	25	30	5	12	81	54	14	7	85	86	3	42	40	116	7	18	41
14	6	8	70	27	6	10	70	51	13	12	30	75	5	19	95	103	8	17	34
9	11	4	25	30	6	20	15	60	4	15	20	86	11	38	40	101	5	61	15
4	5	8	10	31	7	11	85	60	11	18	45	75	6	29	80	107	8	12	71
2	4	10	35	27	7	12	00	53	7	11	15	81	4	24	76	108	8	48	90
6	5	5	00	35	10	10	50	59	6	19	35	82	11	48	75	117	4	34	30
5	3	12	80	25	11	4	75	57	12	12	63	84	2	20	48	111	8	21	80
1	11	4	50	29	13	18	10	50	1	10	40	80	5	25	25	113	3	43	70
12	1	3	50	26	14	8	35	57	8	17	75	78	12	48	15	117	7	38	30
10	6	4	75	25	3	7	63	55	13	8	10	76	8	44	75	103	1	54	35
2	15	8	75	29	1	4	25	57	7	19	80	80	4	10	48	110	5	20	25
10	9	12	80	31	10	12	15	58	15	10	50	79	11	13	35	112	6	14	80
13	10	11	70	28	17	8	10	56	10	14	80	76	9	21	61	103	3	27	60
9	9	18	60	34	2	17	85	55	9	25	75	81	9	10	85	109	3	10	15
15	5	13	80	26	3	10	50	50	2	10	48	79	8	48	75	102	4	41	74
12	12	7	50	32	5	19	70	60	2	18	40	76	10	15	80	108	3	16	50
7	10	16	00	33	5	16	40	59	8	7	75	84	5	10	80	112	9	61	80
11	15	3	75	29	11	13	35	57	14	20	15	81	10	25	50	115	3	12	90
5	1	4	85	28	5	15	10	60	3	12	71	82	6	30	71	118	8	7	80
3	12	15	25	30	17	12	30	59	9	19	85	81	5	10	30	111	5	14	71
14	9	7	60	26	9	10	15	57	11	11	60	83	11	12	40	109	8	10	00
3	5	5	29	35	2	20	66	54	10	10	87	86	12	18	75	100	1	9	75
				25	12	3	30	50	3	21	25	81	6	25	30	111	7	10	02
								52	7	14	25	75	3	14	43				
								51	11	17	00								
		358	30			431	18			512	90			872	40			920	72

ledger. Abstracts of any of the ledgers should prove with the accounts bearing the same names, as kept in the General Ledger. As stated before, these ledgers may be proven with their accounts in the General Ledger, daily, weekly or monthly.

Cash Sales. For each cash sale the cashier receives the required amount of cash and the original sales ticket, which is kept on file until the close of the day or some other convenient time, when all the tickets are assorted according to departments, and are entered on an Abstract of Cash Sales sheet. (*See illustration on page 126.*) These sheets are ruled so that each department receives credit for the sales made from it. Three columns are ruled for each department, one to receive the clerk number, one to receive the ticket number and a third to receive the amount of the sale. The total of the footings of the money columns for the various departments should equal the amount of the cash received by the cashier. The total of each department money column is entered in the Summary of Daily Sales as shown in the illustration on page 124. The Abstract of Cash Sales sheet or sheets are handed to the General Bookkeeping Department with the Cashier's Abstract Statement.

Cashier's Abstract Statement. The cashier's statement in this business is an abstract of other detailed statements. (*See illustration below.*) Detailed statements for each of the ledgers named on the Abstract Statement, and the Abstract of Cash Sales sheet together with the Sales Tickets are sent to the General Bookkeeping Department with the Abstract Statement. After the General Bookkeeper has proven the Abstract Statement with the various detailed statements he records the entries on the Abstract Statement in the Abstract Cash Account as illustrated on pages 128 and 129, and hands the detailed statements to the bookkeeping departments to which they belong.

Detailed Statements. The detailed statements are similar to the Abstract of Time Sales sheets, as may be seen by referring to the illustration of Cash Receipts—A to G Ledger on page 127. When the items on these statements have been entered in the ledgers by the bookkeepers to whom they have been handed, they are filed away in consecutive order.

CASHIER'S ABSTRACT STATEMENT.

July 2, 189

	Disct.					
RECEIPTS.						
On hand,			67246	50		
General Ledger,						
Cash sales,			3095	80		
A to G Ledger,			429	98		
H to M "			813	94		
Mc to R "			289	20		
S to Z "			150	25	71525	67
PAYMENTS.						
General Ledger,			942	50		
Purchase "	37	45	1872	62	2815	12
Balance,					68710	55

CASH RECEIPTS—A TO G LEDGER.

July 2, 189

L. F.			
	Mrs. Henry Bader,	12	40
	Miss Alice Benedict,	13	95
	C. L. Behrns,	18	60
	Mrs. Jno. R. Cassel,	4	29
	R. S. Collins,	12	22
	Henry Combs,	60	54
	C. O. Dinwiddie,	22	60
	Chas. Danenhower,	62	40
	George Engert,	19	20
	Jno. E. Emmett,	70	60
	George Flynn,	7	65
	Jno. R. Gleason,	22	40
	Mrs. A. K. Gilbert,	32	80
	H. J. Glover,	17	75
	Chas. K. Gibson,	8	75
	Dr. D. S. Goble,	3	20
	Miss Bertha Gotman,	9	26
	L. K. Grainger,	12	92
	C. F. Gary,	18	45
		429	98

ABSTRACT

RECEIPTS

Date.		Balance.		General Ledger.		Cash Sales.		A to G Ledger.		H to M Ledger.		Mc to R Ledger.	
189 .													
July	1			67246	50								
	2	67246	50			3095	80	429	98	313	94	289	20
	3	68710	55			3223	83	780	50	620	30	930	20
	6	71266	68			3132	13	1007	20	920	40	326	30
		207223	73	67246	50	9451	76	2217	68	1854	64	1545	70
	L. F.							*8*		*9*		*10*	
	7	46335	61										

Abstract Cash Account. As stated before, this account is kept in the General Bookkeeping Department, and the entries therein are made from the Cashier's Abstract Statement. The numbers in the illustration on pages 128 and 129 written in italics are the folio numbers that indicate to which page of the General Ledger the footings of the columns have been posted. It is not necessary to post the footings of those columns that have no folio numbers. When taking a trial balance the balance of cash as exhibited by this account is to be included.

Pay Roll. The form of Pay Roll illustrated below is one in common use where the custom of paying off weekly is in vogue. In the illustration the clerks' names for but two departments are illustrated. The amount paid out for each department is charged to its account in the General Ledger. The footings of each department are written in red ink to facilitate the finding of the total amount paid out for wages. Study the form carefully.

PAY ROLL.—WEEK ENDING *June 30*, 189

Clerk No.	Names of Employees.	Mon.	Tues.	Wed.	Thur.	Fri.	Sat.	Total Time.	Rate.	Amount.		Remarks and Signatures.
1	Clarence Small,	1	1	1	1	1	1	6	25.00	25	00	manager.
2	William Moore,	1	1	1	½	1	1	5½	18.00	16	50	sick.
3	Miss Jennie Mission,	1	1	1	1	1	1	6	10.00	10	00	
4	Miss Mary Murphy,	1	1	1	1	1	1	6	8.00	8	00	
5	John Newlands,	½	1	1	1	1	1	5½	12.00	11	00	attended a funeral.
6	James O'Neill,	1	1	1	1	1	½	5½	10.00	9	16	
7	Miss Maud Young,	1	1¼	1	1	1	1	6¼	9.00	9	38	worked overtime.
8	Elmer Winter,	1	1	1	1	1	1	6	12.00	12	00	
9	Mrs. Kate Franklin,	1	1	1	1	1	1	6	10.00	10	00	
10	Miss Mamie Robinson,		1	1	1	1	1	5	7.00	5	83	began Tuesday.
11	David White,			1	1	1	1	4	8.00	5	33	" Wednesday.
12	Jas. Abl,				1	1	1	3	6.00	3	00	" Thursday.
										125	*20*	
25	Miss Bertha Steele,	1	1	1	1	1	1	6	25.00	25	00	
26	Miss Lottie Mason,	1	1	1	1	1	½	5½	15.00	13	75	delayed by railroad wreck.
27	Henry Oliphant,	1	1	1	1	1	1	6	15.00	15	00	
28	Chas. Hicks,	1	1½	1	1	1	1	6½	12.00	13	00	worked overtime.
29	Miss Lucy Wade,	1	1	1	1	1	1	6	10.00	10	00	
30	Miss May Greenfield,	1	1	1	1	1	1	6	8.00	8	00	
31	C. C. Cunningham,		1	1	1	1	1	5	10.00	8	33	began Tuesday.
32	John Dwyer		½	1	1	1	1	4½	8.00	6	00	" Tuesday.
33	Joseph Mosby,			1	1	1	1	4	8.00	5	33	" Wednesday.
34	Edward Schriefer,				1	1	1	3	6.00	3	00	" Thursday.
										107	*41*	

Cash Account.

S to Z Ledger.		Total.		Payments. General Ledger.		Discount.		Purchase Ledger.		Balance.		Total.	
		67246	50							67246	50	67246	50
150	25	71525	67	942	50	*37*	*45*	1872	62	68710	55	71525	67
426	30	74691	68	1142	50	*44*	*85*	2282	50	71266	68	74691	68
829	40	77482	11	29720	50	*28*	*52*	1426	00	46335	64	77482	11
1405	95	290945	96	31805	50	*110*	*82*	5581	12	253559	34	290945	96
11						*5*		*12*					

How to Pay Off. Some business houses pay off by check, giving to each employee a check payable to his order for the amount due him. As the check must be endorsed by the employee before he can get the money on it, it becomes a receipt. Other concerns pay off in currency, usually by what is known as the envelope system.

When currency is used the bookkeeper or cashier usually gets from the bank the exact amount of money, and just the kind of denominations and change wanted. To accomplish this he scans his pay roll name by name and records each result as follows: Suppose he has the following records: M. E. Smith, \$68.86, and Frank Kerr, \$75.75. He rules columns on a tablet for 20's, 10's, 5's, 2's, and 1's for dollars, and for fractional currency, 50¢, 25¢, 10¢, 5¢ and 1¢. Commencing with Smith, he enters in his list, 3 in the column headed twenty, 1 in the five column, 1 in the two column and 1 in the one column. $3 \times 20 + 5 + 2 + 1$ equals 68 or \$68. *Fractional:* 1 in 50¢ column, 1 in 25¢ column, 1 in 10¢ column, 1 in 1¢ column. 50¢ + 25¢ + 10¢ + 1¢ equal 86¢. For Kerr—3 twenties, 1 ten, 1 five and 50¢ and 25¢ equals \$75.75. Instead of 3 twenties, 1 fifty and 1 ten could be used; in fact use the largest denominations, then add each kind. When the amount required is ascertained, a check is drawn for that sum, payable, usually, to "Pay Roll" and taken to the bank, together with the memorandum of the change wanted, and cashed. This cash should be kept separate from the other cash on hand, especially where the envelope system is used, so that if any mistakes are made in filling the envelopes they may be detected before paying off. (See form of Pay Roll memorandum on page 130.)

Instead of finding the number of each denomination by the above method the adept bookkeeper scans each amount in the entire pay roll, first, to ascertain how many pennies are required to make the exact change for the entire pay roll. He then ascertains in the same manner the number and amount of nickels, dimes, quarters, halves, 1's, 2's, 5's, 10's, 20's, etc., that are required. These are usually entered on a Pay Roll memorandum as illustrated on page 130, or in the absence of a memorandum sheet, on the back of the check. The total of the memorandum should equal the footing of the pay roll. The objection urged against the first method explained, is that in a pay roll of several hundred names it would require hours to accomplish what can be done by the latter method in a few minutes. It may require considerable practice for some to master this latter method, but its time and labor saving features will be appreciated by all bookkeepers who have had experience with long pay rolls, and who know how precious time often is on pay days.

When the envelope system is used, the envelopes are prepared for filling after the pay roll has been made out for the week or month. This is done by copying on the envelopes from the pay roll the names, or the pay roll numbers, of the employees, together with the amounts due them. The amounts are usually written in a position where they will be covered over when the envelopes are sealed. Some bookkeepers write the amount on the inside of the flap; others on the back (near the lower edge), covering it over by folding the envelope lengthwise before sealing it. When the amount is written on the inside of the flap it will be a convenience to write the name of the employee on the reverse side of the envelope, so that both the name and amount appear on the same side of the envelope. What reason can you assign for covering up the amount of an employee's wages?

The envelopes are filled by placing in each one the amount written upon it, the person filling the same being careful to select the largest possible denominations each time in making up the amount, so as not to run short of change. When the last envelope is reached, the amount of cash remaining should tally exactly with the amount called for on the envelope. If it does not so tally, then a mistake has been made in filling the envelopes. To locate the mistake it will be necessary to recount the cash in the envelopes. The envelopes are usually not sealed until all have been filled and the cash proven as explained above. For the convenience of the one who pays off, the envelopes are arranged in the cash box or on the desk so that the numbers appear consecutively, when the envelopes are numbered, or so that the names appear alphabetically, when names are used. The paying off is usually done by the cashier, bookkeeper, foreman, paymaster, or some one familiar with the names or numbers of the employees.

ALLIANCE BANK,

(Your place here.)

PAY-ROLL MEMORANDUM.

J. A. Luman & Co.

require as follows:

Pennies,	114	1	14
Nickels,	25	1	25
Dimes,	21	2	10
Quarters,	25	6	25
Halves,	40	20	00
Silver Dollars,	67	67	00
2's,	30	60	00
5's,	16	80	00
10's,	23	230	00
20's,	6	120	00
Total		587	74

ABSTRACT OF GOODS RETURNED,
SHOE DEPARTMENT—A TO G LEDGER.

July 6, 189

	L. F.	ACCOUNTS TO BE CREDITED.	AMOUNTS.	
		Jno. Atwood,	12	84
		Geo. P. Bower,	9	20
		Edna V. Bowman,	26	40
		F. J. Brown,	18	96
		A. B. Carr,	12	80
		Mrs. G. Culver,	6	20
		Henry Eames,	13	45
		Frank Fellis,	22	80
		Geo. Gregory,	3	80
		Martin Granger,	14	62
			141	07

Goods Returned. When goods are returned the records to be made are precisely the reverse of those made at the time of sale. In the case of a cash sale, if the cash is refunded, cash account is credited and the department from which the goods were sold is charged, as it has purchased back the goods. When the goods have been sold on time the party who returns them is credited and the department from which they have been sold is charged. This is done by sending a credit ticket or credit memorandum to the counting room for each lot of goods returned. These credit tickets, if for time sales, are entered on a Goods Returned Abstract, as shown in the illustration above. It will be observed that this form is the reverse of the Abstract of Time Sales form illustrated on page 122. The footing of this form is entered on a Daily Summary of Goods Returned, of which no illustration is given, as it is exactly the reverse of the Summary of Daily Sales illustrated on page 124. For each cash sale the credit tickets are entered on the Abstract of Cash Goods Returned form, which is exactly the reverse of the Abstract of Cash Sales illustrated form on page 126.

Credit Memoranda Account. Very often, in the case of cash sales, the money is not refunded at the time the goods are returned, but a credit memorandum is given the party who returns them. In that event the department from which the goods were sold is charged for the amount and Credit Memoranda Account in the General Ledger is credited. When a credit memorandum is received in payment of goods from some other department, the department is credited and Credit Memoranda Account is debited. When all outstanding credit memoranda have been redeemed Credit Memoranda Account should balance. Credit memoranda are in effect Bills Payable, payable on demand either in merchandise or in cash. Is a credit memorandum negotiable or non-negotiable? Give a reason for your answer.

Rebates. When a rebate is allowed to a purchaser of goods on credit, that person's account is credited and the department from which the goods were sold is charged for the amount of rebate allowed. In the case of a cash sale, when the amount of the rebate is refunded, cash account is credited and the department from which the goods were sold is charged. Credit memoranda may be issued for rebates as well as for goods returned, and are treated in the same manner. As the forms used in recording Rebates are in all essential particulars like those used in recording Goods Returned no illustrations of such forms are given.

The student who thoroughly understands the use of the various forms used in recording the sales and purchases in a department store will have no difficulty in designing forms in which to record rebates and goods returned. Study carefully the forms used for recording the sales and purchases.

Sundry Accounts. When a sale is made to a party who is not a regular customer, instead of opening an account with him on a separate page, the entry is made in an account headed Sundry Accounts, or Miscellaneous Accounts, as it is sometimes called, together with other accounts that are not likely to be permanently active. (*See illustration below.*)

You will observe that in the illustration the space occupied by each account takes but two lines—the first for the name, the second for the address. When an account is settled the amount is entered directly opposite and a check mark is placed on the center, triple ruling to show that it is settled in full. When the account is not paid in full a short extension may be made, as shown in the first and last items in the illustration. When desired two Sundry Accounts may be kept—a Sundry Accounts Receivable and a Sundry Accounts Payable.

SUNDRY ACCOUNTS.

	189 .									189 .		
Geo. W. Dodson, Don Juan, Ind.	July.	1	10	8	40				6	July.	6	Cash 5.00
Mrs. Amie Bowen, Avoca, N. Y.		7	12	24	75	✓	24	75			30	Cash
Ben Becker, Rochester, N. Y.		21	14	88	75	✓	88	75	5		30	Cash 50.00; Aug. 5, 38.75
A. P. Root, Kingsville, O.		22	18	72	25							
Jno. Frey, Owensboro, Ky.		25	22	12	26	✓	12	26	8	Aug.	2	Cash
Miss Clara Kaiser, Hester, Mo.		27	29	4	20				9		5	Cash 3.00

WEDNESDAY, JULY 1, 189–.

Investments of the Partners. The firm name of the partnership is to be J. A. Luman & Co., while the business will be known by the general public as the City Department Store. The partners invest the resources of their respective businesses and the liabilities of each are to be paid by J. A. Luman & Co.

J. A. Luman invests the following resources: Cash, $11248.90; Fixtures, $400; Shoes on hand, $16550; due from Joseph Schwartz, $26.50; Albert Basset, $92.40; Lyman Smith, $67.25; Albert Spillman, $32.45; Leroy Gatchell, $12.80. He owes on account as follows: Utz & Dunn, $292.10; Chick Bros., $729.32; Jno. Mundell & Co., $567.49.

H. T. Williams invests as follows: Cash, $9280; Fixtures, $350; Gloves on hand, $21250; due from J. D. Malone, $12.95; Paul Deom, $67.20; George Noble, $132.40; Mrs. Nancy Hicks, $9.80; Mrs. A. Powell, $13.75; J. W. Brady, $19.22. He owes Glover Manufacturing Co., $292.45; Boston Glove Co., $892.40; Chicago Manufacturing Co., $1684.25; H. G. Wells & Co., $321.56.

Thos. H. Betts' resources are: Cash, $11285.60; Fixtures, $525; Hats on hand, $12826; due from W. B. James, $16.80; Cyrus W. Van Winkle, $9.20; Harmon Mosby, $29.56; J. M. Gleason, $14.28; S. E. Walters, $22.65. He owes Jno. B. Stetson Co., $872.40; Rochester Hat Co., $376.89.

C. R. Evans invests as follows: Cash, $17482; Fixtures, $400; Dress Goods on hand, $9126; owing by Miss Josie Nicolay, $76.40; Mrs. L. Lorch, $22.86; Lafayette Miller, $47.29; Chas. F. Marting, $126.50. He owes: Jno. Gibson, $972.40; J. W. Riddle, $269.26.

Abraham Levy makes the following investment: Cash, $17950; Fixtures, $450; Clothing on hand, $9780. He owes Emerald Mills, $3286.40; Jas. Allison's Sons, $1982.62.

Make the entries for the partners' investments in the Journal, similar to the entry illustrated on page 87. Short-extend the cash items as the partners will receive credit for their cash investments on the cashier's detailed statement for the General Ledger. Debit the goods invested by their titles (Shoes, Gloves, Hats, Dress Goods, Clothing) instead of including them all under the general term, Merchandise. This is done so that the gain or loss on each separate kind of goods may be ascertained.

NOTE.—These entries are made in the books of the general bookkeeping department and are all posted to the General Ledger. In every step taken the student should ascertain in what department of the counting room work he is engaged. This is very important if the student desires to gain a clear understanding of the duties of the bookkeepers in the various departments.

Duties of the Partners. As per agreement the duties of the partners are as follows: J. A. Luman will be the Purchasing Agent for the firm; H. T. Williams will be the Credit Man; Thos. H. Betts will be the Treasurer of the concern and will have charge of the cash and finances. C. R. Evans will have supervision of the various Merchandise Departments of the store; and Abraham Levy will be the Advertising Manager and will have charge of the Employment Department. While each of the partners will be in charge of a certain department of the work, they will, nevertheless, assist one another whenever such assistance is required or thought to be advantageous to the mutual interests of the partners.

Employees. The former employees of the partners will be retained in the employ of the new firm. Their names, numbers and wages agreed upon are as follows. Enter their names, numbers and wages per week in the Pay-Roll Book, referring to the instructions and illustration on page 128. Leave two lines blank after the last name in each department.

SHOE DEPARTMENT. Clarence Small (1), manager of department, $25.00; William Curtice (2), $10.00; Miss Jennie Sampson (3), $8.00; Miss Mary Murphy (4), $9.00; John

Nostrand (5), $9.00; James O'Neill (6), $9.00; Miss Maude Youngs (7), $10.00; Miss L. Sweetland (8), $10.00; Miss Kate Franklin (9), $8.00; Miss Mamie LaFever, (10), $8.00; B. R. Rosecrans (11), $8.00; Herbert Downing (12), $11.00; Daniel Murphy (13), $11.00; C. A. Vanduyne (14), $10.00; Chas. Sandwick (15), $9.00.

Glove Department. Miss B. Steele (25), manager of department, $20.00; Miss Lizzie Sullivan (26), $9.00; Orma Blakely (27), $10.00; James Reid (28), $12.00; Chas. Hicks (29), $12.00; Miss Lucy Wade (30), $9.00; Miss Mae Greenfield (31), $9.00; R. W. Burlingham (32), $10.00; Miss Mabel Austin (33), $9.00; John DeWitt (34), $11.00; Harvey Foltz (35), $13.00.

Hat Department. Lawrence Kinney (50), manager of department, $20.00; Elgae Baker (51), $8.00; Miss Sara Hobart (52), $9.00; Miss Addie Stearns (53), $9.00; Claude Loomis (54), $11.00; Wm. Amerman (55), $9.00; Miss Jessie Hunt (56), $8.50; Miss Edna Waters (57), $9.00; Howard Evans (58), $10.00; Miss May Hoagland (59), $8.50; Frank Erb (60), $9.50.

Dress Goods Department. Louis Emerson (75), manager of department, $30.00; Harry Fuller (76), $25.00; Miss M. Lluwellyn (77), $22.00; Miss Helen Waite (78), $18.00; Miss Essie Parks (79), $18.00; Miss Nancy Edmonds (80), $12.00; Mrs. J. H. Bowker (81), $15.00; H. A. Wheat (82), $18.00; L. M. Lillie (83), $18.00; Miss Florence Smith (84), $16.50; Miss Della O. Hawley (85), $16.00; Warren Sherman (86), $16.50.

Clothing Department. Isaac Black (100), manager of department, $25.00; James Corrigan (101), $15.00; Henry Welch (102), $18.00; Jacob Hondorf (103), $12.00; Alfred Rounds (104), $20.00; William Green (105), $14.50; Harold Harding (106), $13.00; Arthur Deitz, Jr. (107), $14.50; C. W. Wilson (108), $15.00; Denton Wood (109), $19.00; Claude Helmer (110), $16.50; Morris Cone (111), $18.00; Clarence Leonard (112), $16.00; Lee Winters (113), $13.50; Gordon Springer (114), $14.50; Edwin Harmon (115), $15.00; Carrol Slade (116), $13.00; W. A. Donald (117), $14.00; H. Patterson (118), $14.00; Lorenzo Glover (119), $13.50.

The names of the partners and of the employees in the counting room are not entered in the Pay Roll, as their salaries are paid monthly and are charged to Expense. The salaries of the partners, as per agreement, are to be $150.00 per month. The employees engaged to do counting room work are: John W. Scull, A to G sales bookkeeper; Caleb Knight, H to M sales bookkeeper; Jas. Hargis, Mc to R sales bookkeeper; and Jno. Patrick, S to Z sales bookkeeper, each of whom is to receive $60.00 per month for his services. No one has been employed in either the Cash or Purchases departments. The student, assisted by the Treasurer and Purchasing Agent, is to do the work in these departments while he is engaged in opening the books. After the books have been opened a cashier, a purchase ledger bookkeeper, a general bookkeeper and necessary assistants will be employed. The student is to receive $10.00 per day, which is considered very ordinary pay for opening books, adjusting accounts or doing any of the work usually done by the expert accountant. The student should not make the mistake of considering himself an *expert accountant*, simply because he is doing a work of a similar nature to that done by expert accountants.

Purchases. The Purchasing Agent has made purchases as listed below; the goods have arrived and are found to agree with the invoices. In business these invoices would be numbered consecutively and filed in a similar manner as soon as entered. Make the entries from the data furnished, in the Abstract Purchase Ledger and also in the Department Charges form. In making the entries be sure to enter the date of the invoice, the

J. W. Harrison, $12.45; 5-7, Richard Smythe, $4.75; 6-2, Andrew McIntyre, $12.65; 5-8, Jos. E. McGregor, $13.85; 6-1, Martin Schneider, $4.15; 6-3, Wm. Henning, $18.40; 1-13, Henry Beaver, $12.30; 7-12, Miss Lillian Betts, $15.50; 7-11, Donald M. Hepler, $12.80; 8-2, Miss Anna Spencer, $4.79; 7-2, Paul Snyder, $14.70; 13-5, Jno. M. McKinley, $9.25; 7-1, Mrs. Kate McKenna, $14.80; 8-11, A. K. Stephenson, $6.30; 1-4, B. W. Hayden, $9.20; 4-8, Dr. C. M. Brucker, $9.50; 13-6, Mrs. Henry Bader, $22.25; 10-5, Thomas Hawkins, $7.45; 2-9, Jno. M. Stone, $9.40; 8-1, Miss Mamie McNeill, $11.45; 4-9, Frank W. Taylor, $4.11; 2-3, Mrs. Geo. Hyde, $7.40; 1-11, Clarence W. Campbell ,$12.50; 9-6, A. B. Jennings, $8.75; 11-14, Wm. Underwood, $4.50; 14-10, Mrs. T. P. McMenamin, $14.85; 14-4, Frank Naylor, $16.85; 13-7, Edgar M. Vail, $12.25; 4-13, Mrs. C. W. Jefferson, $9.25; 5-6, R. S. Collins, $7.80; 11-9, J. E. M. Keller, $12.25; 3-9, Adam Vogel, $12.10; 8-10, Miss Mabel Neilson, $4.50; 4-11, Harvey Nixon, $14.90; 14-12, Frank M. Wagner, $10.12; 3-11, Henry Kempf, $9.25; 11-13, P. Cassidy, $10.00; 13-8, Miss Josie Nicolay, $16.85; 14-2, H. J. Walker, $10.25; 6-11, Lawrence Kiefer, $12.25; 8-3, Ralph E. Cooke, $13.45; 11-12, Wm. Kitchen, $9.40; 9-13, Peter M. Ward, $6.50; 2-7, J. S. Northorp, $13.75; 3-8, H. H. Watterson, $4.50; 12-5, Miss Sarah Keim, $12.50; 15-11, J. W. Clark, $13.75; 7-3, Mrs. H. W. Dickinson, $12.95; 5-9, R. G. Laird, $11.45; 15-8, Frank Zimmer, $4.15; 10-11, William Nye, $19.50; 11-1, Edward O'Connor, $5.25; 2-8, Allen H. Oliver, $18.18; 2-12, Chas. Lake, $9.85; 14-11, C. G. Davis, $7.85; 3-10, Solomon Erb, $19.40; 4-10, D. E. Parsons, $14.21; 14-3, Geo. Eaton, $8.47; 9-12, H. B. Lehman, $14.65; 12-6, H. E. Eastwood, $19.44; 6-12, Alfred Quinn, $7.40; 2-10, Jno. E. Zeigler, $1.75; 4-12, Mrs. G. W. Miner, $14.50; 4-7, Miss Euphemia Faucett, $6.80; 4-6, Geo. E. Munson, $25.50; 6-13, Miss Amie Rathbun, $14.25; 2-11, Jno. R. Fell, $12.40; 14-1, Herman Zumm, $4.55; 3-4, C. H. Remington, $4.65; 15-10, Miss Mary Gilles, $14.65.

Verify your work. Ascertain the footing of the money column on each sheet. Lay aside the sheets for the Shoe Department and head another lot for the Glove Department, following previous instructions. Be sure to carry out these instructions for every department.

Glove Department. 31-11, Mrs. E. McDaniel, $4.64; 26-2, J. W. Harrison, $5.50; 26-4, J. G. Atkinson, $13.20; 27-13, W. E. Schermerhorn, $5.75; 25-17, Geo. McFarlan, $12.30; 31-13, Geo. Heitz, $7.40; 31-2, George Bauer, $3.75; 28-10, Albert E. Shaw, $4.37; 35-14, Edwin Short, $3.65; 27-16, Miss Lillian Betts, $2.60; 32-1, Donald M. Hepler, $7.85; 28-11, Andrew McIntyre, $14.10; 33-15, Jos. E. McGregor, $3.40; 33-7, B. W. Hayden, $12.45; 25-5, Frank Casper, $6.00; 31-15, Paul Snyder, $6.85; 28-7, J. W. Clark, $8.47; 28-8, Mrs. J. G. Hmolf, $4.84; 27-12, Burton E. McGuire, $1.25; 33-17, Thomas Hawkins, $9.80; 31-12, Geo. Eaton, $16.50; 31-8, Miss Anna Spencer, $15.65; 27-14, A. K. Stephenson, $4.25; 27-1, H. E. Eastwood, $7.60; 27-2, Mrs. Geo. Hyde, $4.25; 33-10, Mrs. Kate McKenna, $5.50; 30-10, Geo. W. Jones, $6.40; 31-1, Miss Euphemia Faucett, $4.25; 29-9, Jno. M. Stone, $14.75; 30-13, Miss Lulu Tate, $18.45; 32-14, Jno. R. Fell, $9.25; 29-8, A. B. Jennings, $4.20, 34-7, Jno. M. McKinley, $14.87; 26-15, Mrs. T. P. McMenamin, $45.60; 34-9, Mrs. C. W. Jefferson, $4.50; 26-11, Albert Ginglebach, $12.25; 26-16, Frank W. Taylor, $6.50; 28-9, Morris Thatcher, $31.50; 30-9, Jno. M. Gleason, $12.40; 25-6, Walter Kane, $9.20; 32-13, Miss Mabel Neilson, $10.85; 34-13, Martin Newman, $14.85; 30-14, Miss Josie Nicolay, $1.50; 32-3, Fred W. Townsend, $4.75; 33-8, Edgar M. Vail, $4.50; 28-11, J. E. M. Keller, $7.65; 29-10, Harvey Nixon, $11.70; 31-3, Jno. Noble, $7.80; 31-14, Adam Vogel, $5.75; 25-7, Frank M. Wagner, $4.50; 35-3, Chas. Kaehler, $11.75; 32-4, William Nye, $9.25; 25-16, Edward O'Connor, $14.35; 35-8, Henry Kempf,

$4.20; 29–14, Chas. K. Gibson, $2.50; 32–2, H. J. Walker, $4.25; 33–9, Geo. W. Ottinger, $19.24; 30–11, Wm. Kitchen, $13.25; 28–13, Miss Mary Gilles, $7.25; 31–14, Cora Walters, $8.45; 29–7, Theodore Gilles, $9.45; 35–4, Chas. Lake, $12.50; 30–15, Allen H. Oliver, $9.18; 28–12, C. N. Palmer, $11.40; 35–11, H. B. Lehman, $4.60; 26–10, L. K. Grainger, $11.45; 35–7, A. C. Yates, $4.15; 29–15, D. E. Parsons, $4.25; 27–3, Geo. E. Munson, $10.45; 30–12, Frank Zimmer, $9.50; 27–15, Albert Quinn, $9.75.

Hat Department.—52–2, Miss Pauline Sale, $15.75; 50–11, Geo. Heitz, $4.25; 55–1, Samuel Althoff, $6.40; 52–3, Andrew McIntyre, $4.60; 57–1, Richard Smythe, $3.50; 56–3, Wm. Henning, $4.50; 53–2, Mrs. Geo. Anderson, $7.80; 53–1, Jos. E. McGregor, $8.95; 50–5, Paul Scull, $7.50; 57–3, B. W. Hayden, $5.50; 54–6, J. B. Atkinson, $19.80; 59–13, Jno. M. McKinley, $3.65; 51–16, E. V. Neal, $11.85; 56–4, Mrs. Henry Bader, $14.00; 59–2, Thomas Hawkins, $2.50; 51–3, Edwin Short, $14.85; 53–13, Paul Snyder, $19.50; 53–3, Mrs. M. Jacobs, $4.25; 59–1, Clarence W. Campbell, $7.25; 50–6, Frank Naylor, $4.30; 58–11, Harvey Nixon, $4.95; 55–2, R. S. Collins, $3.40; 56–2, Geo. W. Jones, $4.75; 54–2, Miss Anna Spencer, $4.69; 54–15; A. K. Stephenson, $12.55; 58–13, A. B. Jennings, $3.50; 58–12, P. Cassidy, $7.25; 56–14, Jno. Noble, $3.50; 51.14, Jno. Northorp, $7.50; 50–12, Ralph E. Cooke, $7.85; 58–2, Walter Kane, $3.45; 56–13, Frank W. Taylor, $15.40; 50–10, J. E. M. Keller, $4.75; 56–5, J. W. Clark, $14.26; 52–4, William Nye, $14.85; 51–6, Mrs. H. W. Dickinson, $9.25; 58–14, Chas. Kaehler, $4.75; 59–3, Fred W. Townsend, $12.50; 53–4, Lawrence Kiefer, $14.75; 52–15, C. O. Dinwiddie, $8.60; 51–5, Allen H. Oliver, $14.15; 54–4, Alfred Quinn, $12.80; 51–8, Mrs. Wm. Emery, $4.20; 51–15, Wm. Kitchen, $5.75; 58–10, Wm. Underwood, $10.00; 59–14, Adam Vogel, $6.35; 56–1, Miss Sarah Keim, $9.25; 51–7, R. G. Laird, $5.60; 53–14, Peter M. Ward, $4.25; 54–3, H. H. Watterson, $10.45; 52–10, H. B. Lehman, $9.95; 59–12, Frank Zimmer, $12.25; 54–1, Geo. W. Martin, $3.50; 54–16, Miss Euphemia Faucett, $12.45; 50–13, Jayson Rummel, $12.25; 57–2, Mrs. Lottie Mitchell, $9.40; 51–4, Herman Zumm, $12.15; 51–8, Mrs. G. W. Miner, $9.85; 51–5, Jno. M. Gleason, $9.65.

Dress Goods Department.—84–10, Mrs. Kate McKenna, $145.25; 86–2, Mrs. J. G. Rinolf, $18.25; 85–8, Miss Mary Ambler, $16.85; 83–3, Paul Scull, $19.45; 80–2, Walter W. Stern, $75.43; 84–4, Mrs. Emma Adams, $24.25; 83–2, Mrs. Geo. Hyde, $21.75; 78–3, Jno. M. McKinley, $64.35; 76–3, Mrs. T. P. McMenamin, $148.56; 85–9, Mrs M. Jacobs, $17.45; 78–6, George Bauer, $14.20; 78–4, Miss Lulu Tate, $41.50; 81–7, Albert A. Borton, $17.50; 80–3, Mrs. C. W. Jefferson, $26.75; 82–10, Miss Mabel Neilson, $137.45; 76–5, Henry Kempf, $45.75; 80–1, Frank Casper, $16.20; 81–8, Morris Thatcher, $124.17; 76–1, Mrs. H. W. Dickinson, $17.81; 84–9, Miss Sarah Keim, $19.48; 83–1, Miss Josie Nicolay, $31.25; 78–1, Frank Krauss, $48.90; 76–2, Mrs. Wm. Emery, $38.95; 78–5, Edgar M. Vail, $98.50; 79–10, Miss Euphemia Faucett, $44.23; 85–2, H. B. Lehman, $19.85; 85–1, Jno. Noble, $17.48; 78–2, Mrs. Lottie Mitchell, $74.85; 78–7, Miss M. E. Frost, $35.40; 76–7, J. A. Vanderbelt, $23.50; 75–10, Mrs. A. K. Gilbert, $38.25; 86–1, William Nye, $106.24; 76–6, L. V. Maurer, $34.15; 76–4, C. H. Remington, $26.25.

Clothing Department.—109–2, B. W. Hayden, $14.75; 110–1, Miss Pauline Sale, $2.20; 118–2, Geo. McFarlin, $41.45; 116–5, Mrs. Geo. Anderson, $22.60; 100–2, Dr. C. M. Brucker, $42.50; 104–5, Andrew McIntyre, $47.45; 114–3, Richard Smythe, $18.75; 119–5, Mrs. Geo. Hyde, $17.60; 100–5, A. B. Jennings, $36.55; 113–6, Martin Schneider, $18.95; 118–3, Burton E. McGuire, $15.00; 118–1, Clarence W. Campbell, $36.75; 114–6, R. S. Collins, $29.50; 115–5, Jno. M. McKinley, $51.40; 110–2, W. E. Schermerhorn,

$18.45; 117-8, Mrs. C. W. Jefferson, $34.25; 117-3, Walter Kane, $15.50; 111-2, Albert E. Shaw, $24.75; 110-4, Mrs. T. P. McMenamin, $41.50; 116-6, Jno. W. Clark, $37.45; 110-3, C. O. Dinwiddie, $51.45; 104-1, E. V. Neal, $26.50; 100-3, Edwin Short, $19.50; 106-6, J. E. M. Keller, $24.70; 101-3, Chas. Kaehler, $19.25; 104-3, Paul Snyder, $27.30; 119-2, Frank Naylor, $64.85; 107-1, C. G. Davis, $19.09; 115-6, Martin Newman, $35.60; 108-1, Albert Spare, $34.45; 102-3, A. K. Stephenson, $19.50; 114-4, Harvey Nixon, $29.50; 112-4, Frank W. Taylor, $35.00; 119-3, Jno. Noble, $43.25; 101-2, Morris Thatcher, $135.50; 111-13, Wm. Kitchen, $24.50; 108-2, Wm. Underwood, $18.25; 114-5, Chas. Oakley, $44.11; 112-5, Solomon Erb, $38.60; 115-9, J. A. Vanderbelt, $19.75; 102-2, Frank Krauss, $31.50; 111-9, Frank Vick, $35.40; 119-4, Geo. W. Ottinger, $87.40; 106-7, C. N. Palmer, $19.50; 115-1, Albert Ginglebach, $45.80; 117-1, Adam Vogel, $29.28; 112-3, R. G. Laird, $75.50; 107-9, A. C. Yates, $19.45; 109-1, Chas. Lake, $36.40; 117-2, Frank Zimmer, $14.25; 100-4, Alfred Quinn, $15.45; 113-7, Chas. K. Gibson, $40.75; 119-8, Jayson Rummel, $19.50; 115-8, Jno. E. Ziegler, $25.40; 105-3, Geo. W. Martin, $28.35; 105-12, Herman Zumm, $25.10; 105-4, Valentine Ress, $15.25; 107-2, L. K. Grainger, $58.60; 102-1, L. V. Maurer, $28.90.

Re-add the items on all the sheets to satisfy yourself that the footings are correct. Enter the footings in the Summary of Daily Sales as illustrated on page 124. Ascertain the total sales for each Sales Ledger and enter the amount in the Total column. Find the total time sales for each department. The footing of the Sales Ledger totals should equal the footing of the department sales. If found to agree, assemble the Abstract of Time Sales sheets, place a rubber band around them and put them aside. They are not to be handed to the Sales Bookkeepers until they have been proven with the Clerks' Daily Sales, as taken from the Clerks' Summary sheets.

Cash Sales. The cash sales for the day are listed below. The student should remember that in business a sales ticket is prepared in duplicate, by the sales clerk for every sale, and that the entries would be made directly from the *original* sales tickets, instead of from the data as given herewith. In entering the following sales on the Abstract of Cash Sales be sure to give each department credit for its sales, also credit the clerks by number in the proper column, and specify the number of each sales ticket.

For the convenience of the bookkeepers, in business the Abstract of Cash Sales sheets are loose sheets; in this business for the convenience of the student they are furnished in bound form.

Shoe Department.—1-5, $10.20; 8-4, $4.75; 9-5, $9.40; 9-7, $4.64; 10-4, $10.00; 7-10, $14.80; 1-6, $4.50; 11-8, $9.25; 1-12, $13.25; 5-15, $6.15; 10-3, $11.65; 12-8, $11.50; 11-11, $3.00; 3-7, $4.35; 5-1, $10.60; 5-10, $13.25; 6-10, $7.15; 7-4, $12.40; 8-9, $18.25; 9-1, $10.12; 9-14, $14.75; 11-7, $15.00; 13-4, $14.50; 11-10, $3.50; 7-5, $4.50; 12-7, $15.50; 2-13, $15.30; 12-13, $18.45; 8-13, $4.25; 5-11, $13.45; 11-15, $4.30; 5-2, $12.20; 2-14, $12.25; 11-2, $11.50; 10-10, $6.40; 14-5, $4.50; 3-12, $9.74; 15-6, $15.35; 13-9, $13.55; 15-7, $4.49; 3-6, $9.45; 14-9, $3.24; 15-12, $11.15; 3-5, $9.27; 3-2, $9.28; 2-5, $1.50; 5-4, $3.50; 6-6, $25.25; 1-8, $8.45; 8-6, $14.80; 3-1, $4.50; 1-9, $12.25; 10-2, $9.65; 9-3, $24.80; 6-7, $23.51; 5-5, $7.50; 10-7, $14.44; 11-4, $37.46; 13-2, $17.60; 12-10, $4.45; 13-12, $12.10; 4-3, $4.60; 7-7, $7.85; 13-13, $13.14; 5-14, $95.84; 8-7, $7.81; 2-6, $12.81; 9-1, $4.50; 12-2, $10.25; 15-2, $5.00; 11-5, $4.25; 7-8, $8.45; 10-8, $15.85; 14-7, $14.76; 15-3, $11.80; 4-4, $23.50; 9-10, $12.45; 3-3, $11.50; 13-11, $29.20; 12-9, $27.45; 13-1, $37.40; 15-13, $8.75; 12-1, $39.25; 15-14, $12.25; 12-11, $24.50; 14-6,

$10.15; 4–5, $4.25; 9–11, $12.40; 2–4, $4.75; 6–5, $15.40; 5–3, $8.50; 1–7, $4.25; 7–9, $12.75; 1–10, $6.50; 8–5, $20.40; 1–11, $4.50, 6–8, $7.25; 4–2, $3.50; 9–2, $11.10; 10–1, $8.90; 11–3, $14.50; 15–1, $11.70; 13–3, $4.75; 12–4, $3.50; 13–14, $25.00; 8–8, $14.81; 6–9, $10.00; 7–6, $15.40, 9–8, $9.75; 10–6, $18.70; 14–8, $4.85; 11–6, $6.75; 15–4, $13.51; 5–12, $20.50; 4–1, $18.25; 8–12, $10.50; 5–13, $11.40; 10–9, 7.65; 13–10, $4.75; 12–3, $17.40; 15–5, $3.25; 2–15, $14.75; 10–12, $12.80; 12–12, $20.50; 9–9, $4.50; 15–9, $10.00.

Glove Department.—25–3, $5.75; 29–1, $4.37; 31–10, $3.65; 34–1, $6.85; 28–17, $15.65; 27–11, $4.25; 34–2, $14.75; 29–2, $18.45; 26–3, $6.50; 31–4, $11.50; 32–5, $4.75; 33–11, $4.50; 25–15, $4.25; 33–14, $8.45; 30.16, $4.15; 34–15, $9.50; 29–3, $21.50; 32–6, $2.25; 25–4, $7.65; 33–5, $4.25; 35–9, $8.25; 29–11, $8.56; 27–18, $3.25; 28–5, $3.15; 30–17, $4.00; 26–9, $14.25; 33–16, $4.75; 31–5, $10.15; 35–2, $4.45; 33–6, $10.47; 26–12, $4.25; 27–17, $4.50; 25–8, $5.25; 30–7, $4.75; 28–6, $8.57; 25–9, $9.21; 27–4, $10.12; 31–16, $6.55; 35–12, $3.10; 32–15, $14.85; 30–8, $9.47; 31–17, $6.34; 34–12, $10.45; 27–5, $4.25; 33–12, $4.50; 26–4, $43.75; 33–3, $9.45; 34–3, $6.40; 27–10, $64.50; 35–1, $15.10; 28–3, $46.14; 35–6, $18.20; 30–3, $25.49; 34–4, $10.48; 25–13, $34.10; 29–4, $12.38; 35–5, $36.83; 33–2, $4.25; 26–5, $11.40; 34–11, $19.60; 29–5, $10.12; 25–14, $21.50; 32–7, $4.25; 30–4, $10.13; 33–4, $4.85; 32–8, $7.45; 28–4, $6.48; 34–10, $12.40; 29–12, $2.50; 26–8, $14.85; 31–6, $9.80; 30–5, $8.95; 28–15, $16.40; 27–6, $25.50; 32–9, $4.75; 30–6, $6.25; 31–7, $9.60; 25–10, $4.25; 28–16, $3.60; 30–18, $9.50; 27–7, $5.25; 26–13, $4.75; 35–10, $11.50; 25–11, $4.80; 35–13, $12.40; 29–13, $5.25; 32–16, $6.40; 26–14, $9.50; 25–1, $4.50; 28–2, $10.25; 30–2, $7.80; 32–12, $4.50; 26–7, $12.45; 33–1, $16.20; 29–6, $4.50; 34–6, $11.75; 27–9, $9.81; 33–13, $14.40; 31–9, $20.25; 32–11, $7.60; 25–2, $10.75; 34–5, $11.15; 30–1, $4.50; 32–10, $7.35; 26–6, $12.40; 31–8, $19.20; 28–1, $6.25; 27–8, $4.20; 25–12, $11.48.

Hat Department.—53–6, $10.35; 54–7, $12.45; 55–3, $31.50; 56–6, $4.50; 57–4, $10.00; 50–9, $4.25; 53–5, $13.14; 55–4, $6.70; 52–9, $7.65; 51–2, $12.47; 52–11, $18.50; 58–16, $9.78; 53–11, $8.47; 51–9, $10.50; 56–7, $12.47; 57–5, $18.50; 54–8, $7.65; 51–1, $9.75; 55–5, $6.50; 58–9, $12.50; 52–1, $3.50; 53–12, $14.75; 60–6, $9.55; 59–5, $4.37; 54–14, $7.63; 60–4, $8.95; 51–13, $14.85; 55–6, $11.11; 60–5, $25.50; 59–4, $11.40; 60–11, $4.25; 55–7, $6.91; 60–10, $16.25; 50–7, $12.20; 53–7, $4.16; 60–13, $5.45; 57–13, $4.38; 60–7, $9.25; 52–14, $5.29; 50–8, $14.95; 60–8, $8.47; 59–6, $16.80; 60–9, $4.25; 57–12, $12.40; 50–1, $6.25; 57–8, $5.00; 59–10, $8.75; 55–13, $4.75; 54–9, $11.00; 55–14, $4.25; 57–7, $25.00; 56–9, $12.78; 58–3, $19.81; 52–8, $5.85; 58–15, $11.41; 53–10, $3.45; 59–11, $14.91; 58–8, $21.40; 58–4, $19.70; 56–10, $4.75; 58–7, $21.10; 57–6, $18.25; 58–5, $3.25; 50–14, $19.81; 56–8, $8.54; 52–5, $4.25; 55–8, $11.40; 56–12, $4.50; 52–12, $5.25; 51–12, $4.64; 55–9, $3.45; 56–15, $11.05; 50–2, $11.15; 60–14, $3.45; 54–13, $10.80; 55–10, $4.50; 60–1, $9.45; 53–8, $3.50; 59–7, $6.40; 60–2, $4.50; 57–10, $12.50; 60–12, $4.50; 52–13, $3.25; 59–8, $6.40; 57–14, $4.75; 60–3, $10.05; 59–9, $7.80; 57–11, $4.50; 54–10, $14.50; 57–9, $8.75; 50–3, $3.50; 58–6, $12.00; 52–7, $11.75; 55–12, $4.50; 54–11, $5.25; 55–11, $16.40; 56–11, $7.85; 50–15, $12.30; 51–10, $8.50; 54–12, $7.35; 53–9, $9.50; 51–11, $6.15; 52–6, $11.70; 50–4, $18.40.

Dress Goods Department.—80–5, $28.50; 80–6, $17.64; 78–12, $14.80; 76–8, $9.63; 80–4, $20.75; 83–4, $15.40; 79–11, $18.35; 83–5, $9.24; 76–9, $16.41; 80–12, $4.50; 81–9, $8.47; 83–6, $15.35; 80–7, $12.84; 85–10, $6.38; 82–12, $10.50; 79–8, $8.40; 76–10, $14.85; 75–12, $25.50; 84–5, $19.45; 78–8, $31.15; 81–10, $24.25; 82–5, $17.64; 79–9, $20.40; 78–9, $12.80; 84–6, $18.30; 82–6, $3.46; 75–7, $19.45; 84–7, $6.81; 86–5, $4.50; 75–8, $19.27; 78–10, $10.14; 81–5, $14.25; 82–7, $4.85; 75–9, $7.65; 86–6, $24.85; 82–8, $18.56; 86–7,

$15.25; 82-9, $11.75; 86-4, $5.40; 81-6, $24.80; 84-12, $17.40; 86-8, $3.84; 86-12, $9.63; 86-9, $12.50; 85-5, $10.25; 79-3, $28.25; 85-6, $44.84; 86-10, $12.15; 79-4, $16.90; 77-1, $97.60; 80-10, $11.55; 83-7, $19.09; 77-8, $54.75; 79-5, $21.55; 80-8, $19.25; 77-9, $11.08; 79-6, $46.75; 75-4, $16.45; 81-1, $78.60; 77-10, $24.43; 79-7, $11.21; 77-2, $93.84; 82-3, $14.81; 85-3, $18.91; 82-4, $58.45; 85-4, $16.85; 81-2, $31.50; 85-7, $11.50; 86-3, $25.40; 85-11, $19.81; 75-5, $68.48; 86-1, $12.45; 81-3, $14.50; 84-8, $36.25; 86-11, $84.75; 75-6, $12.10; 84-11, $11.40; 81-4, $11.10; 84-3, $25.40; 82-11, $15.40; 83-8, $21.50; 84-2, $54.60; 80-11, $10.40; 83-9, $19.85; 78-11, $14.10; 76-11, $33.75; 83-10, $36.85; 75-11, $7.40; 75-1, $25.00; 79-1, $11.75; 77-5, $21.40; 84-1, $17.60; 77-6, $10.25; 82-1, $14.11; 77-7, $28.35; 80-9, $51.47; 77-3, $14.85; 79-2, $36.45; 75-2, $19.27; 77-4, $35.34; 82-2, $18.36; 75-3, $12.70.

Clothing Department.—107-3, $18.50; 116-4, $12.40; 118-1, $10.00; 107-4, $5.00; 119-1, $3.50; 106-4, $18.46; 103-1, $19.00; 109-7, $23.85; 106-5, $17.63; 105-5, $10.50; 103-5, $11.40; 118-6, $7.65; 116-3, $9.40; 119-6, $14.80; 119-7, $22.75; 105-6, $20.15; 103-6, $46.20; 101-1, $18.45; 100-8, $26.80; 118-7, $18.75; 100-6, $14.20; 101-8, $20.15; 116-7, $1.64; 102-8, $19.45; 116-1, $18.15; 103-8, $17.48; 105-8, $8.00; 101-5, $10.25; 106-8, $12.40; 107-8, $10.75; 100-7, $11.40; 108-8, $6.25; 117-4, $8.40; 110-8, $29.50; 113-1, $18.24; 111-8, $46.20; 117-5, $4.50; 113-2, $7.25; 112-8, $18.45; 117-6, $16.00; 113-3, $8.40; 117-7, $7.60; 113-4, $4.20; 114-8, $11.40; 103-1, $18.00; 111-7, $26.00; 110-5, $12.00; 115-1, $19.20; 103-2, $10.00; 112-6, $10.50; 115-2, $27.50; 110-6, $54.50; 103-3, $16.40; 107-7, $15.75; 110-7, $33.00; 104-7, $10.95; 112-7, $24.75; 115-7, $12.40; 111-1, $97.65; 104-6, $55.55; 111-4, $12.11; 109-3, $10.15; 102-9, $19.48; 102-4, $94.75; 109-4, $19.27; 102-5, $21.25; 100-9, $10.10; 105-1, $11.40; 108-3, $56.76; 101-6, $40.15; 105-9, $89.25; 108-9, $41.50; 108-1, $14.25; 112-9, $21.25; 114-9, $104.85; 115-3, $15.00; 118-8, $12.85; 111-5, $54.85; 113-5, $37.60; 109-8, $25.00; 111-6, $31.25; 100-1, $10.00; 108-5, $79.40; 113-8, $11.15; 108-7, $96.50; 111-7, $38.45; 108-6, $25.00; 101-7, $28.50; 107-6, $18.00; 106-3, $25.25; 107-5, $11.80; 103-7, $6.75; 114-1, $12.40; 104-1, $16.50; 118-5, $24.75; 114-2, $13.20; 104-2, $11.85; 102-7, $45.80; 105-7, $14.75, 116-2, $10.00; 109-6, $12.85; 112-1, $8.48; 109-5, $17.00; 112-2, $15.25; 106-1, $8.05; 102-6, $14.50; 106-2, $6.50; 101-1, $19.00.

Foot the department columns of the Abstract of Cash Sales sheets to ascertain the total sales of each department for the day. Go over your addition a second time.

Clerks' Daily Sales. In business the clerks hand in their summary sheets to the General Bookkeeping Department once a day, where the daily footings are verified and entered in the Clerks' Daily Sales book. The object of this book or record is explained on page 125. In this business only the daily footings of the Summary sheets are given, which the student will enter in the Clerks' Daily Sales record as illustrated on page 125. Omit two lines after the last name in each department.

Shoe Department. Clerk 1, $140.42; 2, $166.72; 3, $107.97; 4, $152.87; 5, $240.74; 6, $161.19; 7, $116.90; 8, $139.06; 9, $148.31; 10, $142.39; 11, $150.91; 12, $224.69; 13, $232.59; 14, $110.44; 15, $139.80.

Glove Department. 25, $169.84; 26, $228.60; 27, $184.53; 28, $206.03; 29, $134.48; 30, $168.67; 31, $156.68; 32, $110.35; 33, $140.96; 34, $168.95; 35, $150.68.

Hat Department. 50, $143.71; 51, $160.81; 52, $130.74; 53, $126.82; 54, $162.52; 55, $121.77; 56, $132.10; 57, $142.43; 58, $169.05; 59, $121.33; 60, $123.87.

Dress Goods Department. 75, $271.52; 76, $409.61; 77, $391.89; 78, $160.69; 79, $267.24; 80, $298.28; 81, $352.14; 82, $328.34; 83, $219.13; 84, $399.19; 85, $200.17; 86, $359.81.

Clothing Department. 100, $186.50; 101, $291.25; 102, $295.13; 103, $145.23; 104, $196.10; 105, $252.75; 106, $132.49; 107, $209.91; 108, $372.36; 109, $159.27; 110, $242.60; 111, $365.16; 112, $247.78; 113, $176.51; 114, $289.71; 115, $282.05; 116, $114.64; 117, $129.78; 118, $197.20; 119, $273.65.

Find the footings of each department and enter them in red ink. Next find the total of the red ink footings.

Cashier's Statements. The cash receipts (other than cash sales) and payments are listed below. Enter them on the proper detailed statement blanks furnished in your supplies.

Receipts. *Sales Ledgers.* Miss Lillian Betts, $8.10; Paul Snyder, $21.55; Andrew McIntyre, $26.75; Thomas Hawkins, $15.00; Mrs. Geo. Hyde, $24.00; J. W. Clark, $55.00; Miss Anna Spencer, $9.48; Frank Naylor, $55.00; A. K. Stevenson, $25.00; Geo. Eaton, $14.97; Mrs. C. W. Jefferson, $36.00; Mrs. Wm. Emery, $23.15; Miss Lulu Tate, $41.50; Miss Josie Nicolay, $25.00; Frank W. Taylor, $50.00; Miss Euphemia Faucett, $50.00; Henry Kempf, $25.00; Jno. M. Gleason, $10.75; Harvey Nixon, $41.20; Chas. K. Gibson, $20.00; Wm. Kitchen, $21.25; Miss Mary Gilles, $15.00; H. B. Lehman, $30.50; L. K. Granger, $40.00; Edgar M. Vail, $100.00; Allen H. Oliver, $20.00; Mrs. G. W. Miner, $20.00; Geo. E. Munson, $10.00.

Payments. *General Ledger.* The advertising manager has contracted for $\frac{1}{4}$ page space in the leading local papers for one month. The price agreed upon is $1200.00, with a discount of 2 per cent. for cash. It has been paid, less discount; charge the net amount to Advertising account.

Purchase Ledger. Turn to your Abstract Purchase Ledger and ascertain the accounts that will have to be paid *to-day* to take advantage of the discount offered. Enter all such amounts on a Payments-Purchase Ledger statement. Be sure to record the discount in the proper column.

Find the footings of all the statements and enter them on the Cashier's Abstract Statement. Be sure to include the amount of cash sales. Find the balance of cash on hand.

The statements are now ready to be handed to the General Bookkeeping Department, where they will be verified, the items on the Cashier's Abstact Statement entered in the Abstract Cash Account, and the detailed statements handed to the various departments where they belong. This you will now do. Be sure to place the detailed statements in the filing envelopes of the proper bookkeepers.

The footings of the department columns of the Abstract of Cash Sales sheets are entered in the Summary of Daily Sales and the total is ascertained and extended into the Total column. This total should agree with the amount of cash received from the cash sales as exhibited by the Cashier's Abstract Statement.

Note.—In business the Abstract of Cash Sales sheets would be verified with the sales tickets by the General Bookkeeper, after which the sales tickets would be filed away with the Abstract of Cash Sales sheets in consecutive order.

Foot the Department and Total columns of the Summary of Daily Sales and write the footings in red ink. Next compare the footings with the department and total footings of the Clerks' Daily Sales record. If they agree you will place the Abstract of Daily Sales sheets in the proper envelopes for the sales ledger bookkeepers.

Clerks' Time. The time of the clerks is as follows; enter same in the Pay Roll: Clerks numbers 1, 2, 3, 4, 5, 6, 7, 8, 9, 10, 11, 12, 13, 14, 25, 26, 28, 29, 30, 31, 32, 33, 35, 50, 51, 52, 53, 54, 55, 56, 57, 58, 60, 75, 76, 77, 78, 79, 80, 81, 82, 83, 84, 86, 100, 101, 102, 103, 105, 106, 107, 108, 109, 110, 111, 112, 113, 114, 116, 118, 119, have worked full time. Numbers 15, 34, 59, 117 have worked ½ day each. Numbers 27, 85, 104, 115 worked ¾ of a day each. (Numbers 27 and 104 were sick; make a record of it.)

Posting. Open accounts and post to the General Ledger as previously instructed. Post the items on the Payments Purchase Ledger sheet to the Abstract Purchase Ledger. Don't fail to record the discounts in the discount column. The items on the Abstract of Time Sales sheets are not to be posted by the student, as the sales ledger bookkeepers are supposed to do that. Post the total sales for each Sales Ledger as exhibited in the Summary of Daily Sales to its proper account in the General Ledger. Check over the posting. Examine all the filing envelopes to see if all the documents are filed in the proper envelopes.

Present books and filing envelopes for inspection.

The partners have begun negotiations for the purchase of a glove manufacturing plant, which is for sale at a very low price.

FRIDAY, JULY 3, 189-.

Purchases. The purchases to be entered to-day are listed below. Enter them as previously instructed.

CLOTHING DEPARTMENT. Isaac & Garson Co., July 1, 2/10, net 30, $872.40; Strauss & Kohn, July 1, 3/10, net 30, $1282.22.

HAT DEPARTMENT. Jno. Gilles & Sons, July 1, 2/10, net 30, $582.49.

SHOE DEPARTMENT. Martin & Winter Co., July 2, 2/5, net 20, $265.29.

Credit Sales. The credit sales are listed below; enter them on Abstract of Time Sales sheets as previously instructed.

SHOE DEPARTMENT. 12-15, Julius Hanser, $12.00; 6-22, C. L. Behrns, $12.00; 3-19, Jno. C. McCarthy, $12.34; 10-19, Wm. Sassaman, $16.75; 13-17, Richard Smythe, $4.75; 1-21, Geo. McFarlan, $11.00; 14-13, Mrs. Jno. R. Cassel, $9.20; 14-22, C. W. Hammond, $9.50; 13-23, Alonzo Hicks, $13.25; 13-16, Henry Cooper, $18.25; 7-23, Thos. McElwain, $25.30; 2-19, Albert E. Shaw, $9.40; 5-18, Walter Shearer, $4.64; 2-25, Burton E. McGuire, $9.40; 4-19, C. O. Dinwiddie, $15.80; 1-15, Chas. Harrington, $14.75; 2-23, Samuel Halderman, $18.25; 5-19, Chas. Dodson, $8.95; 13-21; Edwin McKenzie, $14.85; 6-21, Edwin Short, $10.00; 12-23, Hiram Simpson, $14.80; 10-21, E. A. McMickle, $11.40; 10-22, Geo. Engert, $19.60; 3-18, Wm. Inman, $9.75; 4-22, Mrs. M. Jacobs, $9.75; 1-17, Jno. E. Eberhard, $9.85; 3-21, E. V. Neal, $13.75; 9-22, Paul Steele, $12.48; 1-18, Walter W. Stern, $11.65; 11-14, Geo. N. Nash, $9.30; 7-24, Gustav Fisher, $13.45; 5-21, J. A. Joseph, $8.15; 7-22, Wm. Johnson, $13.25; 8-23, Jno. B. Fowler, $11.40; 1-16, Andrew J. Nellis, $8.50; 14-23, Fred W. Townsend, $6.15; 10-18, Wm. Vanderpool, $11.25; 15-21, Martin Newman, $9.84; 2-24, Jno. M. Gleason, $15.71; 1-23, Miss Chrissa Katz, $13.45; 3-20, Mrs. A. K. Gilbert, $12.40; 11-25, Benjamin New, $14.80; 3-21, J. A. Vanderbelt, $3.00; 8-22, William Noyes, $13.45; 15-22, Hugh J. O'Brien, $12.84; 3-23, Chas. K. Gibson, $12.75; 12-14, Henry Kurtz, $9.25; 8-21, Chas. Kaehler, $9.50; 5-20, Dr. D. S. Goble, $15.80; 7-27, Geo. W. Ottinger, $7.60; 6-20, Jos. Vernan, $4.35; 14-15, Ira P. Wetzel, $18.25; 6-23, W. S. Osborn, $8.00; 1-25, Theodore Gilles, $14.80; 7-15, Samuel Kelly,

$11.40; 9–23, A. J. Kinneman, $11.40; 5–26, E. G. Osgood, $12.36; 8–25, Cora Walters, $10.60; 15–20, Frank Krauss, $8.65, 5–22, Wm. B. Knight, $4.25; 3–28, Miss Sadie B. Koehler, $14.75, 7–14, A. C. Yates, $10.12; 10–23, Wm. Young, $3.25; 9–26, S. P. Patton, $4.50; 4–20, L. K. Grainger, $9.75; 14–21, L. L. Leaver, $11.40; 8–24, Irving A. Penny, $4.50; 11–22, Jno. Zoll, $7.15; 6–24, Miss Anna K. Seager, $12.40; 6–19, A. Messinger, $13.25; 4–21, Leopold Rice, $16.85.

Glove Department. 27–35, Jno. C. McCarthy, $9.25; 28–18, Wm. Sassaman, $41.50; 26–23, Julius Hauser, $5.65; 27–22, Samuel Althoff, $2.15; 32–17, Miss Mary Ambler, $1.85; 33–25, Wm. Henning, $10.10; 31–24, Richard Smythe, $2.25; 26–24, Ed. McCormick, $13.85; 30–34, Thos. McElwain, $14.25; 30–24, Martin Schneider, $7.65; 31–20, Alonzo Hicks, $4.75; 25–31, Jno. H. Alvey, $5.40; 28–19, Henry Beaver, $4.60; 26–31, Miss Sadie Harlan, $6.50; 34–32, Mrs. W. C. Bostwick, $5.20; 31–18, Judson Brown, $2.50; 28–27, Wm. Inman, $11.20; 35–33, Jno. Stalder, $4.25; 33–24, Miss Ella McMaster, $4.65; 34–33, E. A. McMickle, $19.81; 32–28, Miss Anna K. Seager, $8.25; 35–19, Mrs. M. Jacobs, $7.60; 27–21, Mrs. Henry Bader, $7.50; 25–21, C. L. Behrns, $3.00; 30–26, J. A. Joseph, $10.90; 29–18, Walter Shearer, $8.56; 28–28, E. V. Neal, $9.35; 35–18, Geo. N. Nash, $4.20; 26–33, Edwin Short, $3.25; 25–32, Wm. Johnson, $12.75; 30–23, R. S. Collins, $6.80; 32–20, P. Cassidy, $11.50; 27–29, Miss Chrissa Katz, $5.25; 33–26, Hiram Simpson, $3.15; 26–25, Andrew J. Nellis, $6.85; 28–31, Benjamin New, $9.45; 32–19, Albert Spillman, $4.00; 31–19, Henry Kurtz, $4.25; 29–28, Mrs. Edwin Dalton, $11.75; 34–16, C. O. Dinwiddie, $7.65; 29–20, A. J. Kinnman, $9.85; 27–32, Paul Steele, $2.25; 31–23, Mrs. E. Nichols, $10.55; 30–35, William Noyes, $8.74; 25–22, Walter W. Stern, $4.75; 33–34, Frank Krauss, $10.55; 33–33, C. G. Davis, $9.40; 29–17, W. W. Earnest, $11.40; 25–30, Wm. B. Knight, $9.45; 35–26, Jno. M. Utz, $13.25; 26–26, Wm. Vanderpool, $3.15; 35–15, Geo. Engert, $13.25; 34–17, R. G. Laird, $3.50; 25–31, L. L. Leaver, $9.84; 32–32, Jno. E. Eberhard, $12.34; 35–16, J. A. Vanderbelt, $4.75; 27–30, W. S. Osborn, $11.50; 34–18, E. C. Osgood, $19.38; 25–23, M. C. Parker, $4.00; 31–25, Ira P. Wetzel, $10.15; 31–26, Gustav Fisher, $9.80; 33–23, Mrs. H. H. Martin, $4.25; 31–33, A. Messinger, $7.40; 33–27, Jno. B. Fowler, $9.50; 25–35, C. C. Waite, $4.45; 30–25, S. P. Patton, $12.25; 35–17, Miss Amie Rathbun, $18.50; 27–20, Peter M. Ward, $10.47; 34–26, Mrs. A. K. Gilbert, $9.65; 35–34, Mrs. G. W. Miner, $4.25; 27–19, Dr. D. S. Goble, $11.45; 29–19, Jno. V. Redmond, $12.81; 32–29, Leopold Rice, $11.35; 25–29, Jno. Zoll, $4.25; 32–18, L. V. Maurer, $6.85; 28–29, Valentine Ress, $2.25.

Hat Department. 51–28, Jno. C. McCarthy, $4.50; 58–30, Wm. Sassaman, $6.50; 50–21, J. W. Harrison, $3.50; 52–30, Miss Mary Ambler, $6.75; 56–24, Jno. H. Alvey, $2.60; 51–20, Alonzo Hicks, $4.50; 56–23, Miss Susan Smythe, $12.50; 53–15, Mrs. E. McDaniel, $3.50; 59–25, Ed. McCormick, $8.45; 51–27, Martin Schneider, $3.50; 56–29, Miss Sadie Harlan, $12.25; 51–26, Albert A. Borton, $3.50; 50–30, Geo. P. Bower, $9.50; 57–29, Wm. Johnson, $5.50; 56–30, Jno. Stalder, $14.75; 58–17, Geo. McFarlan, $4.25; 60–23, Thos. McElwain, $13.15; 57–27, Albert E. Shaw, $12.50; 55–18, Henry Kasser, $3.75; 57–26, C. L. Behrns, $6.50; 59–21, Miss Maggie Conway, $27.80; 55–29, Henry Kurtz, $3.50; 59–23, Hiram Simpson, $9.55; 51–17, Burton E. McGuire, $2.50; 58–29, Miss Ella McMaster, $10.25; 57–28, Albert Spillman, $2.50; 58–20, Samuel Kelly, $5.75; 54–25, Henry Cooper, $9.75; 57–25, Mrs. Edwin Dalton, $19.70; 60–22, A. J. Kinneman, $4.50; 53–17, Paul Steele, $5.75; 53–28, Geo. N. Nash, $6.50; 50–24, Andrew J. Nellis, $12.85; 54–24, Jno. M. Stone, $7.63; 50–22, Wm. B. Knight, $11.50; 54–26, C. G. Davis, $12.75; 50–20, W. W. Earnest, $17.60; 54–22, Miss Sadie B. Koehler, $25.00; 60–25, Jno. M. Utz,

$10.50; [illegible]-17, Edgar M. Vail, $15.25; 58-18, Martin Newman, $4.25; 60-24, Benjamin New, $12.65; 59-24, Wm. Vanderpool, $16.25; 55-19, L. L. Leaver, $4.65; 52-26, Solomon Erb, $7.85; 56-25, Geo. Eaton, $21.80; 54-24, A. Messinger, $10.00; 51-18, Jos. Vernan, $12.20; 55-16, William Noyes, $3.75; 58-19, Hugh J. O'Brien, $5.25; 50-25, Ira P. Wetzel, $4.16; 59-22, H. E. Eastwood, $20.00; 56-26, Jno. E. Eberhard, $3.25; 51-19, Jno. R. Fell, $3.50; 50-23, L. V. Maurer, $5.35; 52-28, Frank M. Wagner, $19.25; 51-23, H. J. Walker, $15.47; 60-29, Geo. W. Ottinger, $3.25; 59-29, M. C. Parker, $2.50; 53-16, C. C. Waite, $12.50; 60-30, S. P. Patton, $12.15; 55-15, Miss Amie Rathbun, $19.75; 54-30, Wm. Young, $9.95; 50-31, Jno. B. Fowler, $3.75; 52-27, Mrs. A. K. Gilbert, $6.20; 51-30, Chas. K. Gibson, $1.50; 53-18, Dr. D. S. Goble, $1.50.

Dress Goods Department. 82-15, C. W. Hammond, $45.25; 82-13, Mrs. Geo. Anderson, $29.40; 75-18, Jos. E. McGregor, $44.50; 84-14, Miss Susan Smythe, $38.40; 82-17, Albert E. Shaw, $18.56; 84-11, Miss Ella McMaster, $31.85; 83-17, Henry Beaver, $16.45; 84-13, Chas. Harrington, $26.25; 77-18, Miss Sadie Harlan, $35.20; 86-24, Mrs. W. C. Bostwick, $18.50; 75-20, E. V. Neal, $34.15; 86-16, Frank M. Wagner, $17.75; 80-19, Peter M. Ward, $34.50; 76-18, Hugh J. O'Brien, $47.85; 80-17, Miss Lillian Betts, $24.90; 82-16, Miss Chrissa Katz, $28.40; 79-19, Miss Sadie B. Koehler, $13.50; 75-17, Mrs. Henry Bader, $42.60; 83-19, Mrs. Maggie O'Neill, $49.25; 80-18, Cora Walters, $31.25; 82-14, E. G. Osgood, $43.25; 81-12, R. S. Collins, $18.75; 77-19, Mrs. H. H. Martin, $24.15; 79-15, Alfred Quinn, $19.27; 83-18, Mrs. Jno. R. Cassel, $18.75; 83-24, Miss Maggie Conway, $31.47; 77-17, Miss Amie Rathbun, $10.15; 76-17, Mrs. Edwin Dalton, $28.40; 76-19, Leopold Rice, $10.10; 79-14, Chas. Dodson, $26.76; 78-13, Wm. Young, $40.25; 77-16, Chas. B. Elliot, $48.14; 79-16, Jno. Zoll, $19.75.

Clothing Department.—107-11, Jno. C. McCarthy, $65.00; 115-17, J. W. Harrison, $22.20; 105-11, Wm. Sassaman, $19.25; 105-12, Samuel Althoff, $24.90; 117-16, J. G. Atkinson, $94.80; 117-17, Jno. Stalder, $25.00; 111-14, Geo. Heitz, $25.75; 101-15, Mrs. E. McDaniel, $31.25; 108-12, Jos. E. McGregor, $28.50; 101-14, Wm. Henning, $21.45; 112-16, Hiram Simpson, $28.40; 114-11, Jno. H. Alvey, $17.60; 103-13, Henry Beaver, $32.50; 116-9, Albert Spillman, $25.25; 110-9, Jno. M. Stone, $35.45; 107-17, Alonzo Hicks, $25.30; 111-13, Samuel Halderman, $42.75; 110-17, Andrew J. Nellis, $95.75; 112-13, Benjamin New, $91.25; 108-10, Thos. Hawkins, $14.25; 117-12, J. J. Sweeney, $43.50; 116-10, Judson Brown, $21.75; 105-13, Mrs. Henry Bader, $19.25; 110-10, Fred. W. Townsend, $19.90; 113-17, J. A. Joseph, $45.50; 101-16, Mrs. E. Nichols, $78.40; 112-14, William Noyes, $105.25; 108-11, Henry Kasser, $28.25; 116-8, Wm. Vanderpool, $34.18; 114-10, C. L. Behrns, $27.75; 108-13, Mrs. Jno. R. Cassel, $27.75; 101-10, Ira P. Wetzel, $25.50; 103-11, Henry Kurtz, $21.75; 101-13, Edward O'Connor, $125.50; 109-15, E. G. Osgood, $102.15; 114-12, M. C. Parker, $45.00; 112-12, A. J. Kinneman, $19.75; 111-15, Frank M. Wagner, $25.50; 109-17, P. Cassidy, $47.83; 110-16, Ralph E. Cooke, $37.19; 103-11, H. J. Walker, $28.75; 109-14, L. L. Leaver, $47.80; 106-17, Mrs. H. H. Martin, $14.85; 103-12, S. P. Patton, $17.50; 107-10, Irving A. Penny, $11.40; 104-12, Mrs. G. W. Miner, $45.75; 102-11, Peter M. Ward, $25.25; 112-15, Henry Cooper, $15.55; 101-17, H. E. Eastwood, $21.75; 104-15, W. W. Watkins, $40.00; 100-14, Aug. Morely, $33.75; 100-15, Leopold Rice, $14.25; 101-11, Wm. Young, $19.50; 102-10, Jno. B. Fowler, $13.75; 101-14, Jno. E. Eberhard, $33.43; 109-16, Jacob Froehlich, $75.00.

Foot the columns of the Abstract of Time Sales sheets. Verify your footings and enter them in the Summary of Daily Sales as previously instructed. Prove the totals of the department columns with the sales ledger totals, after which assemble the Abstract of Time Sales sheets and lay them aside as previously instructed.

Cash Sales. The cash sales are listed below. Enter them on the Abstract of Cash Sales sheets as previously instructed. Do not fail to record the clerk and sales ticket numbers for each sale.

SHOE DEPARTMENT.—5-17, $18.70; 2-17, $7.65; 4-16, $4.75; 13-19, $4.50; 8-17, $20.50; 14-17, $12.80; 11-18, $14.75; 7-20, $3.25; 15-17, $17.40; 1-26, $1.75; 10-20, $7.65; 12-25, $11.40; 6-16, $10.50; 15-25, $18.25; 3-14, $13.51; 11-19, $6.75; 4-24, $4.85; 8-26, $18.70; 9-17, $9.75; 15-24, $11.40; 1-18, $10.00; 12-19, $14.81; 4-11, $25.00; 10-13, $23.50; 2-16, $4.75; 15-19, $15.40; 10-25, $8.50; 9-18, $1.25; 7-16, $12.75; 12-18, $26.50; 8-18, $20.40; 13-22, $24.50; 3-16, $7.25; 14-25, $23.50; 10-16, $11.10; 15-26, $8.90; 1-21, $13.50; 9-27, $7.25; 11-26, $14.85; 2-26, $12.60; 7-17, $25.50; 11-27, $16.80; 14-19, $4.75; 5-24, $6.50; 11-23, $4.25; 4-17, $8.45; 2-18, $15.85; 9-21, $4.76; 7-25, $21.80; 6-17, $7.65; 12-16, $3.50; 7-21, $14.76; 11-20, $11.80; 3-22, $23.50; 12-22, $12.45; 8-19, $11.50; 6-25, $4.25; 13-18, $16.80; 9-15, $14.20; 13-25, $3.50; 3-13, $4.11; 14-16, $19.25; 10-24, $21.30; 9-16, $4.15; 15-18, $3.49; 7-13, $18.40; 11-21, $9.85; 10-17, $4.50; 15-23, $12.45; 1-19, $10.00; 3-25, $4.00; 12-17, $3.00; 9-24, $9.75; 12-26, $12.46; 2-21, $9.28; 2-22, $4.50; 3-17, $24.80; 14-26, $12.75; 8-20, $31.50; 4-23, $9.87; 3-27, $3.25; 9-25, $12.15; 1-27, $4.75; 14-24, $18.45; 5-23, $16.90; 15-27, $3.75; 14-20, $21.38; 6-18, $15.25; 4-25, $13.25; 2-20, $6.15; 5-16, $11.65; 8-14, $9.35; 12-24, $6.40; 13-20, $7.38; 14-18, $21.50; 1-22, $12.25; 15-16, $10.10; 10-15, $3.50; 9-20, $8.40; 5-25, $4.75; 7-19, $15.25; 3-26, $9.37; 11-17, $12.85; 8-15, $14.75; 4-26, $12.00; 3-15, $9.95; 6-15, $4.87; 12-21, $16.40; 11-24, $9.12; 7-26, $13.45; 10-14, $4.95; 13-15, $11.15; 15-15, $15.50; 4-15, $18.25; 1-20, $11.50; 12-20, $15.35; 9-19, $13.55; 8-16, $21.25; 11-16, $3.50; 7-18, $4.75; 13-21, $18.40; 4-27, $9.45; 6-14, $20.25.

GLOVE DEPARTMENT.—26-21, $4.50; 25-18, $10.25; 28-25, $7.80; 29-23, $14.80; 27-31, $20-25; 26-28, $7.60; 29-32, $11.48; 34-20, $9.81; 27-28, $7.35; 34-29, $6.25; 33-21, $4.20; 27-24, $19.20; 35-22, $12.45; 33-20, $16.20; 31-29, $11.15; 26-32, $7.35; 29-30, $24.50; 30-19, $5.75; 30-31, $4.37; 26-29, $13.65; 28-32, $6.85; 28-23, $15.65; 27-25, $14.25; 32-27, $14.75; 35-23, $18.45; 30-20, $6.50; 31-31, $11.50; 34-24, $24.75; 25-26, $4.50; 35-24, $14.25; 32-23, $8.25; 30-32, $8.56; 29-26, $3.25; 30-33, $23.15; 34-30, $4.00; 26-19, $10.47; 35-25, $4.25; 31-28, $4.50; 35-35, $15.25; 30-29, $4.75; 26-34, $8.57; 32-24, $19.21; 31-35, $10.12; 28-22, $6.55; 26-22, $4.50; 31-21, $19.45; 28-26, $15.10; 29-31, $24.50; 29-22, $18.20; 34-19, $25.49; 30-27, $10.48; 35-21, $34.10; 29-21, $12.38; 25-24, $4.25; 28-33, $11.40; 35-20, $21.50; 31-22, $4.25; 29-33, $14.85; 25-25, $17.60; 33-30, $16.40; 26-17, $4.25; 33-29, $9.60; 30-28, $11.50; 31-32, $12.40; 34-27, $18.00; 27-23, $4.75; 34-28, $3.25; 33-22, $18.45; 28-20, $15.25; 35-30, $4.25; 29-27, $6.75; 34-25, $9.50; 32-33, $11.50; 26-27, $10.12; 29-29, $4.63; 28-21, $15.25; 29-34, $12.80; 32-21, $4.60; 31-34, $18.45; 29-16, $11.63; 27-33, $25.50; 32-30, $4.75; 28-30, $12.40; 33-28, $3.60; 32-22, $6.40; 31-27, $19.60; 27-34, $20.10; 26-18, $4.50; 33-18, $24.50; 25-19, $18.20; 33-31, $12.40; 32-25, $4.25; 33-32, $10.12; 27-27, $4.60; 28-24, $4.75; 30-22, $3.50; 25-20, $12.40; 35-28, $11.15; 33-19, $4.85; 29-24, $7.63; 34-21, $8.45; 32-31, $9.24; 26-30, $3.76; 35-32, $15.75; 32-26, $12.85; 31-30, $4.15; 34-31, $19.27; 25-28, $9.95; 25-33, $3.50; 34-22, $4.80; 35-27, $11.75; 27-26, $10.90; 35-29, $4.15; 34-23, $19.70; 30-21, $4.95; 35-31, $15.73; 29-25, $3.50; 30-30, $20.25; 26-20, $9.45; 25-27, $15.50.

Hat Department. 56-21, $6.20; 54-29, $15.00; 56-22, $8.75; 51-25, $11.45; 56-20, $6.83; 59-20, $5.85; 57-21, $8.54; 59-19, $14.85; 52-24, $7.85; 59-18, $1.15; 50-19, $19.70; 54-19, $1.75; 54-27, $12.85; 52-25, $21.10; 56-18, $10.80; 53-29, $12.50; 51-21, $5.25; 57-23, $6.40; 52-29, $9.50; 56-19, $12.80; 59-26, $15.75; 52-16, $19.80; 56-27, $1.60; 60-28, $8.75; 54-28, $19.70; 59-27, $1.75; 56-28, $9.45; 55-20, $12.50; 53-19, $10.05; 58-21, $7.80; 51-29, $1.50; 58-22, $3.25; 55-21, $4.64; 60-26, $21.40; 55-22, $11.60; 53-20, $15.50; 60-27, $9.80; 58-23, $11.40; 50-29, $10.25; 54-20, $12.50; 52-31, $9.45; 58-24, $4.75; 53-21, $7.80; 54-31, $3.25; 60-17, $10.35; 52-23, $12.45; 51-24, $1.50; 60-16, $3.50; 56-16, $31.25; 59-17, $6.70; 50-16, $18.50; 54-17, $7.65; 52-22, $14.75; 57-15, $9.55; 60-15, $14.85; 59-16, $16.25; 56-17, $4.80; 50-28, $3.15; 51-22, $7.25; 52-32, $4.16; 54-18, $9.25; 57-16, $8.47; 50-17, $16.80; 52-17, $4.25; 59-28, $12.40; 57-22, $5.45; 59-15, $31.25; 53-30, $7.63; 57-17, $9.85; 56-32, $4.63; 57-18, $18.45; 55-31, $16.70; 50-18, $9.40; 55-23, $18.50; 58-25, $14.75; 57-30, $25.50; 58-26, $4.16; 55-30, $4.25; 53-22, $16.80; 60-31, $11.40; 55-21, $3.50; 60-20, $16.85; 59-30, $4.20; 60-21, $5.29; 55-25, $7.49; 58-31, $19.75; 53-23, $18.60; 56-31, $4.75; 58-32, $8.75; 52-21, $14.50; 60-18, $3.50; 53-27, $12.00; 55-28, $11.75; 58-28, $12.30; 52-20, $6.15; 53-26, $11.70; 58-27, $18.40; 57-20, $9.50; 55-26, $12.30; 57-21, $8.75; 50-26, $16.40; 51-23, $7.35; 52-18, $12.00; 57-19, $9.75; 53-25, $8.65; 55-27, $7.70; 60-19, $11.45; 53-21, $3.65; 52-19, $14.85; 50-27, $10.00.

Dress Goods Department. — 86-11, $10.25; 84-23, $14.55; 86-15, $19.25; 86-23, $11.08; 78-16, $24.43; 83-23, $16.75; 82-18, $18.91; 85-22, $10.25; 79-17, $28.25; 79-23, $44.84; 84-18, $12.15; 77-22, $16.90; 79-18, $97.60; 78-17, $14.55; 86-13, $19.05; 77-13, $54.75; 82-19, $21.55; 84-15, $19.25; 86-17, $11.08; 84-19, $16.45; 77-14, $11.60; 76-20, $14.80; 81-13, $18.90; 86-18, $11.50; 77-20, $25.40; 78-20, $11.21; 77-15, $93.84; 79-20, $68.48; 86-19, $14.50; 84-17, $84.75; 76-23, $14.40; 80-20, $15.40; 81-20, $11.10; 81-14, $19.85; 82-20, $14.15; 76-24, $36.85; 84-16, $8.40; 83-20, $17.60; 79-24, $13.45; 84-20, $15.75; 79-12, $10.00; 80-22, $12.40; 79-13, $10.50; 82-22, $21.75; 78-21, $25.00; 75-13; $14.50; 78-11, $8.75; 79-21, $53.50; 77-21, $12.00; 78-15, $11.75; 80-21; $12.30; 75-14, $28.40; 84-21, $45.90; 83-12, $85.25; 85-17, $10.25; 83-21, $14.75; 76-21, $45.75; 85-18, $10.50; 81-16, $18.40; 85-21, 49-50; 85-19, $12.00; 83-13, $17.64; 86-21, $11.40; 85-12, $31.50; 81-22, $12.15; 77-11, $24.85; 75-21, $27.45; 80-16, $16.84; 86-20, $7.63; 84-22, $10.00; 86-22, $20.50; 77-12, $44.85; 75-19, $12.80; 81-15, $19.20; 80-15, $11.65; 75-23, $20.40; 85-20, $15.65; 78-23, $12.84; 76-12, $37.75; 80-14, $40.45; 79-22, $34.75; 78-22, $95.10; 75-22, $4.60; 76-22, $11.85; 81-23, $19.45; 76-13, $31.15; 83-22, $24.80; 80-13, $12.50; 85-13, $45.90; 81-21, $11.63; 81-17, $19.45; 83-16, $10.84; 85-14, $93.80; 81-18, $19.10; 82-21, $35.34; 75-15, $60.50; 85-15, $18.36; 81-19, $9.71; 85-16, $14.44; 78-18, $12.85; 76-15, $85.75; 83-14, $64.85; 76-16, $10.63; 83-15, $18.90; 76-11, $90.90; 78-19, $8.75; 75-16, $16.40.

Clothing Department. 119-15, $25.00; 115-10, $45.75; 119-16, $49.20; 102-16, $24.75; 115-11, $50.20; 101-9, $18.50; 103-17, $12.75; 119-14, $15.40; 106-9, $24.90; 115-12, $75.75; 109-9, $84.73; 103-9, $10.85; 113-12, $24.70; 114-16, $18.46; 109-10, $19.15; 113-13, $17.45; 100-10, $8.00; 104-8, $10.25; 106-10, $14.50; 103-10, $29.50; 104-9, $11.50; 100-11, $18.25; 111-16, $4.50; 109-11, $15.00; 113-14, $18.45; 106-11, $11.90; 115-13, $20.15; 113-15, $31.50; 119-12, $18.75; 106-12, $24.25; 112-10, $17.88; 104-10, $45.00; 112-11, $10.95; 113-16, $38.30; 106-13, $19.35; 115-14, $48.15; 106-14, $16.75; 104-11, $90.35; 115-16, $11.45; 116-13, $24.80; 106-15, $17.50; 115-15, $18.00;

106-16, $45.25; 108-15, $12.40; 113-10, $9.50; 108.14, $10.00; 116-12, $8.00; 102-15, $18.45; 118-13, $19.00; 118-16, $23.85; 105-15, $17.63; 118-14, $10.50; 101-12, $26.80; 118-15, $46.20; 110-15, $9.40; 107-12, $20.15; 113-11, $19.45; 107-13, $29.50; 114-15, $18.24; 101-13, $28.40; 114-14, $19.25; 107-14, $11.50; 114-13, $10.85; 111-10, $35.50; 117-9, $45.75; 107-15, $22.70; 111-11, $46.20; 107-16, $45.25; 111-12, $18.50; 117-10, $17.63; 100-12, $15.25; 100-16, $20.40; 119-9, $18.95; 117-11, $14.30; 118-10, $10.10; 100-13, $19.50; 117-13, $71.81; 116-16, $8.00; 117-14, $16.80; 117-15, $9.15; 109-12, $12.74; 116-14, $38.30; 119-10, $22.75; 116-15, $35.00; 109-13, $17.75; 118-9, $10.95; 110-12, $19.45; 105-10, $11.65; 118-11, $18.00; 110-11, $48.75; 102-14, $29.50; 103-15, $10.85; 113-9, $45.75; 118-12, $46.20; 110-13, $19.50; 105-14, $16.80; 103-16, $22.75; 110-14, $35.00; 116-11, $17.75; 119-13, $12.50; 102-13, $85.50; 102-12, $60.15; 119-11, $16.40.

Foot the money columns of the Abstract of Cash Sales sheets. Verify your addition.

Clerks' Daily Sales. The daily footings of the Clerks' Summary Sheets are given below. Enter them as previously instructed.

Clerk 1, $139.10; 2, $113.57; 3, $178.48; 4, $169.67; 5, $112.95; 6, $122.77; 7, $211.03; 8, $197.40; 9, $116.59; 10, $147.25; 11, $126.47; 12, $158.32; 13, $137.33; 14, $198.18; 15, $147.97; 25, $154.04; 26, $121.12; 27, $186.72; 28, $189.35; 29, $225.27; 30, $164.35; 31, $167.22; 32, $151.94; 33, $171.92; 34, $218.46; 35, $253.08; 50, $172.41; 51, $79.00; 52, $190.86; 53, $157.63; 54, $175.50; 55, $161.58; 56, $172.01; 57, $166.91; 58, $141.56; 59, $200.70; 60, $173.34; 75, $306.30; 76, $466.18; 77, $401.83; 78, $265.48; 79, $470.65; 80, $212.19; 81, $229.84; 82, $276.56; 83, $417.30; 84, $291.85; 85, $312.15; 86, $202.49; 100, $129.40; 101, $271.55; 102, $287.35; 103, $187.20; 104, $401.78; 105, $139.48; 106, $189.25; 107, $230.80; 108, $121.15; 109, $422.15; 110, $320.69; 111, $198.70; 112, $319.03; 113, $250.60; 114, $157.15; 115, $291.65; 116, $213.03; 117, $338.74; 118, $184.80; 119, $178.95.

Find the footings of each merchandise department and enter them in red ink. Next find the total of the footings.

Clerks' Time. The time of the clerks is as follows. Clerks numbers 1, 2, 3, 4, 5, 6, 7, 8, 9, 10, 11, 12, 13, 14, 15, 25, 26, 27, 28, 29, 30, 31, 32, 33, 34, 35, 50, 51, 52, 53, 54, 55, 57, 58, 59, 60, 75, 76, 78, 79, 80, 81, 82, 83, 84, 85, 100, 101, 102, 103, 104, 105, 106, 107, 108, 109, 110, 111, 112, 113, 114, 115, 116, 117, 118 have worked full time. Numbers 56 and 77 have worked ½ day each. Numbers 86 and 119 have worked ¾ of a day each.

Ascertain the total time of each clerk for the week and extend it in the Total Time column. Next ascertain the amount of wages due each clerk. The managers of the departments are paid for a full week; the other clerks are paid for their actual time. Be very careful in making the calculations and extensions. Find the footings of each department and enter them in red ink. Next find the total amount of the Pay Roll by adding the red ink footings.

Next ascertain the amount of change required of each denomination as explained in the paragraph entitled "How to Pay Off." The total of the various denominations should agree with the total of the Pay Roll. If it does not, go over your work and locate the error.

Cashier's Statements. The cash receipts (other than cash sales) and payments are listed below. Enter them on the proper detailed statement blanks.

RECEIPTS.—*Sales Ledgers.* J. W. Harrison, $17.95; Miss Pauline Sale, $18.00; Samuel Althoff, $21.20; Jno. C. McCarthy, $50.00; Miss Mary Ambler, $20.30; Richard Smythe, $7.25; Geo. Heitz, $23.15; Wm. Henning, $22.90; Paul Scull, $26.95; J. G. Atkinson, $33.00; Mrs. E. McDaniel, $13.04; Geo. McFarlan, $53.75; Henry Beaver, $12.30; Martin

Schneider, $23.10; Donald M. Hepler, $12.65; W. E. Schermerhorn, $24.20; Dr. C. M. Brucker, $52.00; Andrew McIntyre, $52.05; Joseph E. McGregor, $22.80; Mrs. Henry Bader, $36.25; Albert E. Shaw, $29.12; Alonzo Hicks, $25.00; Edwin Short, $38.00; Clarence W. Campbell, $25.00; Burton E. McGuire, $19.25; Paul Snyder, $46.80; B. W. Hayden, $20.00; Frank Casper, $22.20; Mrs. Kate McKenna, $105.00; Jno. M. McKinley, $75.00; P. Cassidy, $17.25; Mrs. J. G. Hinolf, $45.50; Ralph E. Cook, $25.00; Mrs. T. P. McMenamin, $148.56; A. K. Stephenson, $17.60; Mrs. Geo. Hyde, $27.00; Walter W. Stern, $75.43; Henry Cooper, $50.00; E. V. Neal, $41.35; Wm. Inman, $10.95; Jno. M. Stone, $24.15; Mrs. Edwin Dalton, $25.50; Miss Mabel Neilson, $152.80; Andrew J. Nellis, $85.50; Miss Lulu Tate, $18.45; Mrs. M. Jacobs, $21.70; Frank W. Taylor, $11.01; J. A. Joseph, $44.85; Morris Thatcher, $100.00; Geo. W. Jones, $11.15; C. O. Dinwiddie, $60.05; A. B. Jennings, $21.85; Martin Newman, $50.45; C. G. Davis, $26.94; Miss Josie Nicolay, $27.60; Solomon Erb, $58.00; Harvey Nixon, $19.85; Walter Kane, $12.65; Fred W. Townsend, $17.25; Jno. Noble, $55.25; Geo. Engert, $25.00; Wm. Underwood, $32.75; J. E. M. Keller, $19.90; Edgar M. Vail, $30.50; H. E. Eastwood, $27.04; William Nye, $100.00; Mrs. Wm. Emery, $[illegible]0.00; J. A. Vanderbelt, $25.00; Henry Kurtz, $18.40; Adam Vogel, $24.50; Jno. E. Eberhard, $38.87; Edward O'Connor, $19.60; Miss Euphemia Faucett, $12.00; Ira P. Wetzel, $35.25; Chas. Kaehler, $20.50; Henry Kempf, $24.20; Frank M. Wagner, $14.62; Geo. W. Ottinger, $106.64; Jno. R. Fell, $21.65; H. J. Walker, $50.00; Lawrence Kiefer, $27.00; Wm. Kitchen, $31.65; Peter M. Ward, $11.75; Miss. M. E. Frost, $35.40; Allen H. Oliver, $10.00; E. G. Osgood, $125.00; Jno. B. Fowler, $20.00; W. W. Watkins, $20.00; Miss Sarah Keim, $41.23; C. M. Palmer, $30.90; Albert Ginglebach, $58.05; H. H. Watterson, $14.95; Frank Krauss, $80.40; A. C. Yates, $23.60; Jayson Rummel, $15.00; Mrs. A. K. Gilbert, $38.25; D. E. Parsons, $18.46; Chas. K. Gibson, $15.00; S. P. Patton, $35.00; R. G. Laird, $75.50; Alfred Quinn, $25.20; Wm. Young, $45.00; Chas. Lake, $15.00; Theo. Gilles, $9.45; Miss Amie Rathbun, $14.25; Geo. W. Martin, $31.85; Frank Zimmer, $20.00; Geo. E. Munson, $25.95; Jno. E. Ziegler, $30.15; C. H. Remington, $30.90; L. K. Grainger, $30.05; L. V. Maurer, $63.05; Herman Zumm, $16.70; Valentine Ross, $15.25.

PAYMENTS. *General Ledger.* On a Payments-General Ledger sheet enter the amount of the wages for each department as shown by the Pay Roll. Be sure to charge each separate department account with the wages paid for its account.

Purchase Ledger. On a Payments-Purchase Ledger sheet enter all accounts that are to be paid to-day to be entitled to a discount. Make the proper record of the discount.

Find the footings of all the statements and enter them on the Cashier's Abstract Statement. Have you included the amount of cash sales? Find the balance of cash on hand.

As General Bookkeeper you will now verify the work of the cashier. Enter the items on the Cashier's Abstract Statement in the Abstract Cash Account. Carefully lay aside the statements, but do not file them, until the items have been posted to the proper ledgers.

Enter the footings of the Abstract of Cash Sales sheets in the Summary of Daily Sales, and ascertain the total cash sales. Compare it with the cash sales item on the Cashier's Abstract Statement. Foot the department columns of the Summary of Daily Sales in red ink. Compare the footings with the footings of the Clerks' Daily Sales record. If found to agree place the Abstract of Time Sales sheets in the proper envelopes for the Sales Bookkeepers. If you are unable to make the footings agree, report the discrepancy to the teacher, who will advise you how to proceed to locate the error.

Posting. Post to the General and Purchase Ledgers as previously instructed. Be sure to post the totals of the Sales Ledgers from the Summary of Daily Sales to the proper accounts in the General Ledger. Check over the posting. File all documents in the proper receptacles.

Present books and filing envelopes to the teacher for inspection.

Mr. Abraham Levy, one of the partners, died suddenly to-day. As a death causes a dissolution of the partnership, the business can not be continued until matters are adjusted. Mrs. Sarah Levy, his sole heir, has consented to sell the interest of her late husband to the surviving partners at a discount of five per cent. of inventory value. It will be necessary to close the books to ascertain the deceased partner's interest. Preparatory to doing so an account of stock is to be taken. Arrangements have been made whereby some of the clerks have agreed to take account of stock during the holidays (Fourth of July and Sunday) so that the business may be continued without interruption on Monday. These clerks are to receive pay for double time, which will be handed in and recorded on Monday.

NOTE.—The five per cent. discount from the deceased partner's interest is intended to pay for the time and trouble involved in taking an inventory and closing the books, to ascertain his interest.

MONDAY, JULY 6, 189–.

Purchases. Record the purchases listed below as previously instructed.

CLOTHING DEPARTMENT.—Kleinhans & Simmonson, July 2, 2/5, net 30, $982.42; Streng & Thalheimer, July 2, 3/5, net 60, $792.45.

HAT DEPARTMENT.—H. H. Hendricks Co., July 2, 2/5, net 20, $742.98; Wm. Enderlin & Co., July 1, 2/5, net 30, $382.40.

DRESS GOODS DEPARTMENT.—Cahart, Meyers & Co., July 1, 3/10, net 30, $1229.26; Samuel Sloane & Co., July 1, 3/10, net 30, $872.93; Harry Whitehead & Son, July 2, 2/10, net 30, $1222.80; Dobson & Graham, July 2, 3/10, net 60, $1392.19.

Credit Sales. Record the credit sales listed below as previously instructed.

SHOE DEPARTMENT.—14–28, Miss Susan Smythe, $10.34; 1–28, J. G. Atkinson, $76.40; 13–29, Frank R. Heath, $7.45; 8–28, Robt. D. McCoy, $20.25; 9–38, Ed. McCormick, $19.40; 6–27, Jno. Hess, $13.75; 9–28, Mrs. Emma Adams, $12.80; 12–31, Mrs. J. G. Hinolf, $15.50; 2–34, E. J. McLain, $14.60; 10–37, Peter McFetters, $12.37; 11–37, Walter Hallowell, $12.50; 10–36, Geo. P. Bower, $14.60; 10–32, Geo. N. Smith, $4.75; 14–38, Paul Scull, $10.15; 6–28, W. E. Schermerhorn, $12.50; 2–33, George Bauer, $9.00; 5–28, Miss Sadie Harlan, $5.00; 3–36, Mrs. S. S. Neff, $12.25; 13–31, Chas. Oakley, $4.50; 14–29, Edward Jessup, $12.50; 1–33, Walter Kane, $6.25; 9–36, Mrs. W. C. Bostwick, $7.40; 13–28, Miss Frances M. Schreier, $6.25; 10–33, Jno. M. Small, $4.20; 7–37, Judson Brown, $12.00; 12–30, Henry Kasser, $9.25; 6–37, Mrs. Maggie O'Neill, $4.50; 4–38, C. M. Palmer, $9.25; 6–38, Jno. R. Kennedy, $12.80; 3–35, Albert A. Borton, $9.50; 7–35, Albert Spare, $9.50; 11–36, Benjamin Spring, $5.45; 13–30, Mrs. T. F. Campbell, $10.50; 8–29, Mrs. A. S. Klein, $11.48; 14–30, Frank W. Page, $11.60; 2–35, Silas Lapham, $6.25; 1–37, Frank Casper, $8.50; 12–28, Miss Maggie Conway, $9.50; 1–32, J. J. Sweeney, $11.70; 12–29, Miss Lulu Tate, $6.25; 11–38, Wm. Dobbins, $19.75; 3–37, Geo. W. Martin, $7.75; 15–28, Jno. V. Redmond, $14.90; 10–35, M. M. Mahoney, $12.85; 8–27, Mrs. Edwin Dalton, $6.70; 5–29, Benton Thomas, $3.50; 3–38, Jno. M. Utz, $19.81; 15–39, F. J. Earl, $7.80; 6–36, Mrs. Wm. Emery, $27.65; 9–37, Mrs. Lottie Mitchell, $12.65; 7–38, Jayson Rummel, $8.75;

15-29, Mrs. Wm. M. Frantz, $9.75; 2-36, Frank Vick, $14.25; 10-34, Harvey Vincent, $7.64; 12-27, Jacob Froehlich, $12.85; 6-26, Aug. Morely, $14.80; 4-36, Miss M. E. Frost, $7.40; 8-30, C. C. Waite, $8.40; 9-29, Mrs. Emma Wallace, $4.65; 1-39, Albert Ginglebach, $9.40; 7-36, W. W. Watkins, $11.60; 10-38, Walter Reynolds, $12.25; 5-38, A. A. Weaver, $4.25; 9-39, Frank C. Glasser, $9.40; 5-27, L. V. Maurer, $10.50; 4-37, Valentine Ross, $19.24; 8-40, Jos. A. Webster, $9.30.

Glove Department.—35-42, Miss Susan Smythe, $4.50; 30-48, Robt. D. McCoy, $14.75; 26-48, Frank R. Heath, $9.60; 25-36, Mrs. Geo. Anderson, $6.20; 28-48, Mrs. Emma Adams, $6.00; 33-35, C. W. Hammond, $4.25; 26-47, Edwin McKenzie, $11.15; 26-46, Geo. N. Smith, $5.25; 25-49, Paul Seull, $4.75; 33-36, E. J. McLain, $10.85; 31-36, Miss Mamie McNeill, $8.35; 26-39, Alonzo Hicks, $3.60; 31-37, Geo. P. Bower, $6.40; 32-36, Jno. Hess, $9.50; 28-46, Peter McFetters, $4.75; 34-36, Frank Naylor, $7.65; 35-36, Miss Frances M. Schreier, $4.50; 25-1, Jno. M. Small, $3.45; 31-46, Mrs. S. S. Neff, $14.36; 33-46, Chas. Harrington, $9.84; 32-45, Miss Lillian Betts, $3.25; 27-36, Dr. C. M. Brucker, $3.50; 29-45, Samuel Halderman, $4.85; 33-45, Mrs. E. Nichols, $9.86; 27-37, Albert Spare, $4.64; 34-50, Benjamin Spring, $11.05; 28-45, Charles Northrop, $7.47; 34-46, Chas. Oakley, $4.21; 32-47, Walter Hallowell, $5.25; 33-44, Mrs. T. F. Campbell, $6.25; 34-37, Miss Maggie Conway, $4.85; 34-35, William Jackson, $4.25; 30-49, Mrs. Maggie O'Neill, $12.39; 28-35, Henry Kasser, $7.50; 29-47, Ralph E. Cooke, $6.50; 30-46, Samuel Kelly, $7.45; 30-47, C. M. Palmer, $4.25; 32-37, Frank W. Page, $9.21; 33-1, J. J. Sweeney, $3.55; 27-49, Benton Thomas, $4.25; 32-46, O. W. Perry, $4.15; 33-47, Jno. R. Kennedy, $4.75; 35-46, Henry Cooper, $5.25; 29-46, Lawrence Keifer, $6.56; 25-44, D. E. Parsons, $4.25; 25-43, Jos. Vernan, $4.75; 35-2, Frank Vick, $6.55; 35-37, Harvey Vincent, $3.10; 32-49, Irving A. Penny, $9.45; 34-47, Mrs. Emma Wallace, $8.24; 26-1, W. W. Watkins, $8.45; 28-47, Wm. Dobbins, $4.75; 25-45, F. J. Earl, $9.45; 31-48, Mrs. A. S. Klein, $5.25; 31-47, Chas. C. Quick, $4.75; 28-2, H. H. Watterson, $3.15; 26-37, Jayson Rummel, $2.25; 31-38, Mrs. William Emery, $12.70; 32-35, Miss Sarah Keim, $14.44; 28-34, Mrs. Wm. M. Frantz, $12.25; 34-48, A. A. Weaver, $4.15; 32-34, Jacob Froehlich, $6.25; 28-50, Jos. A. Webster, $8.46; 35-49, Walter Reynolds, $21.75; 26-38, Miss Sadie B. Koehler, $10.25; 33-43, Miss Mary Gilles, $3.50; 29-48, C. H. Remington, $19.75; 27-38, Jno. E. Ziegler, $11.15; 31-39, Silas Lapham, $4.80; 26-35, Frank C. Glasser, $4.50; 30-45, Geo. W. Martin, $12.40; 28-36, M. M. Mahoney, $4.20; 26-36, Herman Zumm, $3.20.

Hat Department. 50-37, Julius Hauser, $4.50; 58-41, W. E. Schermerhorn, $10.35; 60-38, Edwin McKenzie, $5.60; 50-44, Mrs. Emma Adams, $9.50; 50-35, Geo. P. Bower, $3.50; 55-32, Miss Mamie McNeill, $15.00; 57-41, Miss Frances M. Schreier, $12.45; 53-34, C. W. Hammond, $5.00; 55-35, Donald M. Hepler, $4.25; 58-43, Miss Anna K. Seager, $15.00; 56-45, E. A. McMickle, $3.45; 60-39, George Bauer, $6.40; 51-44, Miss Lillian Betts, $4.50; 60-37, Peter McFetters, $3.50; 55-33, Walter Shearer, $4.25; 60-41, Mrs. J. G. Hinolf, $12.00; 50-38, Walter Hallowell, $3.40; 56-44, Jno. M. Small, $7.65; 52-44, Mrs. S. S. Neff, $4.75; 57-35, Dr. C. M. Brucker, $12.50; 55-36, Judson Brown, $4.50; 53-44, Miss Mabel Neilson, $6.25; 53-31, Albert Spare, $13.13; 53-35, William Jackson, $2.75; 58-44, J. A. Joseph, $2.55; 58-42, Benjamin Spring, $6.70; 54-43, Mrs. E. Nichols, $4.50; 57-42, Albert A. Borton, $3.50; 57-36, Mrs. T. F. Campbell, $4.50; 57-32, Edward O'Connor, $4.75; 57-33, J. J. Sweeney, $7.65; 59-44, Edward Jessup, $4.85; 51-40, Mrs. A. S. Klein, $15.50; 60-42, Miss Lulu Tate, $12.47, 54-44, Mrs. Maggie O'Neil, $5.35; 55-37, Frank Casper, $7.20; 57-43, Mrs. Jno. R. Cassel, $6.80; 50-36, W. S. Osborn, $24.85; 53-32, Frank Vick,

$18.50; 53–36, Silas Lapham, $14.50; 58–40, Harry Vincent, $7.65; 55–44, Frank W. Page, $4.25; 60–40, Wm. Dobbins, $3.25; 50–40, Chas. Dodson, $11.05; 59–31, D. E. Parsons, $5.50; 55–34, Mrs. Emma Wallace, $10.25; 58–39, M. M. Mahoney, $9.87; 57–34, Jos. A. Webster, $10.35; 58–45, Irving A. Penny, $15.85, 58–37, F. J. Earl, $12.45; 56–43, Chas. C. Quick, $10.50; 52–43, A. C. Yates, $9.75; 59–32, Jno. V. Redmond, $4.50; 60–45; Chas. B. Elliot, $7.80; 60–44, Mrs. William M. Frantz, $4.50; 53–33, Jos. E. Ziegler, $12.45; 50–39, Aug. Morley, $5.25; 51–39, Geo. E. Munson, $5.75; 51–45, C. H. Remington, $6.55; 57–31, Walter Reynolds, $11.25; 55–38, Miss M. E. Frost, $14.25; 58–38, Albert Ginglebach, $4.50; 51–41, Valentine Ress, $15.67; 51–38; Theodore Gilles, $4.75; 58–49, Frank C. Glasser, $10.05.

Dress Goods Department.—75–25, Martin Schneider, $28.50; 79–31, Miss Mary Ambler, $14.90; 79–34, Julius Hauser, $21.25; 77–35, Robt. D. McCoy, $112.35; 81–26, Mrs. E. McDaniel, $33.35; 82–27, Donald M. Hepler, $31.24; 81–24, Jno. H. Alvey, $36.90; 85–28, Miss Frances M. Schreier, $45.25; 85–36, Miss Anna K. Seager, $17.64; 75–36, Geo. P. Bower, $22.55; 86–35, Geo. W. Jones, $16.35; 77–36, Ed. McCormick, $29.90; 79–36, Geo. McFarlan, $48.55; 84–35, Jno. R. Kennedy, $21.75; 81–30, George Bauer, $14.20; 81–25, Miss Anna Spencer, $31.15; 79–32, Fred W. Townsend, $24.25; 84–28, Judson Brown, $9.80; 77–25, Lawrence Kiefer, $11.12; 82–25, E. J. McLain, $41.84; 82–36, Miss Mamie McNeil, $37.75; 80–26, Mrs. A. S. Klein, $50.25; 80–25, Albert A. Borton, $12.25; 85–26, Mrs. T. F. Campbell, $26.50; 78–27, Harvey Vincent, $14.25; 83–27, Mrs. Jno. R. Cassel, $12.45; 86–33, Miss Sadie B. Koehler, $14.65; 76–25, Frank Naylor, $46.45; 79–33, Benjamin New, $75.35; 78–26, Chas. Lake, $41.85; 84–27, P. Cassidy, $18.45; 82–37, A. A. Weaver, $28.50; 78–25, C. G. Davis, $90.80; 85–33, Geo. W. Martin, $35.65; 82–26, Mrs. E. Nichols, $28.30; 86–32, Solomon Erb, $24.37; 81–35, Chas. Oakley, $98.25; 85–32, A. Messinger, $34.10; 75–35, F. J. Earl, $24.15; 77–26, Edward O'Connor, $117.80; 83–36, Jno. R. Fell, $24.75; 85–27, A. C. Yates, $20.75; 86–36, Miss Mary Gilles, $51.40; 83–28, Aug. Morley, $65.05; 83–29, C. M. Palmer, $42.50; 75–37, Theodore Gilles, $24.95; 84–30, O. W. Perry, $14.26; 84–29, Herman Zumm, $19.45; 83–30, Chas. C. Quick, $24.48; 78–28, C. H. Remington, $24.80.

Clothing Department.—104–17, Robt. D. McCoy, $121.60; 105–21, Geo. P. Bower, $42.50; 112–22, Geo. N. Smith, $18.50; 102–18, Frank R. Heath, $41.40; 112–19, Jno. Hess, $18.00; 119–23, Walter Shearer, $74.80; 108–21, George Bauer, $31.50; 104–24, Edwin McKenzie, $19.80; 103–24, E. J. McLain, $45.65; 110–20, Mrs. W. C. Bostwick, $22.50; 110–19, Jno. M. Small, $19.98, 105–18, Walter Hallowell, $21.75; 109–23, Wm. Inman, $37.45; 114–20, Benjamin Spring, $29.35; 112–23, Frank Casper, $19.80; 107–18, Wm. Dobbins, $14.65; 100–21, E. A. McMickle, $27.80; 109–24, Peter McFetters, $51.45; 114–21, Chas. Dodson, $37.87; 110–18, Paul Steele, $56.45; 114–17, Wm. Jackson, $18.00; 105–19, Geo. W. Jones, $98.25; 108–20, Walter W. Stern, $46.20; 103–22, W. W. Earnest, $19.70; 102–25, Mrs. S. S. Neff, $43.50, 106–22, Chas. Northrop, $31.20; 115–24, Geo. Engert, $21.75; 119–24, Benton Thomas, $18.00; 115–23, Wm. Johnson, $25.50; 118–23, Edward Jessup, $24.25; 103–23, Jno. M. Utz, $25.95; 107–19, Geo. Eaton, $37.65; 118–24, William Nye, $41.73; 114–22, W. S. Osborn, $63.64; 101–19, Chas. B. Elliott, $37.85; 105–22, Jos. Vernan, $22.75; 101–25, Samuel Kelly, $35.50; 114–19, C. C. Waite, $28.50; 102–19, Jno. R. Fell, $15.50; 116–22, Frank W. Page, $32.25; 108–18, O. W. Perry, $49.48; 114–18, Gustav Fisher, $24.25; 112–21, Mrs. Emma Wallace, $31.50; 100–20, Jno. R. Kennedy, $34.20; 105–20, Wm. B. Knight, $24.85; 104–16, H. H. Watterson, $18.40; 101–18, M. M. Mahoney, $48.75; 116–23, A. A. Weaver, $19.00; 112–20, Dr. D. S. Goble, $29.70; 106–23,

D. E. Parsons, $55.50; 102–20, Frank C. Glasser, $21.25; 106–24, Jos. A. Webster, $20.15; 108–17, A. Messinger, $15.20; 103–21, Mrs. Lottie Mitchell, $6.50; 108–19, Jno. V. Redmond, $18.00; 102–17, Geo. E. Munson, $44.70; 104–25, Walter Reynolds, $75.00.

Enter the footings of the Abstract of Time Sales sheets in the Summary of Daily Sales as previously instructed. Find the total time sales for each Sales Ledger and also for each department. Lay aside the Abstract of Time Sales sheets.

Cash Sales. Record the cash sales listed below as previously instructed.

SHOE DEPARTMENT.—6–29, $15.40; 10–31, $4.75; 8–31, $6.75; 5–30, $4.50; 7–34, $20.50; 4–28, $12.80; 2–37, $14.75; 9–30, $3.25; 1–34, $17.40; 5–31, $4.75; 5–37, $7.65; 11–35, $11.40; 13–33, $10.50; 2–31, $18.25; 15–35, $20.50; 9–34, $13.51; 3–34, $6.75; 13–37, $4.80; 10–30, $18.70; 14–35, $9.75; 9–35, $15.40; 11–34, $10.00; 14–36, $14.84; 1–29, $25.30; 2–32, $18.75; 13–38, $3.50; 13–32, $7.25; 1–38, $14.35; 11–27, $11.80; 8–38, $9.80; 11–28, $7.63; 14–31, $12.47; 4–35, $9.74; 12–32, $10.47; 8–37, $20.40; 14–37, $6.50; 6–34, $12.75; 12–33, $4.25; 10–29, $18.40; 4–29, $4.80; 13–27, $7.15; 12–34, $9.10; 6–35, $10.12; 13–26, $4.95; 8–32, $9.25; 6–30, $11.15; 12–37, $23.24; 9–32, $9.15; 1–35, $4.49; 3–29, $13.45; 2–38, $15.35; 9–31, $20.74; 7–33, $18.40; 12–38, $14.50; 4–34, $16.40; 9–33, $12.20; 13–34, $14.30; 5–32, $14.50; 7–30, $13.50; 14–34, $11.50; 6–33, $7.75; 5–36, $4.80; 15–37, $12.80; 3–33, $10.10; 15–36, $4.25; 13–36, $15.00; 8–35, $18.25; 10–26, $23.00; 7–28, $24.35; 15–30, $16.30; 10–27, $9.45; 11–29, $7.15; 7–29, $11.65; 11–30, $10.37; 10–28, $9.40; 1–30, $13.75; 11–31, $14.50; 14–32, $22.50; 15–31, $4.90; 4–30, $12.85; 15–32, $19.17; 8–39, $10.00; 15–38, $13.35; 8–36, $17.63; 4–39, $20.40; 15–33, $12.85; 13.39, $24.60; 4–31, $9.75; 6–31, $14.35; 14–33, $12.75; 11–33, $4.80; 3–30, $7.65; 1–36, $24.75; 15–34, $19.80; 6–32, $4.75; 12–36, $8.90; 1–33, $12.40; 7–31, $9.15; 7–32, $12.45; 2–28, $18.45; 3–31, $25.30; 8–33, $12.75; 5–33, $21.25; 2–29, $11.65; 8–34, $9.99; 3–32, $3.50; 5–34, $4.75; 13–35, $19.80; 12–35, $15.00; 11–32, $12.50; 4–32, $18.45; 7–30, $7.65; 5–35, $4.25; 2–27, $11.85; 1–31, $20.75.

GLOVE DEPARTMENT.—34–42, $7.85; 29–40, $12.20; 25–38, $4.25; 27–47, $11.40; 29–49, $7.25; 28–44, $18.30; 33–3, $9.80; 28–41, $7.35; 32–44, $12.25; 34–40, $4.64; 26–42, $3.45; 27–42, $4.75; 33–39, $6.25; 29–50, $9.50; 25–39, $5.25; 27–50, $18.40; 28–49, $14.75; 30–39, $10.27; 33–40, $8.45; 26–49, $16.25; 26–43, $4.50; 34–50, $16.70; 34–39, $8.15; 29–36, $12.84; 29–1, $3.25; 31–43, $8.40; 25–48, $10.48; 29–2, $34.10; 31–44, $3.60; 25–50, $9.50; 29–37, $4.75; 35–50, $11.50; 34–43, $12.40; 28–39, $5.25; 35–1, $14.85; 32–41, $25.50; 35–45, $27.45; 29–38, $5.25; 33–2, $6.40; 25–47, $11.20; 33–50, $4.95; 35–38, $12.00; 31–1, $10.19; 28–40, $4.75; 25–37, $14.75; 29–41, $18.45; 26–40, $6.50; 30–37, $11.50; 33–37, $4.75; 27–40, $4.50; 33–38, $14.25; 29–42, $4.75; 32–43, $21.50; 27–41, $9.50; 26–44, $4.80; 27–48, $10.47; 28–37, $10.12; 30–36, $6.55; 32–38, $3.10; 25–42, $11.85; 32–48, $9.47; 30–43, $6.31; 29–43, $10.45; 33–48, $4.25; 31–40, $20.25; 32–39, $7.60; 29–35, $10.75; 34–34, $11.15; 30–44, $4.50; 34–38, $12.45; 30–38, $5.60; 32–40, $18.75; 31–44, $10.50; 27–39, $11.40; 35–43, $8.45; 34–44, $9.75; 35–47, $3.40; 29–44, $9.40; 35–48, $12.80; 28–38, $19.20; 25–2, $6.25; 31–42, $4.30; 26–50, $11.90; 35–44, $14.63; 25–46, $7.60; 28–1, $9.45; 31–45, $18.80; 31–1, $12.00; 30–41, $4.50; 31–49, $9.45, 27–46, $6.10; 35.41, $60.50; 33–49, $15.10; 28–43, $18.20; 32–50, $25.49; 30–40, $10.48; 26–45, $4.20; 35–40, $8.90; 32–42, $7.50; 28–42, $12.15; 30–50, $18.45; 27–43, $3.50; 34–49, $2.75; 25–40, $11.85; 33–44, $21.50; 29–39, $4.90; 34–41, $11.75; 27–44, $6.50; 35–39, $9.36; 31–45, $12.84; 26–44, $4.75; 33–42, $9.35; 30–42, $11.10; 27–45, $3.25; 25–44, $7.45; 26–2, $13.35; 25–3, $9.85; 27–1, $7.60; 28–3, $8.25; 29–3, $12.00; 30–1, $9.50; 31–2, $8.25.

HAT DEPARTMENT.—53-41, $6.70; 57-46, $12.47; 53-42, $12.40; 54-46, $31.50; 56-41, $6.70; 56-42, $10.00; 51-31, $9.75; 53-43, $4.60; 53-46, $10.50; 51-32, $18.50; 59-38, $4.50; 51-46, $3.25; 54-32, $7.65; 60-34, $12.15; 55-41, $9.55; 60-33, $1.37; 51-33, $7.63; 59-39, $8.95; 55-42, $14.85; 54-33, $11.10; 55-43, $4.25; 59-40, $6.91; 56-33, $16.25; 50-47, $12.20; 54-34, $9.25; 52-47, $5.00; 54-47, $4.60; 56-34, $5.29; 56-47, $14.25; 50-43, $4.25; 54-35, $7.63; 56-35, $3.50; 58-47, $12.50; 52-35, $7.65; 60-47, $19.27; 57-41, $8.95; 60-48, $12.50; 56-36, $11.40; 56-48, $5.45; 57-40, $8.47; 52-48, $4.25; 56-37, $16.80; 59-46, $9.55; 52-36, $12.40; 50-46, $8.75; 50-32, $11.50; 51-45, $5.00; 52-46, $6.25; 60-43, $4.75; 53-45, $11.00; 52-41, $5.85; 54-40, $11.41; 60-35, $3.45; 60-36, $14.91; 54-41, $4.75; 52-42, $19.70; 50-33, $21.10; 55-45, $18.25; 59-33, $3.25; 55-46, $8.54; 54-42, $4.25; 59-34, $11.40; 51-42, $4.50; 59-35, $15.25; 52-45, $4.64; 50-34, $13.45; 59-36, $10.80; 50-45, $4.50; 51-43, $12.50; 59-37, $14.50; 56-46, $6.40; 50-41, $4.75; 57-45, $10.05; 52-33, $7.80; 53-37, $21.40; 57-37, $8.75; 58-46, $11.70; 50-42, $4.35; 57-38, $16.41; 53-38, $12.25; 55-40, $24.50; 57-39, $21.10; 53-39, $18.25; 55-39, $11.80; 60-46, $19.60; 53-40, $3.60; 59-45, $14.20; 52-34, $3.65; 54-48, $15.00; 52-39, $8.75; 53-47, $11.45; 56-40, $6.83; 54-39, $5.85; 58-33, $8.54; 57-47, $19.20; 52-40, $14.85; 58-48, $7.65; 56-39, $4.15; 58-34, $11.70; 51-47, $4.75; 51-34, $12.85; 58-35, $21.10; 54-37, $10.80; 50-48, $12.50; 54-38, $9.50; 59-41, $8.00; 54-36, $11.40; 59-42, $4.60; 51-35, $8.75; 50-49, $4.75; 51-36, $9.45; 59-43, $10.05; 56-38, $12.50; 54-49, $7.80; 52-37, $4.35; 60-32, $11.60; 52-38, $15.50; 58-36, $10.25; 51-37, $3.25.

DRESS GOODS DEPARTMENT.—75-24, $17.64; 82-24, $28.50; 84-34, $14.80; 79-28, $9.63; 80-34, $15.40; 85-23, $18.35; 77-27, $9.24; 79-29, $16.41; 77-28, $14.50; 80-35, $18.47; 79-30, $15.35; 84-26, $12.84; 75-29, $16.38; 85-24, $9.25; 82-23, $10.50; 86-30, $18.40; 85-25, $25.50; 75-30, $14.75; 79-37, $10.10; 82-31, $15.84; 86-31, $18.30; 77-29, $12.80; 76-35, $14.25; 86-34, $36.40; 80-36, $28.70; 81-34, $16.34; 82-32, $12.85; 77-30, $11.63; 82-33, $14.27; 80-28, $12.80; 84-24, $24.50; 76-30, $12.60; 77-31, $24.85; 80-29, $7.60; 82-34, $12.20; 83-26, $14.50; 77-32, $64.25; 84-25, $22.80; 82-35, $12.24; 86-26, $16.80; 77-33, $4.50; 76-31, $24.50; 84-36, $17.40; 83-25, $12.30; 75-26, $17.64; 81-27, $29.38; 84-33, $10.50; 82-29, $12.40; 85-30, $49.75; 76-26, $41.85; 81-28, $10.12; 85-29, $18.47; 75-27, $45.75; 82-28, $48.63; 78-29, $22.50; 76-27, $39.70; 75-28, $18.36; 81-29, $12.24; 84-31, $16.40; 78-30, $10.20; 84-32, $12.50; 77-23, $18.30; 83-31, $15.70; 79-35, $24.75; 83-32, $19.38; 78-31, $21.70; 80-23, $28.05; 82-30, $35.30; 76-28, $18.46; 83-33, $12.24; 77-24, $27.60; 78-32, $24.85; 80-24, $17.40; 83-34, $10.81; 80-27, $28.70; 85-31, $59.75; 78-33, $10.81; 83-35, $44.60; 76-29, $48.47; 86-37, $19.76; 85-34, $25.60; 84-37, $20.00; 85-35, $18.40; 77-34, $23.80; 76-36, $27.60; 86-25, $40.75; 77-37, $12.36; 78-24, $37.85; 79-26, $14.80; 86-38, $16.20; 79-27, $12.85; 86-28, $10.75; 76-34, $24.25; 86-29, $19.45; 80-30, $6.81; 79-38, $18.56; 80-31, $24.85; 75-38, $23.75; 78-35, $10.12; 80-32, $31.15; 81-36, $10.87; 79-25, $14.50; 80-33, $19.45; 81-31, $11.63; 75-31, $24.70; 76-33, $18.00; 81-32, $12.81; 86-27, $21.90; 75-32, $17.63; 81-33, $14.40; 78-34, $24.85; 75-33, $19.81; 76-32, $17.46; 75-34, $11.05.

CLOTHING DEPARTMENT.—111-17, $11.65; 111-18, $24.80; 118-17, $17.00; 116-17, $61.10; 119-17, $35.00; 117-20, $18.36; 116-18, $48.70; 118-18, $90.30; 119-18, $18.00; 111-19, $26.50; 117-21, $13.00; 104-22, $48.50; 118-19, $10.00; 106-25, $12.50; 115-18, $41.20; 117-22, $39.50; 108-25, $19.36; 115-19, $81.90; 110-25, $112.70; 104-23, $40.50; 106-18, $21.25; 100-25, $42.85; 111-24, $98.90; 112-25, $14.30; 115-20, $18.75; 114-24, $16.44; 116-19, $80.50; 106-19, $75.25; 119-19, $14.60; 100-26, $11.74; 114-25, $21.20; 106-20, $38.45; 117-24, $50.00; 117-18, $28.50; 117-26, $17.60; 119-25, $21.75; 117-19,

$28.40; 102-26, $78.15; 118-20, $84.60; 116-21, $16.20; 103-25, $56.80; 105-25, $12.45; 105-26, $27.70; 116-20, $16.00; 100-17, $75.00; 110-22, $14.75; 113-21, $16.84; 111-22, $98.40; 107-25, $12.00; 108-23, $70.15; 113-20, $18.00; 110-23, $22.25; 111-21, $64.70; 108-24, $35.45; 105-23, $10.75; 101-23, $16.40; 109-18, $60.50; 110-24, $45.75; 105-24, $41.50; 100-18, $18.47; 109-19, $71.15; 102-24, $28.40; 105-16, $17.64; 109-20, $38.45; 113-22, $10.00; 100-21, $36.25; 105-17, $19.75; 101-24, $12.40; 115-21, $29.80; 113-23, $11.45; 100-19, $25.00; 103-18, $18.47; 106-21, $68.18; 119-20, $12.80; 111-23, $19.74; 104-20, $33.65; 118-22, $10.05; 113-24, $28.50; 115-22, $14.75; 109-21, $19.89; 118-21, $29.90; 103-19, $48.75; 104-21, $52.85; 107-26, $12.40; 103-20, $11.65; 109-25, $80.70; 110-26, $11.25; 112-26, $17.10; 110-21, $12.00; 101-20, $44.50; 108-22, $18.75; 116-24, $16.83; 102-21, $19.25; 112-24, $34.15; 117-23, $25.85; 101-21, $19.75; 111-20, $12.50; 102-22, $81.18; 107-20, $29.80; 101-22, $12.40; 113-18, $69.75; 102-23, $35.80; 107-21, $97.60; 100-22, $48.85; 107-22, $56.65; 113-19, $91.75; 119-22, $7.64; 104-18, $12.85; 107-23, $38.15; 116-25, $21.20; 114-23, $75.00; 100-23, $87.50; 107-24, $17.96; 117-25, $12.18; 108-16, $7.60; 119-21, $24.75; 112-18, $98.64; 109-22, $11.75; 112-17, $16.80; 104-19, $25.00.

Find the total cash sales for each department. Verify your addition.

Clerks' Daily Sales. Enter the daily totals of the Clerks' Summary sheets listed below as previously instructe...

Clerk 1, $233.04; 2, $169.65, 3, $116.06; 4, $153.48; 5, $89.70; 6, $162.27; 7, $146.00; 8, $170.95; 9, $149.85; 10, $152.36; 11, $116.05; 12, $138.81; 13, $140.55; 14, $146.70; 15, $156.67; 25, $149.13; 26, $127.95; 27, $121.21; 28, $186.30; 29, $197.20; 30, $150.03; 31, $157.25; 32, $192.66; 33, $157.84; 34, $159.93; 35, $229.49; 50, $164.15; 51, $146.35; 52, $135.14; 53, $184.73; 54, $168.89; 55, $155.69; 56, $141.12; 57, $179.15; 58, $178.41; 59, $136.81; 60, $158.12; 75, $327.61; 76, $336.59; 77, $495.00; 78, $334.58; 79, $321.25; 80, $301.88; 81, $331.64; 82, $370.36; 83, $298.76; 84, $235.45; 85, $404.96; 86, $325.48; 100, $373.46; 101, $227.55; 102, $409.73; 103, $233.47; 104, $448.15; 105, $339.89; 106, $322.78; 107, $317.16; 108, $341.69; 109, $371.34; 110, $320.63; 111, $357.19; 112, $299.09; 113, $246.29; 114, $314.25; 115, $233.65; 116, $311.78; 117, $233.69; 118, $337.83; 119, $227.34.

Find the footings of each department; also the total for the day. Next find the total for the month. Verify your work.

Cashier's Statements. Enter the cash receipts and payments listed below as previously instructed.

RECEIPTS. *Sales Ledgers.* Miss Mary Ambler, $23.55; J. W. Harrison, $25.00; Ed. McCormick, $22.30; Robt. D. McCoy, $150.00; Wm. Sassaman, $100.00; Frank R. Heath, $50.00; J. G. Atkinson, $94.80; Geo. McFarlan, $15.25; Miss Pauline Sale, $21.62; Mrs. Emma Adams, $24.25; Julius Hauser, $17.65; Jno. H. Alvey, $25.60; Thos. McElwain, $52.70; Miss Susan Smythe, $50.90; Jos. E. McGregor, $47.90; C. W. Hammond, $54.75; Geo. P. Bower, $9.50; Wm. Henning, $31.55; Burton E. McGaire, $11.90; Richard Smythe, $26.75; Martin Schneider, $11.15; Edwin McKenzie, $35.50; Jno. Stalder, $30.50; B. W. Hayden, $21.90; Geo. Bauer, $17.95; Chas. Harrington, $41.00; Mrs. W. C. Bostwick, $23.70; Jno. M. McKinley, $25.00; Albert E. Shaw, $10.46; Miss Ella McMaster, $36.50; Samuel Halderman, $61.00; Miss Lillian Betts, $24.90; E. A. McMickle, $31.24; Walter Shearer, $13.20; E. V. Neal, $57.25; Judson Brown, $24.25; Walter Hallowell, $30.75; Albert A. Burton, $21.00; Edwin Short, $13.25; Geo. N. Nash, $20.00; Miss Sadie Harlan, $53.95; C. L. Behrns, $35.00; Benjamin New, $125.00; Hiram Simpson, $45.00; Mrs. E.

Nichols, $88.95; Clarence W. Campbell, $31.50; Mrs. M. Jacobs, $17.35; A. B. Jennings, $28.15; R. S. Collins, $50.00; Chas. Northorp, $50.00; Albert Spillman, $31.75; Wm. Noyes, $113.99; Walter Kane, $15.50; Henry Kasser, $32.00; Mrs. Jno. R. Cassel, $55.70; William Nye, $25.00; Paul Steele, $20.48; Chas. Oakley, $44.11; Jno. M. Stone, $43.08; Hugh J. O'Brien, $53.10; J. J. Sweeney, $43.50; J. E. M. Keller, $29.45; P. Cassidy, $59.33; Miss Chrissa Katz, $47.10; Miss Maggie Conway, $55.00; Edward O'Connor, $125.50; Fred. W. Townsend, $26.05; Geo. W. Ottinger, $10.85; Jno. M. Utz, $23.75; Mrs. Maggie O'Neill, $49.25; Wm. Vanderpool, $50.00; Mrs. H. W. Dickinson, $40.01; Samuel Kelly, $17.15; Chas. Dodson, $35.71; W. S. Osborn, $19.50; J. A. Vanderbelt, $26.00; C. G. Davis, $75.00; Jno. R. Kennedy, $25.00; W. W. Earnest, $25.37; A. J. Kinneman, $24.25; Solomon Erb, $10.50; Frank Kranss, $10.00; F. J. Earl, $30.40; Wm. B. Knight, $20.95; Chas. B. Elliot, $50.00; M. C. Parker, $51.50; Jos. Vernan, $20.00; D. E. Parsons, $25.00; Jacob Froehlich, $75.00; Miss Sadie B. Koehler, $83.25; Frank Vick, $55.00; Gustav Fisher, $23.25; R. G. Laird, $20.55; Harvey Vincent, $20.00; Irving A. Penny, $15.50; Adam Vogel, $28.98; Alfred Quinn, $39.47; Frank M. Wagner, $92.50; L. L. Leaver, $40.50; Jno. B. Fowler, $48.40; Chas. Lake, $43.75; Mrs. A. K. Gilbert, $28.25; Leopold Rice, $52.55; C. C. Waite, $40.00; Miss Amie Rathbun, $48.40; Mrs. H. H. Martin, $43.25; Dr. D. S. Goble, $31.75; Valentine Ress, $10.00; Peter M. Ward, $69.22; A. Messinger, $30.65; Miss Mary Gilles, $35.80; Mrs. G. W. Miner, $25.00; Cora Walters, $50.30; A. A. Weaver, $25.00; Jno. V. Redmond, $25.00; August Morley, $33.75; Theo. Gilles, $14.80; Frank Zimmer, $20.15; Jno. Zoll, $31.15; L. V. Maurer, $12.20; Herman Zumm, $25.10.

General Ledger. Enter the following on a Receipts-General Ledger sheet. Miss Josie Nicolay, $76.40; Chas. F. Marting, $50.00; Cyrus Van Winkle, $9.20; S. E. Walters, $22.65; Geo. Noble, $75.00; J. W. Brady, $19.22; Joseph Schwartz, $26.50; Albert Bassett, $50.00.

PAYMENTS.—*General Ledger.* The following accounts have been paid in full; make a full record of them on a Payments-General Ledger sheet. Utz & Dunn, Rochester Hat Co., J. W. Riddle, Boston Glove Co.

Purchase Ledger. On a Payments-Purchase Ledger sheet enter all accounts that are to be paid to-day to be entitled to a discount.

Enter the footings of all the detailed statements on the Cashier's Abstract Statement and find the balance of cash.

As General Bookkeeper you will now verify the cashier's statements. Enter the items on the Cashier's Abstract Statement in the Abstract Cash Account. Lay aside the statements.

Enter the footings of the Abstract of Cash Sales sheets in the Summary of Daily Sales and ascertain the total cash sales. Foot the department columns of the Summary of Daily Sales in red ink. Next add the red ink footings to ascertain the monthly totals. Compare the footings and monthly totals with the footings and monthly totals of the Clerks' Daily Sales record. Report any discrepancies that you may find to the teacher. Place the Abstract of Time Sales sheets in the proper envelopes.

Adjust the interest on the partners' investments. (*See pages 83 and 117.*)

Posting. Preparatory to posting, foot and rule the credit column of the Purchase Ledger, the Department Charges form and the Abstract Cash Account. Post to the General and Purchase Ledgers as previously instructed. Post the totals of the Sales Ledgers from the Summary of Daily Sales to the proper accounts in the General Ledger. Post the total sales of each merchandise department to its proper account in the General Ledger. Likewise post the total purchases as found on the Department Charges form. Post the footings of the columns of the Abstract Cash Account, that are necessary to be posted, to the proper accounts in the General Ledger. The footing of the Discount column is posted to the debit of the Purchase Ledger account and to the credit of Merchandise Discounts account in the General Ledger. Post the total amount of purchases to the Purchase Ledger account in the General Ledger. Have you placed the ledger folio before all items that you have posted? Check over your posting. File all documents in the proper receptacles.

Abstract of Purchase and Sales Ledgers. In business the bookkeepers of the various sub-ledgers render abstracts of their Ledgers to the General Bookkeeper at the time of taking a trial balance or oftener. Below are given the balances of the accounts in the various Sales Ledgers, from which you will write up abstracts on the blanks furnished for that purpose. You will also make an abstract of the accounts in the Purchase Ledger that have not been paid. The total of each abstract should equal the balance of its ledger account in the General Ledger. If a discrepancy exists you will be obliged to locate it before taking a trial balance.

A to G Sales Ledger. Samuel Althoff, \$27.05; Mrs. Geo. Anderson, \$66.00; J. G. Atkinson, \$76.40; Mrs. Emma Adams, \$28.30; Jno. H. Alvey, \$36.90; Henry Beaver, \$53.55; Geo. P. Bower, \$89.55; George Bauer, \$61.10; Mrs. W. C. Bostwick, \$29.90; Miss Lillian Betts, \$17.75; Dr. C. M. Brucker, \$16.00; Judson Brown, \$26.30; Albert A. Borton, \$25.25; Mrs. Henry Bader, \$69.35; C. L. Behrns, \$14.25; Mrs. T. F. Campbell, \$47.75; R. S. Collins, \$16.25; Frank Casper, \$35.50; Mrs. Jno. R. Cassel, \$19.25; P. Cassidy, \$18.45; Miss Maggie Conway, \$18.62; Ralph E. Cooke, \$40.29; Henry Cooper, \$28.80; J. W. Clark, \$18.93; Wm. Dobbins, \$42.40; Mrs. Edwin Dalton, \$41.05; C. O. Dinwiddie, \$23.45; Chas. Dodson, \$48.92; C. G. Davis, \$37.95; W. W. Earnest, \$23.33; Solomon Erb, \$21.72; Geo. Engert, \$29.60; F. J. Earl, \$23.45; Geo. Eaton, \$69.45; Chas. B. Elliot, \$43.79; H. E. Eastwood, \$11.75; Mrs. Wm. Emery, \$40.35; Jno. Eberhard, \$20.00; Mrs. Wm. M Frantz, \$26.50; Miss Euphemia Faucett, \$5.73; Jacob Froehlich, \$19.10; Jno. R. Fell, \$43.75; Gustav Fisher, \$24.25; Miss M. E. Frost, \$21.65; Albert Gingleback, \$13.90; Jno. M. Gleason, \$27.04; Chas. K. Gibson, \$25.50; Dr. D. S. Goble, \$29.70; Miss Mary Gilles, \$26.00; Theodore Gilles, \$29.70; L. K. Grainger, \$9.75; Frank C. Glasser, \$45.20.

H to M Sales Ledger. J. W. Harrison, \$0.70; Frank R. Heath, \$8.45; Julius Hanser, \$25.75; Geo. Heitz, \$25.75; C. W. Hammond, \$9.25; Donald M. Hepler, \$43.49; Alonzo Hicks, \$26.40; Jno. Hess, \$41.25; Chas. Harrington, \$9.84; Mrs. J. G. Hinolf, \$35.05; Samuel Halderman, \$1.85; Thos. Hawkins, \$19.00; Walter Hallowell, \$12.15; Miss Sadie Harlan, \$5.00; William Inman, \$47.45; Wm. Jackson, \$25.00; J. A. Joseph, \$22.55; Geo. W. Jones, \$144.60; Wm. Johnson, \$57.00; Edward Jessup, \$41.60; Mrs. C. W. Jefferson, \$38.75; Walter Kane, \$6.25; Henry Kasser, \$16.75; Henry Kurtz, \$20.35; Chas. Kaehler, \$24.75; Samuel Kelly, \$42.95; Henry Kempf, \$10.00; Jno. R. Kennedy, \$48.50; Lawrence Kiefer, \$17.68; A. J. Kinneman, \$24.25; Mrs. A. S. Klem, \$82.48; Miss Sarah Keim, \$14.44; Frank Krauss, \$9.20; Wm. B. Knight, \$29.10; Miss Sadie B. Koehler, \$24.90; Silas Lapham, \$25.55; L. L. Leaver, \$33.49; Chas. Lake, \$41.85; H. B. Lehman, \$18.55; Geo. W. Martin, \$55.80; M. M. Mahoney, \$75.67; A. Messinger, \$79.30; Mrs. Lottie Mitchell, \$103.40; Mrs. G. W. Miner, \$29.35; Aug. Morley, \$85.10; Geo. E. Munson \$50.45; L. V. Maurer, \$10.50.

Mc to R Sales Ledger. Jno. C. McCarthy, \$41.09; Robert D. McCoy, \$118.95; Mrs. E. McDaniel, \$68.10; Ed. McCormick, \$49.30; Geo. McFarlan, \$48.55; Jos. E. McGregor,

$28.50; Edwin McKenzie, $15.90; Mrs. Kate McKenna, $60.55; E. J. McLain, $112.94; John M. McKinley, $43.52; Miss Ella McMaster, $10.25; Miss Mamie McNeill, $75.55; E. A. McMickle, $31.25; Mrs. T. P. McMenamin, $105.19; Peter McFetters, $72.07; Frank Naylor, $85.10; Mrs. S. S. Neff, $74.86; Miss Mabel Neilson, $6.25; Andrew J. Nellis, $38.45; Martin Newman, $14.09; Benjamin New, $78.50; Mrs. E. Nichols, $12.60; Jno. Noble, $16.78; Jas. Northorp, $9.92; William Noyes, $17.20; William Nye, $66.57; Chas. Oakley, $106.96; Hugh J. O'Brien, $12.84; Edward O'Connor, $122.55; Allen H. Oliver, $11.81; Mrs. Maggie O'Neill, $22.24; W. S. Osborn, $88.49; E. G. Osgood, $52.14; C. N. Palmer, $56.00; Frank W. Page, $57.31; O. W. Perry, $67.89; D. E. Parsons, $40.25; S. P. Patton, $11.40; Irving A. Penny, $25.30; Chas. C. Quick, $39.73; Jno. V. Redmond, $25.21; Jayson Rummel, $27.75; Walter Reynolds, $120.25; C. H. Remington, $51.10; Valentine Ress, $27.16.

S TO Z SALES LEDGER. Wm. Sassaman, $14.00; Miss Susan Smythe, $14.84; Geo. N. Smith, $28.50; Paul Scull, $14.90; Martin Schneider, $28.50; Jno. Stalder, $13.50; W. E. Schermerhorn, $22.85; Miss Frances M. Schreier, $68.45; Miss Anna K. Seager, $53.29; Walter Shearer, $79.05; Jno. M. Small, $35.28; Hiram Simpson, $10.90; Albert Spare, $61.72; Miss Anna Spencer, $46.80; Benjamin Spring, $52.55; Paul Steele, $56.45; Walter W. Stern, $62.60; J. J. Sweeney, $22.90; Miss Lulu Tate, $18.72; Morris Thatcher, $191.17; Benton Thomas, $25.75; Fred. W. Townsend, $24.25; Jno. M. Utz, $45.76; Wm. Vanderpool, $14.83; Joseph Vernan, $24.05; Frank Vick, $19.70; Harvey Vincent, $12.64; Ira P. Wetzel, $22.81; H. J. Walker, $8.72; C. C. Waite, $13.85; Mrs. Emma Wallace, $54.64; W. W. Watkins, $40.05; H. H. Watterson, $21.55; A. A. Weaver, $30.90; Jos. A. Webster, $48.26; A. C. Yates, $40.62; Wm. Young, $27.95; Jno. M. Ziegler, $23.60; Herman Zumm, $22.65.

Compare the footings of the various abstracts with the balances of the respective accounts in the General Ledger. If found to agree you will file the abstracts in the General Bookkeeper's file and take a trial balance of the General Ledger. Present it for approval when finished.

Clerks' Time. Transfer the clerks' numbers and names to pages 20 and 21 of the Pay Roll. Preparatory to ascertaining the liability inventories you will enter the time of the clerks as listed below, and ascertain the amount due them. The time given is the *actual* time; in entering it the student is to double it for Saturday and Sunday. Rule a Total Time column and an Amount column under the Remarks division of the Pay Roll. As the clerks are not paid at this time (the object being to ascertain what is due them) you will extend the total time in red ink, to the column you have ruled for that purpose. Likewise you will ascertain what is due them and record it in red ink. In extending the department managers' time, give them credit for *regular* time (one day) only. As no deduction is made for time they lose, no pay is allowed for extra time.

SATURDAY, JULY 4. Clerks 1, 3, 5, 11, 12, 25, 29, 31, 34, 50, 58, 75, 79, 82, 84, 100, 101, 104, 109, 111, 114, 119 worked full time. Clerks 2, 6 and 53 each worked $1\frac{1}{4}$ days. Clerks 32, 56, 108, and 117 each worked $\frac{1}{2}$ day.

SUNDAY, JULY 5. Clerks 1, 4, 8, 9, 11, 12, 25, 29, 31, 34, 50, 53, 55, 58, 60, 75, 79, 100, 105, 106, 107, 109 and 119 worked full time. Clerks 76, 84, 101 and 111 each worked $\frac{1}{2}$ day. Clerk 82 worked $1\frac{1}{4}$ days. Clerk 114 worked $\frac{3}{4}$ of a day. Clerk 117 worked $1\frac{1}{2}$ days.

MONDAY, JULY 6. All of the clerks worked full time.

Go over your calculations a second time. Foot the amount column of each department.

LIABILITIES.

Shoes, wages due, per Pay Roll,		
Gloves, " "		
Hats, "		
Dress Goods "		
Clothing,		
Expense, salaries due partners (½ month each),		
" " bookkeepers, "		
salary due student (4 days),		

RESOURCES.

Shoes, per inventory sheets,	12791	72
Gloves, " "	17097	48
Hats, " "	14326	39
Dress Goods, " "	9912	53
Clothing, " "	11475	49
Fixtures, cost or investment value,		
Advertising, ½ of one month's advertising not used,		
Expense, ¼ of one month's rent not used,		

You will next write the amounts of the inventories in the proper ledger accounts in red ink. Be sure to enter the liability inventories to the debit of the accounts.

Make a Balance Sheet and have it approved.

Close the accounts showing losses and gains. Bring down the inventories. Liability inventories should appear on the credit side of accounts when brought down.

Present all books and documents for inspection.

The deceased partner's interest has been paid as agreed. Make the entry on the proper detailed statement, on the Cashier's Abstract Statement and in the Abstract Cash Account. In the Journal debit him for the discount and credit Loss & Gain. Post the entries just made. By this transaction the surviving partners have secured control of the entire business. Are their interests greater or less than they were before the decease of the partner? If greater, how much? If less, how much? Explain how you arrived at your result.

Write a credit memorandum on a blank sheet of paper favor of Mrs. Sarah Levy for the salary due Abraham Levy, making it payable Aug. 1.

NOTE.—In business it would either be necessary to draw up a new partnership agreement, or it would be necessary to amend the present partnership agreement by stating that one of the partners had died and that a new partnership had been formed in which the rights and privileges of the surviving partners are the same as those specified in the original agreement.

Notice of the dissolution, and the formation of a new partnership should also be given. The method and form of giving notice are explained on page 86.

Your work of opening the books and adjusting the partnership interests is now completed and you are supposed to turn over the books to Mr. Harvey Luman, who is to be the permanent General Bookkeeper. Render the firm a bill for your services, using a blank sheet of paper.

MANUFACTURING BUSINESS

Glove Manufacturing Plant Purchased. The glove manufacturing plant owned by J. B. Luckey has been purchased by the surviving members of the firm of J. A. Luman & Co. Mr. Luckey has decided to retire from business and has sold the plant for $100,000, which is considerably less than the inventory value, as may be seen by consulting the expert accountant's report on page 165. Each of the partners has contributed $25,000 from his private funds to pay for the glove plant, and it is to be conducted independently of the department store business. You are retained to open the books for the manufacturing business and to conduct them for a time after business hours.

Owing to the advantages of an incorporated business over a business conducted by a partnership the members of the firm have decided to incorporate the glove manufacturing business under the style and title of the Luman Glove Company (incorporated), beginning August 1. In the meantime the business is to be conducted by a temporary partnership, known as the Luman Glove Company (not incorporated).

Object of this Business. The object of this business is to familiarize the student with the forms of books specially adapted to a manufacturing business and the method of keeping them.

Books and Forms. Some of the special books and forms that may be used to advantage in a glove manufacturing business are: Cost Book, Order Sheets, Cutters Stock Book and Stock Tickets. The other books used are the Impression Sales Book, Monthly Pay Roll, and a special column Cash Book; these may be used in any line of business. Separate accounts are also kept with the items that enter into the cost of merchandise, and the balances of such accounts are transferred to the debit of the Merchandise account at the time of closing the books.

Cost of Manufacturing. The question of greatest importance to the manufacturer is: What will it cost to manufacture a commodity? Formerly when there was little competition in the manufacturing business it was sufficient to arrive at the cost by a rough estimate. In these days of close competition it has become necessary to ascertain, as nearly as possible, the exact cost of an article, so that it may be placed on the market at the lowest possible

MERCHANDISE.

	189						189.		
Raw material,	June	30	34227	50	12075	80	July	31	980 doz. sold.
Freight & Cartage,			1404	00	5301	25	Aug.	31	795 " "
Bands, Boxes & Cases,			1404	00	2820	75	Sept.	30	380 " "
Silk,			1778	40	2630	25	Oct.	31	310 " "
Buttons,			468	00	2616	48	Nov.	30	340 " "
Labor,			22183	20	2121	50	Dec.	31	295 " "
Salaries,			3088	80	2280	40	Jan.	31	291 " "
Manuf'g Expenses,			2116	80	13987	50	Feb.	28	1595 " "
Traveling "			1872	00	16548	75	Mar.	31	1701 " "
Discounts allowed,			249	85	14789	45	Apr.	30	1587 " "
Loss & Gain,			*35009*	*10*	12860	41	May	31	1160 " "
					7940	84	June	3	671 " "
					91	87			Discounts received.
					7736	*30*			*Inventory (111¼ doz.)*
			103801	65	103801	65			

price and still yield the desired per cent. of profit. These conditions have led manufacturers to seek the cheapest markets in which to purchase raw materials, to lessen the cost of production by the introduction of labor-saving machinery, and to keep separate, detailed accounts with all items that enter into the cost of manufacturing their products.

In the Merchandise account illustrated on page 159 the sales appear on the credit side of the account, while on the debit side appear the balances of the various accounts, the items of which enter into the cost of manufacturing the merchandise. In business detailed information of such items would be obtained by consulting the accounts with the items. In the glove manufacturing business this detailed information of the preceding years is used as a basis on which to calculate the cost of producing the various articles for the succeeding years.

Cost Book. The purpose of a Cost Book in a manufacturing business is to furnish a detailed record of the cost of manufacturing the various commodities. In the glove manufacturing business it is customary to designate the various styles of gloves by number. In the illustration of the Cost Book below a "men's unlined, outseam glove" is designated as No. 1126. It will be observed that the cost of this style of glove is recorded for eight consecutive years; in business this record may be extended for as many years as the glove is being manufactured. By dividing the cost of the various items on the debit side of the illustrated Merchandise account by the number of dozens sold, the cost of manufacturing No. 1126 for the year 1899 will be found to be the same as that exhibited in the illustration of the Cost Book. In ascertaining the cost of the raw material and labor for any style of glove, the number of dozens manufactured must be divided into the cost of the raw material and labor, and not the number of dozens sold. A similar record of all the other styles of gloves to be manufactured should be kept in the Cost Book. In some lines of business it is an advantage to use loose Cost Sheets instead of a Cost Book. Cost Books or Cost Sheets are designed and ruled differently, to meet the requirements of the business in which they are used.

COST BOOK.

Stock No. *1126* Description, *Men's unlined, outseam glove.*

	1892.	1893.	1894.	1895.	1896.	1897.	1898.	1899.
Raw Material,	4.75	4.20	4.43	3.70	4.05	3.60	3.45	3.30
Labor, Cutting,	1.10	1.10	1.12	1.06	1.10	1.05	1.08	1.06
" Making,	.92	1.05	1.03	1.00	1.00	.95	.90	.90
" Silking,	.36	.40	.44	.45	.40	.41	.40	.41
Freight & Cartage,	.17	.15	.18	.14	.15	.15	.16	.15
Boxes, etc.,	.16	.16	.15	.15	.17	.15	.16	.15
Silk & Thread,	.23	.20	.20	.18	.18	.19	.18	.19
Buttons,	.05	.05	.06	.05	.05	.05	.05	.05
Salaries,	.37	.42	.39	.34	.34	.34	.34	.33
Manufacturing Expenses,	.17	.18	.14	.15	.14	.14	.13	.13
Traveling "	.25	.25	.22	.20	.21	.20	.20	.20
	8.53	8.16	8.36	7.42	7.79	7.23	7.05	6.87
Profit, 20% on cost,	1.71	1.63	1.67	1.48	1.56	1.45	1.41	1.37
Interest, 8 mo. on cost,	.34	.33	.33	.30	.31	.29	.28	.27
Discount, 6% on sales,	.69	.66	.67	.60	.63	.58	.57	.56
Losses, 2% " "	.23	.22	.22	.20	.21	.20	.19	.18
Selling Price,	11.50	11.00	11.25	10.00	10.50	9.75	9.50	9.25

Order Sheets. In this business Order Sheets similar to the one illustrated below will be used. When an order is received that is not to be filled immediately, a detailed record is made on an Order Sheet, which includes the serial number of the order, the name and address of the person or firm ordering, the terms, shipping directions, date of order, the kinds of goods ordered and the number of dozens of each kind. These sheets are kept in consecutive order, usually in a binder, and are indexed. When a part of the goods are shipped, they are deducted from the order when the bill is rendered. When all the goods belonging to an order have been sent the Order Sheet is filed away for reference.

ORDER SHEET.

Ordered by *James Hare,*

Terms, *4/10, 2/30, net 4 months.* Address, *Chicago, Illinois.*

Shipping Directions, *3 doz. Samples by Express. 1-2 at once. Balance Oct. 1.*

DATE.	S.B. F	1216	1211	1209	1206	1126	1111	1106	1101	EXPLANATIONS.
July 1		100	50	50	75	25	40	40	20	dozens ordered
3		3	3	3	3	3	3	3	3	Samples
		97	47	47	72	22	37	37	17	Balance
25		47	22	22	35	10	17	17	7	½ of order.
		50	25	25	37	12	20	20	10	

Impression Sales Book. The Impression Sales Book is a book made of fine tissue paper, and is similar in many respects to the Impression Account Sales Book described and illustrated on pages 101 and 102. When an Impression Sales Book is used the bills are written up and an impression taken of them in this book, by means of a letter press. The amount of each bill is extended to a column ruled for that purpose and posted to the Ledger. What advantage do you see in using this book? As this book is very similar to the Impression Account Sales Book and as no billing is to be done, you will not be required to use an Impression Sales Book in this business.

All entries are to be recorded in a Sales Book similar in form to the one illustrated on page 162. Study the form carefully and note that all goods are designated by number instead of writing the description of the gloves.

Cutters Stock Book. After an order for future delivery is received and recorded in the Order Book or on an Order Sheet, it is also recorded in the Cutters Stock Book. Usually this book is ruled so that there is a division for each month of an entire year. In the illustration on page 162 divisions for but four months are ruled. Five columns are ruled under each division, the first to receive the order number, the second to receive the stock numbers of the goods ordered, the third to receive the number of dozens ordered, while the fourth and fifth are used to record the goods that have been cut and sent to the other departments to be made up. As goods are manufactured, based upon orders or probable sales for each season, it is important to know exactly the kind of goods to be made and in what months they are wanted. If the Cutters Stock Book is properly kept the manufacturer

Sales Book.

Shipping Marks.	F	Name and Address	Ck. Kind.	Doz.	Price.		Amt		Bill Rend.	
R & O		Heywood & Co.,	1101	5	7	50	37	50		
Case		Philadelphia.	1106	5	6	75	33	75		
#17185		117 Adams St.	1115	5	9	50	47	50		
		Aug. 1st, 5 30, 6 10.	1126	5	8	25	41	25		
			1130	5	10	50	52	50		
D			1206	5	9	75	48	75		
1978			1209	5	12	75	63	75		
			1211	5	18	00	90	00		
			1216	5	14	75	73	75	488	75
M D		Hare & Smith,	1016	3	12	40	37	20		
Case		Chicago.	1101	2	7	50	15	00		
#17186		Aug. 1st, 5 30, 6 10.	1208	2	11	50	23	00		
			1216	2	17	00	34	00	109	20
Am X										
Case		Allen & Jewett,	1101	1	7	50	7	50		
#17187		Helena.	1131	1	12	00	12	00		
H R		Aug. 1st, 5 30, 6 10.	1120	1	8	75	8	75		
19 17			1200	1	14	00	14	00	42	25
		Merchandise Cr.		58					640	20

will be able to keep his stock about equal to the demand, without being in danger of running short or of carrying over a large amount of stock from the previous season. When all the goods for a month have been cut and made up the footings of the third and fifth columns should be equal.

Stock Tickets. The object of the Stock Tickets is to keep track of the goods while being manufactured. Suppose that 100 dozens of any one style are cut, that number should

Cutters Stock Book—Beginning *June* 189

June.					July.					August.					September.				
Order No.	Kind.	Doz.	Kind.	Doz.	Order No.	Kind.	Doz.	Kind.	Doz.	Order No.	Kind.	Doz.	Kind.	Doz.	Order No.	Kind.	Doz.	Kind.	Doz.
1	1216	50	1216	100	2	926	75	916	25	6	941	50	953	50	9	916	15	1206	50
	1211	50	1206	50		1100	50	953	15		952	50	1100	25		911	15	1100	20
	1209	50	1211	75		1106	50	1216	25		953	50	1206	35		953	15	911	25
	1206	25	916	25		1216	25	917	75		1100	50	941	25		1100	10	1216	50
	1126	25	926	25	5	916	75	926	25	7	1106	10	952	75	10	1211	50	1211	75
3	1206	75	1209	100		917	25	1100	50		1206	10	1216	25		1216	50	953	30
	1209	75	1206	50		926	25	1216	25		1211	10	1211	25	12	941	25	1106	25
	1211	50	917	25		953	25	917	50		1216	10	936	25		953	25	1209	50
	1216	50	941	25	8	917	100	926	100	10	1211	50	1126	15		1106	10	1101	25
5	916	25	1100	25		926	100	1106	75		1216	50	916	50		1126	10	1211	25
	917	25	953	50		1100	25	953	10	11	936	25	941	50		1206	50	953	10
	926	25	952	25		1106	25	1100	25		941	25	1216	25	13	1209	75		
	953	25	1126	25		1216	25	926	75		952	25	917	50		1211	75		
6	941	25	1209	25			[illegible]	916	50		1126	25	1211	35		1216	50		
	952	25	1211	25					[illegible]		1206	25	1106	10		1101	50		
	953	25								13	916	50	917	25		1106	25		
	1100	25									917	75		[illegible]					
		[illegible]										[illegible]							

pass through the making departments, and when finished, be delivered to the salesrooms. If a less number is delivered to the salesrooms an investigation is made and the loss traced to the proper department. Without some such record it would be possible for dishonest employees to carry away stock without being detected.

Pay Roll Book. The form of Pay Roll illustrated below is one that can be used to advantage in any business where employees are paid off monthly. A column is provided to receive the amounts paid employees on account. This form of Pay Roll contemplates that a detailed record of the employees' time, in the different departments, be kept in each foreman's Time Book, and that only the total amount due each employee be carried to the Pay Roll. The only difference between a Pay Roll Book and a foreman's Time Book is in the size, the latter usually being pocket size.

PAY ROLL BOOK.

NAME.	NAME OF FOREMAN.	DEP'T.	B'K.	JULY.			AUGUST.		
				AMT.	PAID.	BAL.	AMT.	PAID.	BAL.
Amanda Connor,	W. Finch,	Hemming,	A	30 50	10 00	20 50	31 50	10 00	21 50
Carrie Lyons,				34 80		34 80	35 80	5 00	30 80
Lena Frey,	Miss Everson,	Silking,	B	35 50	5 00	30 50	34 60		34 60
Kate Schwartz,				30 70		30 70	30 75	5 00	25 75
Nina Eckler,				31 85	5 00	26 85	30 80	10 00	20 80
Lizzie Patch,				36 00		36 00	33 00		33 00
Erma Price,	Miss Adams,	Cutting,	C	34 25	10 00	24 25	34 05	5 00	29 05
Minnie Dunn,				28 50		28 50	28 50		28 50
Wm. Stump,				31 35		31 35	30 25		30 25
Jos. Helm,	H. Ward,	Making,	D	37 75	5 00	32 75	31 70	5 00	26 70
Arthur Fulmer,				34 25		34 25	35 60		35 60
Daniel Brevier,				30 00		30 00	31 50		31 50
				395 45	35 00	360 45	388 05	40 00	348 05

Cash Book. The Cash Book used in this business is of the ordinary form of special column Cash Book. (*See illustration on pages 164 and 165.*)

Journal. The ordinary form of Journal will be used to record the purchases and credit the proper departments. If the purchases are sufficient in number to warrant it, an Abstract Purchase Ledger and a Charges Department form could be kept, the same as in the department store business.

Student's Records. The student will make his records from a description of the transactions. H. T. Williams, the partner having the management of the manufacturing plant will keep a record of the cash receipts and payments in a Petty Cash Book, from which you will write up the regular Cash Book. The entries in the Petty Cash Book are proved each day with the amount of cash on hand by Mr. Williams, so it will not be necessary for you to prove the cash. The balance of cash on hand on the last day of the month should agree with the amount called for by the regular Cash Book.

Petty Cash Book. This book is usually a coarse, cheap book and the entries in it are generally made in pencil. All entries in this book should be made by the person or persons handling the money. Whenever possible, but one person should be permitted to receive and pay out the cash, and he should be held responsible for the correctness of the same. Being a

CASH BOOK.

DATE.		L. F.	NAMES AND EXPLANATIONS.		DISCOUNTS.		GENERAL.	
June	1		Balance,				7640	81
	6		Collier & Meyer,	Bal. acct. less 5%	74	09	1407	61
			Adams & Son,	Bal. acct. less 3%	22	82	737	68
			Merchandise,	Barnes & Co.'s Sale			197	60
	10		Bills Receivable,	C. V. Hick's note			450	00
			Bills Receivable,	O. S. Snyder's note			500	00
			Jones & Co.,	Inv. of 1st inst. 3%	20	72	669	78
	15		Bills Payable,	Disct. our note 60 da.			550	00
	20		Merchandise,	Wilson & Co.'s sale			300	00
	25		Badman & Son,	Inv. of 2d inst. net			370	50
	30		Munson Bros.	Inv. of 23d inst. less 10%	47	58	428	22
			Mdse. Disct. Dr.		165	21		
							13252	20
June	30		Balance,				7755	40

book of original entry, great care should be exercised in keeping the Petty Cash Book, as it takes precedence over the regular Cash Book when brought into court as evidence. The entries in the regular Cash Book are generally made but once a day; they are taken from the Petty Cash Book and from the stubs of the Check Book. As no Check Book is kept in this business, Mr. Williams will keep a memorandum account with the bank, charging it with all deposits and crediting it with all checks drawn. In this case all checks received and issued will be entered in the Petty Cash Book; ordinarily this is not done in business.

Mill Account. In business it is customary to keep an account with the Mill or Tanning Department, to determine if it is a paying investment. In that event Mill account is debited for all that it receives in the way of labor and chemicals needed in tanning and dressing the raw hides into glove leather, and is credited for the market value of all leather that it produces. If the cost of running the Mill is more than the market value of the leather produced, it would not be a paying investment and would be discontinued, as it would be cheaper to purchase the leather already dressed. As the Mill account would be kept very similar to a Branch Store account, the student is not required to keep a separate account with the Mill in this business.

Division of Labor. The use of more than one Ledger in a business presupposes a division of labor among several bookkeepers. The method of keeping a General Ledger and several sub-ledgers has been fully explained, consequently in this business but one Ledger will

Cash Book.

Date.		L. F.	Names and Explanations.		Disc'ts.		General.		Expense.	
June	1		2 tons coal 10.00	Cleaning office 4.75					14	75
			Labor	Adv. E. Jones			12	00		
			Salary Acct.	Adv. J. Lyon, Supt.			25	00		
	6		Office books 10.00	Pens and ink .50					10	50
			Bower & Co.	Inv. No. 11, May 1st, ck. No. 1	69	03	1311	47		
	10		Labor	Adv. W. Adams			7	50		
	13		Office chairs 12.00	Laundry .40						
			Gas bill 7.50	Stationery 1.50					21	40
			Ellie Erb & Co.	Inv. No. 19, June 1, ck. No. 2	48	53	921	97		
			A. F. Peck	Inv. No. 20, " 1, ck. No. 3			470	50		
	15		Discount	On disct. note			5	50		
	20		Bill for repairing water pipes 29.50	Postage1. 20					30	70
			Johnson Bros.	Inv. No. 21, June 2d, ck. No. 4	58	73	1115	77		
			Allen & Tidd	Inv. No. 28, June 3d, ck. No. 5	19	04	361	71		
			Interest	On note due to-day			3	75		
	25		Bills Payable	Note due to day ck. No. 6			500	00		
			Water tax 18.23	Telegram .50					18	73
	30		Labor Acct.	Bal. of Pay Roll			475	30		
			Salary Acct.	Bal. due Supt.			75	00		
			Freight and Cartage	Bill for Month			15	25		
			J. B. Luckey	Private use			100	00		
			Mdse. Disct. Cr.		195	33	5400	72		
			Expense	For month			96	08	96	08
			Balance,	*In safe* 505.20 / *In bank* 7250.20			7755	40		
							13252	20		

be used. This will enable the student to concentrate his attention on the features that are special to the manufacturing business. It must be remembered, however, that it is customary and necessary to keep more than one Ledger in large manufacturing establishments.

July 7, 189–.

D. T. Paterson, the expert accountant engaged by the partners, to investigate the standing of the glove manufacturing plant owned by J. B. Luckey reports as follows:

July 6, 189–.
(Your place here.)

Messrs. J. A. Luman & Co.,
Proprietors City Department Store, City.

Gentlemen:

Herewith I hand you the report of my investigation of the books of record and financial standing of the glove manufacturing plant, owned and for forty-five years conducted by J. B. Luckey.

1. After a careful research among the records of this (your) County, I am assured that J. B. Luckey is the legal owner of the said glove plant. There are no incumberances of any kind on record, consequently he is able to sell and give good title to the purchasers. Taxes of every description have been paid, as is evidenced by the tax receipts submitted herewith.

2. Inquiries have been made of all former creditors as shown by the books, and their replies submitted herewith are evidence that all obligations of every description have been discharged.

3. Advertisements were inserted in the daily papers in which all creditors were requested to present their claims for payment. No claims, other than those credited on the books were presented, and all presented were paid.

4. The market value of the merchandise on hand is found to be $7536.40. (See Inventory submitted herewith. The machinery, after considering the first cost, repairs, wear and tear, and the decline in the price of machinery, I find (by estimation) to be worth $24818.20. The real estate is inventoried on the books at $52000, which amount I consider it to be worth. Furniture and fixtures are inventoried at $400 and are probably worth more. Accounts Receivable, or amounts due from others, are as follows: Heywood & Co., $4280; R. S. Thomas, $2242.40. Judging from their past records and their present financial circumstances, as reported by the commercial agencies, these accounts will be paid in full as soon as due. Their replies to my letters written to them certify that the claims are just and that it is their intention to honor them.

5. Taking into consideration the fact that this plant has been in successful operation for forty-five years, that its business has steadily increased, that all its obligations have been honestly discharged, and that the yearly sales have averaged fully $75000 in the past fifteen years, I estimate the Good Will to be worth $30000.

6. The actual inventory value of the plant is thus found to be $91277; the value of the Good Will added to this makes the plant worth $121277

Respectfully submitted,

D. T. Paterson.

The above report meets with the partners' approval. The amount asked by Mr. Luckey is $100000, of which each of the partners has paid one fourth. Make the entry in the Journal, debiting Merchandise, Machinery, Real Estate, Furniture and Fixtures, Heywood & Co., and R. S. Thomas for the amounts named in the accountant's report. Debit Good Will for the difference between the net value of the assets and the price paid. Credit each of the partners for his share. For entry of a similar nature see page 87. Open the above accounts as indicated in the index printed on the cover pages of the Ledger. Post and check over your posting.

Mr. H. T. Williams is to be the manager at a salary of $150 per month. With the exception of the bookkeeper, all of the former employees of J. B. Luckey have been retained. The names of the employees will be handed in by the foremen of the different departments at the end of the month. Wm. Cloud, the superintendent of the Mill is to receive a salary of $1500 per year; John Hermann, the traveling representative is to receive a salary of $100 per month, and Jas. Mackey, the shipping clerk is to receive a salary of $40 per month.

The partners have withdrawn $5000 from the department store business to be used in conducting the glove manufacturing business. This amount is borrowed from J. A. Luman & Co., but you are not to make the entry now as Mr. Williams has made a record of it in the Petty Cash Book, from which book it will be transferred to the regular Cash Book.

The kind of gloves to be placed on the market are specified by numbers in the following price list:

No.	Selling Price.	Cost Price.	No.	Selling Price.	Cost Price.	No.	Selling Price.	Cost Price.	No.	Selling Price.	Cost Price.
916	$7.50	$5.57	936	$35.00	$25.92	1101	$9.50	$7.05	1206	$9.75	$7.24
917	6.75	5.02	941	33.50	24.81	1106	8.75	6.50	1209	12.75	9.46
926	7.25	5.39	952	14.50	10.75	1111	7.75	5.76	1211	11.50	8.53
931	5.25	3.91	953	15.75	11.68	1126	9.25	6.87	1216	17.00	12.60

The cost and selling prices of the various numbers on sale were ascertained as shown in the illustrations and explanations of the Cost Book and Merchandise account. (*See pages 159 and 160*). Make a detailed analysis of the cost of No. 1126 so that you will understand how the cost and selling prices are ascertained. Your teacher will assist you, if you are unable to make the calculations. In business this work is usually done by the superintendent of the plant, or by the bookkeeper under his direction.

The inventory of merchandise submitted by the expert accountant is as follows:

MERCHANDISE INVENTORY.

30 dozens, No. 1216,	12.60	378 00	
40 dozens, No. 1211,	8.53	341 20	
20 dozens, No. 1209,	9.46	189 20	
70 dozens, No. 1206,	7.24	506 80	
70 dozens, No. 1126,	6.87	480 90	
70 dozens, No. 1111,	5.76	403 20	
70 dozens, No. 1106,	6.50	455 00	
75 dozens, No. 916,	5.57	417 75	
75 dozens, No. 917,	5.02	376 50	
75 dozens, No. 926,	5.39	401 25	
300 dozens, No. 931,	3.91	1173 00	
20 dozens, No. 936,	25.92	518 40	
20 dozens, No. 941,	24.81	496 20	
50 dozens, No. 952,	10.75	537 50	
40 dozens, No. 953,	11.68	467 20	
89 dozens (odd and broken), worth		391 30	
			7536 40

One order has been received which reads as follows:

MR. J. B. LUCKEY, PHILADELPHIA, PA., July 6, 189-.

(your place here.)

DEAR SIR:

Please deliver the following winter goods as per directions given below at the prices named in your annual quotations.

100 dozens, No. 1216; 50 dozens, No. 1211; 24 dozens, No. 1209; 24 dozens, No. 1126.

Kindly ship one-half of this order during the present month and the remainder on or before Sept. 1. Express sample dozens at once.

Very truly,

HEYWOOD & CO.

This order meets with the approval of the firm, and they have written Heywood & Co., telling them that their order will receive prompt attention. They have also notified them of the change in the proprietorship of the glove plant. Enter the order on an Order Blank, following the directions given on page 161. This order is to be designated as number 1. The terms of this order are the regular terms: 6/10, 5/30, net 4 mos. In business these orders would be filed in consecutive order; in this business you may keep the Order Sheets between the pages of one of your blank books. If a Cutters Stock Book were kept this order would be immediately recorded therein, so that the manufacture of the gloves required to fill the order would begin at once.

The invoice listed below has been checked with the goods received and has been audited. Enter it in the Journal, debiting Silk account and crediting the firm from whom it was purchased. Wm. Austin & Son (No. 1), 2/10, net 30 days, $125.00. Write the explanation of this entry as follows: "Invoice No. 1." In business detailed information of the entry would be obtained by referring to the invoice bearing this number.

The Petty Cash Book contains the following records for the day; enter them in the regular Cash Book. Be sure to short-extend the items to be charged to Expense and extend the amount to the Expense column. All the credit items given below are to be charged to Expense.

J. A. Laman & Co.,	5000 00	Postage, 2.00; pens and ink, .50,	2 50
Heywood & Co.,	4280 00	Set of books,	12 00
		Telegram,	25
		Expert accountant's charge,	100 00

Quotations have been received from A. P. Root & Co. for 25 bales Sisal Buckskins, undressed, at 40% per lb., F. O. B. in New York. Five bales are in port, 10 bales are due by next steamer, and 10 bales are ready for shipment from South America. Order has been placed for the entire lot by wire.

Post the books and check over your posting.

JULY 8, 189–.

The gloves on hand as inventoried on page 167 have been sold to S. T. Standish, Cleveland, terms regular, at an advance of $2.00 per dozen on our inventory price. Make the record in the Sales Book, referring to the illustration on page 162.

An abstract of the orders received is given below.

Jas. Hare, terms 6/10, 5/30, net 4 mos. 50 doz., No. 1216; 100 doz., No. 1126; 50 doz., No. 931. One-half to be shipped as soon as possible; the balance not later than August 1. Samples to be forwarded by express at once. Enter on an Order Sheet.

Henry J. Graves Sons, terms 6/10, 5/30, net 4 mos. 100 doz., No. 1126; 100 doz., No. 1209. Ship one-half by the 25th; remainder in the month of August. Sample dozens to be sent by express. Enter on an Order Sheet.

Following is a record of the goods shipped to-day.

Heywood & Co., sample dozens sent by express. (*See order No. 1.*) Deduct the samples on the order sheet as illustrated below and record them in the Sales Book at the selling prices given on page 166.

DATE.		S. B. F.	1216.	1211.	1209.	1126.	EXPLANATION.
July	7		100	50	24	24	Dozens ordered.
	8		1	1	1	1	Samples per S. B.
			99	49	23	23	Balance to be delivered.

Sample dozens have also been sent to Jas. Hare and to Henry J. Graves Sons. Make the necessary records on the Order Sheets and in the Sales Book.

The following invoices have been received, checked and audited; enter them in the Journal. Be sure to charge the proper accounts and to write a clear but brief explanation of each entry.

A. P. Root & Co. (No. 2), July 7, Sisal Buckskins, 3088 lbs., $1234.00 (Charge Raw Material account).

Wm. Austin & Son (No. 3, July 7, 2/10, net 30 days, $118.75 (Silk account).

George Procter (No. 4), July 7, net 30 days, $29.40 (Bands & Boxes).

The Petty Cash Book contains the following records; enter them in the regular Cash Book. Be sure to make a record of the discounts.

Machinery repairs,	6	25
Expense, broom,		75
" laundry for office,		80
Furniture & Fixtures, desk,	100	00
Wm. Austin & Son, less 2%,	122	50
Traveling Expense, Herman,	100	00
Expense, sample cases,	8	00

Post and check over your posting.

JULY 10, 189-.

Shipped one-half of the following orders, less the samples that have been sent. Henry J. Graves Sons, Jas. Hare and Heywood & Co. Make the proper records on the Order Sheets, then enter in the Sales Book.

NOTE.—The question may arise: How can we be shipping goods when all the goods on hand have been sent to S. T. Standish, Cleveland? It must be remembered that these goods have been manufactured since the orders were placed several days ago.

The Petty Cash Book contains the following records; enter them as previously instructed. Record the wages advanced to employees, by short extending the items and charging Labor for the total amount, the same as given in the Petty Cash Book.

S. T. Standish, less 6%,	9178	54	Labor, adv. H. N. Peck 10.00			
			" Ellen Meunier 5.00			
			" R. Foltz 12.00			
			" Erma Price 5.00			
					32	00
			Wm. Austin & Son,	less 2%	116	37

Post and check over your posting.

JULY 11, 189-.

The following invoices have been received, checked and audited. Be sure to charge the proper accounts when entering them.

Clarence Stoner (No. 5) 2/10, net 30, $1935.00, (Raw Material).

Leroy Davenport (No. 6) cash, $12.00 (Buttons). Record this invoice in the Journal, so that an account with the party will appear on the Ledger.

George Proctor (No. 7), $34.50 (Bands & Boxes).

The Petty Cash Book contains the following records: enter them in the regular Cash Book.

R. S. Thomas	2242	40	Leroy Davenport	12	00
			Expense, advertising	38	75
			Expense, postage 2.00, stationery 4.00 pens .20	6	20
			Expense, repairing water pipes	2	75
			Expense, repairing gas pipes	3	75
			Furniture and Fixtures, chairs	8	50
			Expense, 2 tons coal	13	00

Post and check over your posting.

JULY 15, 189-.

The sales since the 11th inst. are as follows: All of them are to be entered on the regular terms: 6/10, 5/30, net 4 mos.

12th. Henry J. Graves Sons, 10 doz. 1126; 10 doz. 1209.

Jas. Hare, 10 doz. 1216; 10 doz. 1126; 10 doz. 931.

Wm. H. Chamberlain, Evansville, 5 doz. 1126. This order need not be placed on an Order Sheet as it was filled from Wm. H. Chamberlain's order the day it was received.

Fred Sturman & Co., Indianapolis, one-twelfth dozen each of all the numbers on sale for the season. (This entry is to be posted to Sundry Accounts Receivable.)

The Petty Cash Book contains the following records; enter them in regular Cash Book.

Heywood & Co., less 6	1317	41	Expense, cleaning office,	10	50
Jas. Hart, less 6	957	62	Expense, daily paper,	1	50
Henry J. Graves Sons, less 6	1634	00	Clarence Stoner, less 2%	1896	30
			A. P. Root & Co.,	1234	00

Post the books and check over the posting.

JULY 31, 189 .

Enter the following sales in the Sales Book on regular terms.

16th. Wm. H. Lester, Kansas City, 15 doz. 1216; 15 doz. 1211; 15 doz. 1209; 25 doz. 1206; 3 doz. 1126.

17th. Thos. K. Harrington, Cannelton, Ind., 25 doz. 1206; 10 doz. 953; 10 doz. 952; 10 doz. 911.

18th. Wm. H. Chamberlain, Evansville, 5 doz. 936; 5 doz. 926; 5 doz. 917; 5 doz. 916.

19th. Birch & Shelters, Cloverport, Ky., 25 doz. 1101; 10 doz. 1106; 10 doz. 1111.

Post the accounts of Lester and Harrington to Sundry Accounts Receivable.

Henry J. Graves Sons order the following to be shipped by August 5: 25 doz. 1206; 100 doz. 953. Samples to be sent at once by express. Enter on an Order Sheet and make the entry for the samples on the Order Sheet and in the Sales Book.

The time of the employees is listed below. Enter same in the Pay Roll Book referring to the illustration on page 163. Each foreman or forewoman of a department keeps a time book; it is from these time books that the Pay Roll is compiled in business.

SILKING DEPARTMENT, Time Book "A." Amanda Connor, forewoman, $30.50; Carrie Lyons, $28.00; Bertha Polk, $25.50.

HEMMING DEPARTMENT, Time Book "B." Maggie Allard, forewoman, $29.75; Rosa James, $26.75; Ellen Little, $30.50; Ellen Meunier, $28.25; (Record the amount paid on the 10th inst.); Mattie Allen, $28.75; Amanda Little, $25.50.

MAKING DEPARTMENT, Time Book "C." Floyd Long, foreman, $65.50; F. G. Prine, $49.75; Geo. H. Bush, $17.80; R. Folts, $66.25; (Record the amount paid on the 10th inst.)

CUTTING DEPARTMENT, Time Book "D." H. N. Peek, foreman, $16.30; (Record the amount paid); Austin J. Camp, $58.40.

CONTRACT WORK, per Job Book. Mrs. Mary Hostler, $53.50; Maude Elliott, $19.60; Jas. Bell, $28.40; Robt. Jones, $56.75; Bessie Nichols, $40.30; Clara Frey, $27.50; Frank Royce, $25.00; Jessie Weeks, $21.50; Minnie Dunn, $20.75; Erma Price, $18.40; (Record the amount advanced); Lena Frey, $16.50; Thomas Burns, $37.75; Ruehen Doty, $48.50; Lizzie Patch, $58.25; A. K. Chandler, $19.00; Timothy Hunt, $40.70; Geo. Mosby, $27.50.

Ascertain the total amount paid for wages. Rule and Foot the Pay Roll.

A separate Pay Roll is kept at the Mill by the superintendent. In business this Pay Roll would be verified by the bookkeeper before the money is sent to pay it. The amount of the Mill Pay Roll is given in the Petty Cash Book and is also charged to Labor account.

The Petty Cash Book contains the following records: enter them in the regular Cash Book.

Expense, renovating carpets		6	00
Freight and cartage, bill for mo.		75	85
Salary, Herman, $\frac{1}{2}$ mo.	75.00		
Cloud, $\frac{3}{4}$ mo.	93.75		
Mackey, $\frac{1}{2}$ mo.	30.00		
Student, 6 da.	60 00	371	
Williams, $\frac{3}{4}$ mo.	112.50		25
Labor, balance of pay roll		1115	40
Labor, mill pay roll		1021	50

Foot and rule the Cash Book and Sales Book; the cash on hand is: bank \$17353.67, safe \$237.63.

Post the books and check over the posting. Take a trial balance.

Preparatory to closing the books, Mr. Williams has had an inventory taken, of which the following is an abstract.

ABSTRACT OF INVENTORIES, JULY 31, 189–.

Real Estate,	32000	00
Machinery,	44818	20
Furniture and Fixtures,	400	00
Good Will,	8500	00
Traveling Expense, amount not used,	21	70
Silk Account,	110	50
Raw Material,	1083	30
Merchandise, 5 doz. No. 1216; 10 doz. No. 1206; 5 doz. No. 916; 10 doz. No. 931; 5 doz. No. 936; 10 doz. No. 953; 20 doz. No. 941.	944	95

Before making a Balance Sheet in a manufacturing business the inventories are written (in red ink) in the proper ledger accounts. The next step is to transfer the balances of the accounts that enter into the cost of merchandise, to the debit of the Merchandise account. These accounts are then ruled and the inventories (if any) are brought down. It is evident after this is done that the Merchandise account and the accounts that enter into the cost of merchandise will not appear on the Balance Sheet as they appeared in the trial balance.

You may now transfer the inventories given to the proper ledger accounts in red ink. Transfer the balances of the following accounts to the debit of the Merchandise account: Raw Material, Labor, Salaries, Silk, Bands & Boxes, Buttons, Freight & Cartage, Discounts and Traveling Expenses. Next rule these accounts and bring down the inventories.

In making the Balance Sheet use the balance of the Merchandise account (not including the inventory) as given in the ledger account, instead of the balance as exhibited in the trial balance. Likewise carry the inventories of the accounts closed into the Merchandise account, from the Ledger to the Balance Sheet.

In business when the accounts receivable and accounts payable are quite numerous, they are never itemized in the Balance Sheet. You may now ascertain the total of the amounts due the business and enter it on the Balance Sheet, specifying it as "Accounts Receivable." Likewise find the total amount owing by the business, and specify it as "Accounts Payable." Foot the first two columns of the Balance Sheet to satisfy yourself that your work has been done correctly. Enter all the inventories in the Resource column (in red ink) and complete the Balance Sheet.

Close the books and present them for inspection and approval.

MANUFACTURING BUSINESS INCORPORATED.

Corporations. A corporation is an artificial being or person formed by a number of natural persons, and is endowed with the capacity of perpetual succession and of acting in certain respects like a natural person. A corporation derives its existence and power from the state under whose laws it is organized. The business of a corporation is transacted through and by its directors and officers, who are elected by the stockholders for a specified time, usually one year.

Advantages of Corporations. The one great advantage that corporations have over ordinary partnerships is the power of succession. In a partnership the death of a partner, the sale of a partner's interest, habitual intemperance, the doing of things that are detrimental to the other partners' interests, and some other causes operate to bring about a dissolution of the partnership. In a corporation each individual's interest is composed of a certain number of shares, which are evidenced by a certificate of stock. Whenever one of the stockholders dies or he disposes of his stock, the corporation is in no way affected by it. The death of an officer also has no effect on a corporation, as a successor is immediately elected by the directors.

In a partnership the private property of the partners can be held for the debts of the partnership; in a corporation the private property of the stockholders usually can not be held for the debts of the corporation.

When the number of persons interested in a business enterprise is very large, it would be very inconvenient, and almost impossible, to conduct it as a partnership. Every death, sale of interest, etc., would bring about a dissolution of the partnership. As the private property of each partner can be held for the liabilities of the partnership, very few persons are disposed to enter a partnership where the members are quite numerous.

Corporations not only possess advantages over partnerships but are absolutely necessary in conducting the large mercantile, manufacturing and other business enterprises of our time. It would be almost impossible to get along without them.

How Formed. Corporations are formed in two ways, viz., (1) by charter; (2) under general statute. When a corporation is formed by a special act of the legislature of any state or territory, it is said to be formed by charter. Owing to the convenience of the second method most corporations are now formed under general statute laws. The growing demand for a simple method of organizing corporations has led the legislatures of all, or nearly all, the states and territories to enact laws governing the organization of corporations. It is now possible to organize a corporation at any time, without applying to the state legislature, by simply complying with the law governing the incorporation of business enterprises. As the requirements vary somewhat in the different states, the student is advised to consult the statute laws of his own state. For the purpose of illustration, the requirements for incorporation in the State of New York are given on the following pages.

NOTE. Owing to the importance of corporations in the commercial world to-day, it will be well for every student to make a thorough study of them. This may be done by consulting and studying commercial law texts, the statutes of the state in which the student resides, and such other books of reference as may be suggested by the teacher.

Requirements for Incorporation. The first and most important step in incorporating a business enterprise is to secure subscribers for stock. In the State of New York the law requires that at least one-half of the capital stock must be subscribed for in good faith, before the Certificates of Incorporation (two in number) can be filed. In some states

Certificates of Incorporation are designated as Articles of Incorporation. The law further requires that one-half of the capital stock must be paid within one year from the date when the Certificates of Incorporation were filed. Three or more subscribers for stock are necessary in New York State, two-thirds of them must be citizens of the United States, and a majority of them must be residents of the State.

The next step is to hold a preliminary meeting of the subscribers to determine the number of directors to be appointed, and to appoint those who are to serve the first year. The directors appointed at this meeting will be formally elected after the Certificates of Incorporation have been accepted and filed with the proper state and county officials. The number of directors required in the State of New York is not less than three nor more than thirteen, each of whom shall be a holder of at least five shares of stock. At least two of the directors must be residents of the State. A record of the proceedings of this preliminary meeting should be recorded in a Minute Book by the person appointed to act as secretary.

The next step is to draw up and execute two copies of the Certificate of Incorporation, both of which are to be signed and acknowledged by the incorporators. It is a good plan to secure the services of a competent attorney to prepare the Certificates of Incorporation and to advise the incorporators in their proceedings. The form of a certificate used in the State of New York is as follows:

CERTIFICATE OF INCORPORATION.

State of New York. } ss.
COUNTY OF MONROE, }

We, the undersigned, desiring to form a corporation pursuant to the statutes relating to the Business Corporation Law, all being of full age, and two-thirds being citizens of the United States, and a majority being residents of the State of New York, do hereby certify:

I.

The name of the proposed corporation is the Chainless Bicycle Company.

II.

The object for which this corporation is formed is to engage in the manufacture of the chainless bicycles, of which Isaac Wilcox is the patentee.

III.

The Capital Stock of the corporation shall be One Hundred Thousand Dollars ($100000).

IV.

The Capital Stock shall be divided into one thousand (1000) shares, and to be valued at One Hundred Dollars ($100.00) per share.

V.

The location of its principal business office shall be in the city of Rochester, in the County of Monroe, State of New York.

VI.

The duration of the corporation is to be fifty (50) years.

VII.

The number of its directors is to be three (3).

VIII.

The names and post-office addresses of the directors for the first year are as follows:

Isaac Wilcox,	*Rochester, N. Y.*
H. L. Miller,	*Rochester, N. Y.*
J. H. Moore,	*Rochester, N. Y.*

IX.

The names and post-office addresses of the subscribers for stock, and the number of shares for which they subscribe are as follows:

NAMES.	POST-OFFICE ADDRESSES.	NO. OF SHARES.
Isaac Wilcox,	*Rochester, N. Y.*	*Twenty.*
H. L. Miller,	*Rochester, N. Y.*	*Fifteen.*
J. H. Moore,	*Rochester, N. Y.*	*Fifteen.*
W. S. Osborn,	*Detroit, Mich.*	*Ten.*

In witness whereof, *We have made, signed and acknowledged this certificate this first day of August, 189–.*

Isaac Wilcox.
H. L. Miller.
J. H. Moore.
W. S. Osborn.

State of New York,
County of Monroe, } ss.

On this first day of August, 189–, before me personally appeared Isaac Wilcox, H. L. Miller, J. H. Moore and W. S. Osborn, to me personally known to be the persons described in, and who executed the foregoing certificate, and they severally acknowledged to me that they executed the same for the purposes therein mentioned.

Richard Roe,
Notary Public, Monroe Co., N. Y.

After they have been executed by the incorporators, the two copies of the Certificate of Incorporation must be sent to the Secretary of State, accompanied by a bank draft for the amount of the incorporation fee. In New York the incorporation fee is one-eighth of one per cent. of the capital stock. The Secretary of State will attach his certificate, in which he will state that the Certificate of Incorporation has been recorded. One copy will be filed in his office and one copy will be forwarded to the Clerk (in some states the Recorder) of the county in which the corporation is to do business.

The incorporators should next hold a meeting and formally elect the directors chosen before the Certificates of Incorporation were filed with the state and county officials. The directors should then choose the necessary officers from among their number. At this meeting the necessary by-laws for the management of the corporation should be adopted. These by-laws, among other things, should specify the number of officers to be elected and the time they are to serve. A complete record of the proceedings of this meeting should be made in the Minute Book by the Secretary.

The officers of the corporation now being elected, the president (or vice-president) and treasurer (or secretary) will comply with the next requirement of the law, by certifying that one-half of the capital stock has been subscribed for in good faith. This certificate is to be executed and acknowledged in duplicate: one copy to be filed in the County Clerk's office and the other with the Secretary of State. The form of certificate as used in New York State is as follows:

CERTIFICATE THAT ONE-HALF OF CAPITAL STOCK IS SUBSCRIBED.

State of New York, }
COUNTY OF MONROE, } ss.

We, the President and Treasurer of the Chainless Bicycle Company, do hereby certify that one-half of the Capital Stock of the Chainless Bicycle Company has in good faith been subscribed.

In witness whereof, *We have signed and executed this certificate on this Fifth day of August, 189–.*

ISAAC WILCOX, *President.*
J. H. MOORE, *Treasurer.*

State of New York, }
COUNTY OF MONROE, } ss.

On this Fifth day of August, 189–, before me personally appeared Isaac Wilcox and J. H. Moore, to me personally known to be the persons described in, and who executed the foregoing certificate, and severally acknowledged to me that they executed the same.

RICHARD ROE,
Notary Public, Monroe Co., N. Y.

State of New York, }
COUNTY OF MONROE, } ss.

Isaac Wilcox and J. H. Moore, being severally duly sworn, each for himself deposes and says that he, the said Isaac Wilcox, is President of the Chainless Bicycle Company; and that he, the said J. H. Moore, is Treasurer thereof, and that the statements contained in the foregoing certificate are true.

ISAAC WILCOX.
J. H. MOORE.

Severally subscribed and sworn to before me on this Fifth day of August, 189–.

RICHARD ROE,
Notary Public, Monroe Co., N. Y.

The statutes of New York state further require that one-half of the capital stock shall be paid within one year from the date of incorporation, and that two certificates of such payment be executed and acknowledged by a majority of the directors, and filed with the Secretary of State and the County Clerk. Failure to comply with these requirements will tend to dissolve the corporation at the end of the year, and the directors will be held responsible individually and collectively for the acts of the corporation and the debts contracted by it, after the expiration of the first year. Their private property may then be held to discharge any of the liabilities of the corporation, the same as in an ordinary partnership. The form of this certificate for the State of New York is as follows:

CERTIFICATE OF PAYMENT OF ONE-HALF OF CAPITAL STOCK.

State of New York, }
COUNTY OF MONROE, } ss.

We, the undersigned, a majority of the directors of the Chainless Bicycle Company, do hereby certify.

That the amount of the Capital Stock of said corporation is One Hundred Thousand Dollars ($100000), and that one-half thereof has been paid.

In witness whereof. *We have signed and executed this certificate on this Fourteenth day of December, 189–.*

ISAAC WILCOX.
J. H. MOORE.

State of New York, } ss.
COUNTY OF MONROE, }

On this Fourteenth day of December, 189 , personally appeared Isaac Wilcox and J. H. Moore, to me personally known to be the persons described in, and who executed the foregoing certificate, and severally acknowledged to me that they executed the same.

RICHARD ROE,
Notary Public, Monroe County, N. Y.

State of New York, } ss.
COUNTY OF MONROE, }

Isaac Wilcox and J. H. Moore, being duly and severally sworn, each for himself deposes and says that he is a director of the Chainless Bicycle Company, and that the statement contained in the foregoing certificate is true.

ISAAC WILCOX.
J. H. MOORE.

Severally subscribed and sworn to before me on this Fourteenth day of December, 189–.

RICHARD ROE,
Notary Public, Monroe Co., N. Y.

A further obligation resting upon the directors of a corporation organized under the laws of the State of New York is that they are required to make an annual report to the Secretary of State and to the County Clerk, during the month of January. Failure to comply with this requirement will tend to dissolve the corporation, and will also make the directors personally responsible for the acts and debts of the corporation. The form of annual report for New York State is given below:

ANNUAL REPORT.

ANNUAL REPORT OF THE CHAINLESS BICYCLE COMPANY.

We, the undersigned, a majority of the directors of the Chainless Bicycle Company, do hereby make the following report:

The Capital Stock of this corporation is One Hundred Thousand Dollars ($100000).

The proportion of its Capital Stock actually issued is Sixty Thousand Dollars ($60000).

The existing debts of the corporation do not exceed Eight Thousand Dollars ($8000).

The assets of the corporation at least equal the sum of Seventy-five Thousand Dollars ($75000).

Dated January 12, 189–.

ISAAC WILCOX.
H. L. MILLER.
J. H. MOORE.

State of New York, } ss.
COUNTY OF MONROE, }

Isaac Wilcox and H. L. Miller, being duly and severally sworn, each for himself, deposes and says that he, the said Isaac Wilcox, is the President of the Chainless Bicycle Company, and that he, the said H. L. Miller, is the Secretary thereof; and that the statements contained in the foregoing report are true to the best of his knowledge and belief.

ISAAC WILCOX.
H. L. MILLER.

Severally sworn to before me on this Twelfth day of January, 189–.

RICHARD ROE.
Notary Public, Monroe Co., N. Y.

Board of Directors. As stated before, the directors of a corporation are elected by the stockholders. Each stockholder is entitled to one vote for every share of stock he owns. The number of directors that may be chosen is regulated by statute laws in most of the states, and the by-laws of each corporation determine the time for which they are to be elected. The directors are entrusted with the management of the corporation's affairs; and the business is transacted through and by the officers, who are chosen by the directors from among their number.

Duties of Officers. The by-laws of each corporation usually designate the number of officers to be chosen, and the duties of each are also defined. The following officers are usually elected: president, secretary and treasurer.

The duties of the president are, to preside at the meetings of the board of directors, and to carry into execution the wishes of the board. He is the executive officer of the corporation. Sometimes a vice-president is chosen, who acts as president in the absence of the latter.

The secretary attends to the correspondence of the corporation and is the custodian of the corporation seal. The official records of the corporation are kept by him. He attends the meetings of the board of directors and records the proceedings in the Minute Book. He also has charge of the Subscription Book or List, the Stock Certificate and Transfer Book, the Stock Ledger, Dividend Book or Sheet, the Installment Scrip Book, and such other books and records as may be thought necessary to keep the official records of the corporation.

The treasurer has charge of the finances of the business. He supervises the keeping of the regular books of the business, and the bookkeeper, cashier and other assistants are subject to his directions.

Books Used. The regular books of a corporation are of the same form and design as those used in a business, conducted by a partnership or single proprietor. The only difference in keeping them is in the opening and closing entries. No accounts are kept in the general books with the stockholders to represent their investments. In place of such accounts, a Capital Stock account is kept, which is credited for the amount of the capital stock specified in the charter or in the Certificate of Incorporation. The corresponding debit for Capital Stock account is Subscription account, if the full amount of capital stock is subscribed. If it is not all subscribed for, Treasury Stock is debited for the amount not subscribed. If additional stock is subscribed for at any time, Subscription account is debited and Treasury Stock is credited. More stock than the amount of capital stock specified in the charter or Certificate of Incorporation can not be subscribed. It requires a new charter or the filing of a new Certificate of Incorporation to increase the amount of the capital stock of a corporation. The desired amount of capital stock will have to be specified in the new application, and one-half of it will have to be paid within one year from the date of incorporation.

Since the capital stock of a corporation can not be increased or decreased except by the authority of the State, the account with Capital Stock should at all times equal the amount of capital stock specified in the charter or in the Certificate of Incorporation. The net gain or net loss is never transferred to the Capital Stock account. Hence, in closing the books the balance of Loss & Gain account is usually left open, but it may be transferred to Undivided Profits account. The directors then meet to decide what shall be done with the undivided profits. Usually a dividend of a certain per cent. of the subscribed stock is declared, and the amount necessary to pay it is transferred to the credit of Dividend account. When all the dividends are paid the account should balance. The remaining balance of the undivided profits may remain open, or it may be transferred, in full or in part, to the

Official Records. [illegible] by the secretary [illegible]

Minute Book. [illegible] of the directors and stockholders is kept [illegible] by the secretary and signed by him and the president. [illegible] The Minute Book [illegible]

Subscription Book. [illegible] By signing his name he becomes legally pledged [illegible] Every subscription book should [illegible]

[illegible]

Date	Names	Addresses	No. of Shares	Amounts	
[illegible]	[illegible]	[illegible]	[illegible]	[illegible]	[illegible]

[illegible] when payments are made in installments [illegible] Instead of placing these special columns in [illegible] As the installments are collected they are [illegible] is usually furnished [illegible] memorandum form by [illegible]

Installment Scrip Book. The Installment Scrip Book is a book of receipts, which [illegible] the installments are paid. The installment scrip is given [illegible] usually the secretary and the treasurer.

[illegible]

Stock Certificate and Transfer Book. [illegible]

[illegible]

Stock Ledger. [illegible]

Dividend Book. [illegible]

[illegible]

Certificate No.

Shares

Issued 189

To

Received the above described Certificate

For value received I hereby sell assign and transfer Shares of the above described Stock to

Witness my hand this day of 189

In presence of

Returned and Cancelled

189

New Issue No.

To

Manufacturing Business, Continued

August 1, 189–.

To the Student. In order that you may get an intelligent idea of the method of forming a corporation, you will be required to perform the routine work in the order in which it is done in business. To do this it will be necessary for you to keep the books of official record (stock books) as well as the regular books of the business. In business the books of official record are kept by the secretary.

Glove Business Incorporated. At a preliminary meeting held on the 15th day of July, the partners decided to form a corporation under the laws of your state. The name of the corporation is to be the Luman Glove Company, and the capital stock is to be $150000, divided into 1500 share of $100 each. The resources and good will of the glove manufacturing business are to be turned over to the corporation, for which 300 shares of stock are issued to each of the partners. Each of the stockholders (partners) is to serve as a director for the first year, and the officers are to be as follows: H. T. Williams, President; J. A. Luman, Vice-President; Thos. H. Betts, Secretary; C. R. Evans, Treasurer. In business a record of proceedings of this meeting would be made in the Minute Book by the secretary.

Books of Official Record. You may now prepare a Subscription List on the page reserved for this purpose in your blank book, referring to the illustration on page 178. Get your teacher and three other parties to sign for the subscribers, who are: H. T. Williams, J. A. Luman, Thos. H. Betts and C. R. Evans. In business a power of attorney would have to be secured from each of the above named parties, before the parties you secured could subscribe for them.

You may now proceed to prepare the Certificate of Incorporation, or Articles of Incorporation, on a sheet of legal cap paper, referring the illustration on page 173 and also complying with the requirements of the state under whose laws this business is supposed to be incorporated. Ask your teacher to assist you whenever it becomes necessary. In this business it will not be necessary to prepare more than one copy of the Certificate of Incorporation. The same parties who signed the Subscription List should be secured to sign and acknowledge the Certificate of Incorporation. Some one should be secured to sign for "Richard Roe" as Notary Public. "Richard Roe" is a mythical person, used in law for illustrative purposes. It would be a violation of the law for any one but a Notary Public to sign as such. Have the Certificate of Incorporation approved by the teacher; then brief and file it.

We will now suppose that the Certificate of Incorporation has been forwarded to the proper state official, and has been accepted by him, recorded in his office, and a copy of the same forwarded to the proper county official of the county in which the business is located. In business another meeting of the stockholders would now be held to formally elect the directors, who in turn would elect the officers. A record of the proceedings of this meeting would be made in the Minute Book by the secretary. Your next duty will be to prepare a certificate, certifying that one-half of the capital stock has been subscribed, and another that one-half of the capital stock has been paid. The parties who previously signed for the stockholders, and who represent the officials of the corporation, should sign and acknowledge these certificates. Have them approved by the teacher; then brief and file them. In doing this work be sure to comply with laws of the state under which the business is supposed to be incorporated.

As the requirements of the law are now fulfilled, and the stock subscribed has been paid for, you may write up four Certificates of Stock, one for each stockholder. Be sure to make a detailed record on the first part of the stub. Notice that the Treasurer and President have signed these Certificates. Next get the parties representing the stockholders to sign the stubs of the certificates. In business the certificates are detached from the stubs and delivered to the stockholders. In this business you may deliver them to the teacher.

In the Stock Ledger debit Capital Stock account for the amount of the stock subscribed. Credit each stockholder for the amount of stock issued to him. Give ten lines to Capital Stock account and five lines to each subscriber for stock. If desired the number of the shares issued may be written in the explanation column of each account. When entries are made directly in the Ledger, as in the above case, it is a book of *original* entry. This completes the opening entries on the books of official record.

Opening Entries Regular Books. Under date of August 1, make a record in the Journal similar to the following:

"The co-partnership heretofore existing between H. T. Williams, J. A. Laman, Thos. H. Betts and C. R. Evans under the firm name of the Laman Glove Company has this day been dissolved by mutual consent. The members of the late partnership have decided to incorporate the business under the title of the Laman Glove Company. To that end and for that purpose, Certificates of Incorporation have been filed with the proper state and county officials in which are specified that the Capital Stock of the corporation is $150000, divided into 1500 shares of $100 each. The resources and good will of the business are turned over to the corporation, for which 1200 share of stock are issued, 300 to each partner. The remaining 300 shares will remain in the treasury, to be disposed of in the future, and be known as Treasury Stock. The liabilties of the late partnership are to be paid by the corporation."

Following this statement make a Journal entry debiting Subscription account for the amount of stock subscribed and Treasury Stock account for the amount of stock not subscribed. Credit Capital Stock for $150000.

NOTE. In business it is customary to open a new set of books when a partnership is converted in a corporation. In this instance the old books will be used; the accounts representing the investments of the partners will be closed, and accounts with Capital Stock, Treasury Stock and Subscriptions will be substituted.

You will now credit each of the partners with a sufficient amount of good will to make his present capital equal $30000. Debit Good Will account for the total. Be sure to write an appropriate explanation for this entry.

Debit each of the stockholders for the stock subscribed and credit Subscription account for the total. When these entries are posted the Subscription account and the stockholders' accounts should balance. The stockholders' interests in a corporation are evidenced by the Certificates of Stock issued to them and by the accounts in the Stock Ledger. Write an appropriate explanation of this entry.

Post the books. Check over your posting. This completes the opening entries of the books. Excepting the opening and closing entries, the regular books of a corporation are in no wise different from those of a partnership or of a single proprietor.

AUGUST 6, 189–.

The following invoices have been approved, checked with the goods and audited. Enter them in the Journal.

A. P. Root & Co. (No. 8), Aug. 2, 2/10, net 30 days, $2130.70. (Raw material.)

George Proctor (No. 9), Aug. 3, net 30 days, $19.85. (Bands & Boxes.)

Following are the sales for the past week. Make the proper record on the Order Sheets and enter in the Sales Book.

2d, Heywood & Co., regular, 10 doz. 1216; 5 doz. 1211; 2 doz. 1126.

3d, Hare & Smith (successors to Jas. Hare), regular, 5 doz. 1216; 5 doz. 1126; 5 doz. 931. Transfer the balance of Jas. Hare's order to a new Order Sheet. Write on the old order: "Succeeded by Hare & Smith; see order number 5."

The following orders have been received:

3d, Heywood & Co., regular, 10 doz. each of numbers 1209, 1211, 1216, 931, 926, 936, 953, 1101, 1106; to be shipped not later than Aug. 8th.

Hare & Smith, regular, 25 doz. 1211.

Henry J. Graves Sons, regular, 10 doz. 1209; 10 doz. 1216; 5 doz. 931; 2 doz. 916; 1 doz. 1111. Cancel their old order for the remaining 40 doz. of number 1126. This you will do by writing: "Canceled Aug. 5, 189–, by letter," in red ink on the order; then file it away for future reference. In canceling an order always be sure to state whether it was countermanded by letter or in person. In case of litigation an order given by letter would be a question of fact, while an order given in person would require evidence to substantiate it.

The samples sent to Fred. Sherman & Co., on the 14th ult., have been returned by express, charges prepaid. Make an entry in the Journal that will cancel the entry made in the Sales Book at the time the goods were sent. Be sure to write an appropriate explanation of this entry; remember that the explanation is the essential part of every bookkeeping record. In business when goods are returned frequently, a special Goods Returned Book may be provided. An ordinary Invoice Book will serve the purpose, as in it the returned bills may be pasted, and posted to the credit of the proper ledger accounts. The monthly footings would be posted to the debit of Merchandise account.

You and your teacher will each subscribe for 50 shares of the Treasury Stock. Both of you should sign the Subscription List for the proper amount. We will now assume that you have paid for your stock and, hence, are entitled to your Certificates of Stock. Fill in two certificates, numbering them 5 and 6. Be sure to fill the stub properly. Deliver the teacher's certificate, getting him to sign for it on the stub. Detach your certificate after you have signed for it.

Next make the entry in the Stock Ledger, debiting Capital Stock for $10000 and credit yourself and your teacher, each for $5000. This completes the entries in the books of official record.

On your regular books debit Subscription account in the Journal and credit Treasury Stock for $10000. In writing an explanation for this entry, be sure to specify to whom the stock was sold.

The Petty Cash Book contains the following records; enter them in the regular Cash Book:

2	Jas. Hare, July 12th, less 5%,		299	25	2	George Proctor, Invs. No. 4 & 7,	63	90
3	Henry J. Graves Son, July 12th and 31st, less 5 and 6%,		232	97	3	Expense, Inv. of blank books,	35	75
6	Subscription, Teacher	5000			6	Expense, cleaning office 5.00, desk 14.00, postage 1.10,	20	10
	" Student	5000	10000	00		A. P. Root & Co., Inv. No.8, less 2%,	2088	09
	Mdse., Cash sales for week,		314	90				

Post the books and check over the posting.

AUGUST 13, 189–.

The following sales have been made during the week.

8th, Heywood & Co., regular, 25 doz. 1216; 15 doz. 1211; 11 doz. 1209; 5 doz. 1126;

5 doz. 931; 5 doz. 926; 5 doz. 936; 5 doz. 953; 5 doz. 1101; 5 doz. 1106. It will be necessary to make records on both of their orders (numbers 1 and 6). Observe these instructions in the future.

10th, Henry J. Graves Sons, regular, 10 doz. 1209; 12 doz. 1206; 19 doz. 953; 2 doz. 916; 1 doz. 1111.

11th, Hare & Smith, regular, 25 doz. 1126; 10 doz. 1211.

12th, Allen & Jewett (post to Sundry Accounts Receivable), one-twelfth doz. each of the following numbers: 1211, 1209, 1126, 931, 953, 916, 1111, 1101, 1106.

The following invoices have been received, checked with the goods and audited. Enter them.

Sweet, Sharp & Co. (No. 10), Aug. 10, 5 days net, $166.40. (Raw Material.)

B. G. Greenway (No. 11), Aug. 9, net 30 days, $121.78. (Raw Material.)

George Proctor (No. 12), Aug. 11, 30 days net, $83.17. (Bands & Boxes.)

Garson & Wood (No. 13), Aug. 12, 30 days net, $65. (Furniture & Fixtures.)

Clarence Stoner (No. 14), Aug. 8, 2/10, net 30 days, $76.40. (Raw Material.)

The Petty Cash Book contains the following records:

8	Wm. H. Lester, July 16th, less 5%,	$45	74	8	Expense,	gas bill, 4.50		
9	Heywood & Co., Aug. 2d, less 6%,	231	24			matting, 5.75		
	Hare & Smith, Aug. 3d, less 6%,	148	05			stationery, 4.50	14	75
13	Mdse., cash sales for week,	55	21	9	Labor,	advanced H. N. Peck, 15.00		
						Rosa James, 5.00		
						Floyd Long, 10.00	30	00
				11	Salary, advanced bookkeeper,		15	00
				12	Sweet, Sharp & Co., Inv. No. 10, Net.		166	40
				13	Clarence Stoner, Inv. No. 14, less 2%,		74	87
					Expense,	bill for plumbing and repairs,	17	80
					Real Estate, painting mill,		195	00

Post the books and check over your posting.

August 20, 189–.

The sales for the week are as follows; enter them in the Sales Book and on the Order Sheets.

15th, Henry J. Graves Sons, regular, 12 doz. 1206; 10 doz. 1216; 5 doz. 931.

Hare & Smith, regular, 5 doz. 1216; 15 doz. 1211.

The following order has been received:

Henry J. Graves Sons, regular, 25 doz. 1206; 50 doz. 931. Enter on an Order Sheet. They also give instructions to cancel the balance of number 953 on their previous order.

The Petty Cash Book contains the following records:

14	Wm. H. Chamberlain, Inv. of July 12th & 18th, less 5%,	312	31	14	Expense, 12 tons coal,	56	00
15	Thos. K. Harrington, Inv. July 17th, less 5%,	$37	19	17	Expense, carpet for office,	12	18

Post the books and check over your posting.

August 27, 189–.

The balance of the goods due Heywood & Co. have been shipped. Make the proper records on the Order Sheets and in the Sales Book.

The Petty Cash Book contains the following records:

21	Merchandise, cash sale,	34 78	21	Expense, water tax,		8 17
22	Hare & Smith, Inv. Aug. 11th, less 5%,	328 94	23	Labor, advanced A. J. Camp,	5.00	
24	Henry J. Graves Sons, Inv. Aug. 10th, less 5%,	538 17	24	Frank Royce,	5.00	
25	Birch & Shelters, Inv. July 19th, less 5%,	382 37	26	Erma Price,	15.00	25 00
				J. A. Luman & Co., in full,		5000 00

Post the books and check over your posting.

AUGUST 31, 189–.

The following sales have been made; enter them on the Order Sheets and in the Sales Book.

28th, Henry J. Graves Sons, balance of their order.

Hare & Smith, balance of their order.

The following order need not be entered on an Order Sheet as it was filled on the day it was received. Munson & Holly, Aug. 31, regular, 50 doz. 936; 50 doz. 941; 50 doz. 953; 100 doz. 952; 140 doz. 931.

The following invoices have been received, checked with the goods and audited.

Sampson & Co. (No. 15), Aug. 26, 30 days net, $43.75. (Buttons.)

George Procter (No. 16), Aug. 30, 30 days net, $46.50. (Bands & Boxes.)

The time of the employees as taken from the foreman's Time Books is as follows. Enter it in the August column of the Pay Roll Book.

SILKING DEPARTMENT, Time Book "A." Amanda Connor, $40.80; Carrie Lyons, $35.60; Bertha Polk, $50.50.

HEMMING DEPARTMENT, Time Book "B." Maggie Allard, $50.75; Rosa James, $38.40 (record the amount paid on the 9th); Ellen Little, $43.20; Ellen Meunier, $55.30; Mattie Allen, $54.20; Amanda Little, $40.00.

MAKING DEPARTMENT, Time Book "C." Floyd Long, $81.50 (record the amount paid on the 9th); F. G. Prine, $80.75; Geo. H. Bush, $71.40; R. Folts, $70.30.

CUTTING DEPARTMENT, Time Book "D." H. N. Peck, $73.50 (record the amount paid on the 9th); Austin J. Camp, $85.30 (record the amount advanced on the 23d).

CONTRACT WORK PER JOB BOOK. Mrs. Mary Hostler, $51.70; Maude Elliot, $45.25; Jas. Bell, $58.60; Robt. Jones, $80.40; Bessie Nichols, $51.38; Clara Frey, $50.10; Frank Royce, $49.65 (record the amount advanced on the 24th); Jessie Weeks, $49.10; Minnie Dunn, $48.90; Erma Price, $55.00 (record the amount advanced on the 26th); Lena Frey, $41.37; Thos. Burns, $64.38 (record the amount advanced on the 28th); Rueben Doty, $35.50; Lizzie Patch, $64.20; A. K. Chandler, $70.25; Timothy Hunt, $69.15; Geo. Mosby, $55.18; Nina Eckler, $43.20; Kate Schwartz, $46.10 (record the amount advanced on the 28th); Chas. Heald, $61.94; Wm. Stump, $65.13; Jos. Helm, $64.08; Harry Eckler, $55.07; John Dunn, $61.19; D. F. Kellog, $66.30; Arthur Fulmer, $57.18 (record the amount advanced on the 28th); I. H. Covert, $51.28; Daniel Brevier, $55.00.

Foot and rule the Pay Roll. Verify your work by going over it a second time.

The Petty Cash Book contains the following records:

27	Traveling Expense, Hermann,		158 48
28	Labor, advanced Thos. Burns, 20.00		
	" Kate Schwartz, 5.00		
	" Arthur Folmer, 10.00		35 00
29	Expense, painting and papering,		19 89
31	Freight & Cartage, for mo.		156 29
31	Salaries, Cloud,	125 00	
	Herman,	100.00	
	Mackey,	40 00	
	Williams,	150 00	
	Student,	45.00	460 00
31	Labor, balance of pay roll,		2348 08
31	Labor, mill pay roll,		289 20

Foot and rule the Cash Book; the cash on hand is: bank, $20740.00; safe, $122.47. Foot and rule the Sales Book.

Post the books and check over the posting. Take a trial balance and have it approved.

Preparatory to closing the books an inventory has been taken, of which the following is an abstract.

ABSTRACT OF INVENTORIES, *Aug. 31*, 189–.

Real Estate,		32000 00
Machinery,		44818 20
Furniture & Fixtures,		450 00
Good Will,		24512 79
Traveling Expense,	amount not used,	19 50
Silk Account,		15 00
Raw Material,		847 75
Merchandise,	per inventory sheets,	712 50

Write the above inventories in the proper ledger accounts. Transfer the balances of the accounts that enter into the cost of merchandise to the debit of the Merchandise account. Next make a Balance Sheet, following the directions given for the month of July and those given herewith. The amounts of Capital Stock, Treasury Stock and Subscription account are to be transferred to the Resource and Liability columns, directly opposite where they appear in the first and second money columns. When the net gain is ascertained, it is to be added to the footings of the Loss and Liability columns, and is to be designated as "Net Gain."

Close all accounts showing losses or gains into the Loss & Gain account. The Loss & Gain account is not to be closed until the Board of Directors have met and decided what shall be done with the net gain.

In business the Balance Sheet and books would be audited by the treasurer, or some one under his direction, and a certificate attached to the Balance Sheet, similar in form to the following:

Aug. 31, 189–.

Your place here.)

TO THE BOARD OF DIRECTORS:

I hereby certify that the accompanying statement of the business is a correct abstract of the resources and liabilities of the Luman Glove Company. The resources and liabilities were ascertained by estimating and calculating the commodities on hand at their actual cash valuation; the accounts receivable and accounts payable are given as they appear on the Ledger; there have been no bad debts to date and I believe that all amounts now outstanding will be paid in full.

Respectfully submitted,

C. R. EVANS, *Treasurer.*

Write a certificate similar to the above at the foot of your Balance Sheet. Present your books for approval, and get your teacher to sign for C. R. Evans as Treasurer. The Balance Sheet, and such other books as they may wish to see, are now ready to be presented to the Board of Directors for their consideration.

SEPTEMBER 1, 189–.

In business dividends are usually declared annually or semi-annually; in this business, for the purpose of illustration, a dividend will be declared at the end of the first month. At a meeting of the Board of Directors the following resolution was adopted:

.... Sept. 1, 189–.
(Your place here.)

Resolved, That based upon the showing of the previous month's business as exhibited by the Balance Sheet and Books, that there be declared a dividend equivalent to 6 per cent. per annum, or ½ of one per cent. for the past month, and that the remaining balance of the Loss & Gain account be closed to Undivided Profits account.

THOS. H. BETTS, *Secretary*. H. T. WILLIAMS, *President*.

In compliance with the above resolution you will now calculate the dividend on the amount of stock subscribed, as shown by the Subscription Book and the Subscription account in the Ledger. Compile a Dividend Sheet on legal cap paper referring to the illustration on page 179. Next debit Loss & Gain account, in the Journal, for the amount of the net gain, and credit Dividends account for the amount of the dividend, and Undivided Profits account for the balance.

The dividends as exhibited by the Dividend Sheet have been paid and a record made in the Petty Cash Book; enter same in the regular Cash Book, then balance and rule the same.

			Dividends, as per Dividend Sheet,	650

Post the books and check over your posting.

You will now sell your stock to H. T. Williams and get your teacher to sell his stock to some student. Fill in the blank forms of assignment on the back of certificates 5 and 6. You and your teacher will now assign your stock in the presence of a witness.

Paste certificates 5 and 6 to the original stubs and cancel the seals. Fill in the forms of transfer on the stubs, which should be signed by yourself and your teacher, respectively. Fill in the third part of the stubs, then write up the new certificates (numbers 7 and 8), favor of the parties to whom you sold the stock. Get the transferees to sign the first part of stubs 7 and 8. Detach the certificates and deliver them to the teacher.

Make the proper entries for the above transactions in the Stock Ledger, debiting the sellers and crediting the purchasers. These transactions in no wise affect the regular books of the business. Do you see why?

Your teacher will now hand you the certificates of stock left with him, which you will preserve for future reference.

Examine your books thoroughly to see that they are in proper shape to be handed to the regular bookkeeper who is to succeed you. As but a few transactions have been recorded since the Balance Sheet was made, no trial balance will be necessary. Render the corporation a bill for the amount due you.

Present all books and documents for examination and approval.

LIMITED CORPORATIONS AND JOINT STOCK COMPANIES

Limited Corporations. There is another kind of corporation, known as a limited liability corporation. A limited corporation differs from the ordinary corporation, described in the preceding pages, in this: Each shareholder in a limited liability corporation is individually liable to the creditors of the corporation for the amount represented in his certificate, until the full amount of the capital is paid in, and a certificate thereof has been made and recorded with the proper officials as prescribed by law. If judgment is rendered and not paid, proceedings may be instituted against any one of the stockholders for an amount equal to the par value of the stock he owns. Should a shareholder be required to pay a claim, he is entitled to recover from each shareholder such a part of the claim as each shareholder's stock is a part of the capital stock. When the capital is all paid in the liability of the stockholder ceases. Limited liability corporations are required by law to use the word "Limited" after the name of the corporation whenever or wherever the name is used, either written or printed; furthermore, the name of the corporation, with the word "Limited," must be conspicuously posted outside the general office and branch offices. Limited corporations and joint stock companies command a better credit than do corporations. Do you see why?

Joint Stock Companies. Joint stock companies are associations formed for the transaction of business, and are intermediate between corporations and ordinary partnerships. They are in fact partnerships, and are so considered in law, yet they differ from the ordinary partnership in their organization. Formerly these companies were more common than they are at the present time. The legislatures of most states have enacted general laws under which corporations may be readily and easily organized, consequently they have almost entirely taken the place of joint stock companies. Formerly it was necessary in the organization of a corporation to apply to the legislature for a charter. This very often involved much delay and frequently large expense, hence, rather than await the result of such special legislation, the persons interested in the proposed business would risk the responsibility of partners.

Joint stock companies are usually formed in preference to the ordinary partnerships when the number of persons interested is so large as to make it inconvenient to conduct the business as is commonly done in ordinary partnerships. The stockholders forming the company usually draw up an agreement, in which the rights of members, among themselves, are defined and regulated. This agreement usually specifies the manner of forming the company, the amount of the capital stock, the number and value of the shares, the manner in which stock may be transferred, and the election of officers or agents. In this agreement are also included such other provisions as may be deemed necessary for a proper management of the business.

Ordinarily the members of a joint stock company are personally liable for the debts of the company the same as in an ordinary partnership. That is, if the assets of the company are exhausted and there are debts remaining unpaid, each stockholder is liable to the creditors for the full amount of such indebtedness. When no statutory provisions exist regulating the liability of the stockholders, their liability is determined in the same manner as in the case of an ordinary partnership.

The business of a joint stock company is usually transacted by directors or trustees chosen by the stockholders. These companies, unless they are organized under the laws of the State of New York, can not sue or be sued in the name of the officers; suit must be brought against the members individually or collectively.

The books of a joint stock company need in no wise be different from those of a corporation. Books of official record (stock books) are kept, the stock issued is signed by the officials, and the profits are distributed to the stockholders in the form of dividends, the same as in a corporation. The main difference between a corporation and a joint stock company is that the latter is not created by the state. A joint stock company has no right to use a common seal.

Joint Stock Companies in New York. In New York State the formation of joint stock companies and the liability of the stockholders is regulated by statute, and they are given certain corporate privileges. A company so formed may sue and be sued in the name of the president or treasurer, and the members are not individually liable until a judgment has been recovered against the company, and an execution issued thereunder has been returned unsatisfied. These companies are not dissolved by the death of a member or by the transfer of his stock, as is the case in the ordinary joint stock company or partnership.

Carefully review the work, beginning on page 117, and be prepared to answer the following questions:

QUESTIONS.—What is a department store? What advantages are there in keeping a department store? What reason can you assign for subdividing the Merchandise account in a department store business? What is the object of dividing the counting room work in a large business into departments? What reasons can you assign for keeping accounts with all the other ledgers in the General Ledger? What is the nature of the work usually done in the Cash Department? In the Credit Man's Department? In the Time Sales Department? In the Purchases Department? Describe the Abstract Purchase Book. Why is it not a convenient form of record when there are many departments? What forms may be substituted when the departments are numerous? Describe the Department Charges form. What are the advantages of using an Abstract Purchase Ledger? What is the object in keeping track of the due date and discount time limit on bills purchased and sold? Describe the Time Index. What advantage is there in using Sales Tickets? Describe the Clerks' Summary Sheet. What is the object in keeping these Summary Sheets? Describe the routine of a sale on account. What forms may be used to advantage in recording Time Sales? Describe an Abstract of Time Sales sheet. What reason can you assign for making a Summary of the Daily Sales? What is the object in keeping a record of the Clerks' daily sales? Explain how you would determine from what department a sale was made. How are the clerks usually designated in a large establishment? Explain the method of keeping a Sales Ledger. Where do the records in the Sales Ledgers originate? What reasons can you assign for keeping accounts with the Sales Ledgers in the General Ledger? Explain the method of verifying these accounts with the respective Ledgers. Describe the routine of a cash sale. Draw from memory an Abstract of Cash Sales form. From what sources is the Abstract Cash Account compiled? Describe the detailed statements used in the Cash Department. What is the object of a Pay Roll? What is a Pay Roll Memorandum? How are returned goods recorded? Describe the Credit Memoranda account. How are rebates recorded? What is the object of a Sundry Account? What effect does the death of a partner have on a partnership? What is the object of making abstracts of the Purchases and Sales Ledgers before taking a trial balance of the General Ledger? What is meant by a Liability Inventory? Name some accounts that may have Liability Inventories. Explain the method of closing an account that has a Liability Inventory.

Name some of the books especially adapted to the manufacturing business. Why is it customary to keep separate accounts with the items that enter into the cost of merchandise? What is done with the balances of such accounts? What is the object of the Cost Book? What advantages do Order Sheets have over an Order Book? In what way does an Impression Sales Book save labor? What reason can you assign for designating gloves by stock numbers instead of writing a description of same? Describe the Cutters Stock Book. What is the object of Stock Tickets? What is the difference between a Time Book and a Pay Roll Book? Describe the Monthly Pay Roll. What is the object in keeping a Petty Cash Book? What object is there in keeping an account with the Mill or Tanning department of a manufacturing business? Describe the method of closing the books in a manufacturing business When the accounts receivable and accounts payable are numerous how are they entered on the Balance Sheet?

What is a corporation? Name some of the advantages of a corporation. How are corporations formed? Which method is the more convenient and why? Do you know what the requirements for incorporation are in your State? How do they compare with the requirements in New York State? What is a Certificate of Incorporation? What difference is there between a Certificate of Incorporation and Articles of Incorporation? Describe the method of forming a corporation, step by step, in your State. With what officials are the Certificates of Incorporation to be filed? What is the longest time for which a corporation may be formed in your State? How much of the capital stock must be subscribed for before the corporation can do business? What are the further requirements in your State? How is the business of a corporation transacted? By whom are the directors of a corporation elected? Who elects the officers? How is the number of votes that a stockholder is entitled to determined? Name the officers usually elected. What are the duties of the President? Secretary? Treasurer? In what respects does corporation bookkeeping differ from the bookkeeping of a business conducted as a partnership? What is meant by the Capital Stock of a corporation? Treasury Stock? Subscribed Stock or Subscription account? Why are no accounts with the stockholders to represent their investments kept on the regular books? Explain the method of closing corporation books. What are the books of official record and by whom are they kept? Describe the Minute Book. Subscription Book. Installment Scrip Book. Stock Certificate & Transfer Book. Stock Ledger. Dividend Book or Dividend Sheet.

What is a limited corporation? A joint stock company? Why do limited corporations and joint stock companies command a better credit than do corporations? What is the difference between a joint stock company organized under the laws of New York and those organized in other States?

BANKING

FROM

NEW COMPLETE BOOKKEEPING.

BANKING.

A Banker is a dealer in money. The business of banking consists in receiving deposits of money on which interest may or may not be allowed; in making advances of money, principally in the way of discounting notes and other commercial paper; and in effecting the transmission of money from one place to another. The disposable means of a bank consist of the capital paid in by the shareholders; the money deposited with it by its customers; the notes it can circulate; the money it receives in the course of transmission, and which, of course, it must repay in another place. The profits of a bank arise mainly from the following sources: discount, interest, dividends, exchange and collection.

Banking associations are divided into two general classes: Public banks and Private banks. Public banks are also of two classes: Those organized under the laws of the State in which they are located, and those organized under the laws of the United States. The former are called State banks and the latter are called National banks. State banks may be divided into Deposit and Discount banks, Savings banks and Trust companies. Private banks are conducted by individuals and are unincorporated. State and National banks are incorporated institutions.

A National Bank is a bank organized under the National Banking Act. This does not mean that the government owns or conducts National banks, but only authorizes their creation and prescribes their mode of doing business. Every association doing business under this law is governed by the same principles, is subject to the same inspection, uses the same forms in making reports to the Treasury Department at Washington, and is under the same penalties for the violation of any requirement of the National Banking Law.

The National banking system, based on the system of banking in the State of New York in 1862, is the principal banking system in the country, and the only one by which banks now issue notes of their own. By the National banking law banking associations may be formed by five or more persons who must specify in their articles of association the several objects for thus uniting. They must make "an organization certificate" specifying the name assumed by the association; its place of business; the amount of its capital stock and the number of shares into which it is divided; the names and residences of the shareholders and the number of shares held by each; a declaration that the certificate is made to enable them to avail themselves of the advantages of the act.

The association may sue and be sued, elect directors, who, in turn, may elect a president, vice-president, cashier and other officers; discount and negotiate promissory notes, drafts, bills of exchange, and other evidences of debt; receive deposits, buy and sell exchange, coin and bullion; loan money on personal security, issue and circulate its own notes, and make all needful by-laws not inconsistent with the Banking Act.

There must be at least five directors. Each director must own at least ten shares of the stock, and he holds his office until the election and qualification of his successor. Annual meetings are held in January. The capital stock is divided into shares of $100 each, and are transferable. The liability of a shareholder is limited to a sum equal to the par value of his stock. Before beginning business, fifty per cent. of the capital stock of an association must be paid in, and ten per cent. of the remainder monthly until all is paid. After the association is organized and fifty per cent. of the capital stock paid in, the next step is the transmission by the association of a certificate to the Comptroller of the Currency stating that all the provisions of the law with reference to organizing a bank have been observed. The Comptroller of the Currency then makes such an examination as may be thought necessary, and if he finds that the law has been properly complied with, he gives to the association a certificate to that effect, and that it is authorized to begin business. This certificate must be published within sixty days from the time of receiving it.

As a necessary preliminary to furnishing notes for circulation, the Comptroller of the Currency, under the direction of the Secretary of the Treasury, is entrusted with the important duty of engraving plates in the best manner to guard against counterfeiting and fraudulent alterations, and to print therefrom and number so many circulating notes in blank as may be required to supply the banks entitled to receive the same. After these notes have been signed by the president or vice-president, and the cashier, they are issued and circulate as money, and are received at par everywhere in the payment of taxes, excises, public lands, and all other dues to the government, except for duties on imports; and also for all salaries and other debts owing by the United States, except interest on the public debt and in redemption of legal tender notes. They are also a legal tender for any debt or liability to every National banking association. The notes which are issued by National banks are secured by registered United States bonds, deposited with the Treasurer of the United States. Upon a deposit of bonds the association making the same is entitled to receive from the Comptroller circulating notes equal in amount to ninety per cent. of the par value of the United States bonds so deposited, but the total amount of such notes issued to any association may not exceed ninety per cent. of the amount of its capital stock actually paid in.

Many National banks, especially those located in some of the large cities, do not issue notes for the reason that, with the tax of one per cent. a year upon the average circulation, the expense of handling the notes, the expenses of the redemption of the same, the express charges, etc., they find it is not profitable.

A National bank can hold real estate under the following conditions, and no others: The building needful to transact its business; land mortgaged to it in good faith to secure debts previously contracted in the course of business; lands purchased under sales ordered by courts in order to secure debts due to the bank. In the last three cases the real estate cannot be held beyond five years. National banks cannot make loans on the security of their own stock, except to prevent a loss on a debt previously contracted, nor can they pledge their own notes of circulation for the purpose of getting money to pay in their capital stock. They are subject to examination by officers appointed by the government. They must make reports to the Comptroller of the Currency according to the forms which he prescribes, exhibiting in detail the resources and liabilities of the associations at the close of business on any past day specified by him. The Comptroller is required to call for not less than five such reports during each year. These reports must be verified by the oath of the president or cashier and attested by the signatures of at least three of the directors.

In addition to the reports mentioned above, each association is required to make a sworn report within ten days after the declaration of any dividend, of the amount of such dividend, and the amount of the net earnings.

The National banking law provides that semi-annual dividends of the net profits of any National bank may be declared by the directors thereof; but that before each dividend every bank shall carry one-tenth of its net profits of the preceding half-year to its surplus fund until it shall equal twenty per cent. of the capital stock.

For a further explanation of the National banking law, the student is referred to Bolles' Practical Banking, from which excellent work some of the foregoing paragraphs were compiled.

State Banks.—A State bank is a bank organized under the laws of the State in which it is located. The preliminary steps in organizing a bank under the banking law of the State are much the same as those to be taken in organizing a National bank. The subscription list is opened, articles of association and a name are adopted, a Board of Directors and officers are elected, just as in the case of a National bank. In addition to the steps mentioned, it is necessary that a copy of the articles of association be filed with the Bank Superintendent of the State, where there is such an officer, or with the Comptroller, and another copy in the office of the clerk of the county in which the bank is to be located.

Previous to July, 1866, State banks issued notes which circulated as money, but on that date the government imposed a tax of ten per cent. on the circulation of the State banks, which had the effect of withdrawing it as the rate was too high to allow of any profit to the banks on it. Except as to issuing circulating notes, State banks are conducted as they were before the creation of the National banking system. There is very little difference between the internal workings of a National and a State bank. The main function of receiving deposits and of loaning them is performed in essentially the same way by all banks.

It is claimed that State banks possess some advantages over National banks among which are the following: They are not examined so critically; in some cases are not required to make returns to State officials, and in no case are such full returns required as the National law requires to be made. They can certify checks in excess of the amount which the depositor may have at the time of certifying. The National banks are expressly forbidden to do this.

Private Banks.—A private bank is a bank organized and operated by a private individual or by a firm.

In opening a bank by an individual no formality is required, unless restricted by statute; nor in opening one by a partnership, further than is necessary in any partnership formed for business purposes; simply a partnership contract, signed by the partners, setting forth the nature of the business to be transacted, the amount of capital each partner is to furnish, the duties of each partner, the duration of the partnership, and such restrictions upon the acts of the officers as it is thought wise to impose.

The Board of Directors meet at certain specified times to consider the character of the paper offered for discount and referred to them by the president or cashier, and to consult as to general business. In some banks the Board delegates its authority, in the matter of passing upon paper offered for discount, to the president or cashier during the intervals when the Board is not in session. This exercise of authority by the president or cashier is, however, subject to the approval of the Board.

Officers of a Bank.—The officers and clerks of a bank are, usually, a President, Vice-President, Cashier, Receiving Teller, Paying Teller, General Bookkeeper, Individual Bookkeeper, Note Clerk, Messenger, and Porter, together with the necessary assistants in the different departments.

The President is the chief executive officer of the bank and presides at the meetings of the Board of Directors, and generally exercises the authority of the Board during its recess. Some banks have a Vice-President who assumes the functions of the President during his absence.

JOURNAL.

MONDAY.

	Coll. & Exch.		General.	
Monroe County National, Clyde, 211^{92}		50	211	92
Clinton National, 865^{70}	1	00	865	70
Henry D. Wilson & Co., Batavia, 912^{17}		35	912	17
Bills Discounted, 2500, 12000, 2540^{18}	7	92	17040	18
Discount, [illegible]	3	19	40	62
Exchange National, New York,	9	69	9962	95
Deposits,			19831	57
Collection and Exchange,	22	65	22	65
			48887	76

NEW YORK DRAFT

EXCHANGE NATIONAL BANK, NEW YORK.

MONDAY,

No.	By Whom Drawn.	Of What Place.	On What Place.	Face.	Total.
	Balance,				74751 27
3043	First National,	Fort Scott,	Park Bank,	1450 00	
1682	Traders National,	Oakland,	Ninth National,	1912 16	
1142	Third National,	Bancroft,	Metropolitan,	234 91	
877	Exchange Bank,	Mt. Morris,	Bowery,	116 27	
229	Miners Bank,	Coalburgh,	Exchange,	386 34	4129 68
					78880 95

The Cashier, unless there be a Vice-President, ranks next to the President, and has certain specified duties to perform. He is appointed by the Board of Directors and is required to furnish a bond for the faithful performance of his duties. He keeps a record of the meetings of the Board of Directors, for whom he is the acting secretary. The certificates of stock issued to shareholders are signed by him as well as by the President, as also are the notes which circulate as money. Drafts drawn on other banks are usually signed by him, and he indorses personally or by deputy all drafts and notes sent away to other banks for collection. All notes and drafts received from other banks for collection are endorsed over to him. He is the manager of the internal workings of the bank, and has supervision of the clerical force. He is expected to have an intimate knowledge of the system of bookkeeping practiced by his bank, and to see that the work in the various departments is properly performed.

The Tellers.—The Paying Teller pays out all moneys, issues certificates of deposit, certifies all checks that are to be certified, and has charge of that part of the vault containing the working cash of the bank. He must be acquainted with the signature of each depositor and his daily balance, and be rapid and accurate in the handling of money. He is required to give bonds for the faithful discharge of his duties. The Receiving Teller receives all the money coming into the bank, makes the record therefor, and at night turns over all money received during the day to the Paying Teller. He too must be rapid and accurate in counting and handling money, and be able to detect counterfeit money and forged negotiable paper. Like the Paying Teller he is required to give bonds. Sometimes the two offices are combined in one.

JOURNAL.

DECEMBER 12, 189–.

		General.	
	Monroe County National, Clyde, 423^{31}	423	31
	Farmers National, Lincoln, 193^{42} 1215	1408	42
	Traders National, Ontario, 345^{23}	345	23
	Third National, Brighton, 583^{75}	583	75
	Clinton National, 911^{18}	911	13
	Exchange National, New York,	4129	68
	Deposits,	30483	53
	Bills Discounted,	3750	00
		42035	08

REGISTER.

In Account with SECOND NATIONAL COLLEGE BANK,

DECEMBER 12, 189–.

No.	In Whose Favor Drawn.	Exchange.		Face.		Total.	
1626	Drummond Bank, Pittsford,	2	81	4497	19		
1627	Jones Manufacturing Company,	5	63	4500	00		
1628	John Adams,		50	397	84		
1629	Samuel Wallace,		50	450	00		
1630	C. W. Davis,		25	117	92	9962	95
	Balance,					*68918*	*00*
		9	69			78880	95

The Bookkeepers.—The bookkeepers in a bank are known as General bookkeeper and Individual bookkeeper. The General bookkeeper has charge of the General Ledger, which usually contains the main accounts of the bank and also accounts with other banks. The Individual bookkeeper has charge of the Individual or Depositors' Ledger.

The duties of the other clerks of a bank will be stated in connection with the explanation of the books.

Books Used.—The books used in this bank are Journal, General Ledger, Individual Ledger, New York Draft Register, Discount Register, Collection Register, Discount Tickler and Collection Tickler. Other books such as Offering Book, Dealers Discount Book, Dealers Bill Book, Tellers' Books, Certified Check Book, Certificate of Deposit Book and Statement Book are also used in banks.

The Journal sustains the same relation to the banking business that a Main Cash Book does to any mercantile business. On the left-hand side are entered all cash receipts at the commencement of business and afterwards are entered all deposits and collections of whatever kind either in detail or in total. On the right-hand side are entered all payments on deposit account, either in detail or in total, and the amount paid out for notes discounted and for the running expenses of the bank. If balanced the difference between the two sides should show the amount of cash in the vaults of the bank. This balance usually consists of National Bank notes, Treasury Notes, Silver Certificates, Checks on other banks, the notes issued by the bank, Specie and Cash Items. Cash items consist of memoranda of different kinds carried as cash. Sometimes the Journal is balanced daily and the balance rep-

INDIVIDUAL

NAME	Monday, Dec. 12, 189 . Balance	Checks in Detail	Total Checks	Deposits	Balance	Tuesday, Dec. 13, 189 . Checks in Detail	Total Checks	Deposits	Balance	Wednesday, Dec. 14, 189 . Checks in Detail	Total Checks	Deposits	Balance
Adams, John	10301 85	673 00 500 00 397 81	1571 44		8730 41	1000 00	1000 00		7730 41			1171 55	8901 96
Brown, H. J.	32465 06			3500 00	35965 36	500 00 3063 71 1941 82	5505 53		29659 83	1000 00 2500 00 603 42	4103 42		25556 41
Davis, C. W.	6619 99			1846 75	8466 74	93 18 112 50 825 00	1030 68	d1616 76 1500 00	10552 82	1741 96 622 12	2364 08		8188 74
Jones Mfg. Co.	16014 54	4500 00	4500 00	d1743 02 3118 56 910 64	17316 75			2260 00	19576 75	500 00 1074 83 1500 00	2874 83	4325 00	21026 92
*													
Certificates of Deposit,	3000 00				3000 00	3000 00	3000 00					1500 00	1500 00
Certified Checks,								1500 00	1500 00	1500 00	1500 00	1000 00	1000 00
Cashier Account,						448 35	448 35	d448 35		1794 60	1794 60	d1794 60	
TRANSIENT ACCOUNTS. Long, H. S.	918 30				918 30	918 30	918 30						
	232206 37		30483 53	19831 57	221554 11		36111 09	20553 09	205006 41		23677 23	25742 99	208302 17

* Several accounts are here omitted, but the footings of the columns include the results of the accounts as well as those illustrated.

resents the cash on hand, and the Journal as a whole represents the cash account. Usually, however, a Cash account is opened in the General Ledger and the footings of the Journal are posted daily, but the Journal in such a case is never balanced. But whether this balance is made in the Journal or in the Cash Book the proof of the balance found is made in a book called a "Blotter," "Cash Proof" or "Cash Balance." It is compiled as follows: On the right-hand side of a perpendicular line running through the center of a blank page is set down the balance on hand the day previous. To this is added the footing of the left-hand or debit side of the Journal, and from the amount thus obtained is subtracted the footing of the right-hand or credit side; the balance should be the amount on hand. On the left-hand side of said perpendicular line and opposite the work already compiled is made a memorandum exhibiting the following: The total amount of bills on hand, the amount of specie on hand, the amount of cash items and the amount of checks and drafts on hand and treated as cash. The aggregate sum should equal the sum of the other side.

The entries in the Journal are made up almost wholly of totals compiled from other books. The left-hand side has two money columns devoted to "Collection and Exchange" and "General" respectively. The Collection and Exchange column contains all the items to be credited to Collection and Exchange account, and at the end of the day this column is footed and posted direct to this account in the General Ledger. In the General column are

LEDGER.

Thursday, Dec. 15, 189-. Checks in Detail.	Total Checks.	Deposits.	Balance.	Friday, Dec. 16, 189-. Checks in Detail.	Total Checks.	Deposits.	Balance.	Saturday, Dec. 17, 189-. Checks in Detail.	Total Checks.	Deposits.	Balance.	Name.
211 61 63 84 1250 00	1525 45		8976 51				6976 51				6976 51	Adams, John.
675 00	675 00	2250 00	27131 41	365 00 2000 00 183 71 675 00	3223 71	2187 55	26095 25	1500 00	1500 00	d3243 50 651 71	28490 46	Brown, H. J.
1256 88 5000 00	6256 88	575 00	2506 86			4000 00	6506 86	69 35 476 62	545 97	d1841 38	7802 27	Davis, C. W.
175 00 86 40 1000 00	1261 40	1900 00	21665 52	1500 00 794 18 162 35	2456 53	d2452 72 3500 00	25161 71	118 50 500 00 1896 17	2514 67	d4790 84 4942 11	32379 99	Jones Mfg. Co.
			1500 00				1500 00				1500 00	Certificates of Deposit.
			1000 00				1000 00				1000 00	Certified Checks.
				748 37	748 37	d748 37						Cashier Account.
												TRANSIENT ACCOUNTS. Long, H. S.
	20502 87	21933 44	289792 74		13998 24	24365 42	228289 92		11756 50	27292 97	235908 41	
											2 02	(Overdrafts in red ink.)

entered the credits to Bills Discounted, Deposits account and Chemical Bank of New York. The total for credit to Bills Discounted is entered here from the total amount collected during the day on paper owned by the bank, as shown by the Discount Tickler. The total credited to the Chemical Bank is the footing of the New York Draft Register, which represents the aggregate amount of drafts drawn on the Chemical Bank by us during the day and the total credit to Deposits account is from the total footing of the Deposits column in the Individual Ledger. Receipts from other Banks and from other sources are also entered in the General column. On the right-hand side of the Journal are entered the debits to Deposits account, the Chemical Bank of New York, accounts with other Banks and such other accounts as Collection and Exchange, Expense, etc. The entry to Deposits account is compiled from the Total Check column of the Individual Ledger; the total to Chemical Bank from the New York Draft Register, which total represents the remittances for the day to the Chemical Bank; charges to the Expense account are either compiled from the vouchers in the cash drawer at night or from the Expense Book.

When the business is of such magnitude as to necessitate the employment of two clerks upon the Journal, or where two tellers are employed in a bank, the Journal is divided into two books. The right-hand side of the general Journal would be bound into one book and called the Debit Journal and the left-hand side would be bound into a separate book and called the Credit Journal. Sometimes the Credit Journal is called the Debit Cash Book and the Debit Journal the Credit Cash Book.

DISCOUNT

When Dis.		No.	Maker.	Endorser.	Page of B. B.	Where Payable.	Date.	
Dec.	12	555	Harwood Bros.,	W. F. Johnson,	13	Union Bank,	Dec.	12
		556	Ham & King,	Jones Mfg. Co.,	17	West's Bank, Livonia,		11
Dec.	13	557	L. W. Gray,	J. H. Woodward,	19	Second Nat., Lyons,	Dec.	13
		558	Payne & Harris,	C. W. Davis,	20	Union Bank,		7
		559	Henry L. Fowler,	H. Sibley,	15	Our Bank,		2

COLLECTION

When Left.		No.	Payer.	Endorser.	Where Payable.	To Whom Sent.
Dec.	12	919	Samuel Wallace,	J. E. Hill,	Our Bank,	
		920	Union Bank,	D. B. Jones,	Our Bank,	
		921	C. W. Davis,	Jas. Brackett,	Our Bank,	
		922	Our Bank,	Klein & Co.,	Our Bank,	
		923	J. W. Mead,	Jones Mfg. Co.,	Lyons,	Monroe Co. Nat'l.
		924	W. G. Shaver,	D. J. Slocum,	Canton,	Farmers, Canton.
		925	P. A. Wood,	J. H. Woodward & Co.,	Kingston,	Tra. Nat'l, Kingston.
		926	First Nat'l, Newport,	Case & Weaver,	Newport,	3rd Nat'l, Newport.
		927	J. L. White,	R. L. Mason,	2nd Nat'l, Rockford,	1st Nat'l, Rockford.
		928	D. J. Dudley,	Michael Kauffman,	Bath,	

The General Ledger contains all the accounts of the business excepting those with depositors, Certificates of Deposit and Certified Checks. Deposits account in the General Ledger represents the total of all the accounts in the Individual Ledger.

The Individual Ledger is a book of original entry for all cash transactions with depositors, and in using it much labor is saved and errors are less likely to occur. It is made with a very large page—18 x 23 inches not being an unusual size—large enough to contain the accounts of forty or more depositors on a page. The left-hand page is ruled with a column for the names of the depositors, and one for the balances of the depositors' accounts. The remainder of the page is divided into three sets of money columns, each containing four columns. The first or left-hand column in each set is devoted to "Checks in Detail," the second to "Total Checks," the third to "Deposits" and the fourth to "Balances." The right-hand side of the page is the same as the left-hand page, except that the column for the depositors' names is on the extreme right. Sometimes these names are printed in where the book is made, especially where a bank has a certain line of regular depositors. In that case a few blank lines are left after each letter, the names being arranged alphabetically, for the names of new depositors. The name of each depositor is written on each page and the line upon which his name appears represents his account for a period of one week. At the beginning of each week, unless the names are printed, the names are rewritten and the balances carried forward. In some banks, however, the leaves following the first record of names are cut some two inches narrower, so that when a leaf on the right is turned over on to the left-hand page the names are not covered, and the record may be continued without rewriting the names, except upon the first of each month or quarter. (*See form of Individual Ledger, pages 198, 199.*)

REGISTER

TIME.	WHEN DUE.		FACE OF PAPER.		DISCOUNT.		COLL. & EX.		PROCEEDS.		Tickler Check.	FOR WHOM DISCOUNTED.	Post'g Check.	REM'KS.
15 da.	Dec.	30	2000	00	6	00			1994	00	✓	W. F. Johnson.	✓	
10 da.		24	1750	00	3	79	3	19	1743	02	✓	Jones Mfg. Co.	✓	
			✓ 3750	00	✓ 9	79	✓ 3	19	3737	02				
15 da.	Dec.	31	500	00	1	50	1	13	497	37	✓	J. H. Woodward.	✓	
15 da.		25	1620	00	3	24			1616	76	✓	C. W. Davis.	✓	
30 da.	Jan.	4	450	00	1	65			448	35	✓	Henry L. Fowler.		Cash.
			✓ 2570	00	✓ 6	39	1	13	2562	48				

REGISTER

DATE.		TIME.	WHEN DUE.		FOR WHOM COLLECTED.	FACE.		CHECK. T.orCr.	CHECK. Paid	REMARKS.
Dec.	12	Sight,			Monroe Co. National Bank,	211	92	✓	✓	Credited.
"	9	Sight,			Clinton National Bank,	865	70	✓	✓	Credited.
Nov.	13	30 da.	Dec.	16	Farmers, Canton,	Int. 1250	00	✓		
Dec.	9	Sight,			Drummond's Bank, Pittsford,	4500	00			Remitted N. Y. draft.
"	12	Sight,			Ourselves,	423	31	✓	✓	
"	12	Sight,			D. J. Slocum,	193	42			Returned.
"	12	Sight,			J. H. Woodward,	315	23	✓	✓	Credited.
"	10	Sight,			Case & Weaver,	583	75	✓	✓	Credited.
Oct.	14	2 mo.	Dec.	17	R. L. Mason,	285	00			
Dec.	12	Sight,			M. Kauffman,	322	15	✓	✓	Credited.

At the close of banking hours each day, every customer's deposit for the day is added to his balance of the day previous, and from this sum the aggregate of his checks is deducted, and the new balance is extended into the "Balance" column. Each column is then footed, excepting that devoted to "Checks in Detail," and in case there are more than one page of accounts, the footings are carried forward so that the final footings shall exhibit the total amount of checks paid and the total amount of deposits for the day, as well as the aggregate of balances of depositors' accounts. The footing of the column of "Total Checks" is carried to the debit of Deposits on the right-hand side of the Journal, and the footing of the column of "Deposits," to the credit of Deposits on the left-hand side of the Journal.

The advantages of this form of Ledger are: first, the paying teller can more readily ascertain the condition of a depositor's account; second, the necessity for writing all the names on both sides of the Journel every day is obviated; and, third, the bookkeeper has forty or more accounts before him at once, instead of being required to consume a large part of the time turning from one account to another.

The New York Draft Register.—In this book is kept, in detail, the account between the bank and its New York correspondent. On the left-hand page are entered all remittances to the Chemical National Bank for its credit, with the number of the draft or check, the bank or person by whom drawn, the bank or person on whom drawn, and the amount. On the right-hand page are recorded all drafts drawn by the bank on the Chemical National Bank, with the number, the name of the person, bank or firm in whose favor made, the amount of Collection and Exchange and the face of each draft. (*See New York Draft Register, page 196.*) This book is balanced every day and the balance brought down, and while an account is kept in the General Ledger with Chemical Bank, simply to show in the

DISCOUNT TICKLER.

DECEMBER 12 189-

No.	Payer.	Endorser.	Where Payable.	To Whom Sent.	Amount.		Ck.	Remarks.
50	W. P. Johnson.	James Brackett.	Our Bank.		1200	00	1	P. & E.
51	Robert Vaughn.	Lord & Barrett.	Union, City.		2540	18		
			13					
52	H. W. Gloss.	Wm. Raymond.	Brown & Co., Canton.	Farmers, Lincoln.	785	00	1	Protest. P. & E. [illegible]
53	L. W. Davis.	Thos. H. Wilson.	Exchange, City.		3250	00		

COLLECTION TICKLER.

DECEMBER 12 189-.

No.	Payer.	Where Payable.	To Whom Sent.	For Whom Collected.	Amount.		Ck.	Remarks.
833	Arthur Ranney.	Lincoln.	Farmers Bank.	L. J. Farnham.	1215	00		
834	Jacob Hockstra.	Exchange, City.		S. H. Lowe.	918	31	1	Returned.
835	A. M. Hastings.	Yonkers.	Exchange.	W. F. Johnson.	856	62		
			13					
867	Chas. F. Ham.	Clyde.	Monroe Co.	Stillman & Moore.	318	20	1	P. & E.
872	Harvey Brown.	Union, City.		Henry D. Wilson & Co.	942	17		Protested.
886	James Angle.	Our Bank.		Traders National.	1400	00		

quarterly statement all the resources and liabilities of the bank, yet this book represents the current condition of the account with Chemical Bank and is the account consulted when information is wanted regarding the business with the bank. The aggregate of the remittances to Chemical National Bank for the day is charged to that bank on the right-hand side of the Journal, and the aggregate of the drafts made on Chemical National Bank during the day is credited to that bank, on the left-hand side of the Journal. The footing of Collection and Exchange column in this book is credited to Collection and Exchange account on the left-hand side of the Journal. If it is deemed desirable this book may be divided into two books as in the case of the Journal, one devoted to remittances made to our correspondent in New York City (or other commercial center) and the other to the drafts drawn by us upon such correspondents.

Discount Register.—This book is a book of original entry and becomes the basis for all transactions involving Bills Discounted. It contains a complete record of all paper discounted by the bank, which record is made at the time the paper is discounted. The Amount, Discount, Collection, and Exchange, and Proceeds columns are footed each day and ruled as illustrated. (*See Discount Register, pages 200, 201.*)

DEALERS BILL BOOK.

JONES MANUFACTURING COMPANY

When Discounted.	No.	Other Parties Liable.	Discounted for Him	Liable as Payer	Liable as Endorser	When Due.	Remarks.
189[illegible]. Dec. 12	53[illegible]	Hahn & King.	75 [illegible]		175 [illegible]	Dec. 24	

HENRY L. FOWLER

When Discounted.	No.	Other Parties Liable.	Discounted for Him	Liable as Payer	Liable as Endorser	When Due.	Remarks.
Dec. 13	5[illegible]	H. [illegible]	45 [illegible]	45 [illegible]		Jan. 4	

The footing of the Total column represents the total amount of paper, at its face value, bought during the day; the Proceeds column represents the total cost, and the difference between the two amounts represents the amount charged by the bank for discount, collection, and exchange, which amount is shown by the footings of the Collection and Exchange and Discount columns. The footing of the "Amount" column is charged to Bills Discounted on the right-hand (or paying out) side of the Journal and checked in the Discount Register. On the left-hand (or receiving) side of the Journal, Discount, Collection and Exchange are credited for the footings of the Collection and Exchange columns. The items in the Proceeds column in the Discount Register are posted in the Deposits column of the Individual Ledger and then carried to the left-hand side of the Journal, together with other deposits, in one total. Excepting where paper is discounted for cash, each party whose name appears in the "For Whom Discounted" column is credited in the "Deposits" column of the Individual Ledger for the proceeds of the paper discounted (*see explanation of Individual Ledger, page 200*) as shown by the amount in the "Proceeds" column of the Discount Register. The amount when so transferred is checked, using as a check either the page in the Individual Ledger on which the depositor's name is entered or the numerical system, which consists in giving each depositor a number from one to the total number of depositors and entering the depositor's number as a check mark.

For paper discounted for cash, a Cashier's check is given by the Discount Clerk to the party selling the paper. This check is cashed by the Teller and entered to the debit of Cashier's account in the "Checks in Detail" column of the Individual Ledger. For these cash purchases the word Cash is entered after the parties' names and the items are credited to Cashier's account in the Individual Ledger.

The entries in the Discount Register are numbered consecutively. All paper is carefully classified with reference to its maturity so that it may be protected by protest if not paid. This is done by recording each paper by number, name, amount and when legally due in the Discount Tickler under the date of maturity. When so transferred a check mark is made in the Discount Register in the column headed "Tickler Ck." In case the paper is dishonored and protested the word "Protested" is written opposite the record of it in the "Remarks" column of the Discount Tickler, and such other particulars regarding the matter as may be important.

Discount Tickler. As explained above, in this book are entered all the discounted notes or bills, arranged with reference to their maturity. The sphere of the Discount Tickler is to insure the presentation of paper for payment at the proper time.

The Dealers Bill Book, sometimes called "Individual Liabilities," is designed to show in convenient form the amount of discounted paper carried by the bank for each customer. A title page is given to each dealer and the record is compiled from the Discount Register. The book is divided into columns as follows: Commencing on the left there are consecutively given the "Date Discounted," "Number" (which is the consecutive number in the Discount Register), "Other Parties Liable," "Liable as Endorser," "Liable as Payer," "When Due," and "Remarks." Sometimes the dealer's name is the one written at the head of the page, but the rule is to write the name on the strength of which the paper was bought. The book is indexed so that ready reference may be had and the amount on hand, if any, may be ascertained. Some banks observe a very strict record regarding the customers from whom they buy paper. A record is compiled not only like the above for each dealer, but a page is set apart upon which are posted the mercantile reports, synopsis of letters pertaining to the character of the house, opinions of business men regarding the dealer's standing, etc. This record is carefully compiled from day to day. As fast as paper is paid it is marked "Paid" in the Remarks column.

Collection Register.—This book is designed to contain a record of all paper left at the bank for collection, that which is received from abroad for collection, and of all sight paper, payable abroad, received as cash. (*See Collection Register, page 200.*) Being the book of original entry for such paper, the paper is recorded by consecutive numbers. The record of the time paper is then transferred to the Collection Tickler, and when so entered a check mark is made in the column headed "Tickler and Cr. Check" of the Collection Register. All sight paper received from abroad is at once presented for payment, and if paid it is checked in the "Paid" column of the Collection Register. Paper received from a regular correspondent, if paid, is credited to such bank in the Journal and checked in the column headed "Tickler and Cr. Check" of the Collection Register. The proceeds of all paper received from other than regular correspondents are remitted in draft on Chemical National Bank, and when so remitted a memorandum to that effect is made in the "Remarks" column of the Collection Register and the draft is entered in the New York Draft Register.

All checks and sight drafts payable abroad, received as cash, are entered in this book and charged in the Journal to the accounts of the banks to which they are sent for collection. When so charged they are checked in the "T. and Cr. Check" column. All paper payable abroad, received as cash, is charged immediately to the banks where sent for collection.

The Collection Tickler contains a record of all time paper left with the bank for collection, and is compiled from the Collection Register. Like the Discount Tickler all transfers to the Collection Tickler are arranged according to the date of the maturity of the paper. At the beginning of the year a new book is gotten up with printed headings for every week-day of the year; as, "Monday, Jan. 2nd, 1899," etc., one-half of a double page usually being given to each day of the week from Monday to Saturday. On each page are ruled columns headed "For Whose Acct.," "Payer," "When Payable," and "To Whom Sent." A record so kept enables the bank to demand payment promptly on the date of maturity, and if not paid to protest same and notify the endorsers as provided by law. The Collection and Discount ticklers are consulted at the beginning of each day's business, when it can be seen just what paper demands attention. All collections are sent to the bank where made payable or to the correspondents of the bank, except in cases where a long time is to elapse before maturity. But even in case of long time paper such collections should be sent several days before maturity that due notice may be sent the payer by the bank where payment is to be made.

Stock Ledger.—This book contains an account with each stockholder, in which he is credited for all stock paid for, and debited with all stock transferred to other parties. This book is kept by the Secretary or Cashier and therefore is not used here in the memoranda.

Collection Paper is paper received by a bank for collection on account of its depositors, correspondents and others. Such paper does not become the property of the bank as the bank acts only as agent for the owners, charging a fee for its services, called "Collection." The making of collections is an important part of the banking business, and the one which illustrates forcibly the utility of banks. Paper for collection must be drawn or endorsed so that the bank can make the collection.

When paper is received for collection, the bank clerk marks on each note or time draft the date of its maturity. This is called "timing."

All paper received for collection, wherever payable and of whatever kind, is entered in the Collection Register. If it is time paper it is also entered in the Collection Tickler and checked in the Tickler Check column in the Collection Register to show that it has been entered in the Tickler. Every entry is numbered in the Collection Register and the Collection Register number is written on the paper itself, usually in red ink.

Paper from abroad received for collection, if payable at sight, is collected and checked in the "Paid" column in the Collection Register, and credited in the Journal to the bank from whom it was received, and again checked in the Tickler check column to show that it had been so credited. The "Tickler Check" column thus serves the double purpose of checking sight paper when credited and time paper when entered in the Tickler.

After paper received for collection, payable abroad, has been entered in the Collection Register, if time paper, it is also entered in the Collection Tickler and checked in the Tickler Check column, and sent to the place where it is payable, for collection.

There is no uniform rate of charges for collecting paper, the amount charged being largely governed by circumstances: that is, the place where payable, the amount of the paper and the business relations with the customer.

No charge is made for collecting paper payable in the city received from banks which are regular correspondents, nor do such banks make a charge in similar cases. The accommodation is reciprocal. The bank that received the paper for collection usually makes a charge to the party for whom the collection was made, whether or not a charge was made to the bank for collecting the paper. When a charge is made by a correspondent of the bank for making a collection this charge is included in the bank's charges to the party for whom the collection is made.

If paper payable abroad is collected by a bank not a regular correspondent the proceeds are usually remitted by New York draft. If the collection is made by a regular correspondent the proceeds are credited, and a notice is usually sent to that effect.

Sight paper received from abroad, drawn on a depositor, is presented to the payee, who pays it either by giving a check for the amount, or by accepting it payable at the bank. This is not an "acceptance" in the usual sense, but an order on the bank to pay the amount specified in the draft.

Discount Paper includes all the paper discounted or bought by the bank. Such paper is called Bills Discounted, which is the same as Bills Receivable. Unlike collection paper, discounted paper is the property of the bank, and when it is paid Bills Discounted account is credited for the amount of such paper. In addition to the discount on discounted paper payable abroad, charges are usually made for collection and exchange. As the proceeds of each note must be collected and remitted to the bank discounting the paper, if it is collected by a bank not a regular correspondent, the cost of exchange will be deducted, in addition to the charge for collection. Were it not for the reciprocal arrangement for mutual services, like charges would be made by the bank's correspondents. Thus it will be seen that the charges for collection and exchange made the party for whom the paper is discounted, are for services rendered by the bank or its correspondents. When discounted paper payable at the bank where it is discounted, falls due, it is charged direct to the account of the makers if their account is good for it. Previous notice is, however, always sent of the maturity of such paper. Some banks require that such paper be taken up or "lifted," as it is called, by check.

When paper is discounted for a regular depositor, he is usually credited in account with the proceeds. If the party is not a regular depositor, the amount of the proceeds is paid him in cash. In transactions of this kind, the person for whom the paper was discounted is furnished a check signed by the cashier, called a "Cashier's Check," which is immediately cashed by the paying teller and placed among the checks and charged to "Cashier Account." Cashier account is credited for this amount from the Discount Register. This check is drawn for the purpose of serving as a voucher of the transaction, and is used for the accommodation of the bank.

Sight Paper Deposited.—All sight paper deposited becomes the property of the bank and is treated as cash. When this paper is sent away to be collected, the banks to which it is sent are charged for the amount of it at the time it is sent, instead of at the time it is collected, as in the case of sight paper received for collection. Whether received for collection or on deposit, all sight paper is entered in the Collection Register.

Directions for using the Individual Ledger. - Write the names of the depositors in alphabetical order, and Certificates of Deposit, Certified Checks, Cashier and the transient accounts beneath, on the left of the left-hand page and on the right of the right-hand page, being particular to put each name on the same line on each page. Enter the balance of each account in the "Balance" column, opposite the depositor's name. Enter each customer's checks paid during the day in the "Checks in Detail" column, opposite his name, and extend the aggregate of such checks to the "Total Checks" column. Enter each customer's deposit in the "Deposits" column, and also any collection made for him, from the Collection Register or Collection Tickler, and the proceeds of paper discounted for him, not paid in cash, from the Discount Register. Enter the proceeds of discounted paper that was paid in cash also in the "Deposits" column, opposite "Cashier Account." Add each customer's deposit for the day to the last balance of his account, and from that sum deduct the amount of his checks. The difference will show the present balance of his account, and will be extended into the next "Balance" column, opposite his name. When the account is overdrawn, enter the amount of the "overdraft" in *red ink*.

When the balances of all the accounts have been entered as directed, add the "Total Checks," "Deposits" and "Balance" columns.

To prove the correctness of this work, find the difference between the total checks and deposits for the day. This difference will equal the difference between the total balances of the day and the total balances of the day previous. If the "Balance" column contains both black and red ink entries, foot first the black and then the red ink amounts, and place the footings at the bottom of the column in corresponding ink, and exhibit the difference beneath, which difference will be the amount due depositors.

The footing of the "Total Checks" column is debited to deposits in the Journal, and the footing of the "Deposits" column is credited to deposits in the Journal.

As depositors are credited in the Individual Ledger with the proceeds of paper discounted for them, and Deposits account is credited in the Journal for the amount of the deposits, it will be necessary to carry the other results of the Discount Register to the Journal as well, in order that the Journal may show the correct balance of cash. Bills Discounted should, therefore, be debited and Collection and Exchange and Discount credited in the Journal each day for the footings of those columns in the Discount Register.

RESOURCES AND LIABILITIES

OF THE

SECOND NATIONAL BANK.

The General Ledger of the Second National Bank exhibits the following balances of accounts at the close of business, Saturday, Dec. 24th, 189–.

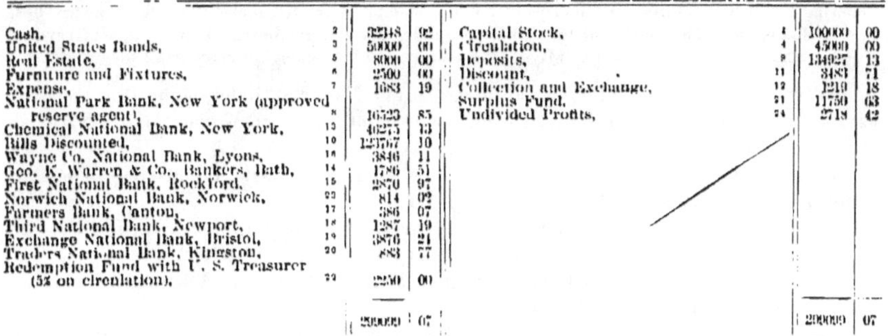

DEBIT BALANCES.				CREDIT BALANCES.			
Cash,	2	22348	92	Capital Stock,	1	100000	00
United States Bonds,	3	50000	00	Circulation,	4	45000	00
Real Estate,	5	8000	00	Deposits,	9	134927	13
Furniture and Fixtures,	6	2500	00	Discount,	11	3483	71
Expense,	7	1683	19	Collection and Exchange,	12	1219	18
National Park Bank, New York (approved reserve agent),	8	16523	85	Surplus Fund,	21	11750	63
Chemical National Bank, New York,	13	46275	13	Undivided Profits,	24	2718	42
Bills Discounted,	10	123767	10				
Wayne Co. National Bank, Lyons,	16	3846	11				
Geo. K. Warren & Co., Bankers, Bath,	14	1786	51				
First National Bank, Rockford,	15	2870	97				
Norwich National Bank, Norwick,	22	814	02				
Farmers Bank, Canton,	17	386	07				
Third National Bank, Newport,	18	1287	19				
Exchange National Bank, Bristol,	19	3876	21				
Traders National Bank, Kingston,	20	883	77				
Redemption Fund with U. S. Treasurer (5% on circulation),	23	2250	00				
		299099	07			299099	07

(Open accounts in the General Ledger with the above balances, as you would if you were opening a new Ledger in any other business, and open them in the order indicated by the number placed before each account. Give the accounts numbered 3, 4, 5, 6, 21, 22, 23 and 24, one-fourth of a page space, and all of the others one-half a page each. Also place the balance on deposit in Chemical Bank in the New York Draft Register, as illustrated on page 196.)

The General Ledger used in this set is the ordinary form of Ledger. Some banks, however, use a form of General Ledger similar to the Individual Ledger illustrated on pages 198 and 199.

The following are the balances of depositors' accounts, as shown by the Individual Ledger. It will be observed that the aggregate of these credits is the same as the amount credited to Deposits account in the General Ledger.

(Credit each depositor in the Individual Ledger, with the amount opposite his name. See directions for the keeping the Individual Ledger, page 200.) *(Arrange the accounts in alphabetical order.)*

W. F. Jameson,	12186	18
Chas. J. Burke,	9173	11
R. L. Mason,	8452	09
D. J. Slocum,	2183	74
Stillman & Moore,	12293	81
Jas. Angue,	4817	04
Thomas H. Wilson,	8117	93
Ray Brothers,	7183	51
Meyer & Kauffman,	6411	31
Johnson Manufacturing Company,	6343	67
William Raymond,	3184	65
Forward,	82147	08

(Credits continued)		
Forward,	82147	08
Maxwell Day,	5946	25
Samuel Wilder,	7216	07
L. J. Farnsworth,	4388	29
Bingham, Field & Ward,	8443	86
Benj. Thomas & Son,	9963	26
Lord & Bennett,	6861	98
T. J. & W. E. Upton,	8298	16
Certified Checks,	1762	19
Total,	134927	13

The following discounted paper, aggregating the amount debited to Bills Discounted account in the General Ledger, in possession of the bank at this date, should be shown by the Discount Tickler. *(See form of Discount Tickler, on page 202. Enter this discounted paper in the Discount Tickler each item under its date of maturity. Add three days of grace to all time paper. Write the dates in order in the Discount and Collection Ticklers, entirely through these books, omitting Sundays and holidays.)*

Since there is no entry or check mark to be made in the Discount Register at the maturity of paper, it is not necessary for you to enter paper on hand at this date in your Discount Register. In business such paper would, of course, be entered in the Discount Register and Discount Tickler at the time it was discounted. All paper maturing on Sundays or holidays should be entered under the date of the first business day following. The statutes of the various States are not uniform in regard to the time of payment of paper maturing on Sundays and holidays. Remember to add three days of grace to all time paper.

No. 489. Note of H. Whitaker, at 30 days from Nov. 23d, indorsed by D. J. Slocum, payable at Second National Bank, Lyons, for 1500.00. Sent to Wayne County National. *Discount Tickler, see page 202.*

No. 486. Note of H. C. Decker, at 90 days from Sept. 24th, indorsed by Wm. Raymond, payable at Exchange Bank, City, for 8750.00.

No. 488. Note of W. S. Chapin, indorsed by W. W. Wheeler, at 2 months from Oct. 23d, payable at Woodruff's Bank, Lyonia, for 500.00. Sent to Woodruff's.

No. 487. Note of Maxwell Day, indorsed by Burt, Brace & Co., at 1 month from Nov. 24th, payable at our bank, for 10000.00.

No. 483. Note of A. O. Bunnell, indorsed by Joseph Cone, at 3 months from Sept. 24th, payable at Exchange Bank, Dansville, for 10500.00. Sent to Exchange Bank.

No. 485. Note of A. M. Hastings, indorsed by Samuel Wilder, at 6 months from June 25th, payable at Union Bank, City, for 5000.00.

No. 484. Note of W. T. Tinsley, indorsed by J. A. Munson and Meyer & Kauffman, at 30 days from Nov. 25th, payable at Wayne Co. National Bank, Lyons, for 7500.00. Sent to Wayne County National.

No. 482. Note of H. Bancroft, indorsed by Samuel Wilder, at 3 months from Sept. 25th, payable at our bank, for 9000.00.

No. 499. Note of J. Wilson & Co., indorsed by Lord & Bennett, at 60 days from Oct. 26th, payable at our bank, for 15000.00

No. 494. Note of P. J. Smith, indorsed by Ray Bros., at 4 months from Aug. 26th, payable at Third National Bank, Newport, for 7200.00. Sent to Third National.

No. 496. Note of Johnson Mfg. Co., indorsed by Freeman Clarke, at 90 days from Sept. 27th, payable at our bank, for 3000.00.

No. 495. Note of R. L. Mason, indorsed by P. J. Moore, at 1 month from Nov. 27th, payable at our bank, for 5000.00.

No. 491. Note of D. W. Smith & Co., indorsed by Jas. Angle, at 6 months from June 27th, payable at Union Bank, City, for 2876.90.

No. 493. Note of L. J. Pratt & Co., indorsed by Jas. Angle, at 30 days from Nov. 27th, payable at Exchange Bank, City, for 1500.00.

No. 492. Note of Bingham, Field & Ward, indorsed by C. D. Cox, at 90 days from Sept. 29th, payable at our bank, for 2150.00.

No. 498. Accepted draft of P. Wise & Son, indorsed by Bingham, Field & Ward, at 10 days from Dec. 18th, payable at Second National Bank, Palmyra, for 1800.00. Sent to Second National.

No. 497. Note of Creed & Wilson, indorsed by Ray Bros., at 3 months from Sept. 28th, payable at Union Bank, City, for 2500.00.

No. 490. Note of Brown & Wood, indorsed by Benj. Thomas & Son, at 60 days from Oct. 29, payable at Third National Bank, Newport, for 1750.00. Sent to Third National.

No. 503. Note of W. F. Jameson, indorsed by James Brackett, at 30 days from Nov. 30th, payable at our bank, for 12000.00.

No. 505. Note of Robert Vaughan, indorsed by Lord & Bennett, at 2 months from Oct. 29th, payable at Union Bank, City, for 2540.18.

No. 504. Note of H. W. Glass, indorsed by Wm. Raymond, at 2 months from Oct. 31st, payable at Brown & Co.'s Bank, Canton, for 785.00. Sent to Farmers.

No. 500. Note of L. W. Davis, indorsed by Thos. H. Wilson, at 4 months from Aug. 31st, payable at Exchange Bank, City, for 3250.00.

No. 502. Note of Meyer & Kauffman, indorsed by Nelson James, at 2 months from Nov. 1st, payable at our bank, for 4500.00.

No. 501. Note of Knapp & Peck, favor of Meyer & Kauffman, at 60 days from Nov. 2d, payable at First National Bank, Auburn, for 3879.60. Sent to First National.

No. 506. Note of L. W. Brigham, indorsed by Samuel Wilder, at 3 months from Oct. 2d, payable at Farmers Bank, Canton, for 1285.42. Sent to Farmers.

The following paper is in possession of the bank at this date for collection for other parties, as shown by the Collection Tickler. (*See form of Collection Tickler, on page 202. Enter this paper in the Collection Tickler, each item under its date of maturity. Remember to add three days of grace to all time paper.*)

Since there is no entry to be made in the Collection Register when the paper matures, excepting to check sight paper when it is paid and credited, you need not enter this paper in your Collection Register.

No. 819. For R. L. Mason, accepted draft at 10 days from Dec. 13th, on J. H. Wing, Lyons, for 584.75. Sent to Wayne County National.

No. 825. For Stillman & Moore, accepted draft at 3 days from Dec. 20th, on Porter Farley, Canton, for 1250.00. Sent to Farmers.

No. 823. For Thos. H. Wilson, John B. Sage's note, at 30 days from Nov. 24th, payable at Geo. K. Warren & Co.'s Bank, Bath, for 817.00, with interest. Sent to Geo. K. Warren & Co.'s. (*Write Int. over the amount in C. T.*)

No. 824. For Meyer & Kauffman, Henry A. Strong's note, at 2 months from Oct. 24th, payable at Union Bank, City, for 215.00.

No. 821. For Wm. Raymond, accepted draft on W. D. McGuire, at 10 days from Dec. 14th, payable at Norwich, for 368.90. Sent to Norwich National.

No. 822. For Samuel Wilder, accepted draft on E. F. Woodbury, Newport, at 60 days from Oct. 26th, for 63.02. Sent to Third National.

No. 820. For Bingham, F. & W., J. E. Booth's note, at 1 month from Nov. 25th, payable at Canton Savings Bank, for 216.25. Sent to Farmers.

No. 829. For Ray Brothers, P. Ford's note at 30 days from Nov. 25th, payable at Rockford County Bank, with interest, for 1483.50. Sent to First National. (*Write "Int." over the amount in C. T.*)

No. 828. For Lord & Bennett, J. M. Harrison's note, at 3 months from Sep. 26th, payable in Bristol, for 1500.00. Sent to Exchange National.

No. 827. For Chas. J. Burke, accepted draft on R. S. Kenyon, at 2 months from Oct. 26th, payable in New York, for 957.65. Sent to Chemical.

No. 826. For D. J. Slocum, A. L. Mabbett's note, at 3 months from Sep. 26th, payable at Lyons, for 88.40. Sent to Wayne County National.

No. 834. For Jas. Angle, J. L. Townsend's note, at 60 days from Oct. 27th, payable at Bath, for 396.15. Sent to Geo. K. Warren & Co.'s.

No. 833. For Johnson Manufacturing Co., accepted draft on F. W. Clark, Norwich, at 3 days from Dec. 24th, for 911.13. Sent to Norwich National.

No. 832. For Maxwell Day, Ward Kelly's note, at 6 months from June 27th, payable at Union Bank, City, for 1350.00.

No. 831. For L. J. Farnsworth, accepted draft on Arthur Ranney, at 1 month from Nov. 28th, payable in Canton, for 1215.00. Sent to Farmers.

No. 830. For S. H. Lowe, Jacob Hoekstra's note, at 6 months from June 28th, payable at Exchange Bank, City, for 918.30.

No. 835. For F. W. Jameson, accepted draft on A. M. Hastings, Yonkers, at 10 days from Dec. 18th, for 856.62. Sent to Chemical.

In case paper is payable where a regular correspondent can collect it more easily than you can, it is better to send it to such correspondent. This explains why No. 835 was sent to Chemical Bank, New York.

No. 836. For R. L. Mason, L. S. Fulton's note, at 2 months from Oct. 28th, payable in Lyons, for 126.90. Sent to Wayne County National.

MEMORANDA OF TRANSACTIONS FOR DECEMBER.

The following transactions are not to be copied but are to be entered in the various books as indicated.

DECEMBER 26, 18—.

Discount No. 486, note of H. C. Decker of $750.00, has been paid. (*Mark this Paid & Entered, or P. & E., in the Discount Tickler, and credit Bills Discounted in the Journal, short extending the amount, that is: writing it inside as illustrated on page 196, as there may be other Bills Discounted to be credited, and in this manner several may be entered on one line and extended in total at the close of the day.*) Received the following paper for collection:

No. 837. For R. L. Mason, sight draft on L. W. Wooden, Nyack, for 432.50. Sent it to Chemical Bank. (*C. R. See explanation of Collection Register and Collection Tickler, page 204*).

No entry, except in Collection Register, is required until notice has been received of the disposition of the paper.

No. 838. For Stillman & Moore, note of L. F. Chappell, at 3 months from Oct. 9th, for 1250.00, payable at Second National Bank of Lyons. Sent to Wayne Co. National Bank, Lyons. (*C. R. and C. T.*)

In entering in Tickler remember to add the three days of grace.

No. 839. For G. H. Perkins, sight draft on W. B. Murdock, Canton, for 926.18. Sent to Farmers Bank, Canton. (*C. R.*)

No. 840. For Jas. Angle, note of David A. Welles, at 30 days from Nov. 26th, for 750.00, with interest, payable at Union Bank, City. (*C. R. and C. T.*)

No. 841. For T. J. & W. E. Upton, sight draft on Daniel Boody, Hoboken, for 119.75. Sent to Chemical Bank. (*C. R.*)

No. 842. For Samuel Wilder, accepted draft on Wm. Haynes, Norwich, at 10 days from Dec. 22d, for 1842.11. Sent to Norwich National Bank. (*C. R. and C. T.*)

No. 843. For Wm. Raymond, sight draft on Peter Bradley, Rockford, for 143.90. Sent to First National Bank, Rockford. (*C. R.*)

Discounted the following paper:

No. 507. For Chas. J. Burke, note of J. D. Winslow, at 30 days from this date, payable at Exchange Bank, City, for 858.90. Discount, 4.72. Proceeds credited. (*D. R., D. T. See explanation of Discount Register, page 202, and Discount Paper, page 206; also forms on pages 200 and 202.*)

No. 508. For D. J. Slocum, note of H. Whitaker, at 30 days from Dec. 24th, payable at First National Bank, Lyons, for 1250.00. Proceeds credited and note sent to Wayne County National Bank for collection. Discount, 6.46; collection, 1.00; exchange, 1.56. (*D. R., D. T.*)

No. 509. For Samuel Wilder, note of A. M. Hastings, at 10 days from this date, payable at Union Bank, City, for 3875.00. Discount, 8.40. Proceeds credited. (*D. R., D. T.*)

No. 510. For Johnson Mfg. Co., their note at 30 days from this date, indorsed by Freeman Clarke, payable at our bank, for 5000.00. Discount, 27.50. Proceeds credited. (*D. R., D. T.*)

The following drafts on New York were received among the deposits, and have been sent to Chemical Bank, New York, for our credit: No. 234, First National of Dayton, on Shoe & Leather, 2875.00; No. 1851, Commercial of Corning, on Metropolitan, 542.75; No. 753, City Bank of Holley, on Broadway, 37.20; No. 115, Seward's of Auburn, on Chemical, 1123.14; No. 1321, Exchange of Geneva, on Third National, 2475.00; No. 4, Steel & Avery, City, on D. Slote & Co., 375.00. (*N. Y. D. R. See form on page 196. See also explanation of N. Y. Draft Register, page 201.*)

Drew the following drafts on Chemical Bank: No. 1585, favor Lord & Bennett, 325.10; exch., 50¢. No. 1586, favor Samuel Wilder, 1200.00; exch., 1.50. No. 1587, favor G. W. Cook, 56.15; exch., 15¢. No. 1588, favor Meyer & Kauffman, 2500.00; exch., 3.13. No. 1589, favor Stillman & Moore, 300.00; exch., 50¢. No. 1590, favor Thos. H. Wilson, 10000.00; exch., 12.50. No. 1591, favor W. F. Jameson, 2000.00; exch., 2.50. (*N. Y. D. R.*)

Paid certified check No. 4392. Amount, 384.16. (*I. L. See page 198.*)

The Teller certifies a check presented for certification, provided the maker's account is good for the amount, and places a slip memorandum on a spindle, giving the name of the maker and the amount of the check. The book keeper debits the depositor for such check from this slip, and credits Certified Checks account. When the check is paid Certified Checks account is debited.

Received the following deposits: Lord & Bennett, 1285.50; Samuel Wilder, 976.00; Johnson Manufacturing Co., 2875.00; Stillman & Moore, 1872.25; Chas. J. Burke, 5460.00; James Angle, 375.00; W. F. Jameson, 926.14; D. J. Slocum, 432.12; Ray Bros., 856.11; Wm. Raymond, 1756.23; L. J. Farnsworth, 493.92; Benj. Thomas & Son, 1250.00; T. J. & W. E. Upton, 2115.00. (*I. L. Enter the above deposits in the "Deposits" column of the Individual Ledger, and the following checks in the "Checks in Detail" column. See form of I. L. page 198.*)

It will be found necessary to write the amounts of checks in very small figures to afford room for all in the space allotted. It is customary in business to leave two or more lines for one account, if it be a very active one involving the entry of more checks than could be entered on one line.

Deposits are entered from Deposit Tickets made out and brought to the bank by the depositors. The teller, after checking the deposits on the Deposit Tickets and examining the footings, places the tickets on a spindle from which the bookkeeper takes them and makes the proper entries.

Paid the following checks: Bingham, Field & Ward, 375.00, 926.50, 1000.00; Lord & Bennett, 2118.00, 325.60, 92.15; Samuel Wilder, 2025.00, 37.50, 325.00, 150.00; Wm. Raymond, 200.00, 480.00, 3115.00; Meyer & Kauffman, 4275.00, 85.00; Thos. H. Wilson, 8000.00; Stillman & Moore, 2500.00, 187.50, 300.00; R. L. Mason, 3250.00, 132.00, 247.18; W. F. Jameson, 2000.00, 312.75, 1175.00. (*I. L. See "Directions for using I. L.," page 206.*)

Collection and Exchange, from Teller's Memorandum, 7.25. (*J. See form of Journal, page 195.*)

The items of Collection and Exchange on sight drafts and foreign checks received on deposit are entered in the Teller's Memorandum at the time the deposits are made, and are either paid in cash by the depositors or deducted from the deposit tickets. Collection and Exchange is credited in the Journal at the end of the day for the sum of such items.

You will now balance the New York Draft Register (*see form on pages 196, 197*), and carry the aggregate of the drafts drawn on Chemical National Bank to the credit of that bank on the left-hand side of the Journal, the footing of the Collection & Exchange column to the Collection & Exchange column on the left-hand side of the Journal, and the aggregate of remittances to Chemical National Bank to the debit of that bank on the right-hand side of the Journal (*see form of Journal, pages 196, 197*). Add and rule the columns in the Discount Register (*see form on pages 200, 201*), and enter the footing of the column containing the amount of paper discounted to the debit of Bills Discounted on the right-hand side of the Journal, the footings of the Discount and Collection & Exchange columns to the credit of those accounts on the left-hand side of the Journal. The items in the Proceeds column should be credited to the parties for whom discounted, in the Individual Ledger, writing the amounts over the deposits in cases where deposits have been made this day, and placing the letter "d" against the amount as illustrated in the form of Individual Ledger shown on page 196. Check each posting in the Discount Register as illustrated on page 201.

Extend the balances of depositors' accounts into the "Balance" column in the Individual Ledger, and foot the column; foot the "Total Checks" and "Deposits" column, and carry the footings to the Journal. (*See "Directions for using I. L.," page 206.*) Rule the Individual Ledger at the bottom of the page.

You will also add and rule the Journal, carrying the footings of the Collection & Exchange into the General column. (*See form of Journal on pages 196 and 197.*) Post all the items in the General column on the left-hand page to the credit of the respective accounts in the General Ledger, and the footing of the Collection & Exchange column to the credit of Collection & Exchange account in the General Ledger, and those in the General column on the right-hand page to the debit of the respective accounts. Debit Cash account in the General Ledger with the footing of the left-hand page of the Journal, and credit it with the footing of the right-hand page.

DECEMBER 27, 189–.

Received advice from Wayne County National Bank, Lyons, that collection No. 819 has been paid and placed to our credit. (*J. & I. L. Charge W. C. N. Bank, 584.75, and credit R. L. Mason, 584.25, and Coll. and Ex., 50c. Check Paid and Entered, or P. & E. in the Collection Tickler. See next to last paragraph on page 205.*)

Also received notice from Farmers Bank, Canton, that collection No. 825 has been paid and placed to our credit. (*J. & I. L. Charge Farmers Bank, 1250.00, in J., and credit Stillman & Moore, 1249.00, in I. L. and Coll. & Ex., 1.00 in J. Check P. & E. in C. T. See next to last paragraph on page 205.*)

Collection No. 824 has been paid. (*I. L. Credit Meyer & K., 215.00, and check P. & E. in C. T. See third last paragraph on page 205.*)

Discount No. 487 has been placed among the checks, and will be charged to the account of the maker, Maxwell Day, at the close of business for the day. (*J. Check P. & E. in D. T. See last paragraph on page 205.*)

Since this note was made by one of our depositors, and his account is good for the amount, it is only necessary to credit Bills Discounted, 10000.00, at this time, and place the note among the vouchers that are to be charged to depositors. See list of checks paid, below.

Received advice from Wayne County National Bank, that discount No. 489 has been paid and placed to our credit. (*J. Credit Bills Discounted and debit W. C. N. Bank 1500.00, and check Paid and Entered, or P. & E., in the Discount Tickler.*)

Received draft No. 161, on Sixth National Bank, New York, from Woodruff's Bank, Livonia, for proceeds of discount No. 488, less 25¢ collection and 25¢ exchange. (*J. Credit Bills Discounted, 500.00, and debit Coll. & Ex., 50¢.*)

The draft received will be charged to Chemical National Bank, in the N. Y. Draft Register, later in the day, with other drafts received during the day.

Received the paper described below, from the following banks, for collection and credit: From Norwich National Bank, H. B. Cook & Co.'s sight draft for 4150.00, on N. Fisher & Co., City, dated Dec. 26. Presented, collected and credited. (*C. R., J. Credit N. N. Bank, 4150.00, and check in both columns in the Collection Register.*)

From Exchange National Bank, Bristol, D. J. Loomis' check on Union Bank, City, dated Dec. 26, for 493.18. Collected. (*C. R., J. Credit Exchange N. Bank, Bristol, 493.18. See sixth paragraph on page 205.*)

From Traders National Bank, Kingston, A. B. Wilson's sight draft on Johnson Mfg. Co., dated Dec. 26, for 573.90. Presented, accepted and placed among the checks. (*C. R., J. Credit Traders N. Bank, Kingston, 573.90. See last paragraph on page 205. See list of checks for this date.*)

Received remittances in drafts on New York from the following banks, on account. No. 943, First National of Rockford, on Broadway Bank, for 2500.00; No. 341, Geo. K. Warren & Co., Bath, on Union Trust Co., for 1500.00. (*Credit the banks from which the drafts are received at once, in the Journal, and enter the drafts on the left-hand side of the N. Y. Draft Register, with other drafts, later in the day.*)

The following sight drafts, dated this day, on individuals and firms, received on deposit from our customers, and included in deposits enumerated below, have been sent to our correspondents for our credit:

W. F. Jameson, on D. B. Hill, Lyons, for 225.00. Sent to Wayne Co. National, and charged to their account. (*C. R., J. Debit Wayne Co. National, 225.00. In "For Whom Collected" column in C. R. write "Cash," as this was received as a cash deposit. See "Sight Paper Deposited," page 206.*)

As this item is included in the amount of W. F. Jameson's deposit mentioned later no entry should be made to his credit at this time.

Johnson Mfg. Co., on P. G. Warren, Bristol, for 2800.00. Sent and charged to Exchange National Bank, Bristol.

Maxwell Day, on D. L. Price & Co., Kingston, for 340.00. Sent and charged to Traders National Bank, Kingston.

Jas. Angle, on A. A. Wildman, Rockford, for 1350.00. Sent and charged to First National Bank, Rockford.

Discounted the following paper: For Johnson Mfg. Co., P. L. Paine's accepted draft, at 30 days from Dec. 24th, payable at First National Bank, Lyons, for 4325.00. Discount, 21.63; collection, 4.00; exchange, 5.41. Sent to W. C. N. Bank. (*D. R., D. T.*)

For Maxwell Day, D. H. Davis' note, at 3 months from Oct. 23, payable at Woodruff's Bank, Livonia, for 1500.00. Discount, 7.50; collection, 1.00; exchange, 1.88. Sent Woodruff's Bank. (*See first paragraph on page 206.*)

For Samuel Wilder, Isaac Willis' note, at 60 days from Nov. 18, payable at Farmers Bank, Canton, for 2394.80. Discount, 9.58; collection, 2.00; exchange, 2.98. Sent Farmers Bank.

For Thomas H. Wilson, J. D. Shultz' note, at 30 da. from date, payable at Corning's Bank, Richmond, for 398.50. Discount, 2.19; collection, 50¢; exchange, 50¢. Sent Corning's Bank.

For R. L. Mason, T. G. Lord's note, at 4 months from Sept. 17, payable at Norwich National Bank, for 960.00. Discount, 3.84; collection, 50¢; exchange, 1.20. Sent Norwich National Bank.

Received the following paper for collection: From W. F. Jameson, draft at 10 days from date, on W. L. Peters & Co., Hoboken, for 918.75. Sent Chemical Bank. (*C. R., C. T.*)

From Jas. Angle, note of W. F. Burroughs, at 2 months from Nov. 8, payable at Exchange Bank, City, for 1290.00.

From Ray Bros., note of Miller & Co., at 2 months from Nov. 8, payable at First National Bank, Kingston, with interest, for 482.60. Sent Traders National, Kingston.

From Meyer & Kauffman, draft at 15 days from date on Wendell & Holmes, Canton, for 1194.83. Sent Farmers Bank, Canton.

Certified Lord & Bennett's check for 2500. (*I. L. See note at bottom of page 211.*)

Drew the following drafts on Chemical Bank: No. 1592, favor Lord & Bennett, 1141.80; exch. 1.00. No. 1593, favor Bingham, F. & W., 132.20; exch., 25¢. No. 1594, favor Wm. Raymond, 437.00; exch., 50¢. No. 1595, favor Johnson Mfg. Co., 6444.00; exch. 6.00. No. 1596, favor Ray Bros., 4196.00; exch., 4.00. No. 1597, favor R. L. Mason, 4246.00; exch., 4.00. (*See last paragraph on page 211. See form on pages 196, 197.*)

The following drafts on New York, received during the course of to-day's business, have been remitted to Chemical Bank for our credit: No. 161, Woodruff's Bank of Livonia, on

Sixth National, 499.50; No. 943, First National of Rockford, on Broadway Bank, 2500.00; No. 341, Geo. K. Warren & Co., Bath, on Union Trust Co., 1500.00; No. 108, Ward's Bank of Union, on Third National, 86.90; No. 347, First National of Butler, on Chemical, 583.11; No. 4043, Second National of Byron, on Broadway Bank, 2586.74; No. 48, Clark's Bank of Warsaw, on Sixth National, 138.18. *(See last paragraph on page 201.)*

Received the following deposits: T. J. & W. E. Upton, 1175.00; Benj. Thomas & Son, 435.57; Bingham, Field & Ward, 2850.00; Samuel Wilder, 894.13; Maxwell Day, 2948.75; Johnson Mfg. Co., 3480.00; Meyer & Kauffman, 550.00; Thos. H. Wilson, 2294.18; Jas. Angle, 1840.00; D. J. Slocum, 486.78; W. F. Jameson, 1500.00. *(See I. L. page 198.)*

Paid the following checks: Bingham, Field & Ward, 132.40, 1892.18, 450.00; Wm. Raymond, 500.00, 437.50, 140.00; Johnson Mfg. Co., 6450.00, 573.90; Maxwell Day (note), 10000.00; Ray Bros., 115.00; 973.62, 4500.00; Thomas H. Wilson, 56.75, 1394.11, 250.00; Stillman & Moore, 7500.00; R. L. Mason, 4250.00, 1400.00; Lord & Bennett, 2500.00, 1142.80, 177.14. *(See I. L. page 198.)*

Collection and Exchange, from Teller's Memorandum, 6.94. *(See note, page 212.)*

Paid cash for office stationery, postage, etc., 12.18. *(Expense.)*

Rule, foot, and post as instructed for the previous day.

DECEMBER 28, 189–.

Received advice from Chemical National Bank, New York, that collection No. 841 has been paid. *(Check in "Paid" column of C. R. Charge Chemical Bank in N. Y. D. R., 119.75. Credit T. J. & W. E. Upton, 119.25 in I. L.; Coll. & Exch., 50c., in J. See "Collection Paper," page 205.)*

Received notice that collection No. 837 has also been paid. *(Charge Chemical Bank, 432.50, N. Y. D. R., and credit R. L. Mason, 432.00, and Coll. & Exch., 50c. See "Collection Paper," page 205.)*

Received advice from First National, Rockford, that collection No. 843 has been paid. *(Charge First National Bank, Rockford, 143.90. Credit Wm. Raymond, 143.40; Coll. & Exch., 50¢.)*

Received advice from Geo. K. Warren & Co., Bath, that collection No. 823 has been paid. *(Check P. & E. in C. T. Charge Geo. K. W. & Co., 817.00, and 33 days' interest, 4.49; total, 821.49. Credit Thos. H. Wilson, 820.99; and Coll. & Exch., 50c.)*

From Norwich National Bank, that collection No. 821 has been paid and credited. *(Credit Wm. Raymond, 368.40, and Coll. & Exch., 50c.; and charge Norwich National, 368.90.)*

From Farmers Bank, Canton, that collection No. 839 has been paid. *(Open an account with G. H. Perkins on first vacant line in I. L., and credit him 925.68; credit Coll. & Exch., 50c., and charge Farmers Bank 926.18 in J.)*

Received from Exchange National Bank, Dansville, their draft, No. 1486, on Bowery Bank, New York, for 10494.75, proceeds of discount No. 483, less their charge for collection, 5.25. *(J. Check P. & E. in D. T. Credit Bills Discounted, 10500.00, and debit Coll. & Exch., 5.25, in the Journal. The difference represents the draft received, which will be sent and charged to Chemical Bank with others at the close of the day.)*

The Exchange National Bank of Dansville, not being a regular correspondent, charges us one-twentieth per cent. for collecting paper sent them. This charge is about one-half of that made by us to the customer for whom we discounted the note, the difference showing our profit in that transaction from collection alone.

Discounts Nos. 485, 482 and 499, payable in the city, have been paid. *(See "Discount Paper," page 205.)*

Received the paper described below, from the following banks, for collection and credit: From Geo. K. Warren & Co., Bath, A. L. Underhill's draft on Harvey Brown, dated this day, at 2 days' sight, 942.17. The drawee accepts the draft upon presentation, payable at Union Bank, City. *(C. R., C. T.)*

From First National, Rockford, Brooks & Smith's sight draft on O. W. Lansing, city, 1455.00. Collected and credited to First National Bank, Rockford, 1455.00. *(C. R., J.)*

From Farmers, Canton, S. P. Stevens' sight draft on M. M. Ward, 32.18. Collected and credited to Farmers, Canton, 32.18.

From First National, Belleville, B. T. Jones & Co.'s sight draft on Yeoman & Blake, 411.75. Collected and remitted draft No. 1598 on Chemical Bank for 411.50. Collection, 25c. *(Enter in C. R. only at this time. Enter the collection in the Exchange column in N. Y. D. R.)*

This draft will be entered to the credit of Chemical Bank, in the N. Y. D. R., with others, at close of banking hours, and the collection will be credited to Coll. & Exch. at the same time by being entered in the Exchange column in that book. These entries will be made from the stub of the draft book. Since the First National Bank of Belleville is not a regular correspondent, we make a charge for collecting the foregoing draft, but only one-half of the charge we would make to an individual. No charge for exchange. See list of drafts drawn on Chemical Bank.

Received remittances from our correspondents, on account, as follows: From Wayne Co. National, draft No. 4142, on Fifth National, New York, for 5000.00. From Third National, Newport, draft No. 372, on Bowery Bank, New York, for 1287.19. *(J. Credit the banks making these remittances.)*

These drafts, with others received during to-day's business, will be remitted to Chemical Bank at the close of banking hours, and at that time will be charged to Chemical Bank in the N. Y. D. R.

Remitted our draft, No. 1599, on Chemical Bank, for 3000.00, to Norwich National Bank, on account.

This will be credited to Chemical Bank, with others, at the close of the day. This could be entered in the N. Y. D. R. at once, but these drafts are usually torn from a stub when issued, and are entered in the N. Y. D. R from the stubs at the close of the day.

The following sight drafts on individuals and firms, received on deposit, have been sent forward for collection and credit: Lord & Bennett, on W. H. Atwater, Lyons, 211.50; sent and charged to Wayne Co. National. Wm. Raymond, on W. Dunn, Corning, 275.50; sent to Livingston's Bank, and charged to Livingston's Bank in Sundry Banks and Bankers accounts. *(See "Sight Paper Deposited," page 206.)*

Livingston's Bank not being a regular correspondent, we do not wish to open a separate account with it. We therefore open an account with Sundry Banks and Bankers, and debit that account for the amount of the draft sent Livingston's Bank. Debit Livingston's Bank in the Journal, and place S. B., the initials for Sundry Banks and Bankers, after the entry, and post the item to Sundry Banks and Bankers account in the General Ledger. When the proceeds are received, credit Livingston's Bank for the face of the draft, and post it to the credit of Sundry Banks and Bankers account, on the same line with the debit to Livingston's Bank, and debit Coll. & Exch. in the Journal for the collection.

Discounted the following paper: For D. J. Slocum, Ward & Cobb's note, at 30 days from date, for 3000.00, indorsed by Jas. Jackson, Jr., payable at Second National Bank, Lyons; sent Wayne Co. National for collection. Discount, 16.50; collection, 3.00; exchange, 3.75.

For Jas. Angle, Young & Baldwin's note for 380.00, at 15 days from date, payable at Union Bank, City. Discount, 1.14.

For L. J. Farnsworth, T. K. Scott's note for 1800.00, at 1 month from 23d inst., payable at Exchange Bank, City. Discount, 8.70.

For Bingham, Field & Ward, Wm. Raymond's note for 1450.00, at 5 days from this date, payable at our bank. Discount, 1.93.

For Meyer & Kauffman, their note at 20 days from this date, for 2000.00, indorsed by W. M. Bond, payable at our bank. Discount, 7.67.

Received the following paper for collection: From D. J. Slocum, his sight draft on Ward & Holmes, Lyons, for 149.44; sent Wayne County National.

From Samuel Wilder, his sight draft on King & Co., Canton, for 856.90; sent Farmers Bank, Canton.

From Chas. J. Burke, his sight draft on Warren & Co., Belfast, for 1492.00; sent First National Bank, Belfast.

From L. W. Perry, his sight draft on Wilson & Caldwell, Newport, for 364.87; sent Third National, Newport.

From Thos. H. Wilson, his sight draft on Nellis & Knox, Rockford, for 182.50; sent First National, Rockford.

Drew the following drafts on Chemical Bank: No. 1598, favor First National, Belleville, 411.50; exch., 25¢. No. 1599, favor Norwich National, 3000.00. No. 1600, favor T. J. & W. E. Upton, 400.00; exch., 50¢. No. 1601, favor Lord & Bennett, 52.25; exch., 15¢. No. 1602, favor Samuel Wilder, 1790.26; exch., 2.24. No. 1603, favor Johnson Mfg. Co., 5992.50; exch., 7.50. No. 1604, favor D. J. Slocum, 74.75; exch., 15¢.

Remitted to Chemical Bank, for our credit, the following drafts on New York, received during the day: No. 1486, Exchange National Bank, Dansville, on Bowery Bank, 10494.75; No. 4142, Wayne County National Bank, Lyons, on Fifth National, 5000.00; No. 372, Third National, Newport, on Bowery Bank, 1287.19; No. 1009, First National, Memphis, on Broadway, 63.94; No. 416, Wheeler's Bank, Belleville, on Second National, 489.43; No. 3142, Richmond's Bank, Batavia, on Chemical, 6300.00; No. 113, Ray Bros. on Cook & Lane, New York, 987.00.

Received the following deposits, as shown by deposit tickets filed: Lord & Bennett, 3000.00 Benj. Thomas & Son, 1790.00; L. J. Farnsworth, 315.00; Wm. Raymond, 775.00; Johnson Mfg. Co., 5275.00; Ray Bros., 2910.00; Thos. H. Wilson, 1800; Stillman & Moore, 6150.00; R. L. Mason, 8219.40; Chas. J. Burke, 3926.42.

Paid the following checks: T. J. & W. E. Upton, 242.69, 400.00; Lord & Bennett, 52.75, 146.90, 2234.46; Bingham, Field & Ward, 824.50, 640.00, 1138.55; Samuel Wilder, 2134.30, 86.25; Johnson Mfg. Co., 896.81, 27.50, 6000.00; Ray Bros., 4500.00; Jas. Angle, 1690.00, 47.25; D. J. Slocum, 75.00, 1792.63, 250.00.

Collection & Exchange, from Teller's Memorandum, 16.92.

Rule and foot the New York Draft Register, the Discount Register, and the Individual Ledger, and carry the results to the Journal. Rule, foot and post the Journal, as directed on page 212.

DECEMBER 29, 189–.

Received advice that the following collections have been paid: No. 822; Coll. & Exch., 25¢. No. 820; Coll. & Exch., 50¢. No. 829; Interest, 8.16; Coll. & Exch., 1.00. (*J. & I. L.*)

Collection No. 840 has been paid. (*Credit Jas. Angle, 750.00, and 38 days' interest, 4.13; total, 754.13. I. L.*)

Be careful to make the proper check mark in the C. T.

Received advice from Wayne County National Bank that discount No. 484, has been paid, 7500.00.

Discount No. 496, payable at our bank, has been charged to the account of the maker. (*See "Discount Paper," page 206.*)

Received 3000.00 on deposit from W. G. Snyder. Issued him a Certificate of Deposit. (*Credit Certificates of Deposit in the Individual Ledger. Open an account with Certificates of Deposit.*)

W. G. Snyder is not a customer, and instead of crediting him for his deposit, we, at his request, issue him a Certificate of Deposit, and credit Certificates of Deposit account. A Certificate of Deposit is a paper headed with the name and location of the bank, and the date, stating that Mr. ——— has deposited ——— dollars in this institution, payable to himself, or order, upon return of this certificate properly indorsed, and is signed by the president or cashier, or both.

Received the paper described below, from the banks named, for collection and credit:

From Farmers, Canton, P. G. White's sight draft, dated 28th, on Jas. Angle, for 94.16. Presented, accepted, and placed among the checks. (*Credit Farmers, Canton, 94.16.*)

From D. G. Lamson's Bank, Belfast, C. A. Stone's sight draft, dated 27th, on Hart & Shepard, for 298.75. Collected. Remitted our draft on Chemical Bank for the amount, less 25¢. for collection. (*C. R.*)

This draft will be entered in the N. Y. D. R. at the close of business hours. No entry at this time excepting in the C. R.

From Wayne County National, Weaver & Janes' sight draft on Peter Wallace & Co., for 873.25, dated 28th. Collected. (*See third last paragraph on page 205.*)

From Traders National, Kingston, Jas. Angle's note, at 3 months from Sept. 30th, indorsed by E. H. Mott & Co., for 1400.00, payable at our bank.

From Wisner & Clark's Bank, Clyde, W. A. Hood's note, indorsed by C. A. Parry & Co., for 375.00, at 30 days from Dec. 10th, payable at Exchange Bank, City.

From Norwich National, Warren & Sharp's sight draft on L. W. Gage for 162.11, dated Dec. 28th. Collected.

The following described paper, received on deposit, has been sent to the banks named, for collection, and charged to their respective accounts: Samuel Wilder's sight draft on Tubbs & Co., Kingston, for 191.50; to Traders National, Kingston. D. J. Slocum's sight draft on Norman Lacy, Rockford, for 34.17; to First National, Rockford. Johnson Mfg. Co.'s sight draft on B. A. Cole, Livonia, for 86.40; sent to Woodruff's Bank, Livonia. (*Charge Woodruff's Bank in Sundry Banks and Bankers account. See note on page 216.*)

Benj. Thomas & Son's sight draft on M. F. Burgess, Newport, for 316.94; sent Third National, Newport. Lord & Bennett's sight draft on L. M. Newton, Bath, for 732.81; sent Geo. K. Warren & Co., Bath. Bingham, Field & Ward's sight draft on Newman & Gregg, Bristol, for 17.39; sent Exchange National, Bristol.

Received the following paper from our customers and others for collection: From Ray Bros., sight draft on G. H. Wilson & Co., Holley, for 182.90; sent City Bank, Holley. From Thos. H. Wilson, Hadley & Holmes' note, at 3 months from Oct. 4th, for 918.92, payable at First National, Lyons; sent Wayne County National, Lyons. From Dunn & Cole, sight draft on D. F. Coates, Geneva, for 863.50; sent Exchange, Geneva.

Discounted the following paper: For R. L. Mason, Havens & Co.'s note for 450.00, at 30 days from this date, payable at Union Bank, City. Discount, 2.48.

For Samuel Wilder, his note for 1500.00, indorsed by J. A. Lindsay, at 30 days from the 28th inst., payable at our bank. Discount, 8.00.

For Meyer & Kauffman, Robert Moore's note for 2200.00, at 20 days from this date, payable at First National, Lyons. Discount, 8.43; coll., 2.00; exch., 2.75. Sent to Wayne County National.

For J. A. Bush, Philip Warner's note for 500.00, indorsed by John Rice, at 30 days from this date, payable at Union Bank, City. Proceeds paid in cash. Discount, 2.75. (*Write "Cash" after Bush's name in the "For Whom Discounted" column in the Discount Register, so that it will be posted to Cashier Account instead of to the account of the customer; see checks below. See second paragraph on page 206.*)

For Wyman & Fisher, their note, indorsed by J. H. Price, at 1 month from the 24th instant, for 600.00, payable at Farmers, Canton. Proceeds paid in cash. Discount, 2.90. Coll. & Exch., 1.50. Sent Farmers Bank.

For Johnson Mfg. Co., Darwin & Kent's note for 1500.00, at 1 month from the 24th inst., payable at Norwich National, Norwich. Discount, 7.25; coll. & exch., 2.88. Sent to Norwich National.

Drew the following drafts on Chemical Bank: No. 1605, favor Johnson Mfg. Co., 998.75; exch., 1.25. No. 1606, favor D. C. Allison, 17.00; exch., 15c. No. 1607, favor W. F. Jameson, 244.50; exch., 50c. No. 1608, favor L. S. Lansing, 116.00; exch., 25c. No. 1609, favor D. J. Slocum, 4993.75; exch., 6.24. No. 1610, favor P. J. Dudley, 73.50; exch., 15c. No. 1611, favor Meyer & Kauffman, 2496.87; exch., 3.12. No. 1612, favor W. B. Sage, 1000.00. exch., 1.25. No. 1613, favor Lord & Bennett, 1598.00; exch., 2.00. No. 1614, favor D. G. Lamson's Bank, 298.50; exch., 25c.

Remitted to Chemical Bank, for our credit, the following drafts on New York, received during the day: No. 1042, First National, Princeton, on Bowery Bank, 192.82; No. 213, Woodruff's, Livonia, on Sixth National, 1482.90; No. 194, Ward's Bank, Union, on Third National, 18.25; No. 1516, Exchange National, Dansville, on Bowery, 411.07; No. 2104, Commercial, Corning, on Metropolitan, 1242.16; No. 13492, First National, Waverly, on Union Trust Co., 27.90; No. 826, City Bank, Holley, on Broadway, 146.83; No. 1513, Exchange, Geneva, on Third National, 875.00; No. 482, First National, Butler, on Chemical, 218.11.

Received the following deposits: W. F. Jameson, 584.00; D. J. Slocum, 1395.18; Jas. Angle, 2873.00; Thos. H. Wilson, 843.10; Meyer & Kauffman, 4200.00; Johnson Mfg. Co., 5125.00; Samuel Wilder, 943.92; Bingham, Field & Ward, 550.00; Benj. Thomas & Son, 1975.00; Lord & Bennett, 2400.00.

Opened an account with J. H. Wentworth & Co., and received a deposit of 1250.00.

Paid the following checks: Johnson Mfg. Co. 1000.00, 396.00, 2584.00, 3000.00; T. J. & W. E. Upton, 985.00, 146.32, 75.00, 843.90; W. F. Jameson, 245.00, 2940.00, 133.25; D. J. Slocum, 5000.00; Jas. Angle, 3500.00, 200.00, 75.00, 186.90, 94.16; Thos. H. Wilson, 2735.50; Meyer & Kauffman, 2500.00, 1500.00, 49.26; Lord & Bennett, 85.00, 242.50, 1600.00; G. H. Perkins, 925.68, Cashier, 497.25, 595.60.

Collection and Exchange, from Teller's Memorandum, 27.85.

Rule, foot, and post, as heretofore instructed.

DECEMBER 30, 18

Received advices that the following collections have been paid: No. 861; coll. & exch., 50c. No. 862; coll. & exch., 50c.

Received from First National Bank of Belfast a draft, No. 8046, on Ninth National Bank, for proceeds of No. 863, less 50c, for collection. (*Credit Coll. & Exch., 50c., the difference between our charge and that of Belfast Bank; and credit Chas. J. Burke, 1491.00; see third last paragraph on page 205.*)

No. 864; coll. & exch., 50c. No. 865; coll. & exch., 50c.

Credit L. W. Perry, in Individual Ledger, under "Transient Accounts," for the proceeds of collection No. 864

Collection No. 832 has also been paid. (*I. L.*)

Discounts Nos. 495, 491 and 493 have been paid. (*See "Discount Paper," page 206. At this time credit Bills Discounted only.*)

Received the following described paper, from the banks named, for collection. All of the sight drafts were paid upon presentation.

From Third National, Newport, Clark & Co.'s sight draft, dated 28th, on J. H. Rich, for 197.46.

From Exchange National, Bristol, L. M. DePuy's sight draft, dated 29th, on M. W. Cheney, City, for 388.19.

From Wayne County National, J. F. Osgood's note at 90 days from Oct. 4th, indorsed by W. P. Follett, payable at Union Bank, City, for 1385.00.

From Cascade Bank, Portage, Norman Seymour's sight draft, dated 28th, on W. F. Lawrence, City, for 843.90. Remitted draft No. 1615, on Chemical Bank, for the proceeds, less 25¢ for collection.

From Traders National, Kingston, Duncan Jones' sight draft, dated 28th inst., on H. P. Randall, for 246.83.

The following paper, received on deposit, has been sent to the banks named for our credit: D. J. Slocum's sight draft, dated 29th, on Frank W. Brown, Corning, for 382.00; sent Livingston's Bank, Corning. (*Charge Livingston's Bank, in Sundry Banks and Bankers Account, for the draft.*)

Maxwell Day's sight draft, dated 30th, on Wing & Walker, Rockford, for 181.40; sent and charged to First National Bank, Rockford. J. H. Wentworth & Co.'s sight draft, dated 29th, on Holmes & Co., Geneva, for 23.82; sent Exchange Bank, Geneva. (*Charge Sundry Banks for the draft sent Exchange Bank.*)

Wm. Raymond's sight draft, dated 30th, on H. A. Miller, Lyons, for 392.50; sent Wayne County National. R. L. Mason's sight draft, dated 30th, on M. F. Griffith, Canton, for 49.80; sent Farmers.

Discounted the following paper: For H. W. Phillips, his note, indorsed by H. Chase and Andrew Springer, for 1000.00, at 30 days from this date, payable at Wayne County National, Lyons. Discount, 5.50; coll., 1.00; exch., 1.25. Proceeds paid in cash. (*See second paragraph on page 206.*)

For R. L. Mason, Shelby & Co.'s note, at 30 days from the 28th, payable at Norwich National, for 575.00. Discount, 2.97; coll. 50¢; exch., 72¢.

For Samuel Wilder, Jones & Hardy's note, at 30 days from the 29th, payable at Union Bank, City, for 173.91. Discount, 93¢.

For Morgan & Seelye, H. A. Wood's note, indorsed by L. M. Lay, at 20 days from this date, payable at Exchange Bank, City, for 1485.00. Discount, 5.69. Proceeds paid in cash.

Drew the following drafts on Chemical Bank: No. 1615, favor Cascade Bank, Portage, for 843.65; exch., 25¢. No. 1616, favor Chas. J. Burke, for 9990.00; exch., 10.00. No. 1617, favor R. L. Mason, for 2188.00; exch., 2.74. No. 1618, favor R. W. Bush, for 18.50; exch., 15¢. No. 1619, favor A. B. Ward, for 142.00; exch., 25¢. No. 1620, favor Jerome Sackett, for 82.19; exch., 15¢.

Remitted Chemical Bank the following drafts and checks on New York, received during the course of to-day's business: No. 8046, First National, Belfast, on Ninth National, 1491.50; No. 1143, Second National, Westboro, on Bowery, 188.63; No. 896, Grangers Bank, Jackson, on Metropolitan, 864.50; No. 693, Exchange Bank, Norwich, on Sixth National, 92.18; No. 13482, Manufacturers Bank, Middletown, on Ninth National, 1143.75; No. 132, F. W. Richmond, Goshen, check on Chemical, 945.00.

Received the following deposits: D. J. Slocum, 1294.11; Wm. Raymond, 2250.00; Maxwell Day, 3960.12; L. J. Farnsworth, 3118.07; Lord & Bennett, 6190.83; T. J. & W. E. Upton, 4114.60; J. H. Wentworth & Co., 8673.95; R. L. Mason, 5000.00.

Paid the following checks: Chas. J. Burke, 10000.00, 546.50, 1850.00; R. L. Mason, 134.65 (note), 5000.00; Jas. Angle, 314.98, 1165.00, 123.16, 85.00; Stillman & Moore, 3500.00, 1492.50; Johnson Mfg. Co., 1122.50, 97.00, 2462.75; Samuel Wilder, 186.42, 1729.03; Bingham, Field & Ward, 916.40, 2422.76; Benjamin Thomas & Son, 10000.00; Cashier, 992.25, 1479.31.

Collection and Exchange, from Teller's Memorandum, 11.96.

Add, rule and post, as heretofore directed.

DECEMBER 31, 18--.

Received advices that the following collections have been paid: No. 828: coll. & exch., 1.00. No. 827: coll. & exch., 50¢. No. 826; coll. & exch., 25¢. No. 834; coll. & exch., 50¢.

Received from Exchange Bank, Geneva, their draft No. 910, on First National Bank, New York, for proceeds of Collection No. 880. Amount of draft, 863.25, collection, 25¢. *(Credit Dunn & Cole, in Individual Ledger, 863.00; and credit Collection & Exchange account, 25c. Be careful to make the proper check mark in the C. R. Charge Chemical Bank in N. Y. D. R. for Collection No. 827.)*

Collection No. 830, payable in the city, has been paid. *(Credit S. H. Lowe in I. L., under "Transient Accounts" 918.30.)*

Received from Woodruff's Bank, Livonia, draft No. 317, on Sixth National, for proceeds of Collection No. 874, less charges for collection. *(Credit Woodruff's Bank in Sundry Banks account for 86.40, and debit Collection & Exchange, 12c.)*

Collection No. 859 has been returned protested, and the drawers, Lord & Bennett, to whom it was credited, have given us their check for its face, 211.50, and the cost of protest, 1.35. *(Credit the bank to which it was sent for the total amount, 212.85. L. & B.'s check for the same amount will be charged up with others at the close of the day. Mark the paper "Protested" in the "Remarks" column in the C. R.)*

Collection No. 878 has been returned dishonored. *(Mark it "Returned" or "Ret." in the "Remarks" column in the C. R. See "Collection Paper," page 205.)*

No entry is required. The paper was received for *collection*, hence it is only necessary to return it to the drawers, Ray Bros. It is not customary to make a charge for our trouble unless the collection is made.

When a sight draft is left for collection, it is customary for the owner to request the bank not to protest it if it is not paid. In such a case a "No Protest" is attached to the draft, and if not paid the draft is returned to us and we return it to the owner. When we receive a draft on deposit, we protest it if not paid, to hold the drawer.

Discount No. 492 has been paid.

Discount No. 497 not having been paid, has been protested. (*Mark "Protested" in D. T.*)

Many banks have an account with Protested Paper, debiting Protested Paper and crediting Bills Discounted for dishonored Bills Discounted; but the custom is becoming general to leave all discounted paper in the Bills Discounted account until it is paid, a judgment obtained, or it is found to be worthless. In case judgment is obtained, Judgment Account is debited for the entire amount, face of note, interest and costs, and Bills Discounted is credited for face of note, and Interest for the interest upon it. In case the judgment proves to be worthless, Loss and Gain is debited and Judgment account credited.

Received advice that Discount No. 494 has been paid.

Received the following described paper, from other banks, for collection and credit, all of which was paid upon presentation: From Wayne County National, W. L. Coot's sight draft on Myron G. Peck, dated 30th, for 934.18, and Henry J. Lansing's sight draft on Maxwell Day, dated 29th, for 74.75. Presented the latter to drawee, who has accepted it, payable at our bank. The draft was placed among the checks. (*See list of checks paid.*)

From Norwich National, Jacob Sterling's sight draft on Newman & Barry, dated 29th, for 13.40.

From First National, Rockford, Dwight Weaver's sight draft on Colton & Manning, dated 30th, for 97.80.

From First National Bank, Jefferson, Homer Sprague's sight draft on Wm. H. Lyon, dated 29th inst., for 114.93. Collected, and remitted our draft No. 1621, on Chemical Bank, for 114.78. Collection, 15¢. (*C. R. No entry at this time in N. Y. D. R.*)

The following paper received on deposit, payable abroad, has been sent to the banks named for collection: Samuel Wilder's sight draft, dated to-day, on W. D. Jones, Newport, for 136.92; sent to Third National, Newport. James Angle's sight draft, dated to-day, on I. W. Woolson, Bristol, for 23.44; sent Exchange National, Bristol. James Angle's sight draft, dated to-day, on Hurd & Thomas, Canton, for 61.27; sent Farmers Bank, Canton.

Received the following paper for collection: From T. J. & W. E. Upton, Warren Lee's note, at 90 days from Oct. 12th, for 500.00, payable at Union Bank, City. From Johnson Mfg. Co., H. Burt's note, at 30 days from Dec. 13th, for $73.40, payable at Lansing's Bank, Lyons; sent Wayne County National. From David Gray, his sight draft on Geo. H. Newell, Chester, dated this day, for 94.50; sent First National, Chester.

Discounted the following paper: For Henry Sears, Thomas Brooks' note, indorsed by Frank Woodbury & Son, at 30 days from date, payable at Union Bank, City, for 525.00. Discount, 2.89. Paid cash for proceeds.

For Stillman & Moore, Fanning & Peck's note, at 20 days from date, payable at Exchange Bank, City, for 1500.00. Discount, 5.75.

For Wm. Raymond, Ellis & Hayden's note, at 30 days from the 27th inst., payable at First National, Lyons, for 2650.00. Discount, 12.81; coll., 2.00; exch., 3.31. Sent Wayne Co. National.

Drew the following drafts on Chemical Bank: No. 1621, favor First National, Jefferson, 114.78; exch., 15¢. No. 1622, favor D. J. Slocum, 200.00; exch., 50¢. No. 1623, favor Johnson Mfg. Co., 3500.00; exch., 4.38. No. 1624, favor J. H. Wentworth & Co., 100.00; exch., 25¢. No. 1625, favor L. J. Farnsworth, 3000.00; exch., 3.75.

Remitted Chemical Bank the following drafts on New York, received among the deposits: No. 1009, Howard's Bank, Dundee, on Bowery, 446.94; No. 464, First National, Preston, on Manufacturers and Traders, 132.29; No. 104, J. H. Clark's Bank, Woodville, on Croton, 273.91; No. 1264, Second National, Plainville, on Ninth National, 2500.00; No. 749, Lamont & Thomas, Morrisville, on Sixth National, 382.46; No. 6891, First National, Williamstown, on Chemical, 11.18; No. 317, Woodruff's Bank, Livonia, on Sixth National, 86.28; No. 910, Exchange Bank, Geneva, on First National, 863.25.

Received the following deposits: Samuel Wilder, 1947.80; D. J. Slocum, 375.00; R. L. Mason, 1200.00; Stillman & Moore, 900.00; Jas. Angle, 1349.62; Lord & Bennett, 4480.00; Bingham, Field & Ward, 682.11; J. H. Wentworth & Co., 2963.42; Benj. Thomas & Son, 1646.92.

Paid the following checks: D. J. Slocum, 182.41, 943.86, 100.00, 200.00; L. J. Farnsworth, 3000.00; Wm. Raymond, 162.50, 394.05, 873.13; Lord & Bennett, 4000.00, 1263.44, 212.85; Johnson Mfg. Co., 3500.00, 150.00, 150.00; J. H. Wentworth, 1829.38, 163.90, 100.00; T. J. & W. E. Upton, 112.73, 986.09, 250.00; Bingham, F. & W., 3375.00; Maxwell Day (draft), 74.75; Cashier, 522.11.

Collection and Exchange, from Teller's Memorandum, 23.45.

Remitted National Park Bank, currency, 25000.00.

Paid salaries for month as follows: Cashier, 200.00; Teller, 150.00; Bookkeeper, 100.00; Assistant Bookkeepers, 75.00, 50.00; Messenger, 25.00; Janitor, 25.00.

Add, rule and post, as heretofore directed.

You may now take a trial balance of the General Ledger to ascertain whether it is in balance, and also a proof of the Individual Ledger to ascertain whether the difference corresponds with the difference between the sides of the Deposits account in the General Ledger. If correct, your results will agree with the following:

STATEMENT OF SECOND NATIONAL BANK,

AT CLOSE OF BUSINESS, SATURDAY, DECEMBER 31, 18–.

Cash,	67005	29	Capital Stock,	100000	00
United States Bonds,	50000	00	Circulation,	45000	00
Real Estate,	8000	00	Discount,	3679	82
Furniture and Fixtures,	2500	00	Collection and Exchange,	1451	17
Expense,	2320	37	Surplus Fund,	11750	63
Loans & Discounts (Bills Discounted),	78141	31	Undivided Profits,	2718	42
Redemption Fund,	2250	00	Due Depositors,	143740	77
Due from other Banks and Bankers,	98266	43	Due other Banks and Bankers,	142	59
	308483	40		308483	40

You will next close all accounts exhibiting gains and losses into the Loss and Gain account, except the accounts with Real Estate and Furniture and Fixtures, which are inventoried at cost. The net gain is 2810.62.

You will next close the net gain into Surplus Fund account, Dividend account and Undivided Profits account, by a Journal entry, instead of through the Loss and Gain account, crediting Surplus Fund account, 281.06 (*see last paragraph on page 194*), Dividend account, 2500.00 (which will amount to 2½ per cent. upon the capital stock), and Undivided Profits account, 29.56 (the remainder of the net profit, as shown by the balance of Loss and Gain account); and debiting Loss and Gain account for the sum of these items or the net profit, 2810.62. When this Journal entry is posted it will close Loss and Gain account and transfer the gain to the several accounts named. Foot and rule the Journal again.

When the dividend is credited to the stockholders or paid to them in cash, Dividend should be debited in the Journal for the amount thus credited or paid.

QUESTIONS.

What is a banker? Of what does the business of banking consist? From what principal source do the profits of a bank arise? Into how many general classes are banking associations divided? What are they? What is a State bank? A National bank? A private bank? Under what law are National banks organized and governed? Describe some of the requirements of this law. How are State banks organized? Do State banks issue circulating notes? Explain. What are the duties of the Board of Directors? What are the officers and clerks of a bank? State the duties of each. Name the books used in a bank? Describe the books used in this bank. State what is done with paper received for collection. What is the difference between Collection Paper and Discount Paper? What is done with Discount Paper payable abroad? What entries are made when the proceeds of discount paper are paid in cash? What is done with sight paper received as cash and payable abroad? Review the explanations and instruction given throughout the set.

CLEARING HOUSE FORMS.

(D)

Rochester Clearing House Proof, *Aug. 15, 189-.*

NO.	BANKS.	DUE R. C. H.	BANKS DR.	BANKS CR.	DUE BANKS.	NO.
1	Central Bank,	1631 42	10273 18	8641 76		1
2	Commercial National Bank,	4944 04	15217 90	10273 86		2
3	Flour City National Bank,	703 05	14217 17	13514 12		3
4	German-American Bank,		14741 56	20552 87	5811 31	4
5	Merchants Bank,		17585 00	24497 18	6912 18	5
6	Bank of Monroe,		9385 50	18515 50	9130 00	6
7	Trust and Safe Deposit Company,	8246 25	20121 50	11875 25		7
8	Traders National Bank,	8101 28	18615 93	10514 65		8
9	Union Bank,	262 14	26351 12	26088 98		9
10	Powers Bank,		10500 00	25850 50	15350 50	10
11	Rochester Savings Bank,		10500 00	11907 20	1407 20	11
12	Monroe County Savings Bank,	16732 10	28442 50	11710 40		12
13	Mechanics Savings Bank,		11718 40	13718 49	2000 09	13
		40671 28	207682 76	207682 76	40671 28	

(A)

EXCHANGE SLIP

No. 1.

From No. 4,

German-American Bank.

12	50
100	50
500	62
487	78
46	42
1147	82

CLEARING HOUSES.

A Clearing House is an association of banks called into existence by the necessity of the times, to facilitate daily settlements between banks. The aggregate amount of exchanges represents the clearing for the day. "Clearing," says Lloyd, "is the settlement of mutual claims by the payment of differences."

At large trade centers a certain number of banks associate themselves together under articles more or less comprehensive, as the magnitude and volume of trade may demand. Officers are elected and committees are appointed to conduct the affairs of the association. The officers are a President, Vice-President, Manager, and Committee of Management, sometimes called the Clearing House Committee, a Committee on Conference, a Nominating Committee, a Committee on Admission and an Arbitration Committee. The Manager, under control of the Managing Committee, has full charge of the business at the Clearing House so far as the manner of conducting its business transactions is concerned. He has full charge of the clerical force employed and of the settling clerks and messengers from the banks while at the Clearing House.

To enable the student to appreciate the use of the illustrated forms, they will be explained in their order commencing at "A." (See page 234.)

In the daily routine of banking work the teller classifies his exchanges according to the bank at which they are made payable. This is usually done by assorting them in pigeon-

CLEARING HOUSE FORMS.

No. 4. (B)

Rochester Clearing House Association

FROM

GERMAN-AMERICAN BANK.

Settling Clerk's Statement, Aug. 15, 18—.

NO.	BANKS.	TOTAL DEBITS	BANKS CREDIT	NO.
1	Central Bank,	[illegible]	[illegible]	1
2	Commercial National Bank,	[illegible]	[illegible]	2
3	Flour City National Bank,	[illegible]	[illegible]	3
4	German-American Bank,			4
5	Merchants Bank,	[illegible]	[illegible]	5
6	Bank of Monroe,	[illegible]	112 64	6
7	Trust and Safe Deposit Company,	[illegible]	[illegible]	7
8	Traders National Bank,	[illegible]	[illegible]	8
9	Union Bank,	[illegible]	[illegible]	9
10	Powers Bank,	[illegible]	[illegible]	10
11	Rochester Savings Bank,	[illegible]	[illegible]	11
12	Monroe County Savings Bank,	[illegible]	[illegible]	12
13	Mechanics Savings Bank,	[illegible]	[illegible]	13
	Footings,	[illegible]	[illegible]	
	Balance,		[illegible]	
	Proof,		[illegible]	

Balance Ticket.

No. 4 (C) *Rochester Clearing House,*
Aug. 15, 18
From German American Bank
Amt. Rec'd, $[illegible]
Amt. Dr'd, $14,741 [illegible]
Debit Balance Due Clearing House
Credit Balance due Bank $[illegible]11 31.
J. K. Jones, Settling Clerk

Manager's Receipt.

No. 1 (E) *Rochester Clearing House,*
Aug. 15, 18
Rec'd from Central Bank, $1631 42.
Sixteen Hundred Thirty one $\frac{42}{100}$ *Dollars*
in full for the balance due the associated banks.
[illegible] Smith, Manager

holes, and at the end of the day's business Exchange Slips are made out against the different banks for the amount of exchangeable paper held for collection against them. In the illustrated forms the Exchange Slip "A" shows five different pieces of paper, aggregating 1147.82, which is the amount of exchanges carried by the German-American Bank to the Clearing House against No. 1, the Central Bank. There are different slips for each bank, and when ready for clearing the amount of exchange against each bank is placed in a large envelope with the Exchange Slip on the outside. When these slips are made out at the bank, an Exchange Slip is made out also for such other banks as collections are held against, and the aggregate of each is entered on another blank called the Settling Clerk's Statement (*see illustrated form "B"*). In this is entered the total debit against each bank. It will be seen by consulting the form (B) that the Settling Clerk of the German-American Bank took to the Clearing House on Aug. 15, collections aggregating 20552.87, as shown by the column headed "Total Debits." At the time of his arriving there no entries have been made in the column headed "Banks Credit." This is to be used during the interval between the opening and closing of the Clearing House.

Just before the hour of opening each settling clerk delivers to the other clerks their envelopes of exchanges which he has against them.

A credit ticket is made out by the settling clerk and handed to the manager, instructing him to credit the German-American Bank with exchanges aggregating 20552.87. The manager at once enters it in a blank called "Clearing-House Proof" (*see illustration D*). When all are entered the manager foots the column headed "Bank Cr.," which shows the total clearing to be made.

At a given hour, usually at 10 o'clock A. M., the signal is given to clear and the clerks deliver their exchanges, if not already done. The settling clerks now enter in the credit column of the Settling Clerk's Statement (B), the total credit opposite each bank for the amount left against his bank.

The settling clerk of the German-American Bank foots the credit column of his statement and finds that there is an aggregate of 14741.56 against his bank, and that there will be due the German-American Bank 5811.31. He now fills out a Balance Ticket (C), showing debits, 20552.87; credits, 14731.56; balance, 5811.31, and passes it up to the manager. (*See illustration C.*)

The manager fills out the Clearing-House Proof and finding that the columns headed "Dr. Banks" and "Cr. Banks" foot equally, and also the columns headed "Due Clearing House" and "Due Banks" foot equally he announces the result "correct."

This completes the exchanges for the day, and the debit banks have one hour in which to pay their balance to the manager, and at 1:30 the credit banks receive from the manager their balances, which are paid either in checks or Clearing House certificates. Thus millions of dollars of settlements are made and balances are paid without moving specie or transferring a dollar in legal tender. The checks are deposited for clearing the next day and the certificates are used to adjust subsequent balances.

In Cincinnati the system was introduced and since has obtained in several of the Western cities to settle at once with the credit banks by drawing manager's checks upon the debit banks. By looking at "Clearing-House Proof" (D) it will be seen that should the manager give the German-American Bank a check for the balance due of 5811.31 upon No. 12, the Monroe County Savings Bank (whose debit balance is 16752.10), there would be a balance due from No. 12 of 10940.79.

APPENDIX.

SINGLE ENTRY BOOKKEEPING.

Purely Single Entry is a system of bookkeeping which contemplates such a record, or the filing of such documents for reference only, as will enable the proprietor to determine at any time those resources and liabilities of his business which cannot be found by taking an inventory.

Personal Accounts. For this purpose the practice is to debit or credit and post personal accounts only. Hence, the distinguishing feature of purely single entry bookkeeping is that only personal accounts are kept.

No Purely Single Entry in Business. Purely single entry books are seldom kept in business, for the reason that almost every business man desires to keep an account of his cash, his expenses and the goods in which he is dealing. Quite frequently other accounts than those mentioned are kept; but when such is the case it ceases to be single entry, as in purely single entry only personal accounts are kept. To the extent that single entry books contain other than personal accounts they approach double entry, but they will still lack many of the valuable features of the double entry method.

Rules for Debiting and Crediting. The rules for debiting and crediting personal accounts in single entry are exactly the same as in double entry. (*See rules 1 and 2 on page 1, rules 5, 6, 7, 8, 9, and 10 on page 10 and rules 15 and 16 on page 18.*) The posting is also done in the same manner as in double entry.

Compared with Double Entry. In double entry bookkeeping, other accounts than those with persons are kept, and an entry involving equal debits and credits is made in the Journal or some other posting book, for every business transaction. When such entry has been posted equal amounts will have been entered on both sides of the Ledger, hence, the name *double entry.* In purely single entry bookkeeping only personal accounts are kept, and an entry, usually involving either a debit or a credit and sometimes both, is made in the Journal or other book of original entry only when a personal account has been affected. When such entry has been posted a single amount will have been entered on but one side of the Ledger, hence, the name *single entry.*

No Trial Balance. A single entry ledger, then, differs from a double entry ledger in that it contains only personal accounts. Since but one amount is posted for each entry in single entry, it will be apparent that the totals of the ledger debit and credit balances will not be equal, and that no trial balance of a single entry ledger can be taken.

No Balance Sheet. Since no accounts showing losses and gains are kept in single entry, it follows that an itemized statement exhibiting the sources of the losses and gains of the business cannot be obtained. The net gain or net loss of the business can be determined, however, and as accurately as in double entry by taking an inventory of the resources and liabilities as explained and illustrated on pages 33 and 34, and in the following paragraph.

Inventory of Resources and Liabilities. It has been explained that the resources of a business consist of the property belonging to the business and the debts owing to it; the liabilities consist of the debts owing by the business. Since the property belonging to the business can be ascertained at any time by taking an inventory, it follows that the only records which it is absolutely necessary to make in order to be able to determine the results of the business, are of such transactions as affect personal accounts, and of such as cause the issuing of Bills Payable. The latter record is in the form of a memorandum.

Books used in Single Entry. In purely single entry all the books necessary are the Day Book-Journal and the Ledger. Very often the Ledger is the only book of record and is then known as an Original Entry Ledger. A convenient form of original entry ledger is the ordinary journal ruling and is illustrated on page 93. (*See illustration of Customers' Ledger page 93.*) In business when it is desired to make records other than those affecting personal accounts, any of the books used in double entry may be employed to advantage, but when that is done it approaches double entry. The forms of the books used in single entry need not differ from those used in double entry; in fact they are generally the same.

The Day Book-Journal. The Day Book-Journal contains debits and credits to persons arising from transactions with such persons. Such debits and credits should be accompanied by sufficiently clear and complete explanations of the transactions giving rise to the entries as to enable any one, whether familiar with the circumstances or not, to readily understand all important facts regarding them. (*See form of Single Entry Day Book-Journal below.*)

SINGLE ENTRY DAY BOOK-JOURNAL.

MARCH 1, 189-.

L. F.				
	Wm. Wood, Commenced business, investing cash.	Cr.		5000
	3			
	J. W. Winter, Bo't on acct, 400 bu. Oats, 600 " Corn,	Cr. 25¢ 40¢	 100 240	340
	S. W. Snow, Bo't on acct., 400 brls. Flour,	Cr. 3.50	 1400	1400
	4			
	Jas. Spring, Sold on acct., 500 bu. Corn,	Dr. 50¢	 250	250
	6			
	J. W. Winter, Paid him on acct.	Dr.		250
	8			
	M. Sumner, Sold on acct., 400 brls. Flour,	Dr. 4.00	 1600	1600
	Jas. Spring, Rec'd $200 on acct.	Cr.		200
	10			
	M. Sumner, Rec'd his note in full of acct.	Cr.		1600
	12			
	S. W. Snow, Gave him my note on acct.	Dr.		1000
	15			
	Wm. Wood, Drew for private use.	Dr.		75

Single Entry and Double Entry Journal Compared. Compare the single entry day book-journal illustrated on the opposite page with the model double entry journal on pages 2 and 3. Observe that the single entry form does not contain the second, third and fourth entries as given in the model; the reason being that no personal accounts are affected by transactions of that kind, consequently no record is required in single entry.

Make a neat copy of the single entry journal on a sheet of journal paper, observing every detail as given. In making an entry in a single entry journal, first write the name of the personal account to be debited or credited together with the abbreviation Dr. or Cr., beginning at the L. F. column and place the amount in the second money column. On the line below beginning about one inch to the right, write the explanation of the transaction and place the items in the first money column.

Posting. Open accounts with the proper persons on a sheet of ledger paper and post the debits and credits of your journal. Check over your posting in pencil. It will be imposible to take a trial balance to test the accuracy of the posting. Why?

Business Results. Counting the cash on hand, Mr. Wood finds that he has $4676.50; the merchandise on hand consists of the articles enumerated in the Merchandise Inventory illustrated on page 33; there is a note of $1600 on hand and a note outstanding for $1000. These are all the resources and liabilities that can be ascertained by taking an inventory; the remainder of the resources and liabilities consist of amounts owing from persons and amounts owing to persons and are to be ascertained from the books.

Make an Inventory of the Resources and Liabilities of Wm. Wood's business using the inventories as given above and the balances of the ledger accounts. Your Inventory of Resources and Liabilities should be identical with the illustration on page 34. By subtracting Wm. Wood's capital as shown by his account in the Ledger from his present capital, we have the gain. As there are no accounts kept with property, it will be impossible to ascertain the sources of the losses and gains, which is usually done in double entry by making a balance sheet.

Changing to Double Entry. You will now open accounts with the property on hand—Cash, Merchandise, Bills Receivable and Bills Payable in the ledger and post the balances of these accounts as exhibited by the Inventory of Resources and Liabilities. Carry the net gain to Mr. Wood's account. Do not forget to postmark in the folio column of the Inventory of Resources and Liabilities. Your ledger should now be in balance. To test the accuracy of your work take a trial balance. Your books are now in condition to be kept by double entry.

Present your work for inspection and approval.

WM. BURKE'S BUSINESS.

To the Student. You will now assume that you are engaged during the day and that you contract with Wm. Burke, a dry goods dealer, to keep his books by single entry, after business hours. Mr. Burke will make a complete record in a Day Book of all the business he transacts during each day from which you will write up the books each evening. To begin with Mr. Burke wishes you to keep a *purely* single entry set of books. Remember, then, to make no entry of a transaction in the Journal unless a personal account is affected by such transaction. The following is a copy of Wm. Burke's Day Book from which you will write up a Single Entry Day Book-Journal.

MAY 20, 189–.

Particulars	Rate		$	¢
I, Wm. Burke, commence the dry goods business with the following resources:				
Cash in Union Bank,		3000		
Store and fixtures at 463 Jefferson St.,		5200		
Paid for Office Furniture, Books, Stationery, etc.,			124	
Paid for postage,			2	50
Bo't an invoice of dry goods for cash,			422	60
21				
Bo't an invoice of dry goods for casu,			318	25
Sold for cash,				
10 pcs., 583 yds., American Prints,	6¼¢			
Rec'd an invoice of dry goods from Dunn & Son on acct.,			612	27
22				
Sold to M. Casper on acct.,				
5 pcs., 212¼ yds., Hamilton Stripe,	9½¢			
3 " 125 " Piedmont C. Drills,	7¢			
Bo't invoice of dry goods from A. P. Fenn & Co. on acct.,			871	50
Sold to M. Casper on acct.,				
4 pcs., 150 yds., York Denims,	12½¢			
3 " 102 " Royal S. Flannel,	26¢			
Rec'd on acct. from M. Casper,			20	
Paid Dunn & Son on acct.,			200	
Rec'd an invoice of dry goods on acct. from Becker & Son,			112	40
24				
Rec'd M. Casper's note to apply on acct.,			50	
25				
Sold to Dodson & Payne on acct.,				
20 pcs., 795½ yds, Manchester Gingham,	5¾¢			
Bo't an invoice of dry goods from Root, Mills & Co., on acct.,			118	29
Gave Root, Mills & Co. my 30-da. note,			75	
Sold to Dodson & Payne on acct.,				
20 pcs., 746¼ yds., Vermont C. Cheviot,	12½¢			
26				
Rec'd on acct. from Dodson & Payne,			100	

MAY 26, 189–.

Gave Becker & Son on acct.,				50	
Sold T. A. Cody & Co. on acct., 20 pcs., 849½ yds., Hamilton Stripe,	9½¢				
Rec'd on acct. from T. A. Cody & Co.,				25	
27 Gave Becker & Son my note at 30 days to balance acct.,					
Bo't an invoice of dry goods from Jos. Frey, Jr., on acct.,				161	40
28 Gave Jos. Frey, Jr., on account,				50	
Rec'd an invoice of dry goods from Minor, Patrick Co. on account,				379	42
29 Sold to J. F. Brown on acct., 40 pcs., 1209½ yds., Kellog Flannel,	30¢				
Drew for private use,				30	
Sold to T. A. Cody & Co. on acct., 50 pcs., 2014½ yds., Birmingham Ticking,	7½¢				
Rec'd T. A. Cody & Co.'s 30-da. note on acct.,				100	
31 Cash sales to date amount to				782	64
Paid drayage bill to date,				7	80
Sold to J. F. Brown on acct., 40 pcs., 2287½ yds., American Prints,	6½¢				
I find that I have the following property on hand:					
Cash,				2760	39
Bills Receivable,				150	
Real Estate,				5200	
Mdse. per Inventory Book,				1767	46
Office Furniture,				100	
My notes outstanding amount to				137	40

Present your Day Book-Journal for approval.

Posting. In opening accounts in the Ledger, place five accounts on a page, beginning on page 37. Post and check over the posting.

Business Results. Prepare an Inventory of Resources and Liabilities, using the inventories given above and the balances of the accounts on your Ledger.

Have your inventory approved, after which make a neat transcript of same on page 14 of the Cash Book. Carry the Net Gain or Net Loss to the proprietor's account, and bring the balance below the ruling so as to show his Present Capital at a glance.

SINGLE ENTRY CASH BOOK.

189 .		L. F.					
Jan.	1		C. W. Hammond, invested,	5000			
			Cash sale,	324			
	3		Cash sale,	766			
	8		A. P. Batson, on acct.	200			
	16		Frey & Thomas, " "	600			
	20		H. B. Phillips & Co., " "	150		7040	
				7040			
						7040	
Jan.	31		Balance on hand,			3797	25

CONTINUATION OF WM. BURKE'S BUSINESS.

Cash Book. You will now discontinue keeping a purely single entry set of books, as Mr. Burke desires you to make a systematic record of the cash received and paid out, so that the cash can be proven each day if he so desires it. Since Cash is a property account, and since only personal accounts are kept in *purely* single entry bookkeeping, it is apparent that it ceases to be single entry whenever an account with property of any kind is kept. Compare the single entry form of Cash Book given on pages 232 and 233 with the double entry form illustrated on pages 42 and 43. Note that the items (personal accounts) to be posted in single entry are made prominent by short extending the items (property and expense accounts) that are not to be posted.

WM. BURKE'S DAY BOOK (continued).

JUNE 1, 189–.

Sold to L. B. Moffet on acct., 50 pcs., 2123 yds., Bombay Gingham, 8½¢			
Paid gas bill for month of May,		1	27
Cash sales for the day amount to,		126	40
2			
Rec'd from L. B. Moffet on acct.,		75	
M. Casper paid me in full of acct.,			
Paid for postage,		2	
Paid A. P. Fenn & Co. on acct.,		500	
Bo't invoice of dry goods from King, Long & Co. on acct.,		212	37
Cash sales for the day,		131	40
3			
Sold to W. B. Hicks on acct., 80 pcs., 3281 yds., Piedmont C. Drills, 7¢			
Bo't invoice of Mdse. from W. W. Rorer & Co. on acct.,		147	29

SINGLE ENTRY CASH BOOK.

189–.		L. F.					
Jan.	1		Cash purchase,	900			
			Cash purchase,	720			
			Cash purchase,	500			
	2		Office books,	17	75		
			Rent,	90			
	9		Redfield & Son, on acct.,	300			
	17		H. Knefely & Son, " "	250			
	22		A. Paul, Jr., " "	300			
	29		C. W. Hammond, private use,	100			
	31		Student's salary,	50			
			Drayage bill,	15		3242	75
				3242	75		
			*Balance on hand,**			*3797*	*25*
						7040	00

* Italics indicate red ink.

JUNE 3, 189–.

Rec'd from W. B. Hicks on acct.,			100	
Paid for washing windows,				75
Paid Minor, Patrick Co. on acct.,			100	
Cash sales for the day,			117	48
4				
Bo't mdse. on acct. from Minor, Patrick Co.,			248	90
Sold on acct. to W. B. Hicks, 50 pcs., 2252 yds., Passaic Prints, 4⅝¢				
Rec'd from J. F. Brown on acct.,			200	
Paid A. P. Fenn & Co. in full,				
Cash sales for the day,			207	82
6				
Rec'd of Dodson & Payne their note to balance acct.,				
Gave King, Long & Co. my note to apply on acct.,			125	
Sold on acct. to L. B. Moffet, 100 pcs., 4522 yds., Washington Cambric, 4⅝¢				
Cash sales for the day,			192	40
7				
Rec'd of W. B. Hicks his note to apply on acct.,			150	
Paid Dunn & Son in full,				
Paid for drayage,			1	75
Drew a draft on J. F. Brown favor of W. W. Rorer & Co. for the amount I owe W. W. Rorer & Co.,*				
I desire to have my books kept by double entry; ascertain the net gain or loss, using the following inventories, then proceed to change to double entry.				
Real Estate,	5200			
Mdse. on hand,	1392	40		
Bills Rec. on hand,	339	05		
Bills Pay. outstanding,	262	40		
Furniture & Fixtures,	100			

* When two personal accounts are affected by a transaction, one a debit and the other a credit, make the journal entry as follows in single entry:

W. W. Rorer & Co.,	Dr.	100
J. F. Brown,	Cr.	100

Present your Journal and Cash Book for approval.

Posting. Post the entries from the Journal, then balance and rule the Cash Book and post all items affecting personal accounts. Check over the posting.

Business Results. Make an Inventory of the Resources and Liabilities of the business, using the balances of the Ledger accounts and the amounts of the inventories given by Mr. Burke. The balance of cash you will ascertain from the Cash Book The difference between the resources and liabilities is Wm. Burke's present capital. Subtract his capital, as shown by his account in the Ledger, and you have the Gain. Present your Inventory of Resources and Liabilities for approval, after which make a neat copy of same on page 15 of the Cash Book.

Changing to Double Entry. Open accounts in the Ledger with Merchandise, Real Estate, Furniture & Fixtures, Bills Receivable and Bills Payable. Post the balances of these accounts as exhibited by the Inventory of Resources and Liabilities. Post the Net Gain to the credit of Wm. Burke's account. Balance and rule his account and bring down the Present Capital. Your books are now in condition to be kept by double entry. Take a trial balance to make certain that you have made no error. Be sure to include the balance of cash on hand in your trial balance. Copy same neatly on page 16 of the Cash Book. Present all books for inspection and approval.

Omissions in Business. In business, when the books have been kept by Single Entry, it is often impossible to obtain a correct inventory of the resources and liabilities at any given time, owing to the incompleteness of that system; and hence the net gain or net loss of the business for that period, and the proprietor's present capital, as shown by the inventory, will not correctly represent the facts. For instance: If a note had been issued, and no record made of it, and the note was unpaid and not thought of at the time of making the inventory, the liabilities would be the amount of the note too small. This omission would have the effect of increasing the net gain or decreasing the net loss, which in turn would make the present capital greater than it should be, or the net insolvency less than it should be. The omission of a resource at the time of making an inventory would have just the opposite effect of the above results.

How Corrected. There are two ways of correcting such omissions. One way is to change the inventory at the time the omission is discovered, and then make the necessary changes in the Ledger. The other and better way is to make such an entry in the Journal, or other principal book, as will cause the account to which the omitted item belonged to show its true relation to the business, and the proprietor's account to show his true present capital, so far as it can be determined at that time. If a resource had been omitted from the inventory, debit the account to which it belonged and credit the proprietor's account; if a liability, debit the proprietor and credit the liability. The advantage of the second method will be apparent when it is stated that several items are liable to be omitted from the inventory; and the omission may not be discovered until some time after the books have been changed to Double Entry. If these items were discovered at different times, as is generally the case, it would necessitate changing the inventory that number of times by the first method, while by the second only so many entries on the Double Entry books would be necessary.

It is necessary to debit or credit the proprietor's account, as the case may be, for the amount of the omitted item, or items, for two reasons: First, to cause his account to show his true worth at the time of changing the books, and second, to be able to determine the actual gain or loss for the period following the change. This is very important in case a partner had been admitted at the time the books were changed. If the Loss and Gain account had been debited or credited for the omitted items, as is sometimes done, that account would not show the actual gains or losses for the period during which the account remained open, and the new partner would be debited with a greater net loss or credited with a greater net gain than he should be.

Single Entry as practiced in Business. Single entry as practiced in business may be defined as any system of bookkeeping in which an equality of debits and credits is not preserved, thereby making it impossible to take a trial balance. Very often all or nearly all the labor saving forms used in double entry are employed, and accounts with the different kinds of property and allowances are kept, thus enabling the bookkeeper or proprietor to ascertain the sources of the losses and gains, the same as in double entry, the only difference being that it is impossible to apply the test which the trial balance affords in double entry.

QUESTIONS. Define Single Entry. Explain the difference between Double and Single Entry. What are the only records absolutely necessary in Single Entry? Why is it not customary to keep books by the purely single entry method in business? Describe the method of making an entry in the Single Entry Day Book-Journal. Why is it impossible to take a trial balance in single entry? Can you make a balance sheet in Single Entry? How do you change to Double Entry? How can you tell when a set of books is in condition to be kept by Double Entry? How do you ascertain the Net Gain or Net Loss in Single Entry? Which method do you prefer, Single Entry or Double Entry? Give a good reason for your answer to the above. Explain the method of correcting an error or omission in the Inventory of Resources and Liabilities.

MISCELLANEOUS TOPICS.

Business Statement — Analytical Form. The Balance Sheet used throughout this book is not universally used in business. It has been given the preference over other forms of business statements because it tends to develop the mental faculties of the student better than other forms would. To persons conversant in the art and science of double entry bookkeeping, a Balance Sheet or business statement of any kind is unnecessary, as the facts desired can (or ought to be) obtained from the Ledger. The objection urged against the Balance Sheet is that it conveys little, if any, information to those who are not skilled in the art and science of accounting.

The form of Business Statement illustrated on page 237, while furnishing comprehensive information, is so simple that it may be understood by those who do not understand bookkeeping. You will observe that it contains, in compact form, the same information that is given in the illustrations on pages 4, 6, 36 and 38. This form of statement is usually made in the Journal, and with slight modifications and abridgments, is used in a large per cent. of the business offices in this and foreign countries.

The forms of business statements given in this book are intended to instruct the beginning student, and not the expert accountant. The statements used in business are of numerous designs and many of them are of a complicated nature. The student who is fitting himself as a professional bookkeeper is advised to consult the higher, technical works on accounting for further information concerning the various forms of statements that may be used in business. Ask your teacher to advise you what books of reference to consult. Every bookkeeper should read one or more of the periodicals devoted to the interests of the bookkeeping profession.

Suspense Account. With many firms it is the custom to close all doubtful accounts receivable into a Suspense Account. This account is ordinarily kept similar to the Sundry Accounts Receivable illustrated on page 131; it is debited each time an account is closed into it, and credited for all receipts (if any) directly opposite the parties' names who made the payments. This method is considered objectionable by some business men, as there is a possibility of giving offense to strictly honest customers, who may be temporarily unable to meet their obligations, yet intend to pay as soon as able. To overcome this objection the following method of treating doubtful accounts is given.

Inventory of Doubtful Resources. Before closing the books a list should be made, in the Inventory Book or Journal, of all accounts on which it is not expected that the full amount will be realized. Next have the proprietor, or some one able to judge, make an estimate of what is expected to be realized on each account and place this amount opposite the total amount of each account on your list. Foot the two columns and carry the difference between them to the debit of the Loss & Gain account, in red ink, specifying it as "Doubtful Resources." Should the losses turn out to be less than what was expected, the above Liability Inventory will help to increase the gains at a subsequent closing of the books. By this method all accounts receivable remain open and there will be no probable chance of persons learning that their accounts are considered doubtful.

C. O. D. Account. Some firms do a large business on orders sent C. O. D. When goods are so sent a C. O. D. account is opened, which is similar in form to the Sundry Accounts Receivable account, and the parties ordering goods are charged therein. When remittances are received the proper parties are credited. Often, however, these C. O. D.

sales are charged direct to the Express Company, but as it is responsible only in trust and not absolutely, the principle is wrong. The heading, C. O. D. Account, would be strictly in accordance with the facts.

Statement of Wm. Wood's Business, Mar. 15, 189-.

Trial Balance.			
Wm. Wood,			4925 00
Cash,		4676 50	
Merchandise,		70 00	
Expense,		18 50	
J. W. Winter,			90 00
S. W. Snow,			400 00
Jas. Spring,		50 00	
Bills Receivable,		1600 00	
Bills Payable,			1000 00
		6415 00	6415 00
Resources.			
Cash on hand,		4676 50	
Merchandise, per inventory,		332 00	
Bills Receivable, good notes,		1600 00	
Accounts Receivable, Jas. Spring,		50 00	
			6658 50
Liabilities.			
Bills Payable, he owes on notes,		1000 00	
Accounts Payable, he owes others,		490 00	1490 00
Wm. Wood's Present Capital,			*5168 50*
Gains.			
Merchandise, Sales (Ledger credit),	1990.00		
" Inventory,	332.00		
" Sold and on hand is worth,		2322 00	
" " " Cost (Ledger debit),		2060 00	
" Gain,			262 00
Losses.			
Expense, Cost (Ledger debit), no inventory,			18 50
Wm. Wood's Net Gain,			*243 50*
Wm. Wood's Capital Account			
Wm. Wood's investment (Ledger credit),		5000 00	
" " withdrawals (Ledger debit),		75 00	4925 00
" " gain (Ledger credit),			243 50
" " *Present Capital,*			*5168 50*
Trial Balance After Closing.			
Wm. Wood,			5168 50
Cash,		4676 50	
Merchandise,		332 00	
J. W. Winter,			90 00
S. W. Snow,			400 00
Jas. Spring,		50 00	
Bills Receivable,		1600 00	
Bills Payable,			1000 00
		6658 50	6658 50

DICTIONARY OF COMMERCIAL WORDS AND PHRASES.

Acceptance.—Agreeing to the terms proposed; the acceptor's name written on the face of a bill of exchange or draft, usually with the word "Accepted"; bill of exchange or draft when accepted.

Accommodation Paper.—Notes or acceptances drawn for the purpose of being discounted, and not founded on an actual sale of goods; notes or bills signed and accepted without consideration; notes drawn by merchants for like amounts and exchanged for their mutual accommodation.

Account Current.—A running account. A detailed statement of the transactions between two persons or firms, usually expressed in the form of debtor and creditor.

Account Sales.—An itemized statement of sales and expenses, sent by a commission merchant to his principal. It exhibits the quantities and prices of the goods sold, the commissions and other charges, and the net proceeds.

Accrued.—Interest accumulated and unpaid.

Acknowledge.—In commercial correspondence, the term by which the receipt of a letter, remittance, or order, is admitted.

Acknowledgment.—A formal admission made before an officer, that the act described was voluntarily done. The officer's certificate of the admission is also called an acknowledgment.

Administrator.—One who is appointed by the court to settle an estate.

Ad Valorem.—According to value. A custom house term, relating to the estimating of duties upon the value of imported goods.

Affidavit.—A written declaration under oath.

Appraisal.—The act of placing a value on goods.

Arbitration.—The adjustment of a disputed point by a person or persons chosen by the parties in dispute.

Assets.—A term commonly used in trade to designate the funds, property, or effects, that is, the stock in trade, cash, and all the available property of a merchant, in contradistinction to his liabilities or obligations.

Assignee.—A person to whom the property of a bankrupt or an insolvent debtor is transferred for the benefit of the insolvent's creditors.

Assignment.—The act of transferring property to the assignee.

Attachment.—A warrant for the purpose of seizing a man's property.

Auditor.—One who examines accounts; an officer appointed by the government, or by any corporation, to examine claims upon the treasury, and to investigate the treasurer's accounts.

Auxiliary.—Applied to various account books that are kept as aid to the principal books.

Balance of Trade.—The difference between the value of the commercial imports and exports of any country.

Bank Book.—A pass book carried by a depositor, in which the teller of a bank records deposits, and in which the bookkeeper enters the paid checks at stated intervals.

Bank Bills or Notes.—Promissory notes printed by the government and issued by national banks, payable on demand, and used as money.

Bankrupt.—One who is unable to pay his debts, and who fails in business.

Bill.—A statement in writing, as a list of items bought or sold, or of services rendered. The common term applied to a note or draft.

Bill of Exchange.—An order for the payment of money, usually drawn on a person living in a foreign country, the term draft being used to designate bills that are payable in the same country in which they are drawn.

Bill of Lading.—A written account of goods shipped and the conditions of shipment, having the signature of the carrier's agent, and given to the shipper as a receipt.

Bill of Sale.—A writing given by the seller to the buyer, transferring the ownership of personal property.

Board of Trade.—An association of business-men for the regulation and advancement of commercial interests.

Bonded Goods.—Those which are stored in a bonded warehouse, or in bonded cars, the owner having given bonds securing the payment of import duties or of internal revenues, upon their removal, or their arrival at some inland city of entry, and before a specified time.

Bonus.—A premium given on a loan, or for any favor shown.

Broker.—An agent who effects sales or purchases or who makes loans and contracts for another. Also a term applied to one who deals in stocks. A broker does not usually have possession of the property which he sells or buys as agent.

Bullion.—Uncoined gold or silver.

Business.—Exchange of commodities and of commercial values. Also a term representing one's occupation.

Capital.—The investment in business.

Cash Sales.—The sales made for ready money in contradistinction to sales on which credit is given.

Certificate.—A written voucher attesting to some fact; as a certificate of deposit, a certificate of stock.

Certified Check.—One which has been certified or accepted by the bank on which it is drawn, making the bank responsible for its payment.

Charter.—A paper from government defining the rights and privileges of corporations. To hire or let an instrument of transportation; as, a ship, a railway car.

Chattel.—Any kind of property except real estate; as, merchandise, notes and accounts, animals, leases of real estate, etc.

Check.—An order on a bank drawn by a depositor.

Clearing House.—A kind of banking exchange, established in some of the large cities for the convenience of daily settlements; the drafts and checks on each other are mutually exchanged without the individual presentation of each at the banks, and a balance struck, which balance only is paid in cash.

Collaterals.—Pledges of stocks, notes, or chattels, for security of loans and other indebtedness.

Commerce.—The business of exchanging commodities between different places; mercantile business in general, as carried on between individuals or companies of different countries, or of the same country; and in a restricted sense, the shipping which belongs to a country.

Commercial Paper.—Bills of exchange, drafts, and notes, given in the course of trade.

Commission.—A percentage given for the sale or purchase of goods, or the transaction of other business; the order or authority by which one person transacts business for another.

Common Law.—Law based upon the precedent of usage, and not contained in the statutes enacted by legislative bodies.

Company.—A corporation. A term used in a firm name to designate other partners whose names are not given.

Compound, or Compromise.—To settle a claim by paying or receiving only a part of the amount. To agree upon a settlement based upon mutual concessions.

Consignee.—One to whom goods are sent.

Consul.—An agent for a government, residing at a seaport in a foreign country, and guarding the commercial interests of his own country.

Contra.—On the opposite side.

Copartnership.—The joining of two or more persons into one firm for the purpose of carrying on any enterprise. It has the same meaning as partnership.

Copyright.—The right granted by government to an author to control the publication of any book or work.

Counterfeit.—A spurious bank bill; a forgery.

Counting room.—A room in which merchants keep their accounts and transact business.

Coupon.—An interest note or a certificate attached to a bond which is cut off from the bond and collected when due.

Course of Exchange.—The sum merchants pay for bills of exchange to enable them to make remittances from one country to another.

Credentials.—Testimonials giving authority.

Creditor.—One giving credit; one whom we owe.

Currency.—The paper money or the coin which constitutes the circulating medium of a country; that which passes for money in a country.

Days of Grace.—In some states negotiable promissory notes or bills of exchange, payable at a certain time, are entitled to three days delay beyond the time expressed, which are called days of grace, unless "without grace" is expressed on the paper. These days were so called because they were formerly gratuitously allowed. But now, in some of the states of the United States and in England, they are demanded of right, the custom having passed into law. In a number of states days of grace have been abolished by law.

Debtor.—One who owes a debt.

Deed.—A written contract under seal, usually transferring the ownership of real estate.

Defalcation.—Deduction or discount. Embezzlement of money by an officer having it in charge.

Deposit.—To commit to the care of another; especially to place money in bank subject to our order.

Dishonor.—A failure to pay an obligation when due. A failure to accept a draft when presented for acceptance.

Dividend.—The portion allotted to each stockholder in the division of profits.

Dower.—The right of a widow to a life interest in one third of all the real estate owned by her husband at any time after their marriage.

DUE BILL.—A brief written acknowledgment of a debt, having the effect of a promissory note.

DUNNING.—Soliciting payment for a debt; or the urgent pressing of the payment of a debt.

EARNEST.—Part of purchase money paid, or part of goods delivered to bind a verbal contract.

EMBEZZLEMENT.—A fraudulent appropriation of money entrusted to one's care.

EMPORIUM.—A commercial center.

ENDORSE, OR INDORSE.—To write one's name on the back of a commercial paper. To receipt a partial payment on the back of a note or bill.

ENGROSS.—To copy in manuscript.

EQUITY.—The science of right and justice, which often corrects the application of law in a particular case.

EXCHANGE.—The giving of one value for another. The process of remitting money values by means of bills and drafts. The discount or premium arising from the purchase or sale of different classes of paper.

EXECUTION.—A written direction given to an officer authorizing him to enforce a judgment. The act of signing and sealing a legal instrument.

FAC SIMILE.—An exact copy.

FEE SIMPLE.—The absolute ownership of real estate.

FINANCIER.—One having charge of the public revenues. One skilled in money matters.

FISCAL.—Pertaining to the public treasury or revenue. As, the fiscal year, meaning a financial year as reckoned by the department of finance.

FIXTURES.—The furnishings of a store or office that are not movable.

FOLIO.—The page of an account book.

FOOTING.—The amount of a column of figures.

FORGERY.—The act of fraudulently writing or altering a written document.

FREE TRADE.—Commerce between nations unrestricted by duties or tariff regulations.

FREIGHT.—Merchandise being transported. The price paid for transportation.

GAUGING.—The process of measuring the contents of casks.

GOOD WILL.—The reputation and patronage that pertains to an established business. The good will of a business is very frequently the subject of purchase and sale.

GREENBACKS.—United States notes, as distinct from national bank notes.

GROSS WEIGHT.—Weight of merchandise, including the case or wrapping.

GUARANTEE, OR GUARANTY.—A surety for the performance of a contract, in case the party making the contract fails to keep it. A security against loss.

HONOR.—To accept a draft, or to pay it when due.

INDEMNITY.—Security against loss, such as may occur, or has occurred, by reason of some particular or specified event, as in case of ordinary insurance against loss by fire, etc.

INDENTURE.—A mutual agreement in writing between two or more parties.

INDORSEMENT.—A writing on the back of any commercial paper.

INFRINGEMENT.—To trespass upon the rights of another, especially when granted some special right by law, such as a copyright, a patent, or a trade mark.

INJUNCTION.—A writ or process by which a party is required to do or refrain from doing a special act.

I. O. U.—I owe you—an acknowledgment of indebtedness, by the signer to the holder, for the amount.

INSOLVENCY.—The condition of one who is unable to pay his debts or meet his commercial obligations.

INSTALLMENT.—Part of a sum of money paid or to be paid.

INSTANT.—Referring to the present month; as, the sixth instant means the sixth day of the present or current month. Abbreviated *inst.*

INTESTATE.—Dying without having made a will.

INVENTORY.—A schedule or list of the goods, wares and merchandise generally, credits and assets of a merchant, made out in minute detail, each article being set down separately, and separately valued, usually, according to its then cash value; the whole list being then entered in a book called an inventory book.

INVOICE.—An itemized bill of merchandise bought, sold or shipped.

JOBBER.—A wholesale merchant who buys goods from the importers and manufacturers, and sells to country or other merchants and to retailers.

JOINT STOCK.—Property held in common by a company of men, each of whom is called a stockholder.

JUDGMENT.—The decree of a court enforcing a contract or redressing a wrong.

LAW MERCHANT.—Commercial law, or such customs and usages in commercial transactions, as being recognized by the higher courts as establishing rules of action, thus acquire the force of law.

Lease.—The letting of land and other property for hire. The contract for such letting, usually written, but sometimes verbal when the contract terminates within a year.

Legacy.—A gift of property by will.

Legal Tender.—That kind of money which legally can be offered in payment of a debt.

Letter of Credit.—A letter, usually addressed to banking houses in foreign cities, authorizing the holder to receive credit for a stated amount. They are used mainly by travelers.

Liabilities.—The pecuniary obligations of a merchant, which includes his bills payable and all his other debts.

License.—Permission or liberty to prosecute business or to sell.

Lien.—The right of holding or detaining the property of another until some legal claim be satisfied.

Liquidate.—To pay or settle a claim.

MAKER.—The signer of a note.

Manifest.—An invoice or schedule of a ship's cargo.

Maturity.—The date when commercial paper becomes payable.

Merchandise.—In its most comprehensive signification embraces every article dealt in by a merchant.

Money.—Any coin or currency lawfully employed as a representative of value in buying and selling.

Monopoly.—The sole right to make or sell a certain article. The exclusive control of anything.

Mortgage.—The written pledge of real estate or chattels to secure payment of a debt.

NEGOTIABLE.—A term applying to commercial paper, that may be transferred by endorsement, or simply by delivery

Net.—Clear of all charges. The exact weight or amount after all deductions are counted out.

Net Proceeds.—The proceeds of a sale after all expenses are deducted.

Notary, or Notary Public.—An officer who acknowledges deeds and other commercial papers; but whose chief business is to protest paper for non-acceptance and non-payment.

OPEN ACCOUNT.—A running account on a merchant's books, of debits or credits, with an individual or firm.

Open Policy.—One intended to cover all goods shipped by a certain person within a specified time; each special shipment and the amounts of insurance to be indorsed upon the policy, as the shipments are made.

Outlawed.—A term applied to a debt which has run beyond the time when the law will enforce its payment.

Overdrawn.—To draw a greater sum than one has to his credit.

PAR.—Equal in value. Any paper is at par when it is worth its face value, without premium or discount.

Parol.—Oral, not written. Also applied to written contracts not under seal.

Partnership.—The association together of two or more persons in any occupation.

Par Value.—The nominal value; usually the printed or written value of any paper.

Pass Book.—A book in which a trader enters articles bought on credit. It is usually carried by the purchaser, and is presented for record when the purchases are made.

Patent.—An official document securing to a person for a term of years, the exclusive right to an invention.

Pawn.—A deposit or pledge, given as security for a loan. The term only applies to chattels or money, and not to real estate.

Payee.—The one to whom payment is to be made; especially in whose favor a paper is drawn.

Payer.—The one who pays or is under obligations to pay.

Personal Property.—All property except real estate; chattels.

Plaintiff.—One who brings a personal action in law against another party who is called the defendant.

Power of Attorney.—A written instrument giving an agent authority to act for his principal. An agent thus empowered is called an Attorney in Fact.

Preferred Stock.—Stock taking preference over the ordinary stock of a corporation. A dividend is declared and paid on preferred stock before any can be declared on common stock.

Prima Facie.—At first view. Prima facie evidence is that evidence which is sufficient unless rebutted.

Promissory Note.—A written promise to pay a certain sum of money unconditionally, at a specified time.

Pro Rata.—A proportional distribution.

Protective Tariff.—Rates of duty fixed higher than the uniform rates, on certain imported commodities, for the protection of home manufacturers.

Protest.—A formal declaration made by a notary public, of the non-payment of a note, or non-acceptance and non-payment of a draft.

QUARANTINE.—Restraint of intercourse to which a ship, dwelling, or town is subjected on account of being infected with some contagious disease.

QUOTATIONS.—The published prices of merchandise, rates of freight, rates of exchange, etc.

RATIFY.—To sanction or approve; usually applied to a principal's approval of an agent's transactions.

REBATE.—A discount, or an allowance from the stipulated price, made in consideration of prompt payment, or for other reasons.

RECEIVER.—A person appointed to take charge of the affairs of a corporation on its dissolution, and to distribute its property according to law.

REMITTANCE.—The act of transmitting money values from one place to another. The value sent is called a remittance.

RESOURCES.—Money, property, or that which can be converted into property; as, claims against other people, either on writen or verbal promises.

REVOCATION.—The recall of authority conferred on another; as the revocation of an agency.

SALVAGE.—An allowance made by law to those who save a ship's cargo from a wreck or fire.

SET-OFF.—A counter claim. A claim which the debtor or defendant brings to reduce the claim of a creditor or plaintiff.

SOLVENT.—Being able to pay one's liabilities.

STATEMENT.—A list of resources and liabilities. A report of an agent's transactions sent to his principal. An itemized list of the debits and credits of any personal account; as, monthly statements sent by merchants to their customers.

STATUTE.—A law enacted by a legislature.

STOCKHOLDER.—One who owns shares of the capital stock of a corporation.

SUE.—To bring an action against one in law.

SURETY.—A person who has made himself responsible for the contract of another.

SYNDICATE.—A number of capitalists who unite together to dispose of a large loan, or to conduct some great financial enterprise.

TACIT.—That which is understood or implied.

TARE.—An allowance made for the weight of boxes, barrels, or wrappings of merchandise. The remainder after deducting the tare is called net weight.

TARIFF.—A list of prices; as, a freight tariff. A list of duties or customs on imports or exports.

TELEGRAM.—A dispatch or message received or transmitted by the electric telegraph.

TELLER.—One who receives or counts. A bank officer who receives or pays out money.

TICKLER.—A book containing memorandums of notes and debts, arranged in the order of their maturity.

TRADE DISCOUNT.—A discount from certain list prices, or from the amount of purchases, made to a dealer on account of a change in the prices, or on account of cash payments.

ULTIMO.—The last month preceding the present; as, on the twentieth ultimo, meaning the twentieth of last month. Abbreviated *ult.*

USURY.—Interest in excess of the highest rate allowed by law.

VALID.—A term applied to a contract that is properly executed; that is, legal or binding.

VOID.—Having no legal or binding force.

VOUCHER.—A document or paper proving that some transaction occurred; as, a receipt or a canceled note is a voucher for the payment of money.

WARRANTY.—An agreement to become responsible, if certain facts do not turn out to be as represented.

WAY BILL.—A paper containing a list and description of goods sent by railroad.

WHOLESALE.—To sell goods in quantity; usually, in unbroken or whole packages.

ABBREVIATIONS AND CONTRACTIONS.

a or @ (L. *ad*). To *or* at.
A. or *Ans.* Answer.
A 1. First Class.
Acc., *Acct.*, or ℅. Account.
Acct. Cur. Account Current.
Acct Sales. Account of Sales.
Agt. Agent.
Admr. Administrator.
Admx. Administratrix.
Adv. Advertisement; Advocate; Advent; Adverb.
Ala. Alabama.
A. M. (L. *Artium Magister*). Master of Arts.—(L. *Ante Meridiem*). Before noon.—(L. *Anno Mundi*). In the year of the world.
Am., *Amer.* America, American.
Amt. Amount.
Ans. Answer.
App. Appendix.
Apr. April.
Ariz. Arizona Territory.
Ark. Arkansas.
Ass'd Assorted.
Asst. Assistant.
Aug. August.
Bal. Balance.
Balt. Baltimore.
B. B. Bill Book.
Bbl. or *brl.* Barrel, Barrels.
Bdls. Bundles.
Bgs. Bags.
B. I. British India.
Bk. Bank; Book.
Bkts. Baskets.
B/L Bill of Lading.
Blk. Black.
Bls. Bales.
Bot. Bought.
Bro't Brought.
B/S Bill of Sale.
Bu. Bushel.
Bx. Box or Boxes.
c. ¢ Cents.
c/o In care of.
Cal. California; Calendar.
Capt. Captain.
Cash. Cashier.
C. B. Cash Book.
C. H. Court-House; Custom-House.
Cks. Casks.
Clk. Clerk.
Co. Company; County.
C. O. D. Cash (or Collect) on Delivery.
Coll. College; Collector; Colleague.
Con. (L. *contra*). Against; In opposition.
Conn. or *Ct.* Connecticut.
Cor. Sec. Corresponding Secretary.
Cr. Credit; Creditor.
Ct. or *ct.* Cent.—(L. *Centum*). A hundred.
Cts. or *cts.* Cents.
Cwt. or *cwt.* (L. *Centum*, 100, and E. *weight*). A hundred weight.
D. B. Day Book.
D. C. District of Columbia.—(It. *Da Capo*). Again, *or* From the beginning.
d. d. Days after date.
Dec. December.
Del. Delaware; Delegate.
Dept. Department; Deponent.
Dft. or *dft.* Draft; Defendant.
Disct. Discount.
Div. Dividend; Division; Divide; Divided; Divisor.
Do. do. or ". (It. *Ditto*). The same.
Doz. or *doz.* Dozen.
Dr. Debtor; Doctor.
Dray. Drayage.
d. s. Days after sight.
ea. Each.
E. and O. E. Errors and omissions excepted.
Ed. Editor; Edition.
E. E. Errors excepted.
e. g. (L. *exempli gratia*). For example.
Esq. or *Esqr.* Esquire.
Etc., *etc.*, or *&c.* (L. *et cæteri*, *cætera*, *cætera*). And others; and so forth.
Exch. Exchequer; Exchange.
Exec. or *Exr.* Executor.
Execx. or *Ex'x* Executrix.
Ex. Express; example.
Exp. Export; Exporter; Expense.
Feb. February.

Fir. or *fir.* Firkin.
Fla. Florida.
Fo. or *Fol.* Folio.
F. O. B. Free on Board.
Fo'd Forward.
Fr't Freight.
Ft. or *ft.* Foot; Feet; Fort.
Fth. Fathom.
Fur. or *fur.* Furlong.
Ga. Georgia.
Gal. or *gal.* Gallon; Gallons.
Gr. or *gr.*. Grain; Grains.
Hdkf. Handkerchief.
Hf. chts. Half Chests.
Hhd. or *hhd.* Hogshead.
Hon. Honorable.
Hund. Hundred.
I. B. Invoice Book.
I. e. or *ie.* (L. *Id est*). That is.
Ill. Illinois.
In. Inch; Inches.
Ind. Indiana; India; Indian; Index.
Ind. T. Indian Territory.
Ins. Insurance.
inst. Instant,—in the present month.
Int. or *int.* Interest.
In trans. (L. *In transitu*). In the passage.
Inv. Invoice.
Inv't. Inventory.
I. O. U. I owe you—an acknowledgment for money.
Jan. January.
Jr. Junior.
Kan. Kansas.
Ky. Kentucky.
Kg. Keg.
L., *lb.*, or lb. (L. *Libra*). A pound, in weight.
L., *l.*, or £. A pound sterling.
La. Louisiana.
Lat. or *lat.* Latitude.
L/C Letter of Credit.
Led. Ledger.
L. F. Ledger Folio.
L. S. Left side.—(L. *Locus Sigilli*) Place of the Seal.
Man. Manitoba.
Manuf. Manufacture; Manufacturer
Mar. March; Maritime.
Mass. Massachusetts.
Md. Maryland.
Mdse. Merchandise.
Me. Maine.
Mem. Memorandum.
Messrs. or *MM.* (F. *Messieurs*). Gentlemen; Sirs.
Mich. Michigan.
Minn. Minnesota.
Miss. Mississippi.
Mme. Madame.—*Mmes.* Mesdames.
Mo. Missouri.
Mo. or *mo.* Month.
Mon. Monday.
Mont. Montana.
Mr. Master, *or* Mister.
Mrs. Mistress, *or* Missis.
MS. Manuscript.
MSS. Manuscripts.
N. A. North America.
N. B. New Brunswick.—(L. *Nota Bene*). Note well, *or* take notice.
N. C. North Carolina.
N. Dak. North Dakota.
Neb. Nebraska.
Nev. Nevada.
N. F. New Foundland.
N. H. New Hampshire.
N. J. New Jersey.
N. Mex. New Mexico Territory.
No. or №. (L. *Numero*). Number.
Nov. November.
N. P. Notary Public.
N. S. Nova Scotia; New Style (since 1752).
N. Y. New York.
O. Ohio; Old.
%. Per cent.
Oct. October.
O. K. All Correct.
Ont. Ontario.
Oreg. Oregon.
Oz. or *oz.* Ounce *or* ounces.
P. or *p.* Page; Pint; Pole; Part.
℔. Per.
Pa. Pennsylvania
Payt. Payment.
Pd. Paid.
Per an. or *per an.* (L. *Per annum*). By the year.
Per cent., *per cent.*, *Per ct.*, or *per ct.* (L. *Per centum*). By the hundred.
Pk. or *pk.* Peck.
Pkg. Package.
P. M. Post Master; (L. *Post Meridiem*). After-noon.
P. O. Post Office.
P. O. D. Pay on Delivery.
P. O. O. Post Office Order.
pp. Pages.
Pr., *pr.*, or ℔. (L. *per*). By.
prox. Proximo; the next month.
Prem. Premium.
P. S. (L. *Post scriptum*). Postscript.
Pcs. Pieces.
Pub. Public; Publisher.

Pwt. or *pwt.* Pennyweight.
Qr. or *qr.* Quarter (28 pounds); Quire.
Qt. or *qt.* Quart; Quantity.
Recd. Received.
Ret'd Returned.
R. I. Rhode Island.
R. R. Railroad.
$. Dollar; Dollars.
S. A. South America; South Africa.
S. Dak. South Dakota.
Sat. Saturday.
S. B. Sales Book.
S. C. South Carolina; Small Capitals.
Sep. or *Sept.* September.
Shipt. Shipment.
Sr. Senior.
SS. (L. *Scilicet*). Namely.
S. S. Steamship.
St. Saint; Street; Strait.
Str. Steamer.
Sun. or *Sund.* Sunday.
Sunds. Sundries.
Supt. Superintendent.
Tenn. Tennessee.
Tex. Texas.
Thurs. Thursday.
Treas. Treasurer.
Ult., *ult.*, or *ulto.* (L. *ultimo.*) Last, *or* of the last month.
U. S. A. United States of America; United States Army.
U. S. M. United States Mail.
Va. Virginia.
Vice Pres. Vice President.
Viz. or *viz.* (L. *videlicet*). Namely; To wit.
Vol. or *vol.* Volume.
Vt. Vermont.
W/B Waybill.
Wash. Washington.
Wed. Wednesday.
W. I. West India; West Indies.
Wis. Wisconsin.
Wt. or *wt.* Weight.
W. Va. West Virginia.
Wyo. Wyoming.
Y. or *Yr.* Year.
Yd. or *yd.* Yard.

FORM 1.

ARTICLES OF COPARTNERSHIP.

Articles of Copartnership, *made the first day of March, one thousand eight hundred ninety-——, between C. R. Evans, of Woodbury, N. J., of the first part, and Geo. E. Martin, of Philadelphia, Pa., of the second part, witnesseth as follows:*

Whereas *the parties hereunto, having mutual confidence in each other, do this day form with each other a copartnership under the firm name of C. R. Evans & Co., for the purpose of conducting a general merchandising business at 122–124 Main St., Woodbury, N. J., under the following terms and conditions, to wit:*

1. That the said C. R. Evans of the first part shall contribute the entire resources of his late business located at 122–124 Main St., Woodbury, N. J., as per bill of sale executed under even date, less the liabilities which are to be paid by the firm of C. R. Evans & Co., making a total net investment of Seven Thousand Eight Hundred Forty Dollars.

2. The said Geo. E. Martin of the second part shall contribute cash to the amount of Seven Thousand Eight Hundred Forty Dollars.

3. The capital so formed is to be used and enjoyed in common between them for the prosecution and management of said business, to their mutual benefit and advantage.

4. Both parties shall devote their entire time to the business and shall share gains and assets equally, and bear losses equally. Each partner is entitled to draw One Hundred Dollars per month for private use.

In Witness Whereof, *the parties hereto have hereunto set their hands and seals, in duplicate, the day and year first above written.*

Signed, sealed and delivered in the presence of THOS. H. BETTS.

C. R. EVANS. [L. S.]
GEO. E. MARTIN. [L. S.]

NOTE.—Articles of Copartnership are not executed under seal in all states. You are to conform with the requirements of your state in writing legal forms of any kind. Consult your commercial law text book and the teacher whenever in doubt.

FORM 2.

ARTICLES OF AGREEMENT.

Articles of Agreement, *made the first day of April, one thousand eight hundred ninety-——, between F. J. Schwartz and Andrew Schwartz, of the firm of F. J. Schwartz & Co., parties of the first part, and A. P. Fenn of the second part, all of Tell City, Indiana, witnesseth as follows:*

1. The parties above named have agreed to become copartners in business, and by these presents do agree to be copartners together under and by the firm name of F. J. Schwartz & Co., in the business of merchants and dealers in general merchandise, at the said city of Tell City, State of Indiana, the partnership to commence on the date of this agreement and continue five years, unless sooner dissolved by consent of all the partners.

2. To that end and purpose the said parties of the first part shall contribute the resources of their late business, located at 642 Jefferson Street, as per bill of sale executed under even date herewith, less the liabilities which are to be paid by the new firm, making a net investment of Thirty Thousand Dollars, of which each invests one half, and the said party of the second part shall contribute Ten Thousand Dollars in cash.

3. At all times during the continuance of their copartnership they and each of them shall give their attendance, and use their and each of their best endeavors, and to the utmost of their skill and power exert themselves for their joint interest, profit, benefit and advantage, and truly employ, buy, sell and merchandise with their joint stock, and the increase thereof in the business aforesaid, and also that they shall and will at all times during the said copartnership bear, pay and discharge equally between them all rents and expenses that may be required for the management and prosecution of said business; and that all gains, profits and increase that shall come, grow or arise from or by means of their said business shall be equally divided between the said partners, and all losses by bad commodities, uncollectible debts or otherwise shall be borne and paid between them equally.

4. Owing to their unequal investments each partner is to be allowed six per cent interest on the sum or sums by him invested, and to be charged six per cent interest on all withdrawals, said interest to be adjusted at the time of closing the books.

5. Each of the parties may draw from the cash of the joint stock One Hundred Fifty Dollars per month for his own use, the same to be charged on account, and none of them shall take any further sum for his own use without the consent of the other partners in writing.

In Witness Whereof, *the parties hereto have hereunto set their hands and seals, in duplicate, the day and year first above written.*

Signed, sealed and delivered in the presence of
CHAS. M. BRUCKER.

F. J. SCHWARTZ. [SEAL.]
ANDREW SCHWARTZ. [SEAL.]
A. P. FENN. [SEAL.]

NOTE.—Read note under form 1.

FORM 3.

QUIT-CLAIM DEED.

This Indenture, *made the first day of May, in the year of our Lord one thousand eight hundred ninety——, between J. B. Luckey (unmarried) and W. V. Chambers (unmarried) of the city of Louisville, County of Jefferson and State of Kentucky, of the first part, and Chas. F. Grainger of the same place, of the second part.*

Witnesseth, *That the said parties of the first part, in consideration of the sum of Three Thousand Two Hundred Fifty Dollars ($3250) to them in hand paid by the said party of the second part, the receipt of which is hereby confessed and acknowledged, have bargained, sold, remised and quit-claimed, and by these presents do bargain, sell, remise and quit-claim unto the said party of the second part and to his heirs and assigns forever, all that tract and parcel of land situate in the city of Louisville, County of Jefferson and State of Kentucky, and more particularly distinguished as lots numbers sixteen (16) and seventeen (17) as laid down in the original plat of the city of Louisville, Ky. Said lots are situate on the south side of Main street, and are seventy (70) feet in width front and rear, and are one hundred sixty (160) feet deep. Together with all and singular the hereditaments and appurtenances thereto belonging, or in any wise appertaining, and the reversion and reversions, remainder and remainders, rents, issues and profits thereof, and all the estate, right, title, interest, claim and demand whatsoever, of the said parties of the first part, either in law or equity, of, in and to the above bargained premises, with the said hereditaments and appurtenances, to have and to hold the said premises to the said party of the second part, his heirs and assigns, to the sole and proper benefit and behoof of the said party of the second part, his heirs and assigns forever.*

In Witness Whereof, *The parties of the first part have hereunto set their hands and seals the day and year first above written.*

Signed, sealed and delivered in the presence of G. P. WEEDMAN.

J. B. LUCKEY. [SEAL.]
W. V. CHAMBERS. [SEAL.]

NOTE.—Whenever required the acknowledgment is the same as in a warranty deed. *(See form 100 on your Voucher File.)*

FORM 4.

BILL OF SALE.

Know All Men by These Presents, *That we, C. O. Dinwiddie and Chas. T. Platt, of the city of Rochester, County of Monroe, and State of New York, of the firm of C. O. Dinwiddie & Co., parties of the first part, in consideration of the sum of Nine Thousand Dollars to us in hand paid by Jno. R. Cassel, of the firm of C. O. Dinwiddie & Co., of the city, county, and state aforesaid, of the second part, the receipt of which is hereby acknowledged, have bargained and sold, and by these presents do grant and convey, unto the said party of the second part, our interest in the following resources of the firm of C. O. Dinwiddie & Co., to wit: Cash on deposit in the Merchants Bank, $10000; note drawn by Geo. Smith, $500; note drawn by Edwyn Leibfreed, $400; amount due from Frank E. Schwartz, $280; amount due from Jno. D. Malone, $640; amount due from Jas. S. Wilson & Son, $325; shipment made to Grainger & Co., Louisville, Ky., $625; shipment made to Brown & Co., Philadelphia, $392; making a total of Thirteen Thousand One Hundred Sixty-two Dollars ($13162). On condition that the said party of the second part assumes the following liabilities of the firm of C. O. Dinwiddie & Co., to wit: Note drawn by the firm of C. O. Dinwiddie & Co., favor of Ferd. Becker, $1500; amount due R. C. Howell, $1000; amount due Philip Smith & Co., $500; amount due Theo. Schwartz, $1162; making a total of Four Thousand One Hundred Sixty-two Dollars.*

To Have and to Hold *the same unto the said party of the second part and his legal representatives forever.*

The said parties of the first part hereby covenant and agree to and with the said party of the second part that they are possessed of the full right and title to their interest in the property hereby conveyed, and that they will warrant and defend the same in the quiet and peaceful possession of the said party of the second part against the lawful claims of all persons whomsoever.

In Witness Whereof, *we have hereunto set our hands and seals this first day of May, in the year of our Lord one thousand eight hundred ninety ——.*

C. O. DINWIDDIE. [SEAL.]
CHAS. T. PLATT. [SEAL.]

FORM 5.

PARTNERSHIP AGREEMENT.

Articles of Agreement, *made the tenth day of May, one thousand eight hundred ninety ——, between J. W. Graves, of Galveston, Texas, of the first part, and L. W. Warrick, of the same place, of the second part, witnesseth as follows:*

1. The parties above named have agreed to become copartners in business, and by these presents do agree to be copartners together, under and by the firm name of J. W. Graves & Co., in the business of merchants and dealers in groceries, at the said city of Galveston, the partnership to commence on the date of this agreement and to continue until dissolved by mutual consent of the partners.

2. To that end and purpose the said party of the first part shall contribute the cash and other resources and the good will of his late business located at 640 Chestnut Street, amounting to Ten Thousand Two Hundred Eighty Dollars ($10280), out of which the liabilities of the said business, amounting to Three Thousand Dollars ($3000) are to be paid, making a net investment of Seven Thousand Two Hundred Eighty Dollars ($7280), as per bill of sale executed on even date herewith. And the said party of the second part shall contribute his share of the resources of the late firm of C. W. Hammond & Co., amounting to Eleven Thousand One Hundred Eighty Dollars ($11180), out of which the liabilities of the late firm, amounting to Three Thousand Nine Hundred Dollars ($3900), shall be paid, making a net investment of Seven Thousand Two Hundred Eighty Dollars ($7280), as per bill of sale executed on even date herewith; the capital so formed to be used in common between them for the prosecution and management of the said business to their mutual benefit and advantage.

3. And it is agreed by and between the said parties that if any of the resources invested by either of the partners shall prove worthless in full or in part, such worthless resources shall be charged to the partner investing same.

4. Each of the partners may draw from the cash of the firm the sum of Twenty-five Dollars ($25) per week for his private use, and neither of them shall take any further sum for his own separate use without the consent of the other in writing; and any such further sum, taken with such consent, shall draw interest at the rate of six per cent. per annum, and shall be payable, together with the interest due, within one month after notice in writing given by the other party requiring such payment.

5. The said parties shall share gains, losses and assets equally.

6. The said party of the first part shall devote his time to the management of the store, make the purchases, and give the remainder of his time and attention to the business as salesman, and the said party of the second part shall devote his time and attention to the business as salesman and shall keep the books of account, to which both parties shall have access at all times.

In Witness Whereof, *the parties hereto have hereunto set their hands and seals, in duplicate, the day and year first above written.*

Signed, sealed and delivered in the presence of

R. D. McCoy.

J. W. Graves. [SEAL.]
L. W. Warrick. [SEAL.]

FORMS OF ENDORSEMENT.

(Blank).

JAMES W. MOODY.

(Full).

Pay to the order of Erastus F. Jones.

JAMES W. MOODY.

(For Money Paid).

$150.00. Received on the within note One Hundred and Fifty Dollars.
Oct. 15, 189–.

(Without Recourse).

Pay to Henry Sherwood, or order, without recourse.

JAMES W. MOODY.

(For Collection).

Pay to Seventh National Bank, Green Island, for collection.

JAMES W. MOODY.

INDEX.

www.ingramcontent.com/pod-product-compliance
Lightning Source LLC
Chambersburg PA
CBHW021351230426
43666CB00006B/488

* 9 7 8 3 3 3 7 1 4 3 9 8 5 *